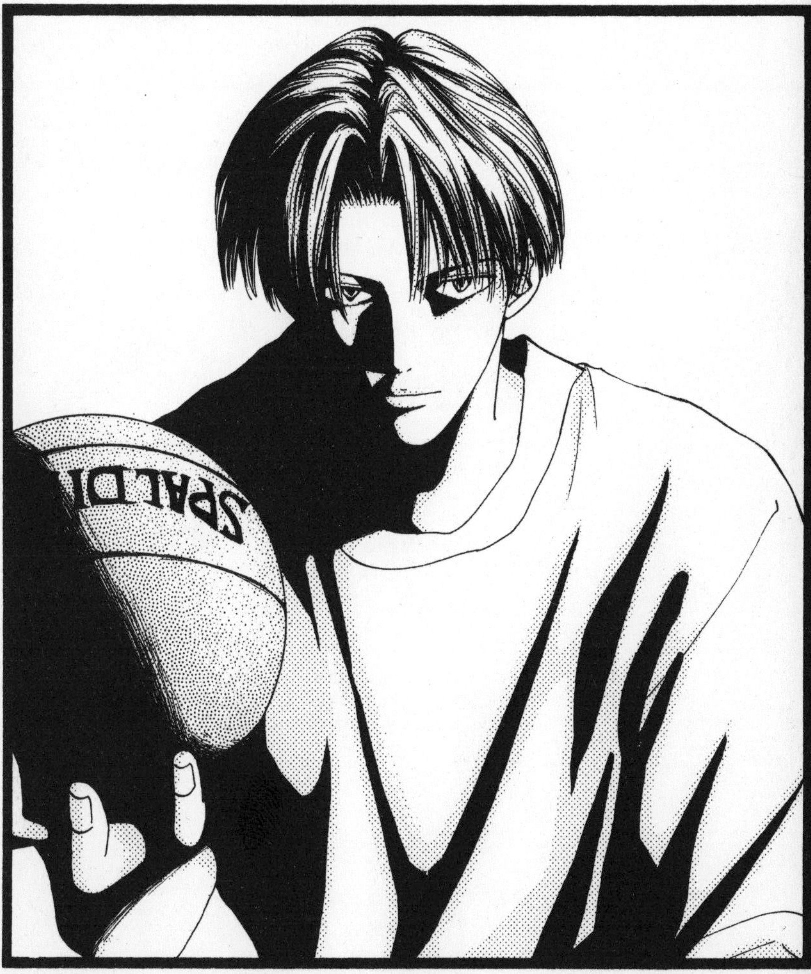

Hands Off! Vol. 3
Created by Kasane Katsumoto

Translation - Asuka Yoshizu
English Adaptation - Lianne Sentar
Copy Editor - Suzanne Waldman
Retouch and Lettering - Benchcomix
Production Artist - Jason Milligan
Cover Design - Seth Cable

Editor - Lillian Diaz-Przybyl
Digital Imaging Manager - Chris Buford
Pre-Press Manager - Antonio DePietro
Production Managers - Jennifer Miller and Mutsumi Miyazaki
Art Director - Matt Alford
Managing Editor - Jill Freshney
VP of Production - Ron Klamert
Editor-in-Chief - Mike Kiley
President and C.O.O. - John Parker
Publisher and C.E.O. - Stuart Levy

A  Manga

TOKYOPOP Inc.
5900 Wilshire Blvd. Suite 2000
Los Angeles, CA 90036

E-mail: info@TOKYOPOP.com
Come visit us online at www.TOKYOPOP.com

ISBN: 1-59532-155-1

First TOKYOPOP printing: May 2005
10 9 8 7 6 5 4 3 2 1
Printed in Canada

Volume 3

by

Kasane Katsumoto

HAMBURG // LONDON // LOS ANGELES // TOKYO

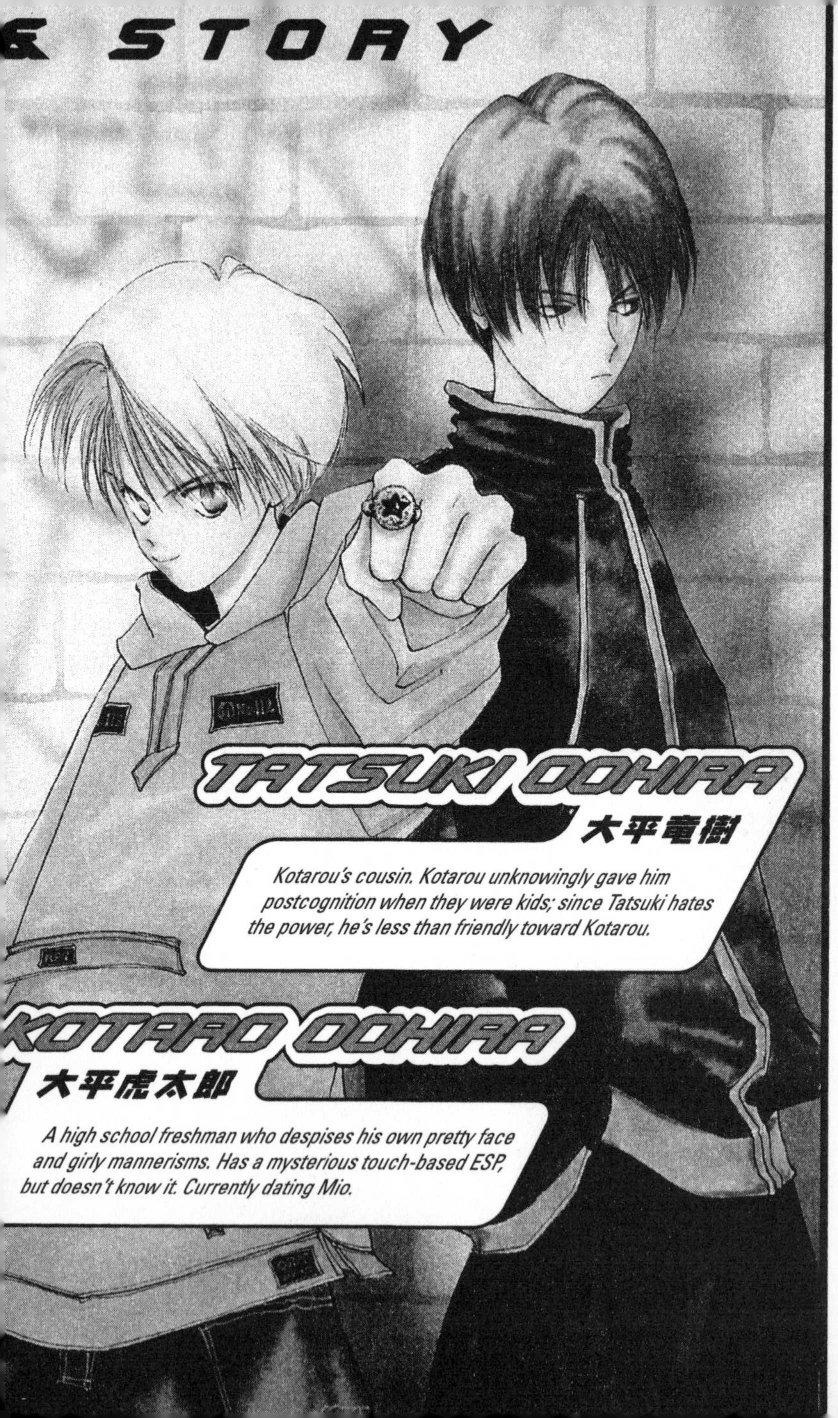
& STORY
TATSUKI OOHIRA
大平竜樹
Kotarou's cousin. Kotarou unknowingly gave him postcognition when they were kids; since Tatsuki hates the power, he's less than friendly toward Kotarou.
KOTARO OOHIRA
大平虎太郎
A high school freshman who despises his own pretty face and girly mannerisms. Has a mysterious touch-based ESP, but doesn't know it. Currently dating Mio.

CHARACTERS

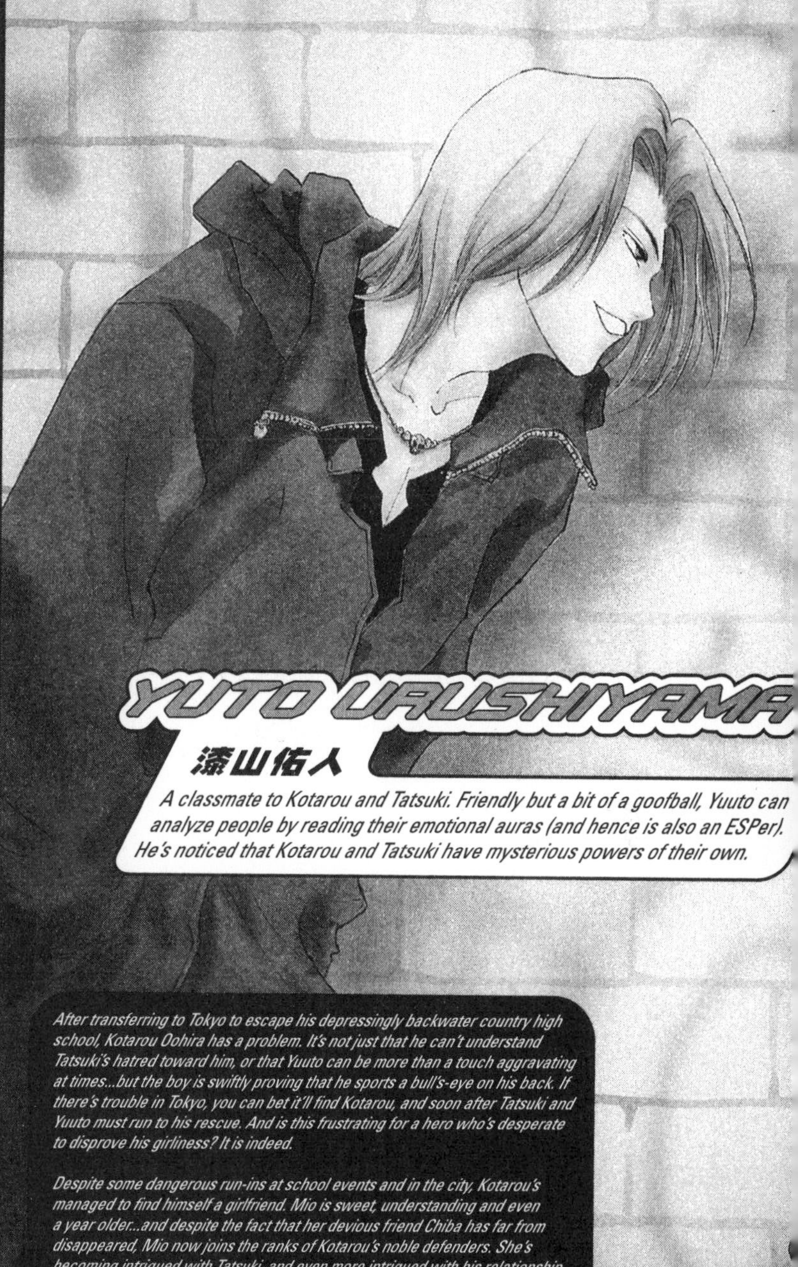

YUTO URUSHIYAMA

漆山佑人

A classmate to Kotarou and Tatsuki. Friendly but a bit of a goofball, Yuuto can analyze people by reading their emotional auras (and hence is also an ESPer). He's noticed that Kotarou and Tatsuki have mysterious powers of their own.

After transferring to Tokyo to escape his depressingly backwater country high school, Kotarou Oohira has a problem. It's not just that he can't understand Tatsuki's hatred toward him, or that Yuuto can be more than a touch aggravating at times...but the boy is swiftly proving that he sports a bull's-eye on his back. If there's trouble in Tokyo, you can bet it'll find Kotarou, and soon after Tatsuki and Yuuto must run to his rescue. And is this frustrating for a hero who's desperate to disprove his girliness? It is indeed.

Despite some dangerous run-ins at school events and in the city, Kotarou's managed to find himself a girlfriend. Mio is sweet, understanding and even a year older...and despite the fact that her devious friend Chiba has far from disappeared, Mio now joins the ranks of Kotarou's noble defenders. She's becoming intrigued with Tatsuki, and even more intrigued with his relationship to her loving little boyfriend...

CONTENTS

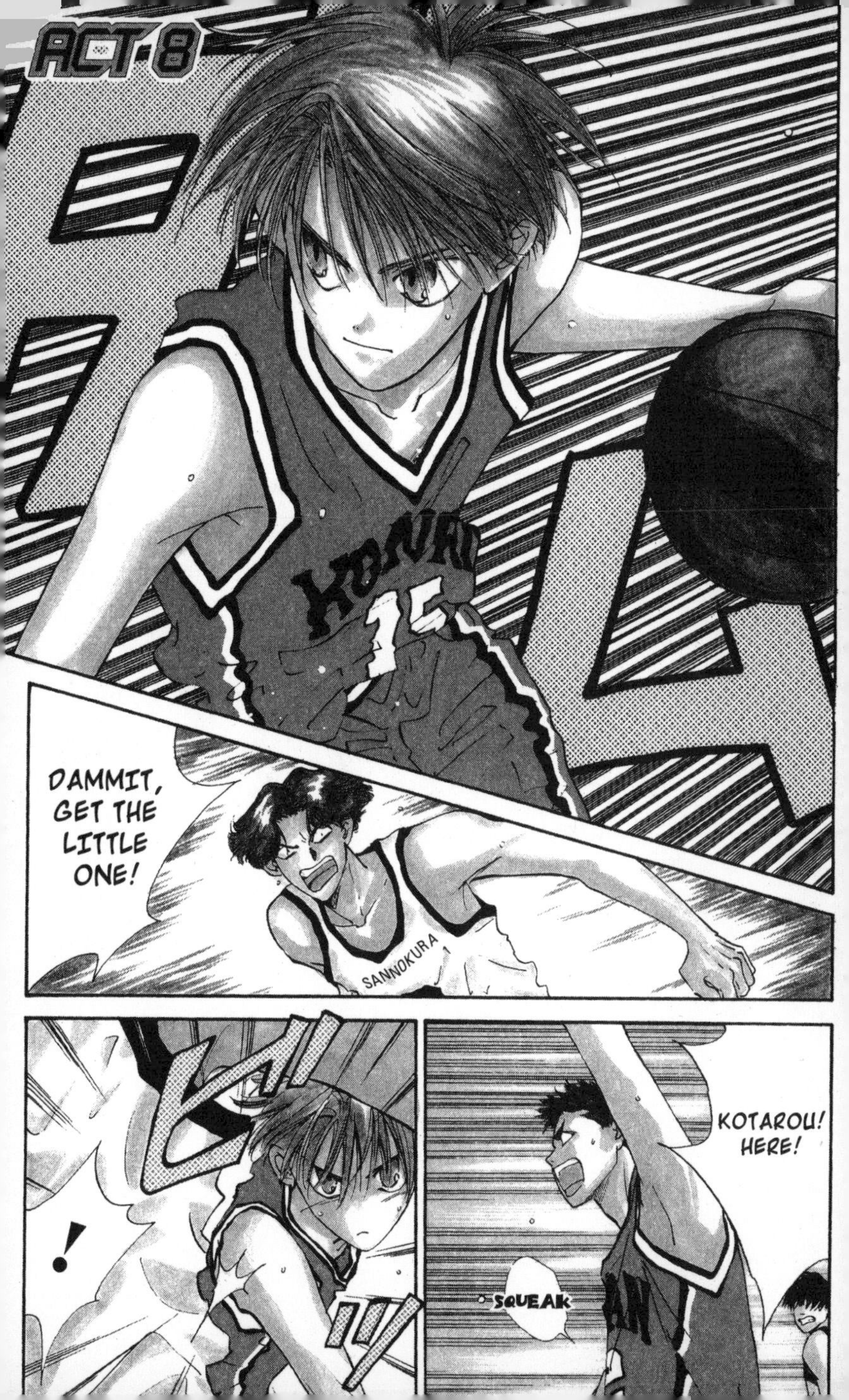
ACT 8
DAMMIT, GET THE LITTLE ONE!
SANNOKURA
KOTAROU! HERE!
SQUEAK
!

ACT 8

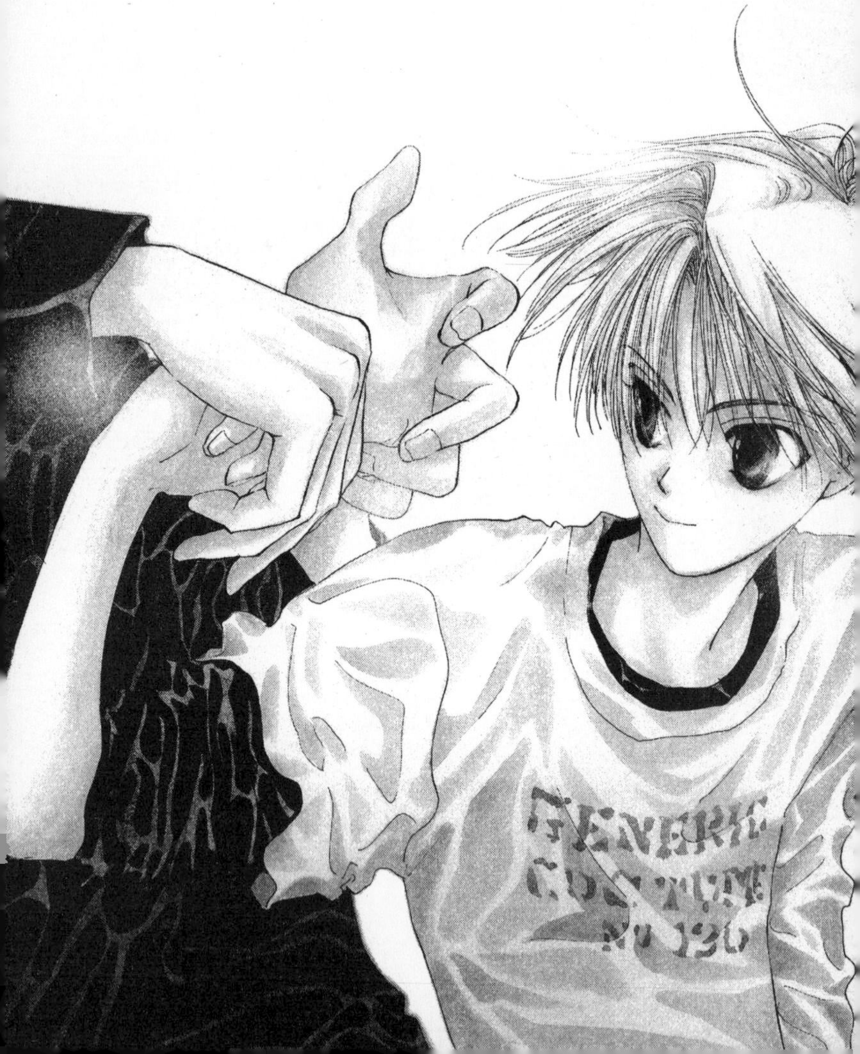

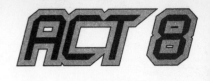

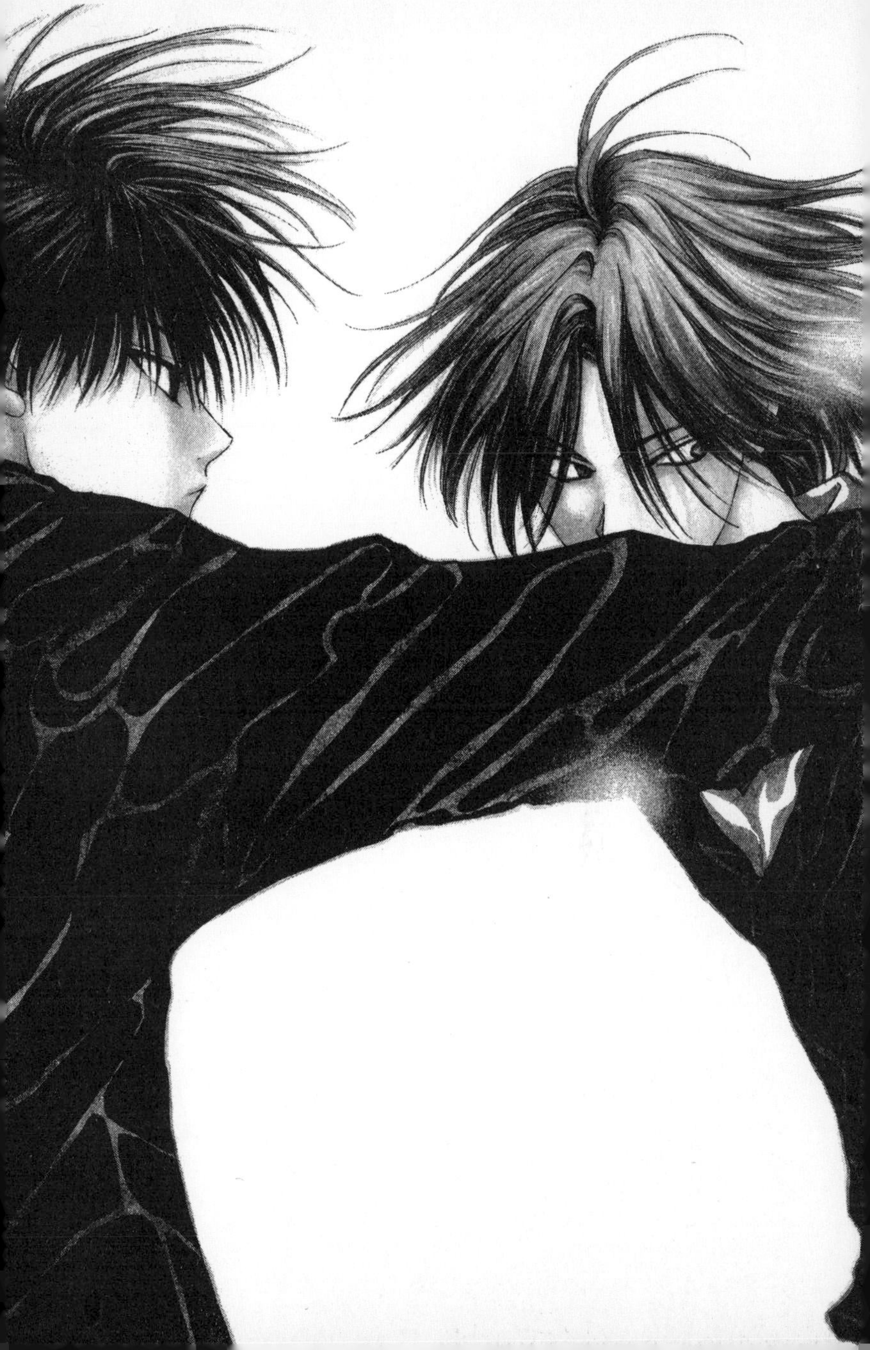

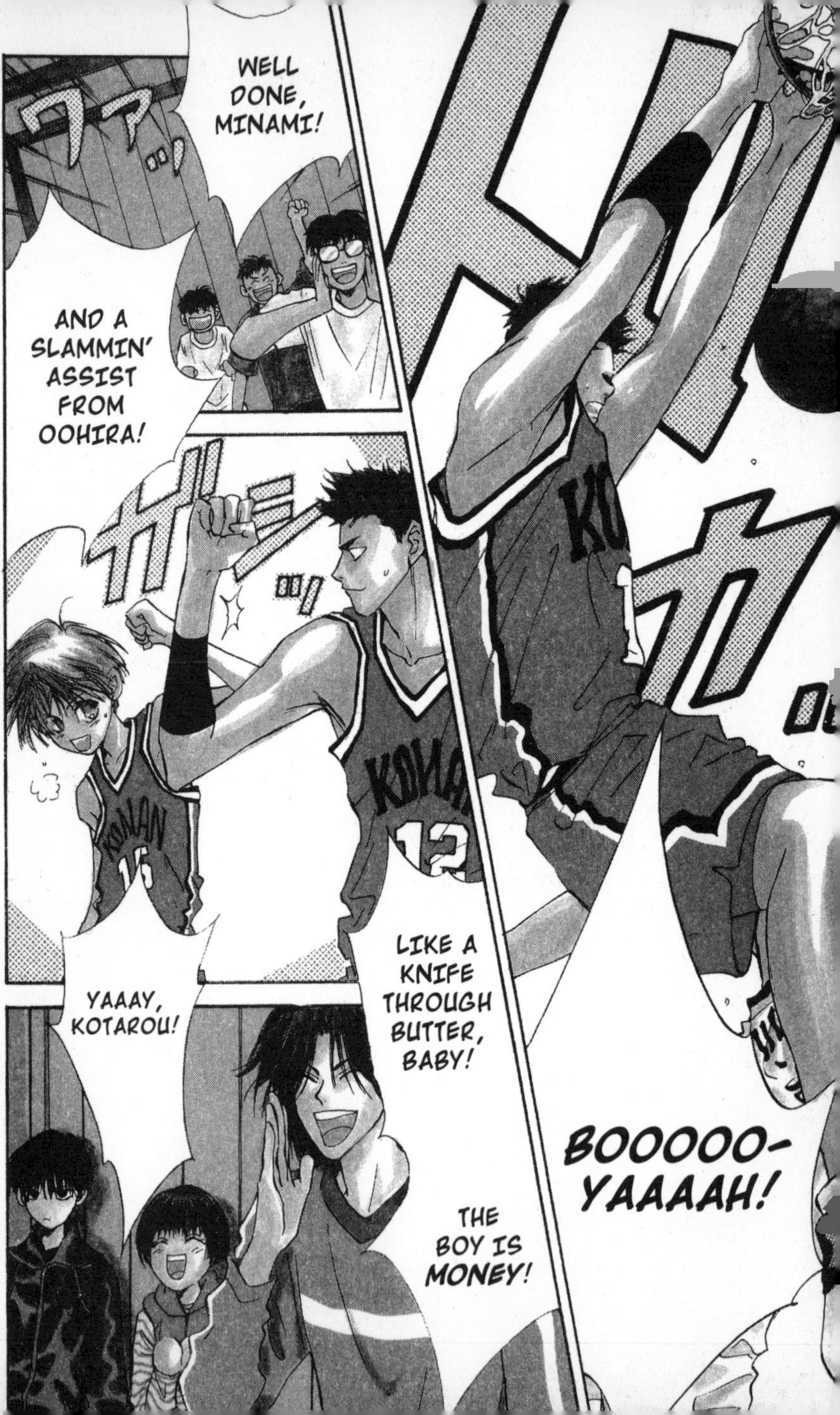
BOOOOO-YAAAAH!
WELL DONE, MINAMI!
AND A SLAMMIN' ASSIST FROM OOHIRA!
LIKE A KNIFE THROUGH BUTTER, BABY!
YAAAY, KOTAROU!
THE BOY IS MONEY!

ACT 8

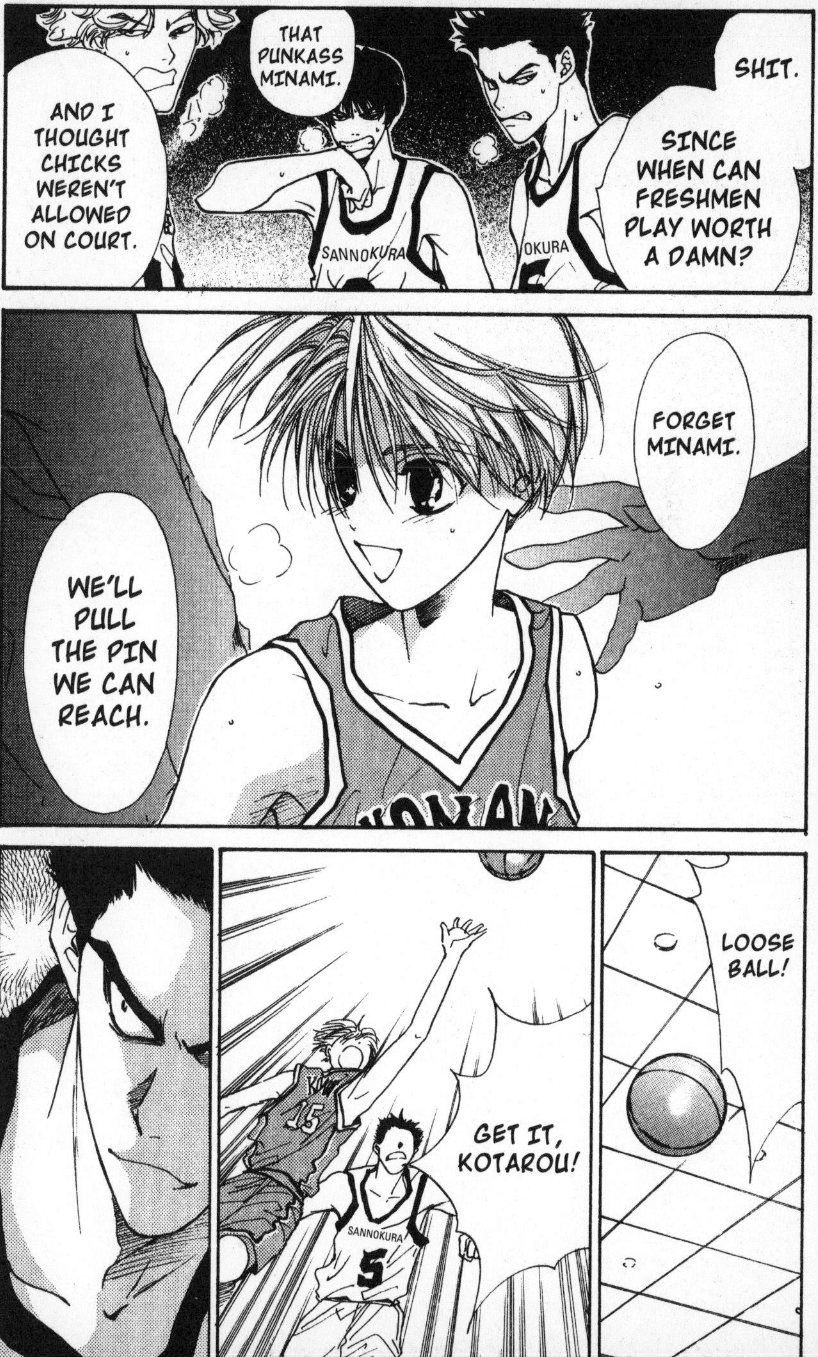
SHIT.
SINCE WHEN CAN FRESHMEN PLAY WORTH A DAMN?
THAT PUNKASS MINAMI.
AND I THOUGHT CHICKS WEREN'T ALLOWED ON COURT.
FORGET MINAMI.
WE'LL PULL THE PIN WE CAN REACH.
LOOSE BALL!
GET IT, KOTAROU!

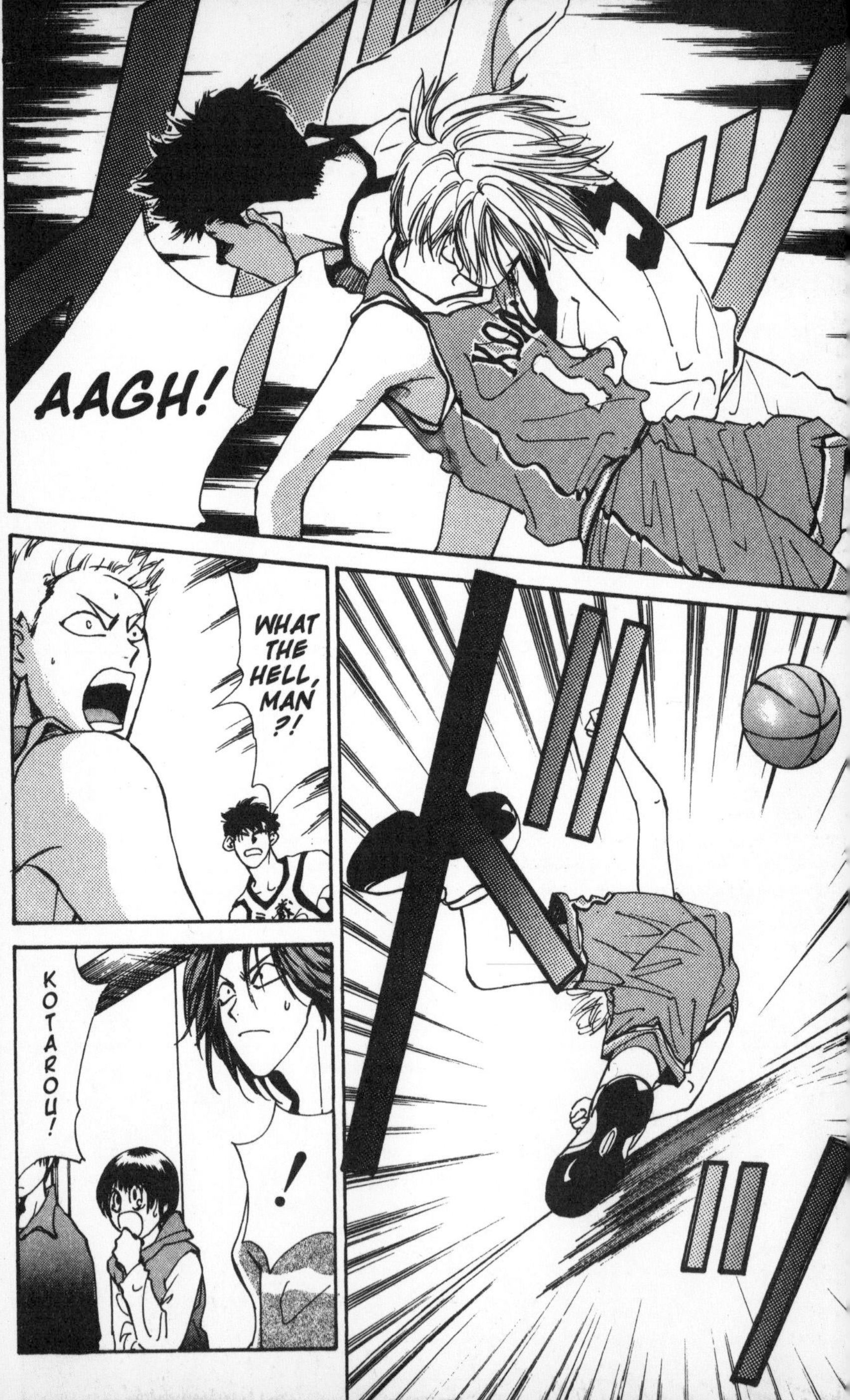
AAGH!
WHAT THE HELL, MAN?!
KOTAROU!
!

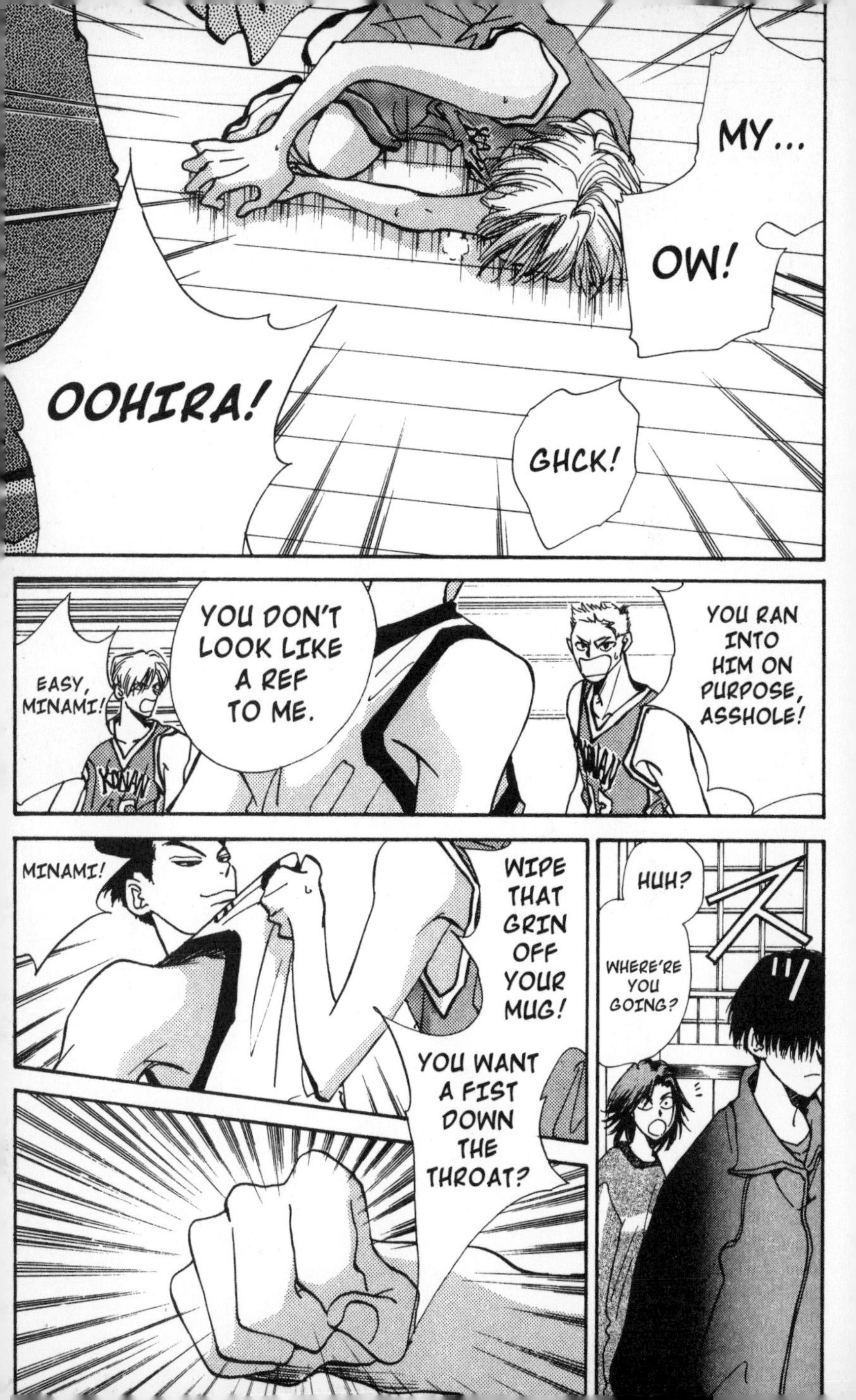
MY...
OW!
GHCK!
OOHIRA!
YOU RAN INTO HIM ON PURPOSE, ASSHOLE!
YOU DON'T LOOK LIKE A REF TO ME.
EASY, MINAMI!
HUH?
WHERE'RE YOU GOING?
WIPE THAT GRIN OFF YOUR MUG!
MINAMI!
YOU WANT A FIST DOWN THE THROAT?

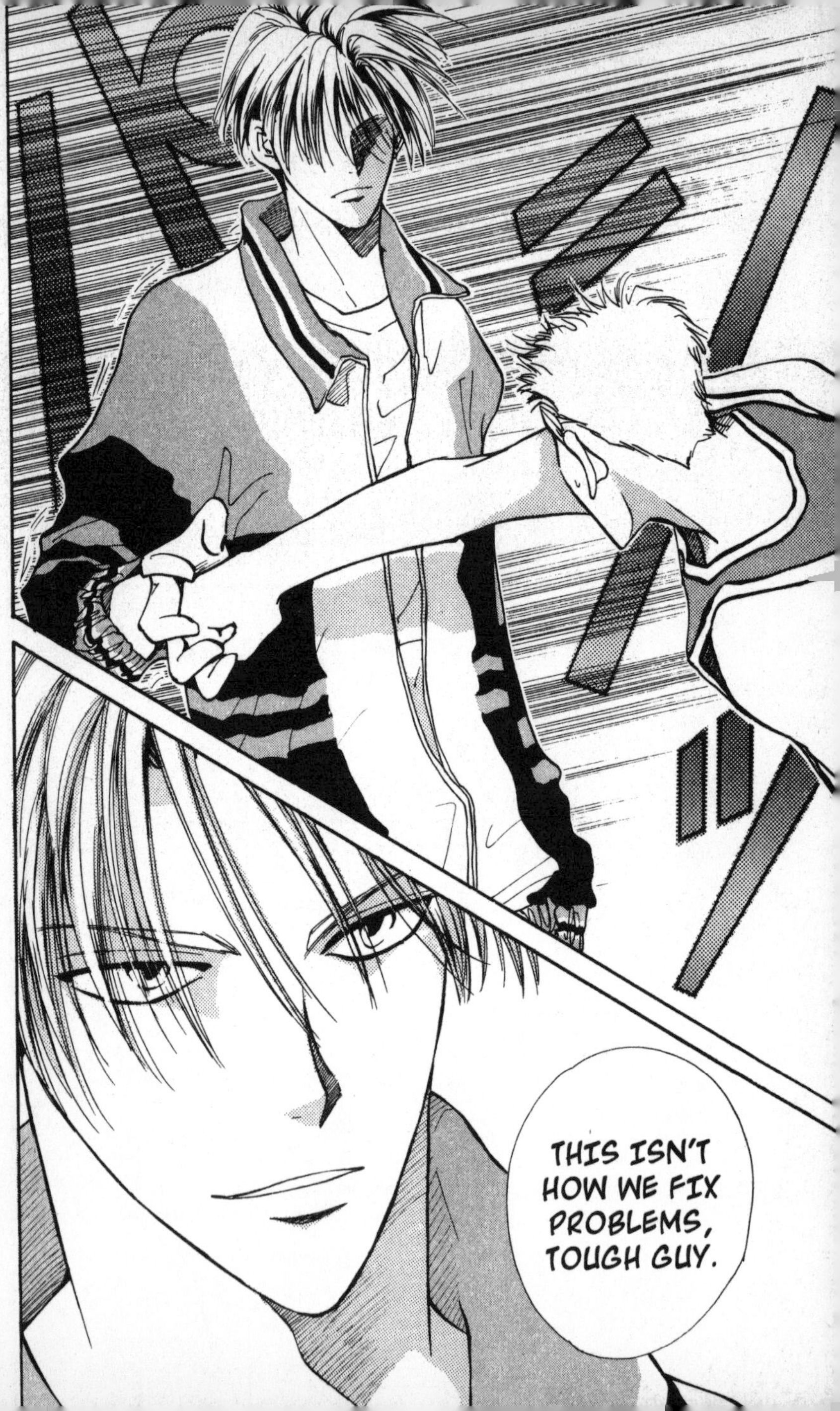
THIS ISN'T HOW WE FIX PROBLEMS, TOUGH GUY.

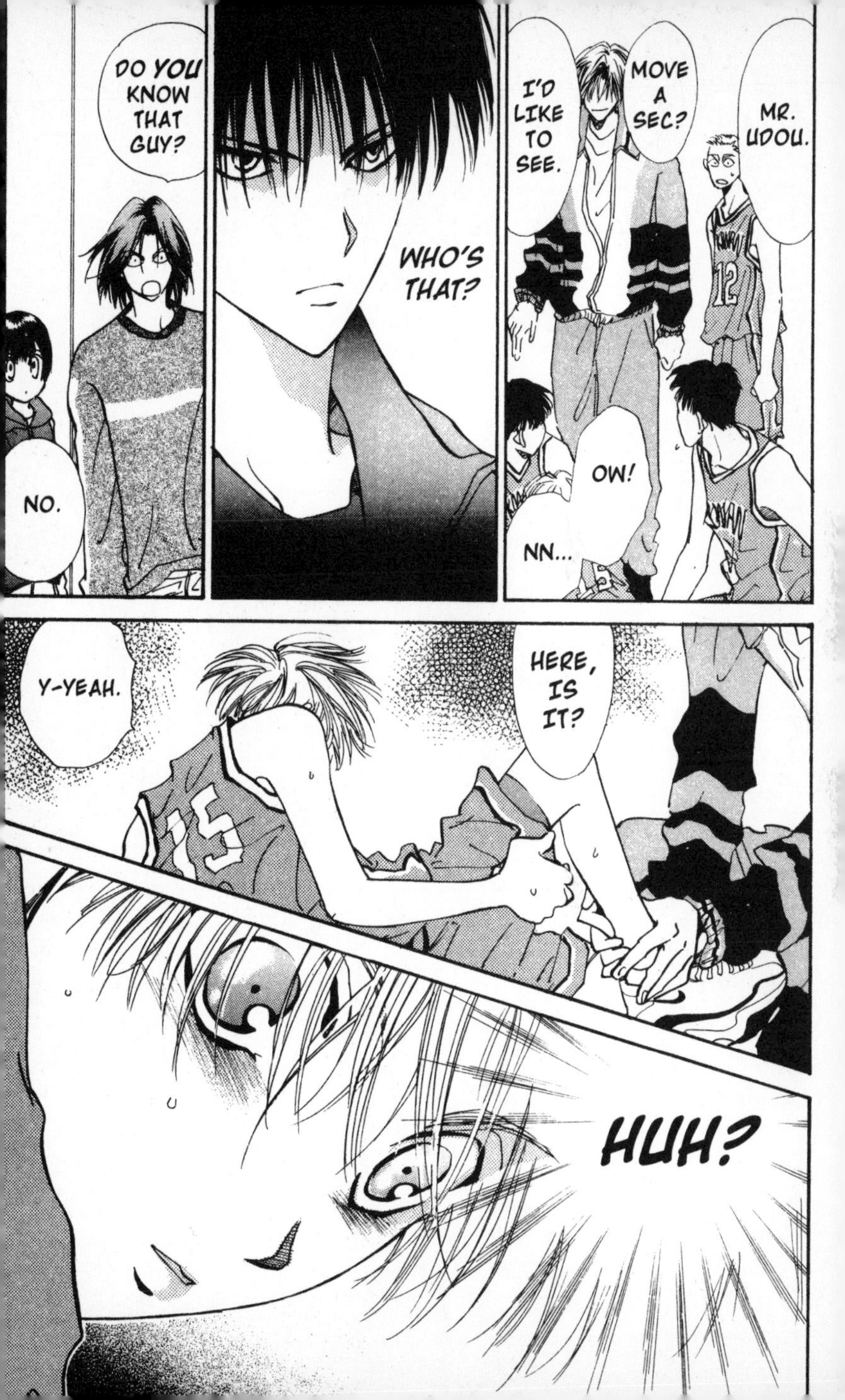
MR. UDOU.
MOVE A SEC?
I'D LIKE TO SEE.
OW!
NN...
WHO'S THAT?
DO YOU KNOW THAT GUY?
NO.
HERE, IS IT?
Y-YEAH.
HUH?

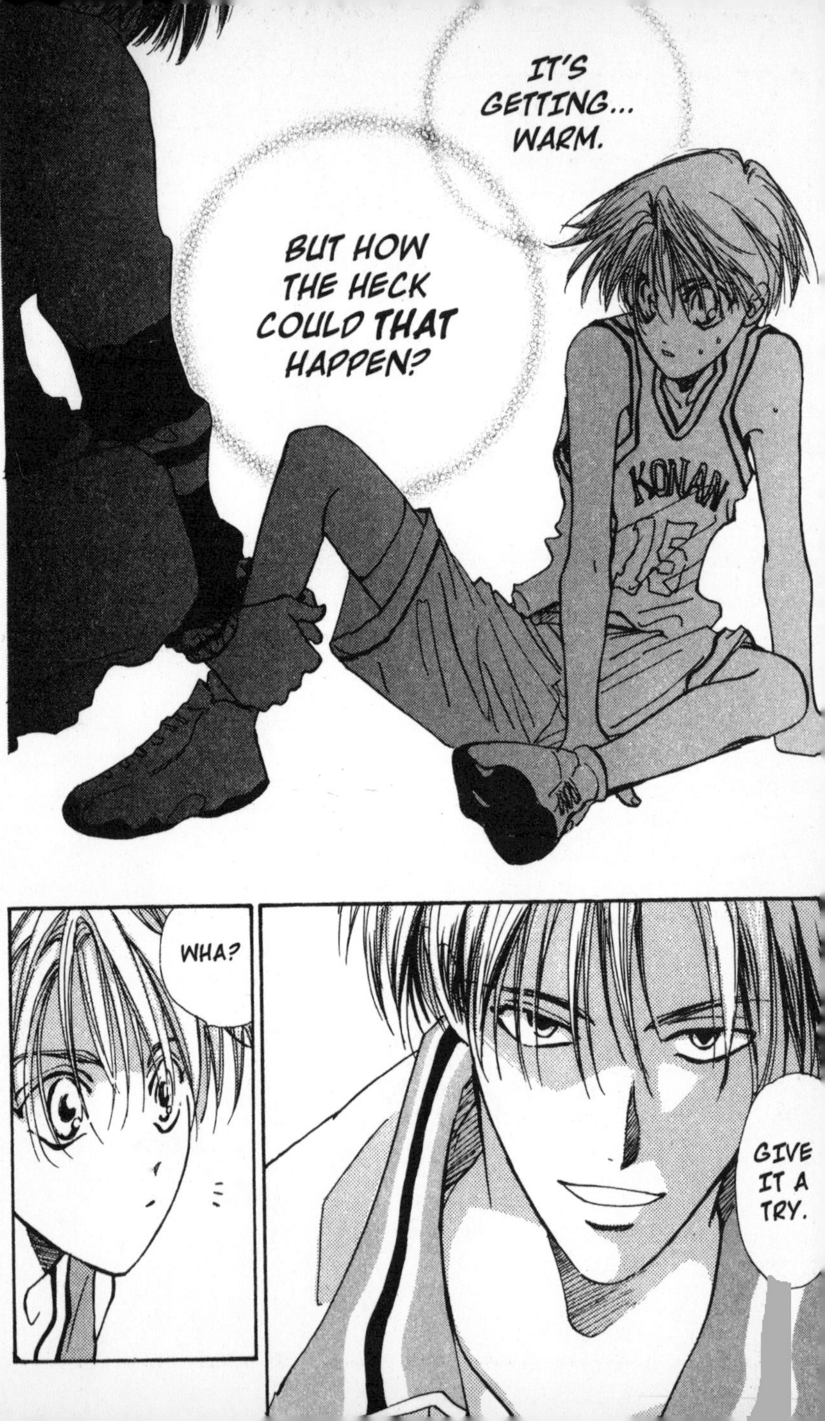
IT'S GETTING... WARM.
BUT HOW THE HECK COULD THAT HAPPEN?
GIVE IT A TRY.
WHA?

ACT 8

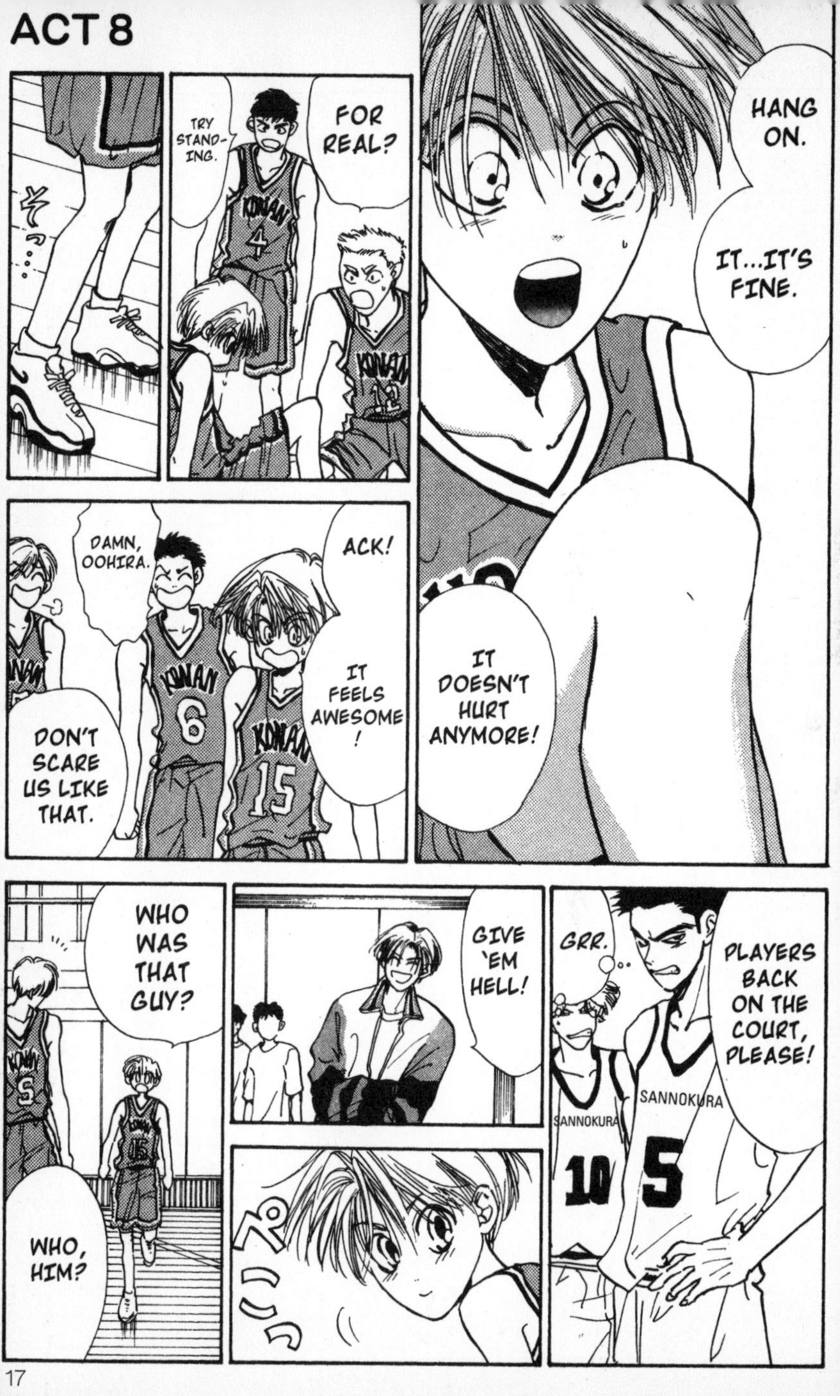
HANG ON.
IT...IT'S FINE.
IT DOESN'T HURT ANYMORE!
FOR REAL?
TRY STAND-ING.
そっ…
ACK!
IT FEELS AWESOME!
DAMN, OOHIRA.
DON'T SCARE US LIKE THAT.
PLAYERS BACK ON THE COURT, PLEASE!
GRR.
SANNOKURA
SANNOKURA
GIVE 'EM HELL!
ぺこっ
WHO WAS THAT GUY?
WHO, HIM?

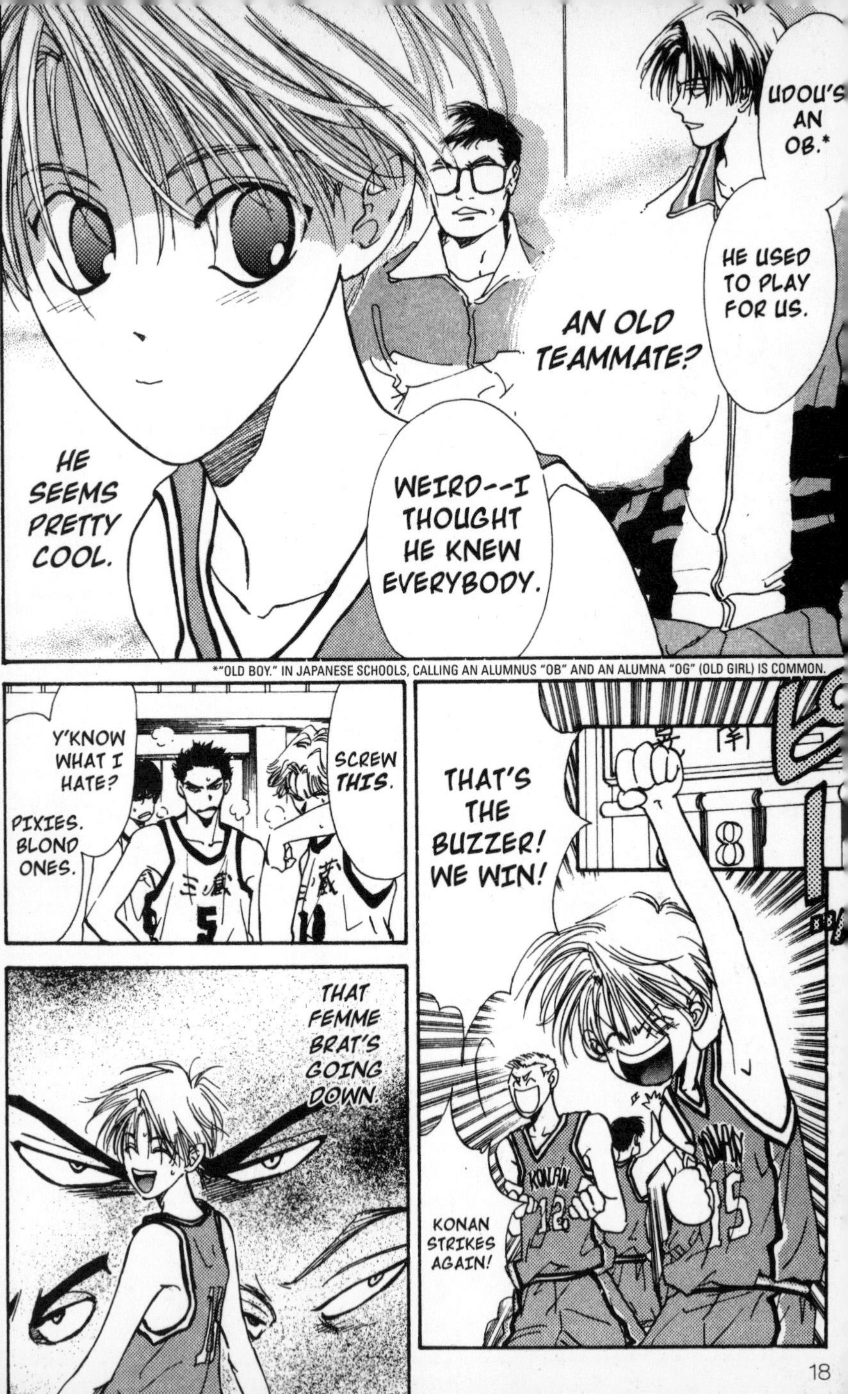
UDOU'S AN OB.*
HE USED TO PLAY FOR US.
AN OLD TEAMMATE?
WEIRD--I THOUGHT HE KNEW EVERYBODY.
HE SEEMS PRETTY COOL.
THAT'S THE BUZZER! WE WIN!
KONAN STRIKES AGAIN!
SCREW THIS.
Y'KNOW WHAT I HATE?
PIXIES. BLOND ONES.
THAT FEMME BRAT'S GOING DOWN.

*"OLD BOY." IN JAPANESE SCHOOLS, CALLING AN ALUMNUS "OB" AND AN ALUMNA "OG" (OLD GIRL) IS COMMON.

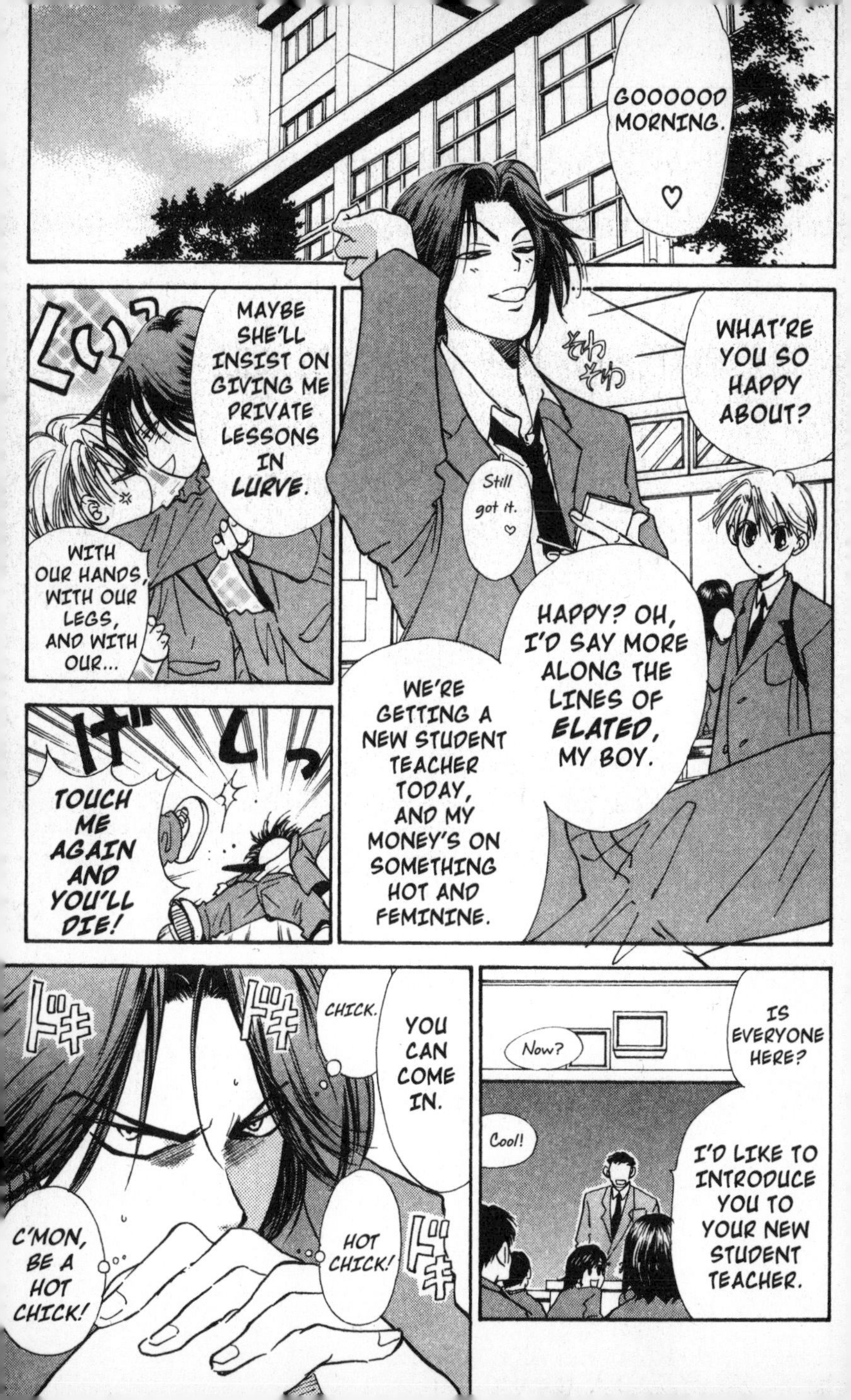
GOOOOOD MORNING. ♡
WHAT'RE YOU SO HAPPY ABOUT?
そわ そわ
Still got it. ♡
HAPPY? OH, I'D SAY MORE ALONG THE LINES OF ELATED, MY BOY.
WE'RE GETTING A NEW STUDENT TEACHER TODAY, AND MY MONEY'S ON SOMETHING HOT AND FEMININE.
MAYBE SHE'LL INSIST ON GIVING ME PRIVATE LESSONS IN LURVE.
WITH OUR HANDS, WITH OUR LEGS, AND WITH OUR...
TOUCH ME AGAIN AND YOU'LL DIE!
IS EVERYONE HERE?
Now?
Cool!
I'D LIKE TO INTRODUCE YOU TO YOUR NEW STUDENT TEACHER.
YOU CAN COME IN.
CHICK.
ドキ
ドキ
HOT CHICK!
ドキ
C'MON, BE A HOT CHICK!

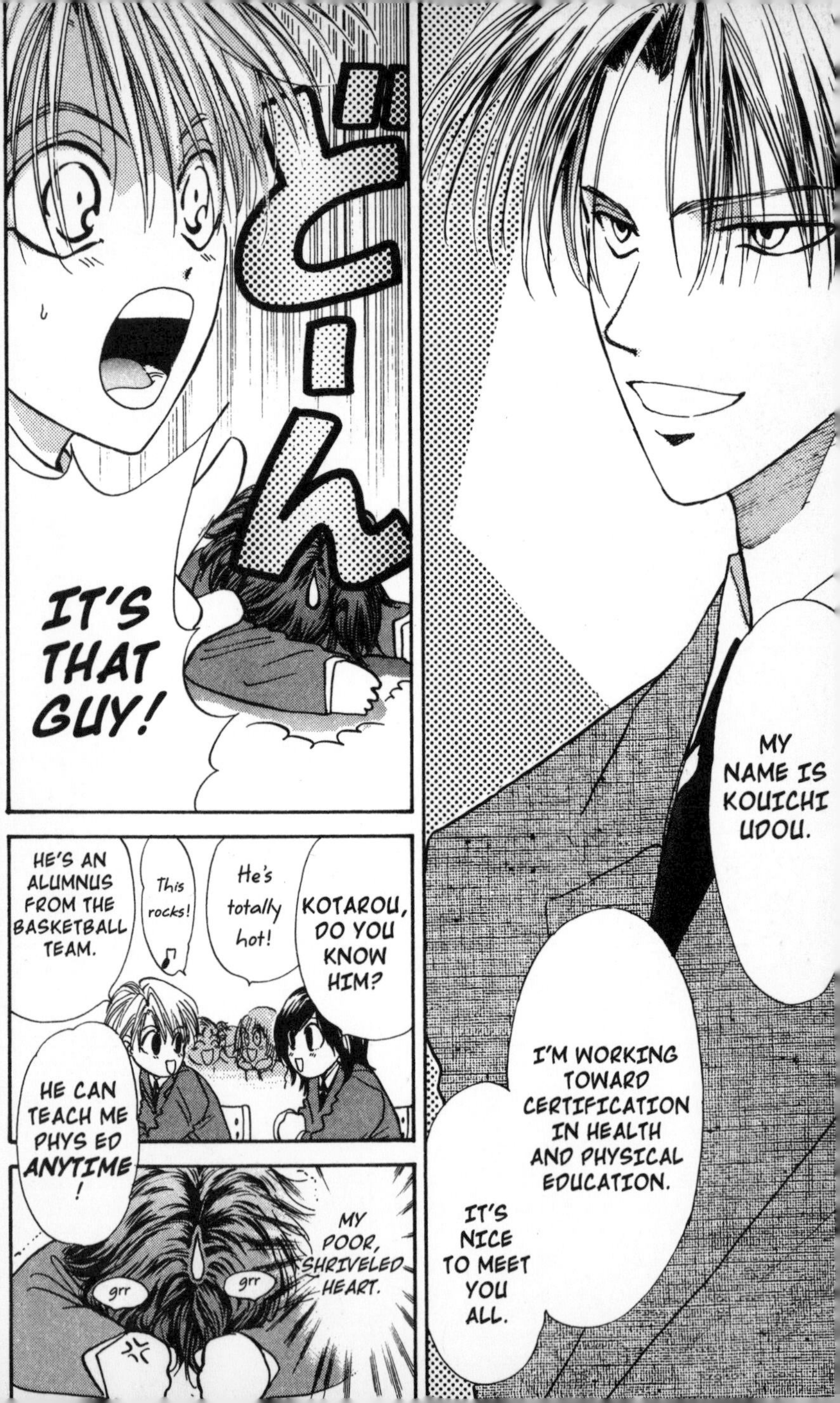
MY NAME IS KOUICHI UDOU.
I'M WORKING TOWARD CERTIFICATION IN HEALTH AND PHYSICAL EDUCATION.
IT'S NICE TO MEET YOU ALL.
どーん
IT'S THAT GUY!
KOTAROU, DO YOU KNOW HIM?
He's totally hot!
This rocks!
HE'S AN ALUMNUS FROM THE BASKETBALL TEAM.
HE CAN TEACH ME PHYS ED ANYTIME!
MY POOR, SHRIVELED HEART.
grr
grr

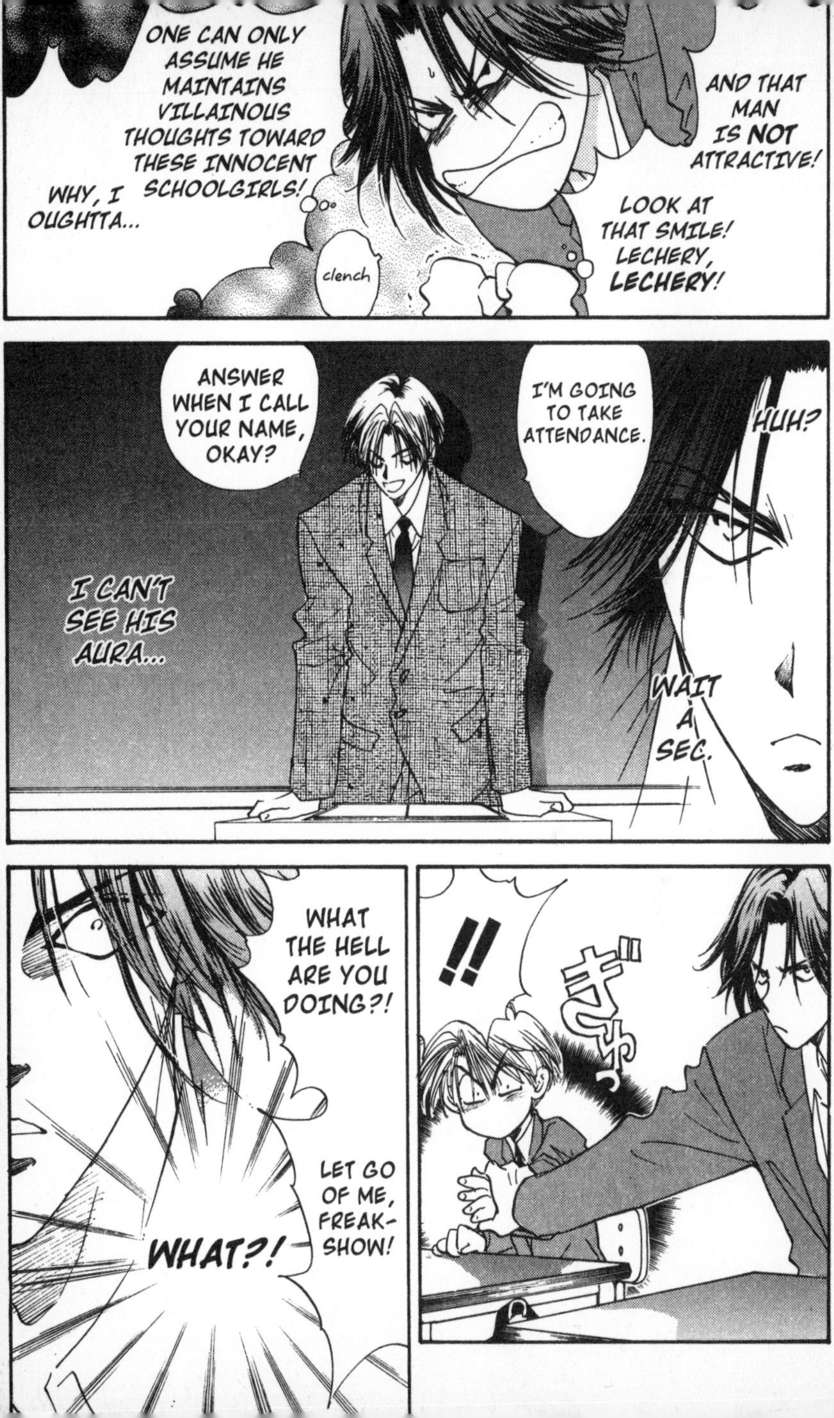

AND THAT MAN IS NOT ATTRACTIVE!
LOOK AT THAT SMILE! LECHERY, LECHERY!
ONE CAN ONLY ASSUME HE MAINTAINS VILLAINOUS THOUGHTS TOWARD THESE INNOCENT SCHOOLGIRLS!
WHY, I OUGHTTA...
clench
HUH?
I'M GOING TO TAKE ATTENDANCE.
ANSWER WHEN I CALL YOUR NAME, OKAY?
WAIT A SEC.
I CAN'T SEE HIS AURA...
!!
ぎゅっ
WHAT THE HELL ARE YOU DOING?!
LET GO OF ME, FREAK-SHOW!
WHAT?!

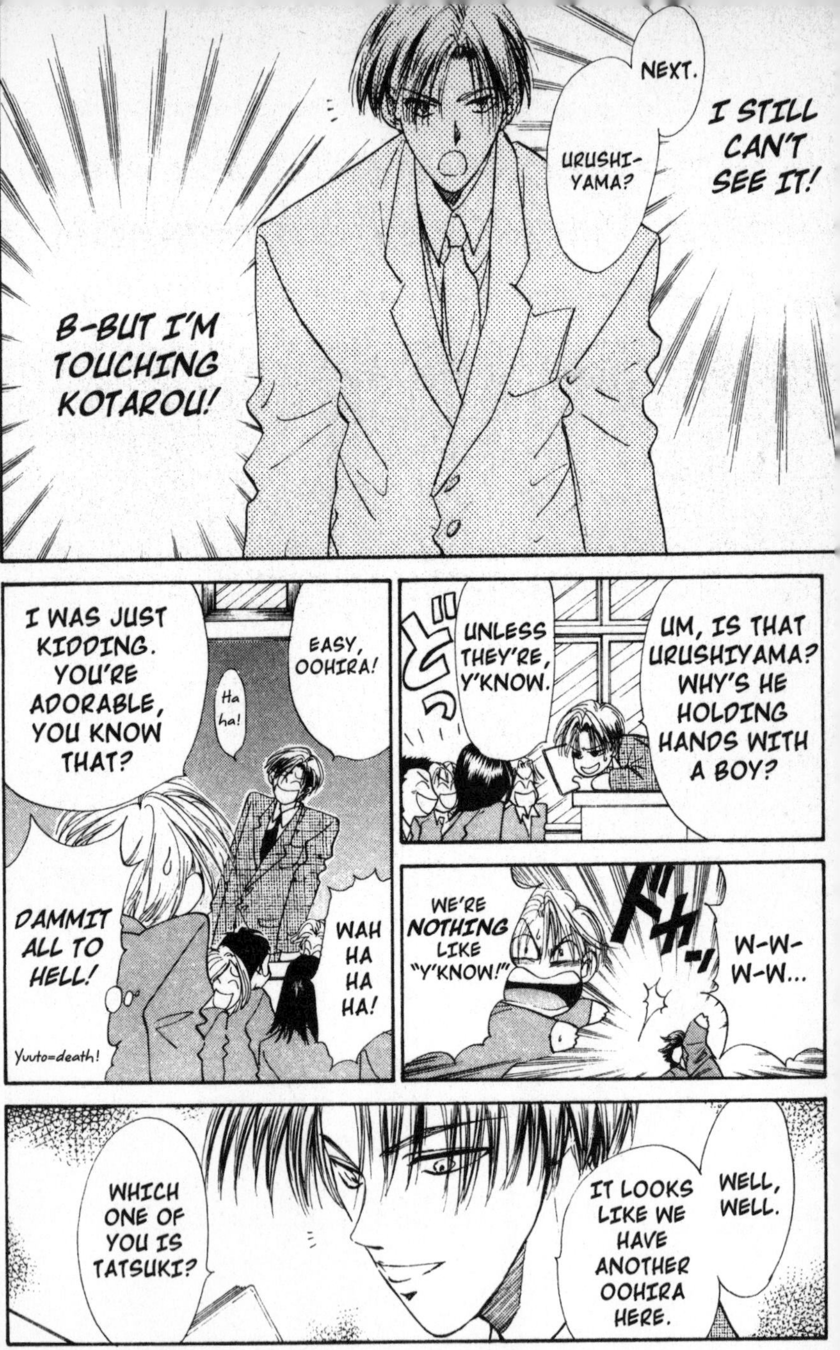
I STILL CAN'T SEE IT!
NEXT.
URUSHI-YAMA?
B-BUT I'M TOUCHING KOTAROU!
UM, IS THAT URUSHIYAMA? WHY'S HE HOLDING HANDS WITH A BOY?
UNLESS THEY'RE, Y'KNOW.
W-W-W-W...
WE'RE NOTHING LIKE "Y'KNOW!"
EASY, OOHIRA!
I WAS JUST KIDDING. YOU'RE ADORABLE, YOU KNOW THAT?
Ha ha!
WAH HA HA HA!
DAMMIT ALL TO HELL!
Yuuto=death!
WELL, WELL.
IT LOOKS LIKE WE HAVE ANOTHER OOHIRA HERE.
WHICH ONE OF YOU IS TATSUKI?

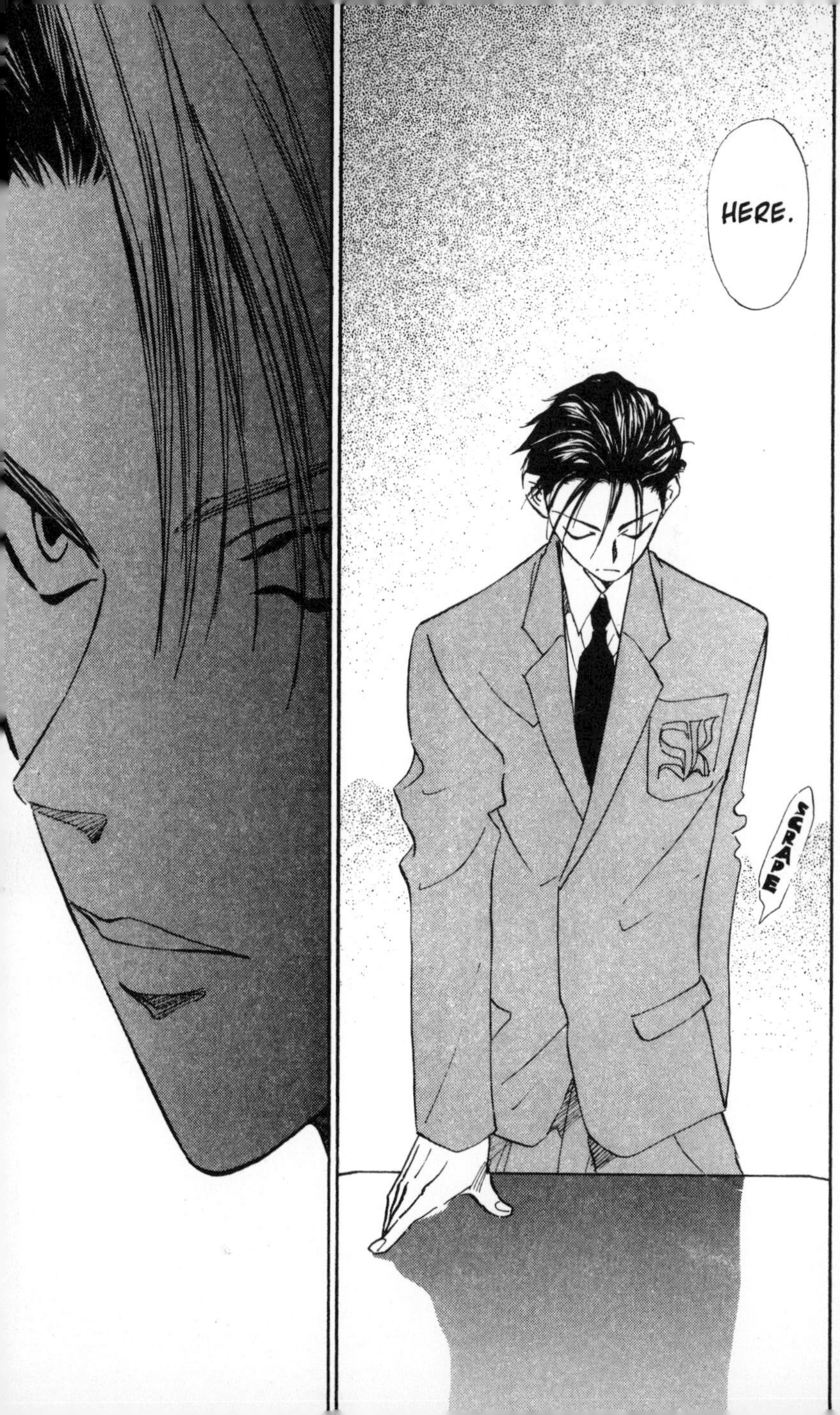
HERE.
SCRAPE

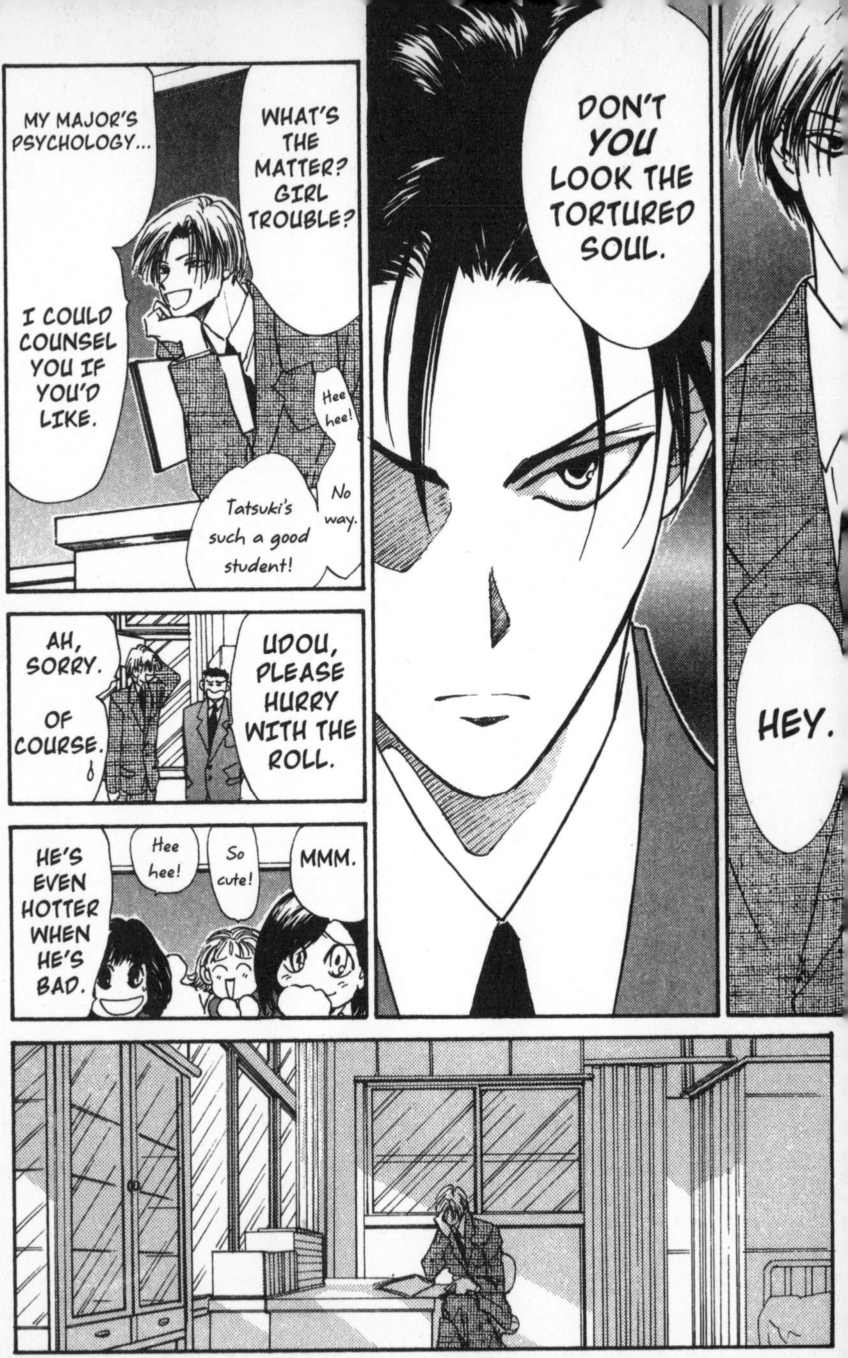
HEY.
DON'T YOU LOOK THE TORTURED SOUL.
WHAT'S THE MATTER? GIRL TROUBLE?
MY MAJOR'S PSYCHOLOGY...
I COULD COUNSEL YOU IF YOU'D LIKE.
Hee hee!
No way.
Tatsuki's such a good student!
UDOU, PLEASE HURRY WITH THE ROLL.
AH, SORRY.
OF COURSE.
MMM.
So cute!
Hee hee!
HE'S EVEN HOTTER WHEN HE'S BAD.

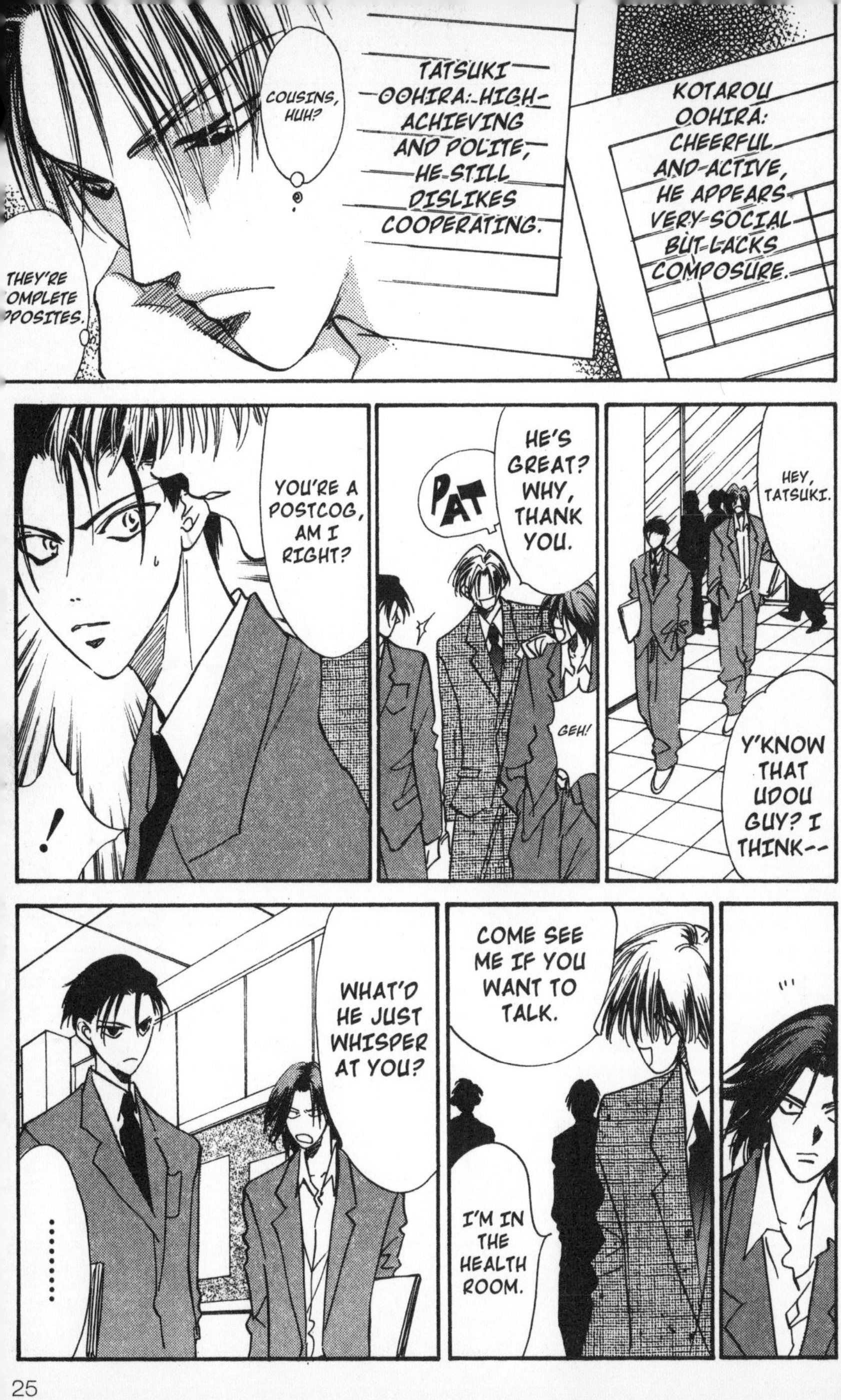
KOTAROU OOHIRA: CHEERFUL AND ACTIVE, HE APPEARS VERY SOCIAL BUT LACKS COMPOSURE.
TATSUKI OOHIRA: HIGH-ACHIEVING AND POLITE, HE STILL DISLIKES COOPERATING.
COUSINS, HUH?
THEY'RE OMPLETE PPOSITES.
HEY, TATSUKI.
Y'KNOW THAT UDOU GUY? I THINK--
PAT
HE'S GREAT? WHY, THANK YOU.
GEH!
YOU'RE A POSTCOG, AM I RIGHT?
!
COME SEE ME IF YOU WANT TO TALK.
I'M IN THE HEALTH ROOM.
WHAT'D HE JUST WHISPER AT YOU?
....

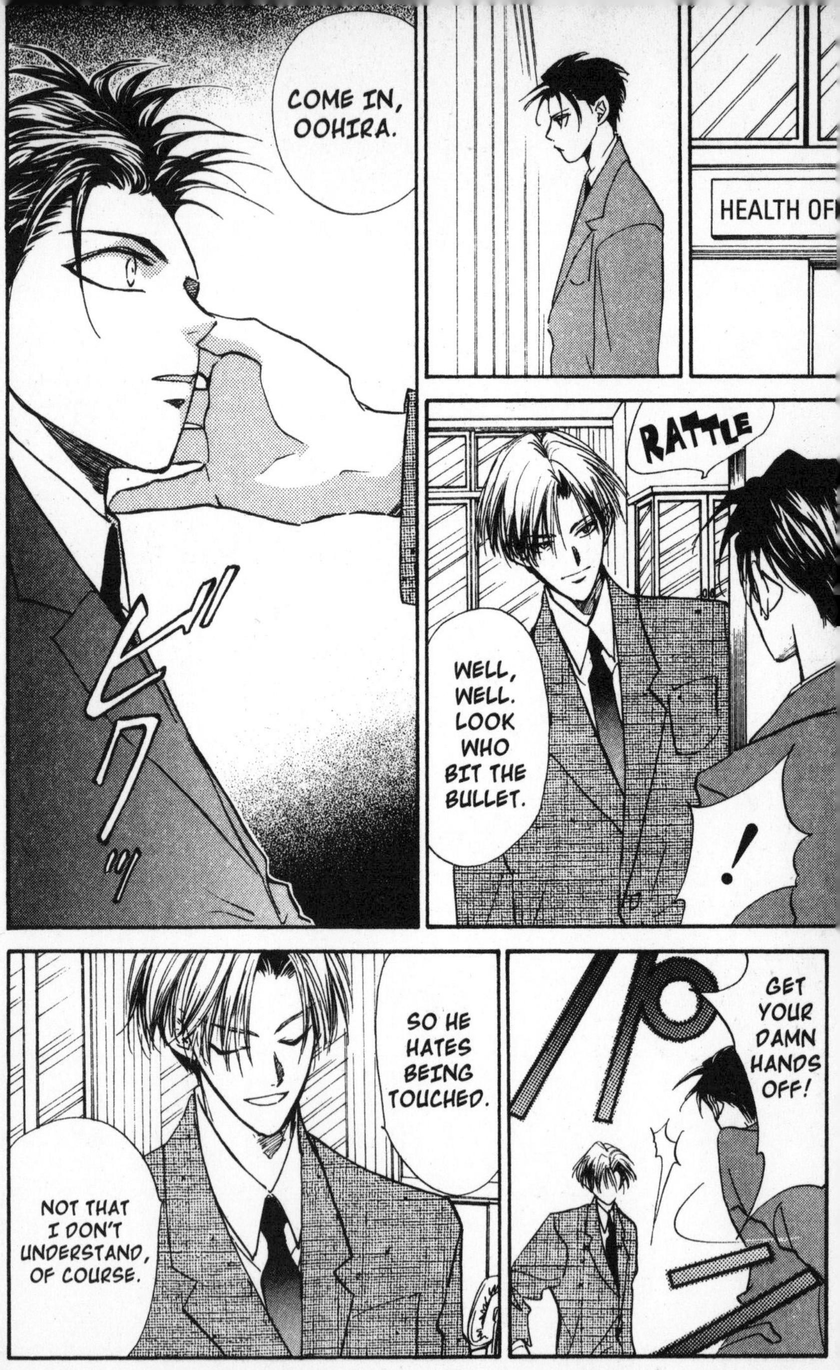
HEALTH OF
RATTLE
WELL, WELL. LOOK WHO BIT THE BULLET.
!
COME IN, OOHIRA.
ビクッ
GET YOUR DAMN HANDS OFF!
SO HE HATES BEING TOUCHED.
NOT THAT I DON'T UNDERSTAND, OF COURSE.

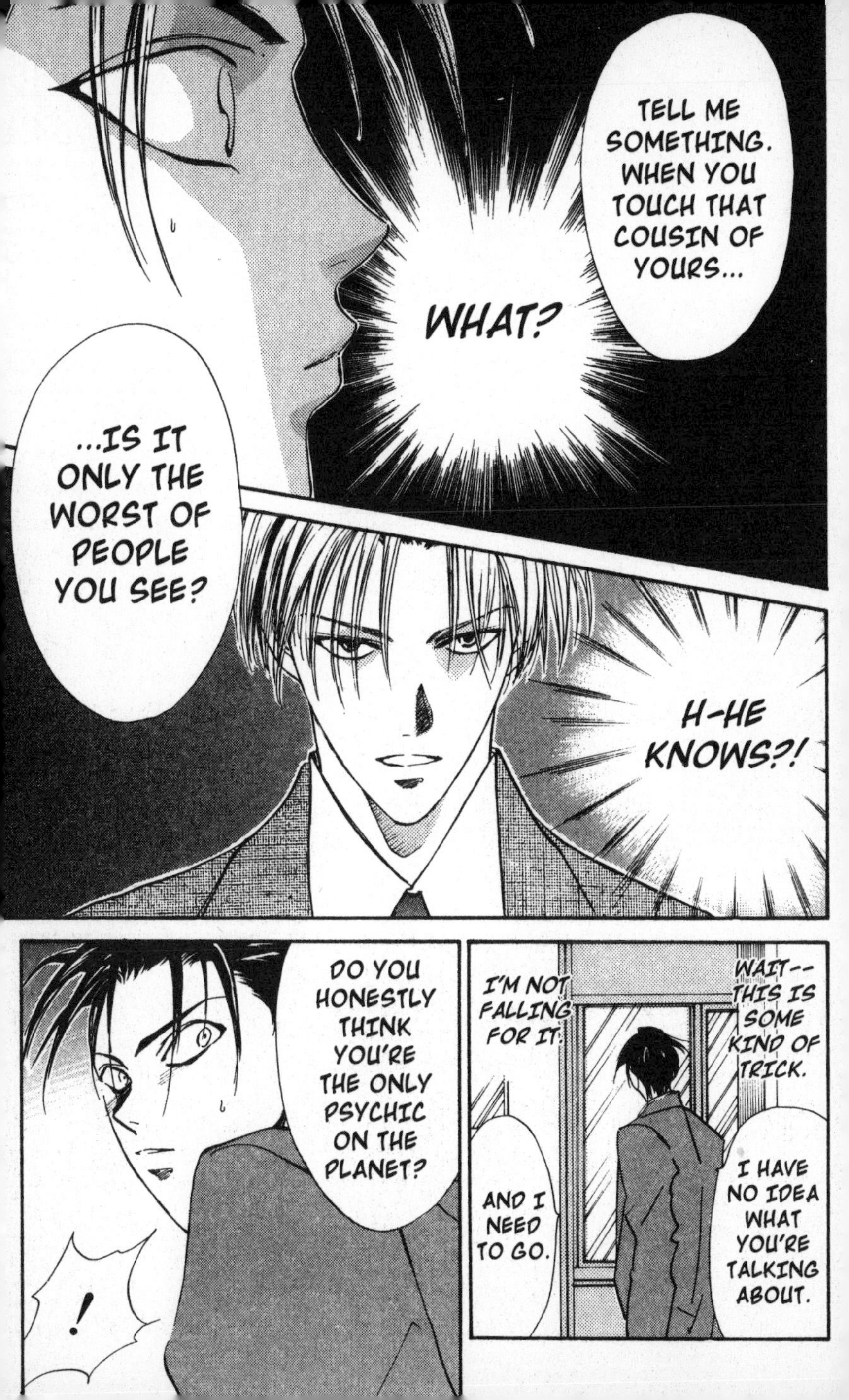
TELL ME SOMETHING. WHEN YOU TOUCH THAT COUSIN OF YOURS...
WHAT?
...IS IT ONLY THE WORST OF PEOPLE YOU SEE?
H-HE KNOWS?!
WAIT-- THIS IS SOME KIND OF TRICK.
I'M NOT FALLING FOR IT.
I HAVE NO IDEA WHAT YOU'RE TALKING ABOUT.
AND I NEED TO GO.
DO YOU HONESTLY THINK YOU'RE THE ONLY PSYCHIC ON THE PLANET?
!

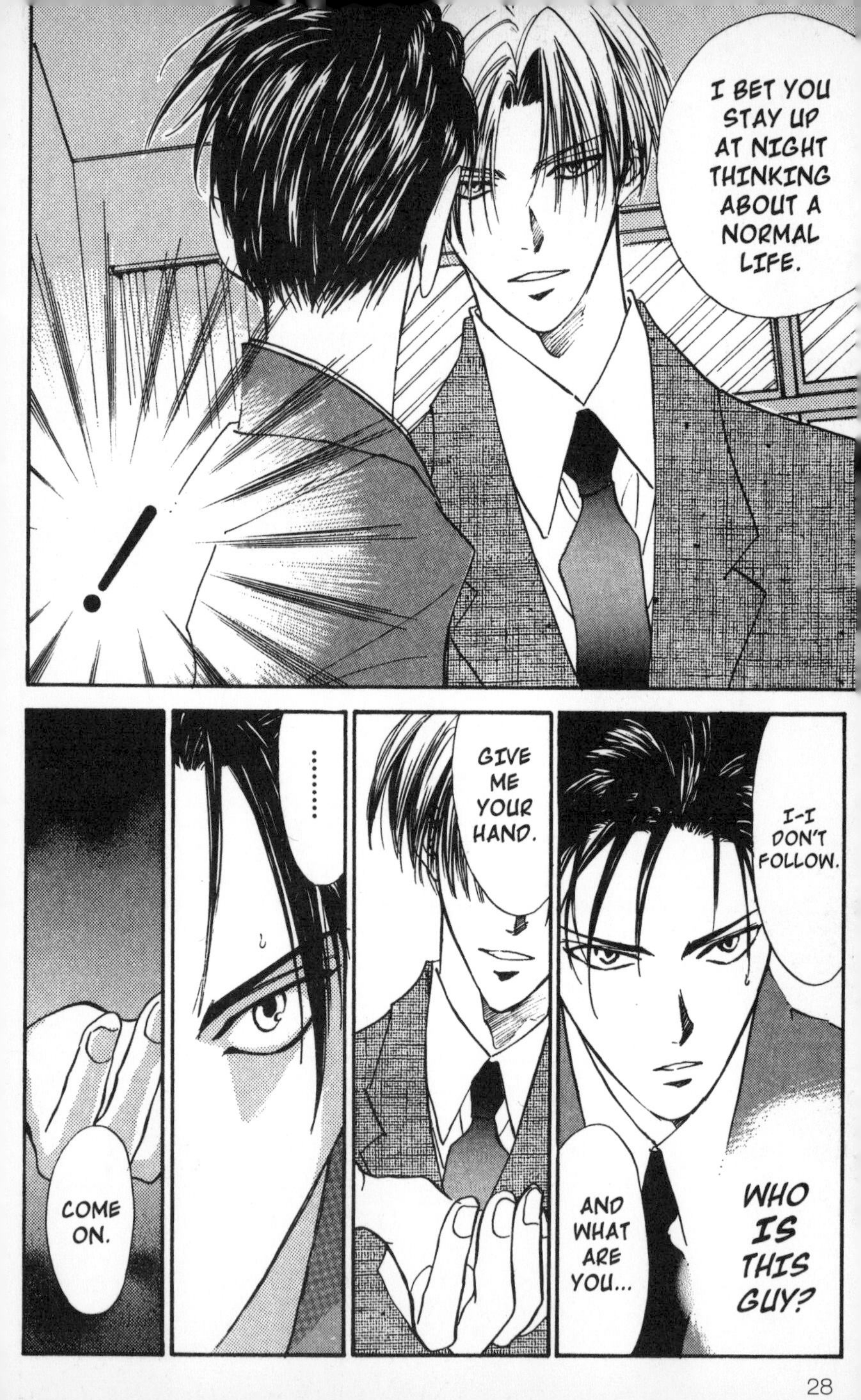
I BET YOU STAY UP AT NIGHT THINKING ABOUT A NORMAL LIFE.
!
I-I DON'T FOLLOW.
WHO IS THIS GUY?
AND WHAT ARE YOU...
GIVE ME YOUR HAND.
....
COME ON.

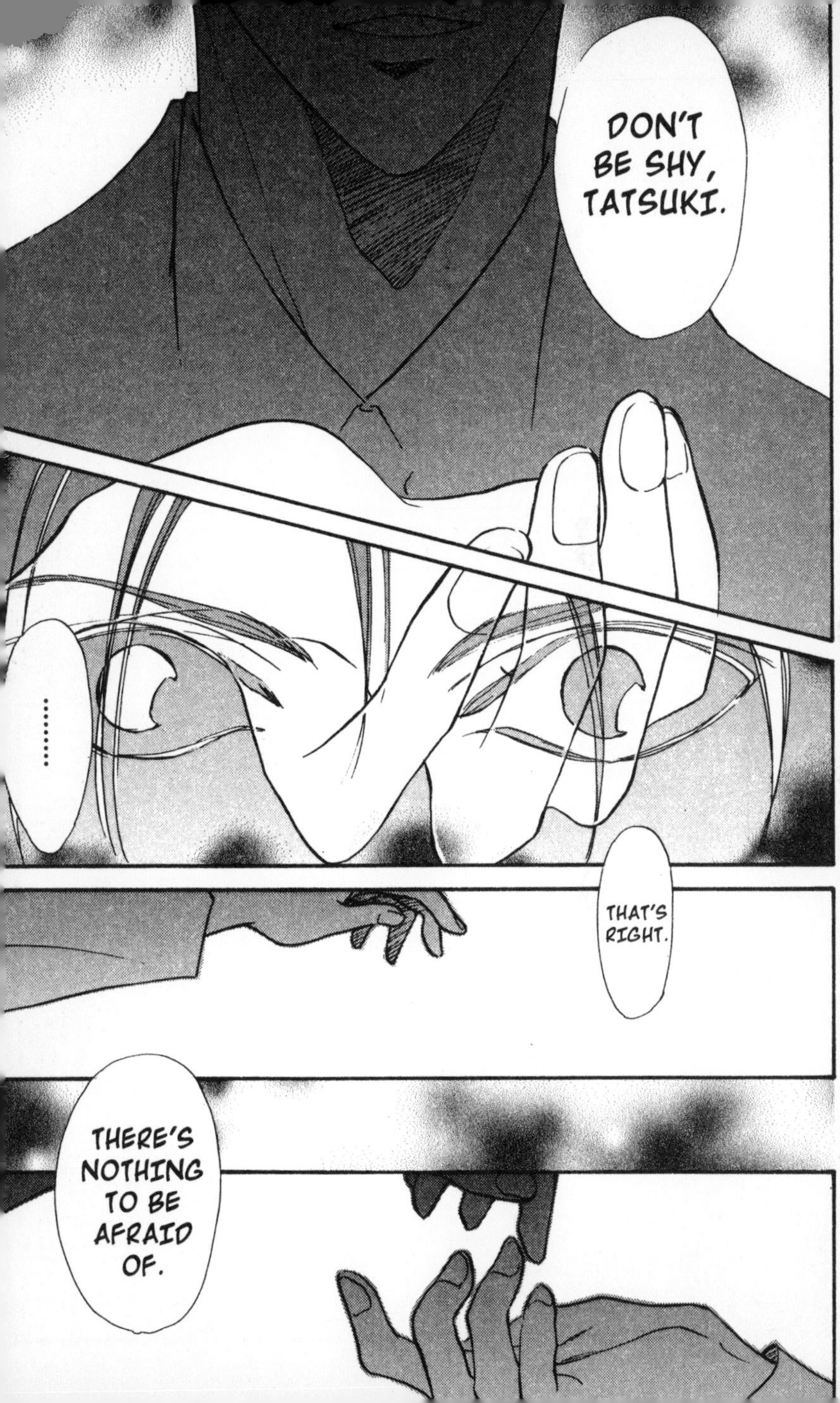
DON'T BE SHY, TATSUKI.
....
THAT'S RIGHT.
THERE'S NOTHING TO BE AFRAID OF.

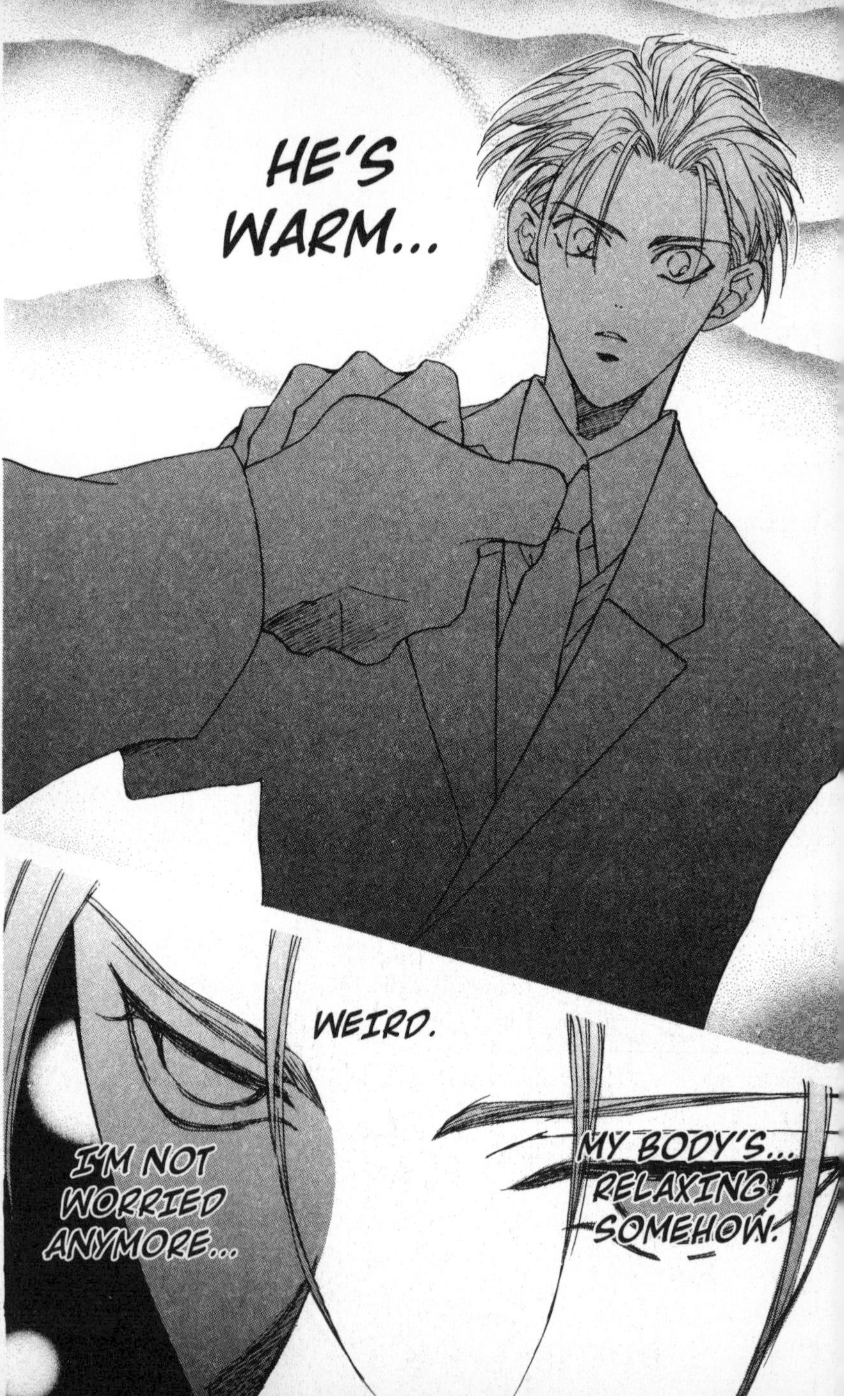
HE'S WARM...
WEIRD.
MY BODY'S... RELAXING, SOMEHOW.
I'M NOT WORRIED ANYMORE...

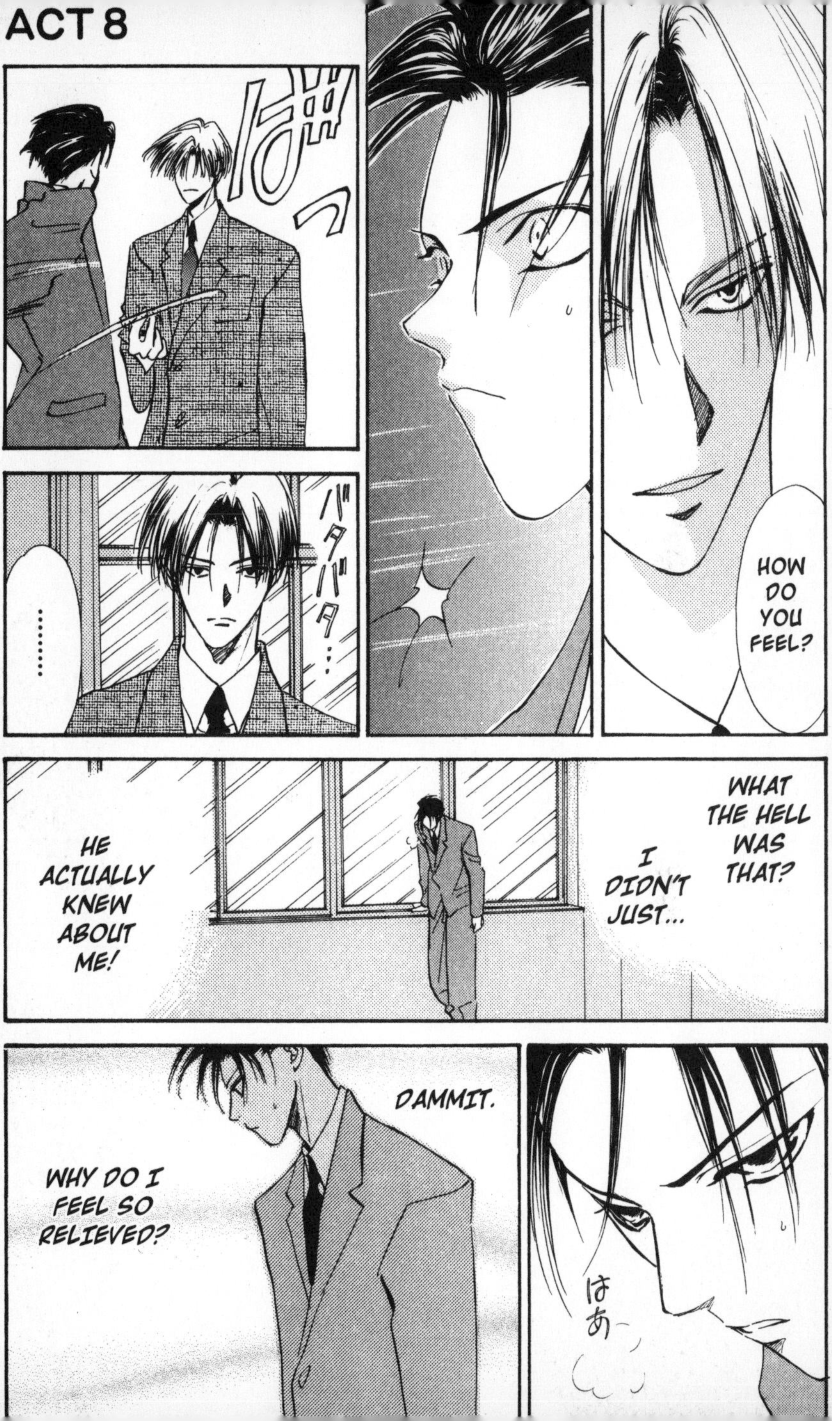
HOW DO YOU FEEL?
はっ
バタバタ…
……
WHAT THE HELL WAS THAT?
I DIDN'T JUST...
HE ACTUALLY KNEW ABOUT ME!
はあ
DAMMIT.
WHY DO I FEEL SO RELIEVED?

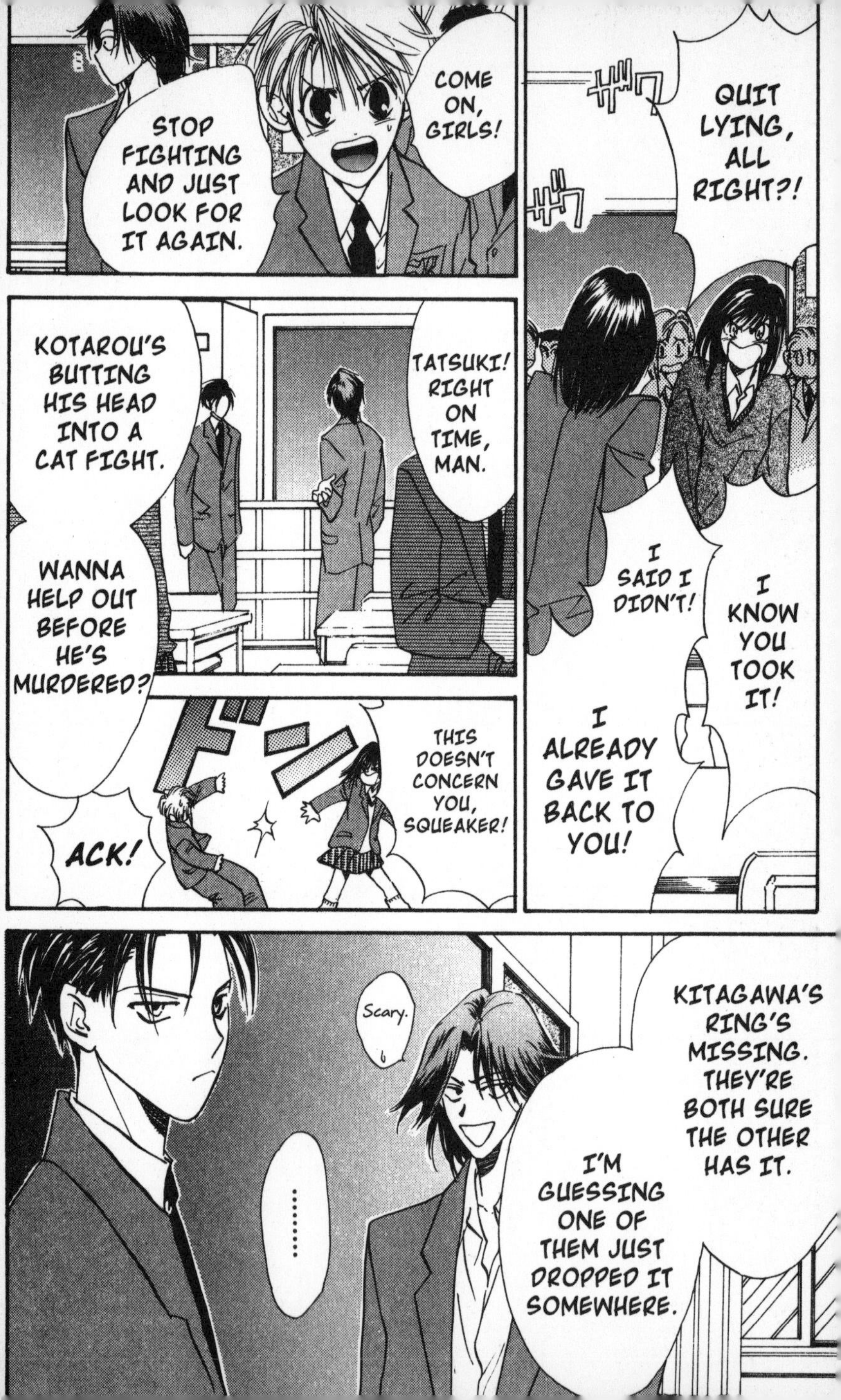
QUIT LYING, ALL RIGHT?!
I KNOW YOU TOOK IT!
I SAID I DIDN'T!
I ALREADY GAVE IT BACK TO YOU!
COME ON, GIRLS!
STOP FIGHTING AND JUST LOOK FOR IT AGAIN.
TATSUKI! RIGHT ON TIME, MAN.
KOTAROU'S BUTTING HIS HEAD INTO A CAT FIGHT.
WANNA HELP OUT BEFORE HE'S MURDERED?
THIS DOESN'T CONCERN YOU, SQUEAKER!
ACK!
KITAGAWA'S RING'S MISSING. THEY'RE BOTH SURE THE OTHER HAS IT.
I'M GUESSING ONE OF THEM JUST DROPPED IT SOMEWHERE.
Scary.
....

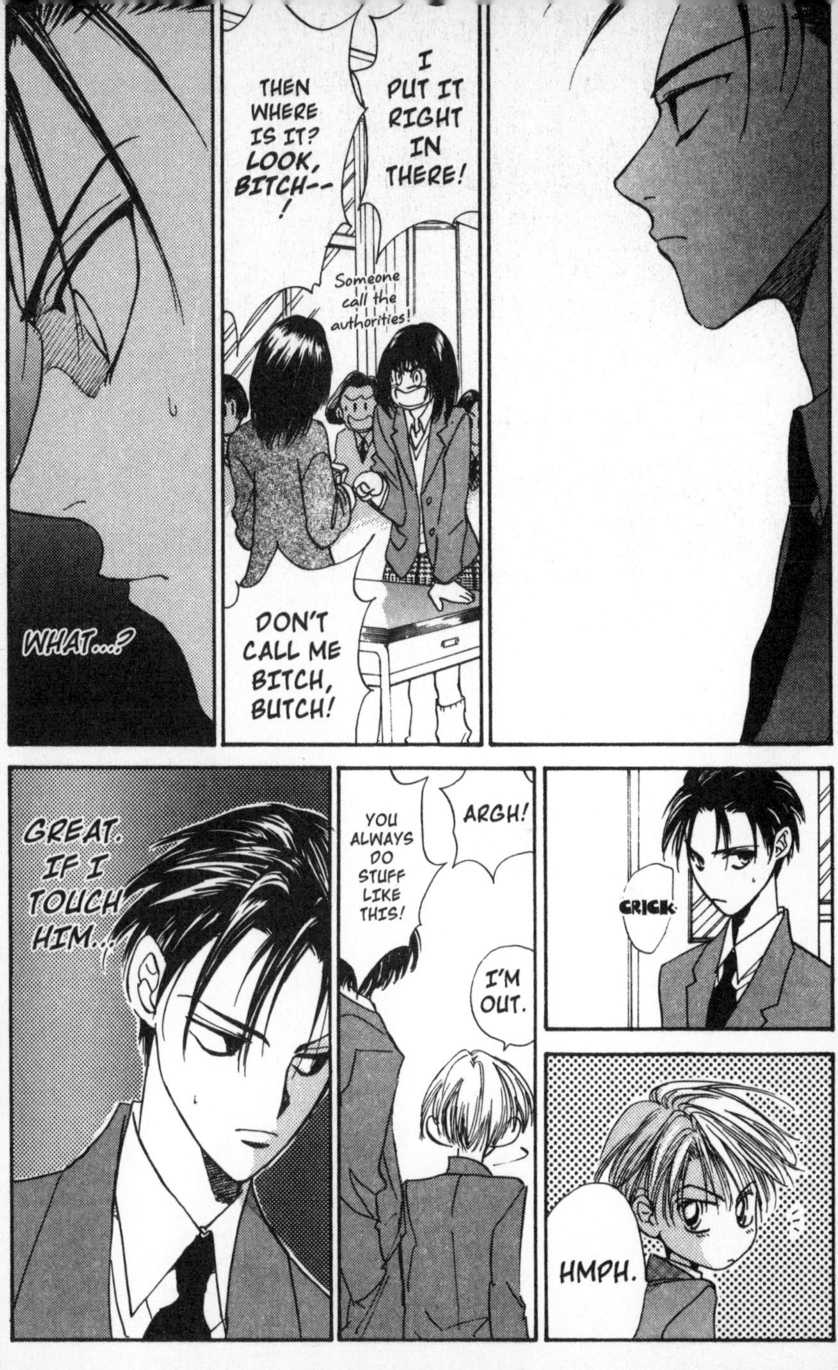
I PUT IT RIGHT IN THERE!
THEN WHERE IS IT? LOOK, BITCH--!
Someone call the authorities!
DON'T CALL ME BITCH, BUTCH!
WHAT...?
CRICK
HMPH.
ARGH!
YOU ALWAYS DO STUFF LIKE THIS!
I'M OUT.
GREAT. IF I TOUCH HIM...

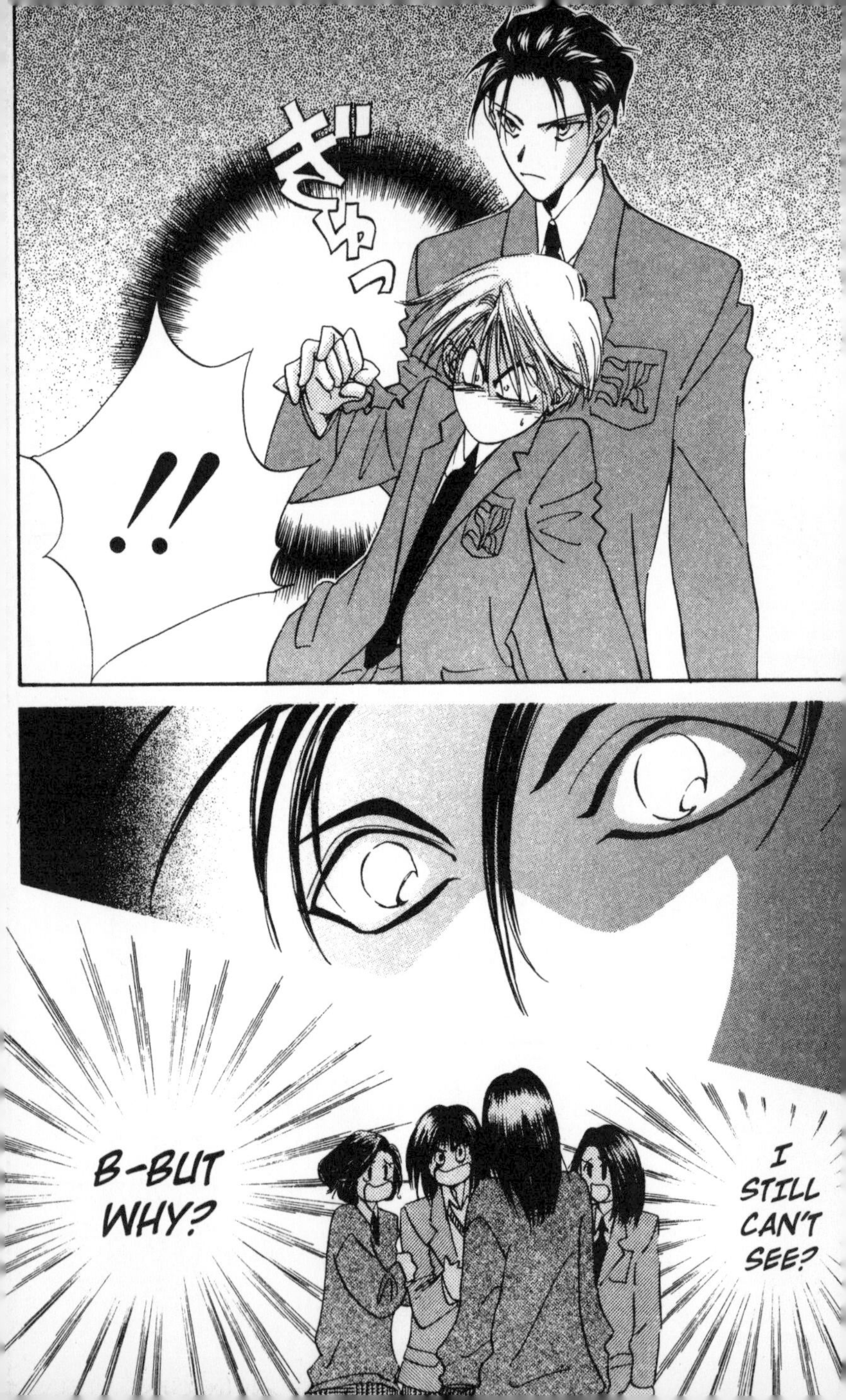
ぎゅっ
!!
I STILL CAN'T SEE?
B-BUT WHY?

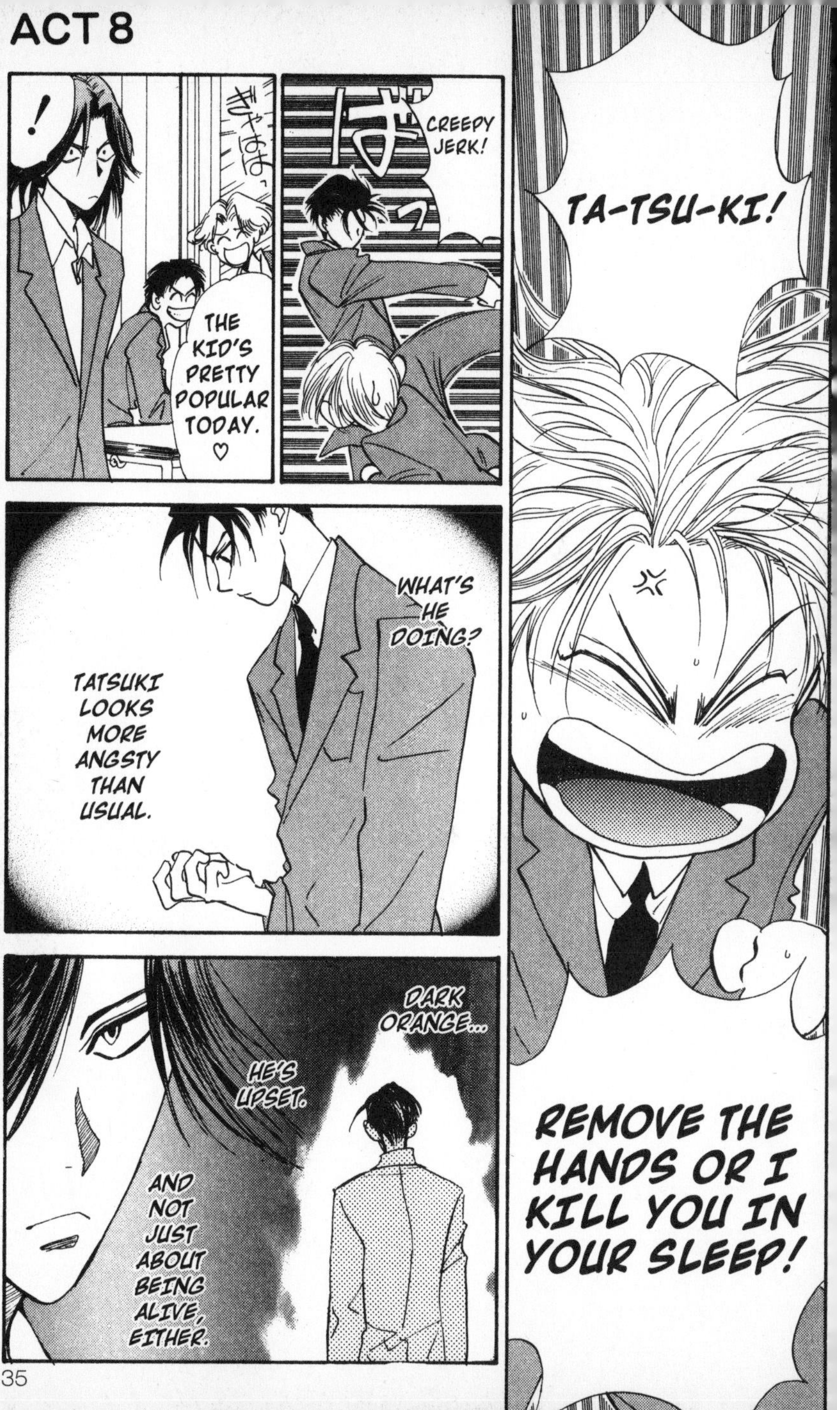
TA-TSU-KI!
REMOVE THE HANDS OR I KILL YOU IN YOUR SLEEP!
ばっ
CREEPY JERK!
ぎゃはは、
!
THE KID'S PRETTY POPULAR TODAY. ♡
WHAT'S HE DOING?
TATSUKI LOOKS MORE ANGSTY THAN USUAL.
DARK ORANGE...
HE'S UPSET.
AND NOT JUST ABOUT BEING ALIVE, EITHER.

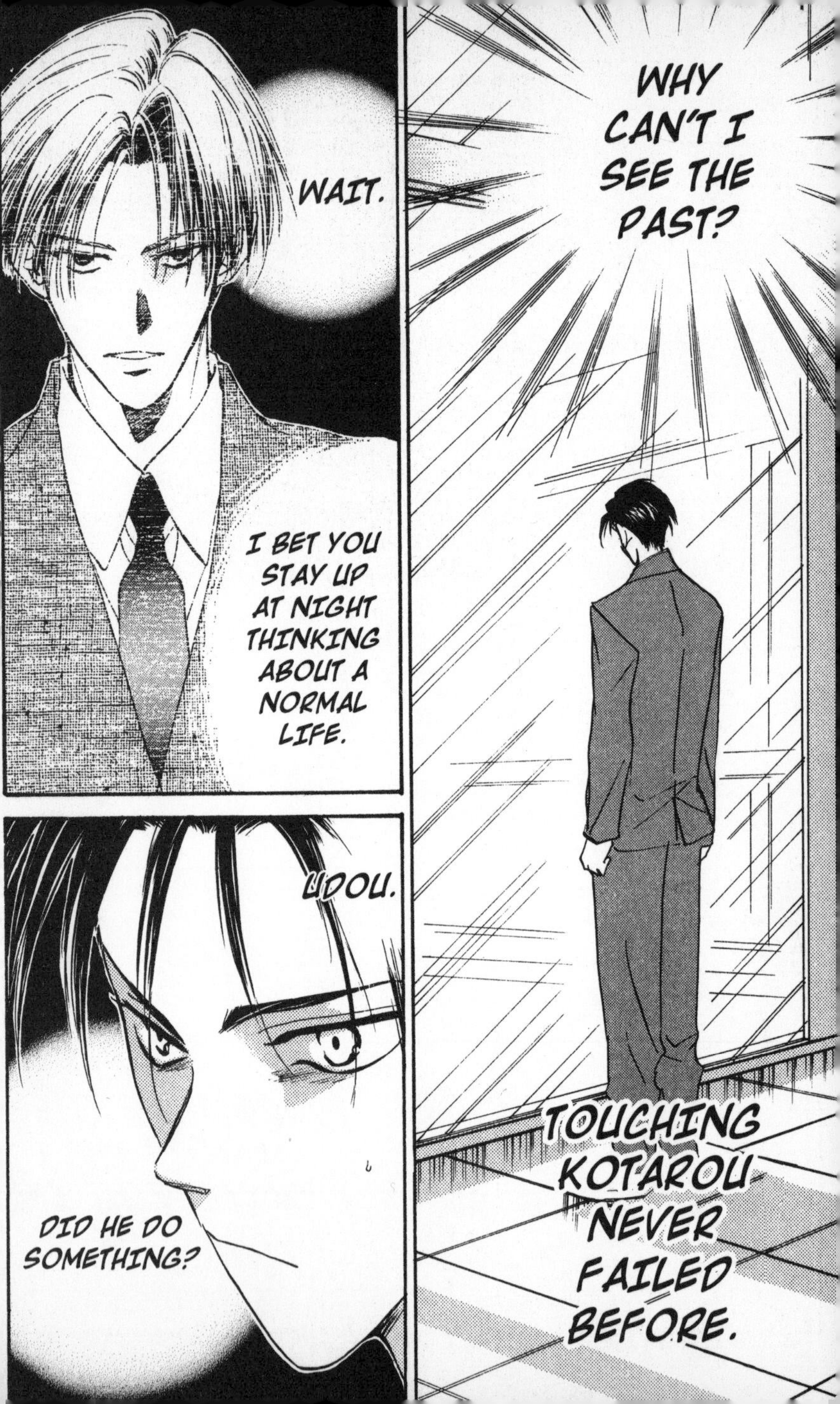
WHY CAN'T I SEE THE PAST?
TOUCHING KOTAROU NEVER FAILED BEFORE.
WAIT.
I BET YOU STAY UP AT NIGHT THINKING ABOUT A NORMAL LIFE.
UDOU.
DID HE DO SOMETHING?

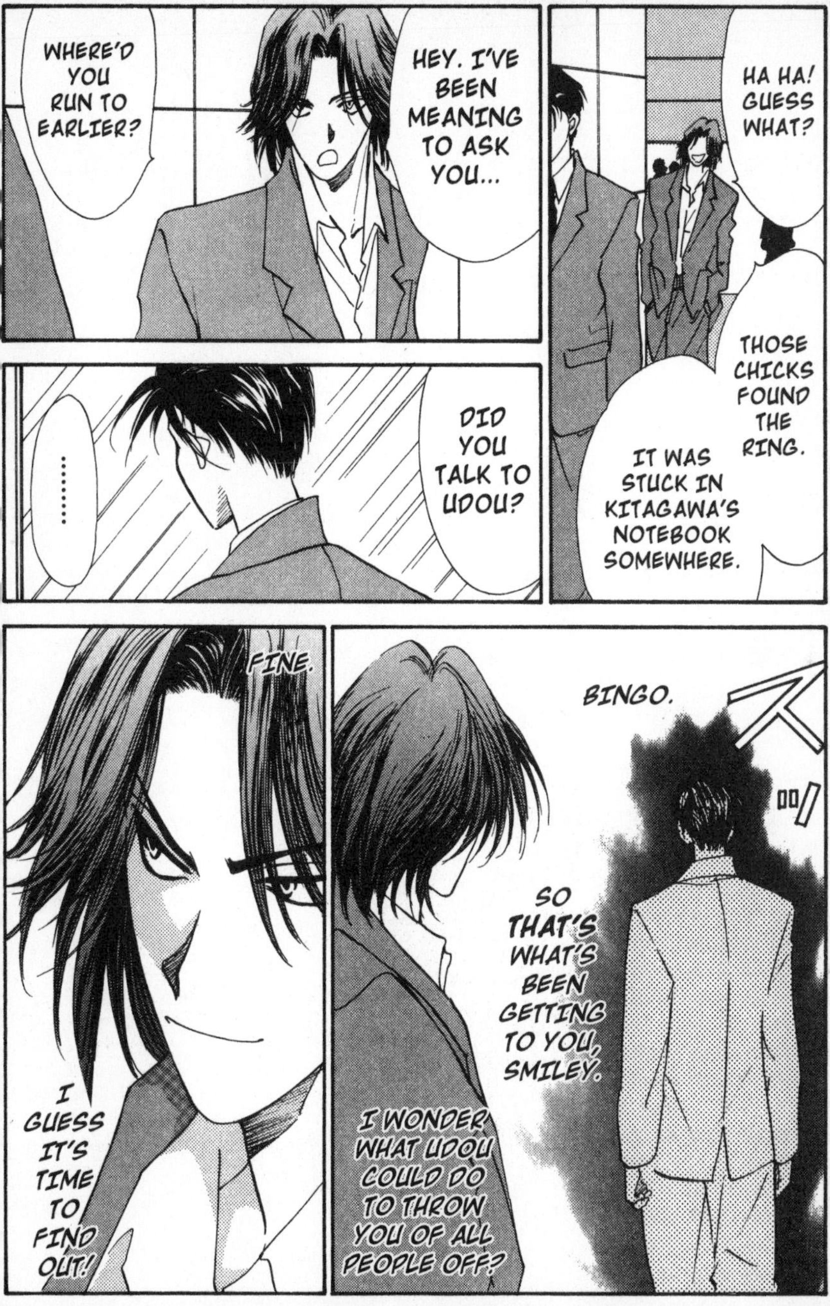
HA HA! GUESS WHAT?
THOSE CHICKS FOUND THE RING.
IT WAS STUCK IN KITAGAWA'S NOTEBOOK SOMEWHERE.
HEY. I'VE BEEN MEANING TO ASK YOU...
WHERE'D YOU RUN TO EARLIER?
DID YOU TALK TO UDOU?
....
BINGO.
SO THAT'S WHAT'S BEEN GETTING TO YOU, SMILEY.
I WONDER WHAT UDOU COULD DO TO THROW YOU OF ALL PEOPLE OFF?
FINE.
I GUESS IT'S TIME TO FIND OUT!

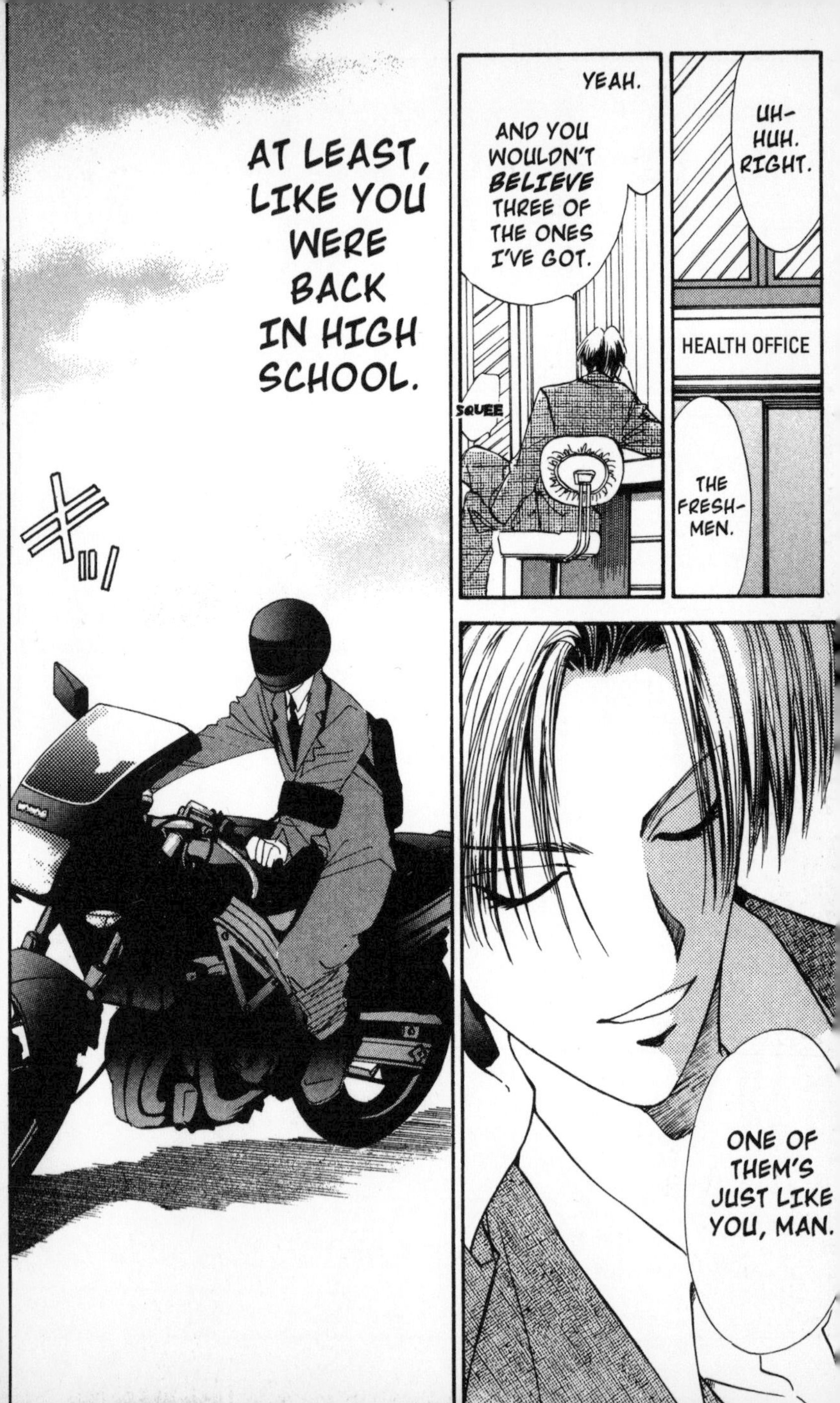
UH-HUH. RIGHT.
HEALTH OFFICE
THE FRESHMEN.
YEAH.
AND YOU WOULDN'T *BELIEVE* THREE OF THE ONES I'VE GOT.
SQUEE
ONE OF THEM'S JUST LIKE YOU, MAN.
AT LEAST, LIKE YOU WERE BACK IN HIGH SCHOOL.

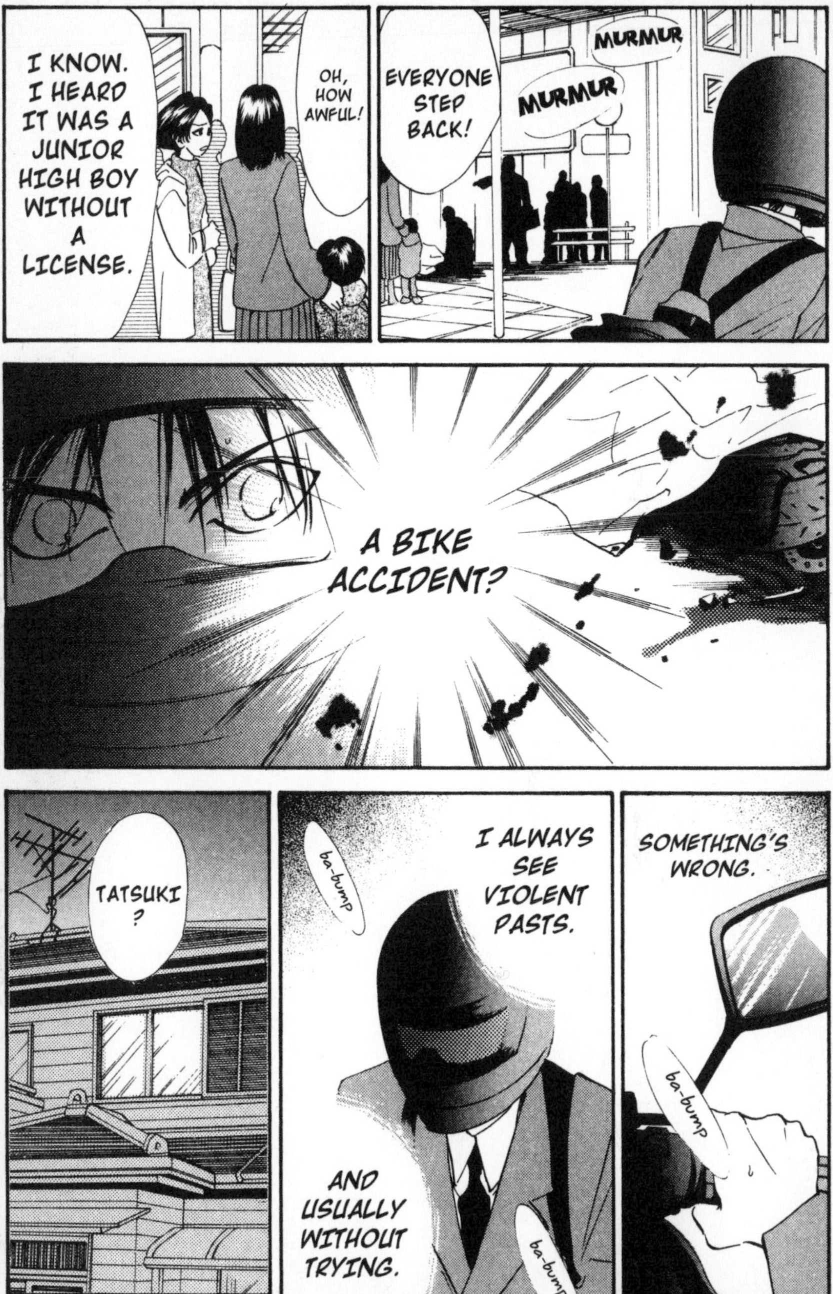
MURMUR
MURMUR
EVERYONE STEP BACK!
OH, HOW AWFUL!
I KNOW. I HEARD IT WAS A JUNIOR HIGH BOY WITHOUT A LICENSE.
A BIKE ACCIDENT?
SOMETHING'S WRONG.
ba-bump
I ALWAYS SEE VIOLENT PASTS.
ba-bump
AND USUALLY WITHOUT TRYING.
ba-bump
TATSUKI?

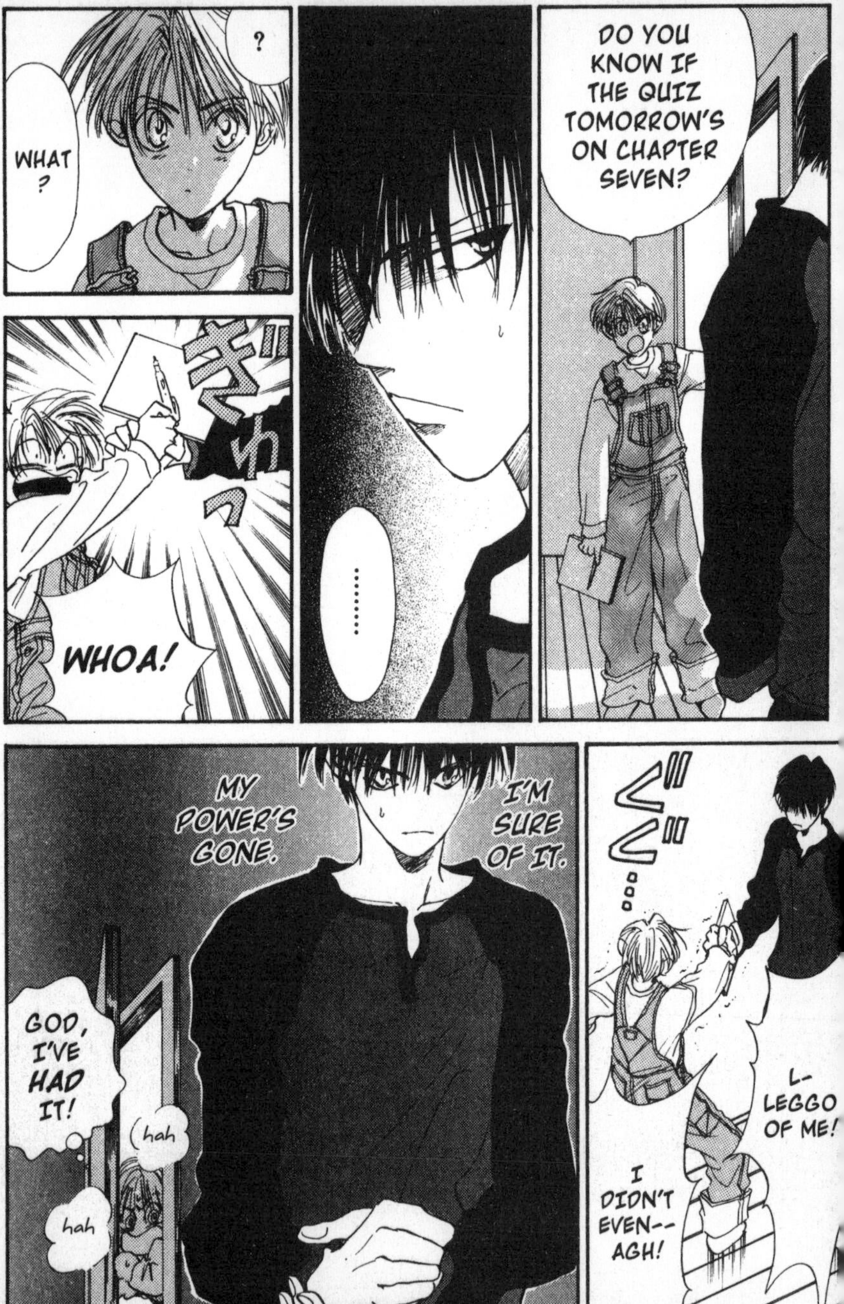
DO YOU KNOW IF THE QUIZ TOMORROW'S ON CHAPTER SEVEN?
....
?
WHAT ?
ぎゅっ
WHOA!
ぐぐ
...
L-LEGGO OF ME!
I DIDN'T EVEN--AGH!
MY POWER'S GONE.
I'M SURE OF IT.
GOD, I'VE HAD IT!
hah
hah

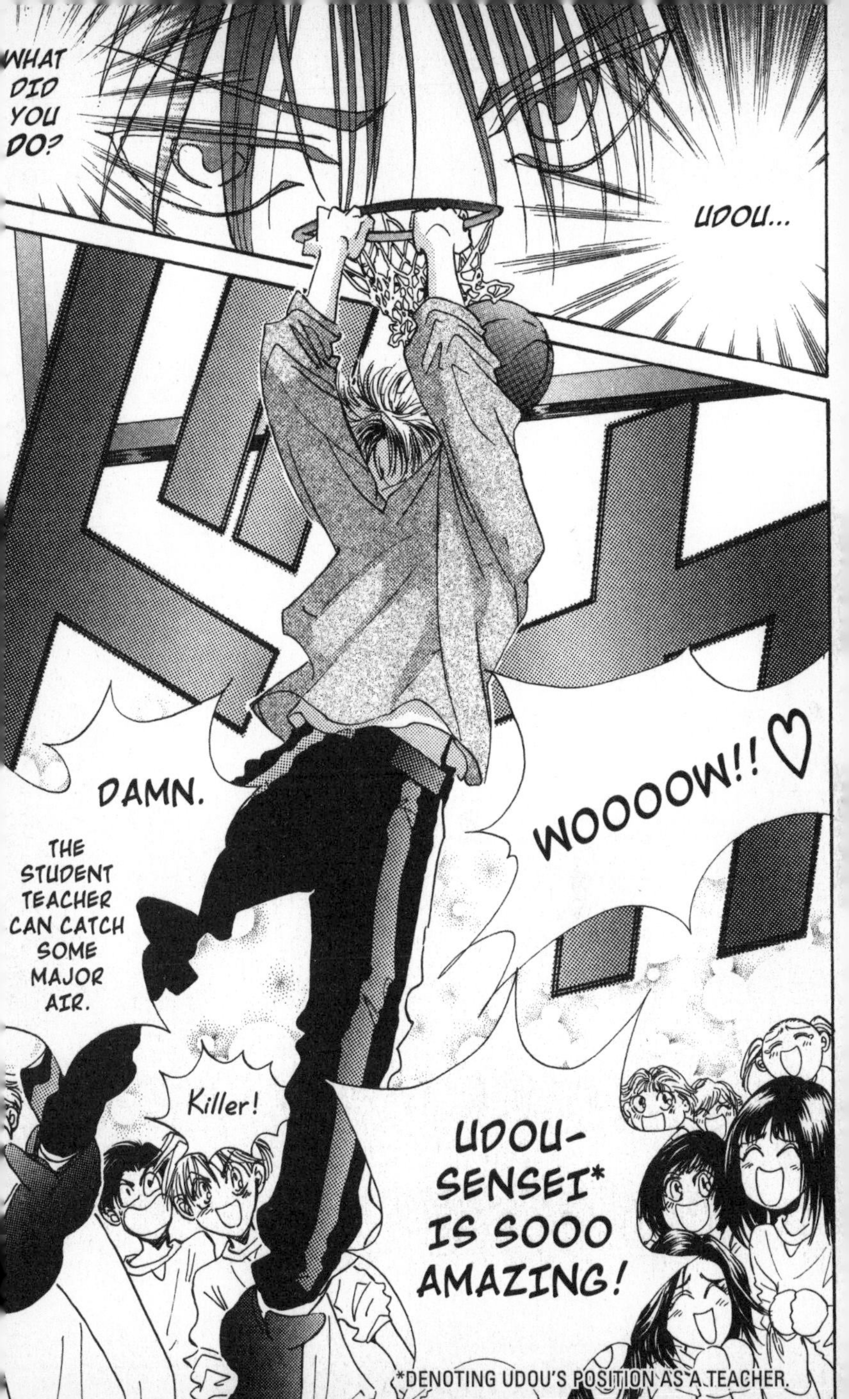
UDOU...
WHAT DID YOU DO?
WOOOOW!! ♡
DAMN.
THE STUDENT TEACHER CAN CATCH SOME MAJOR AIR.
UDOU-SENSEI* IS SOOO AMAZING!
Killer!
*DENOTING UDOU'S POSITION AS A TEACHER.

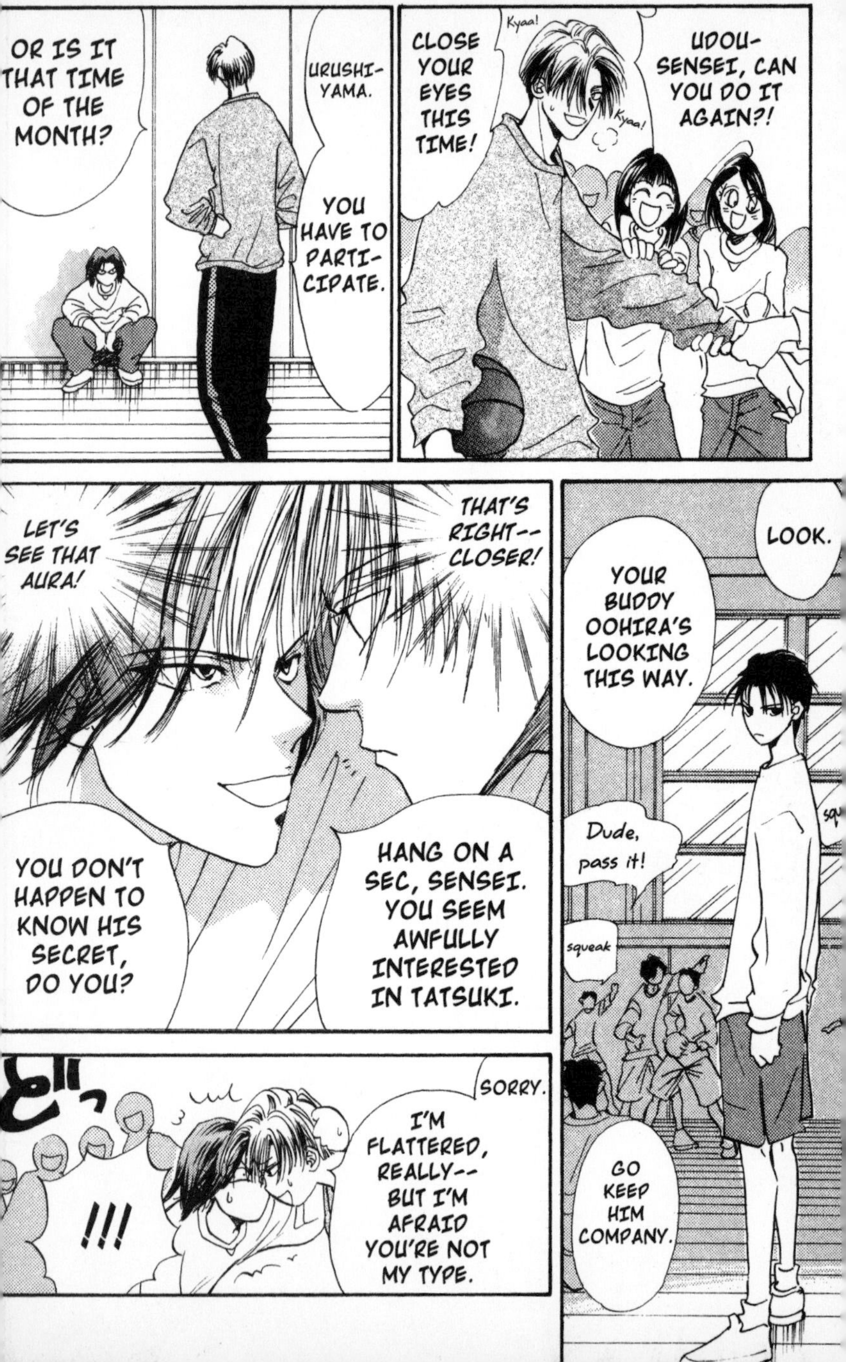
UDOU-SENSEI, CAN YOU DO IT AGAIN?!
Kyaa!
Kyaa!
CLOSE YOUR EYES THIS TIME!
URUSHIYAMA.
YOU HAVE TO PARTICIPATE.
OR IS IT THAT TIME OF THE MONTH?
LOOK.
YOUR BUDDY OOHIRA'S LOOKING THIS WAY.
Dude, pass it!
squeak
GO KEEP HIM COMPANY.
THAT'S RIGHT--CLOSER!
LET'S SEE THAT AURA!
HANG ON A SEC, SENSEI. YOU SEEM AWFULLY INTERESTED IN TATSUKI.
YOU DON'T HAPPEN TO KNOW HIS SECRET, DO YOU?
SORRY.
I'M FLATTERED, REALLY--BUT I'M AFRAID YOU'RE NOT MY TYPE.
!!!

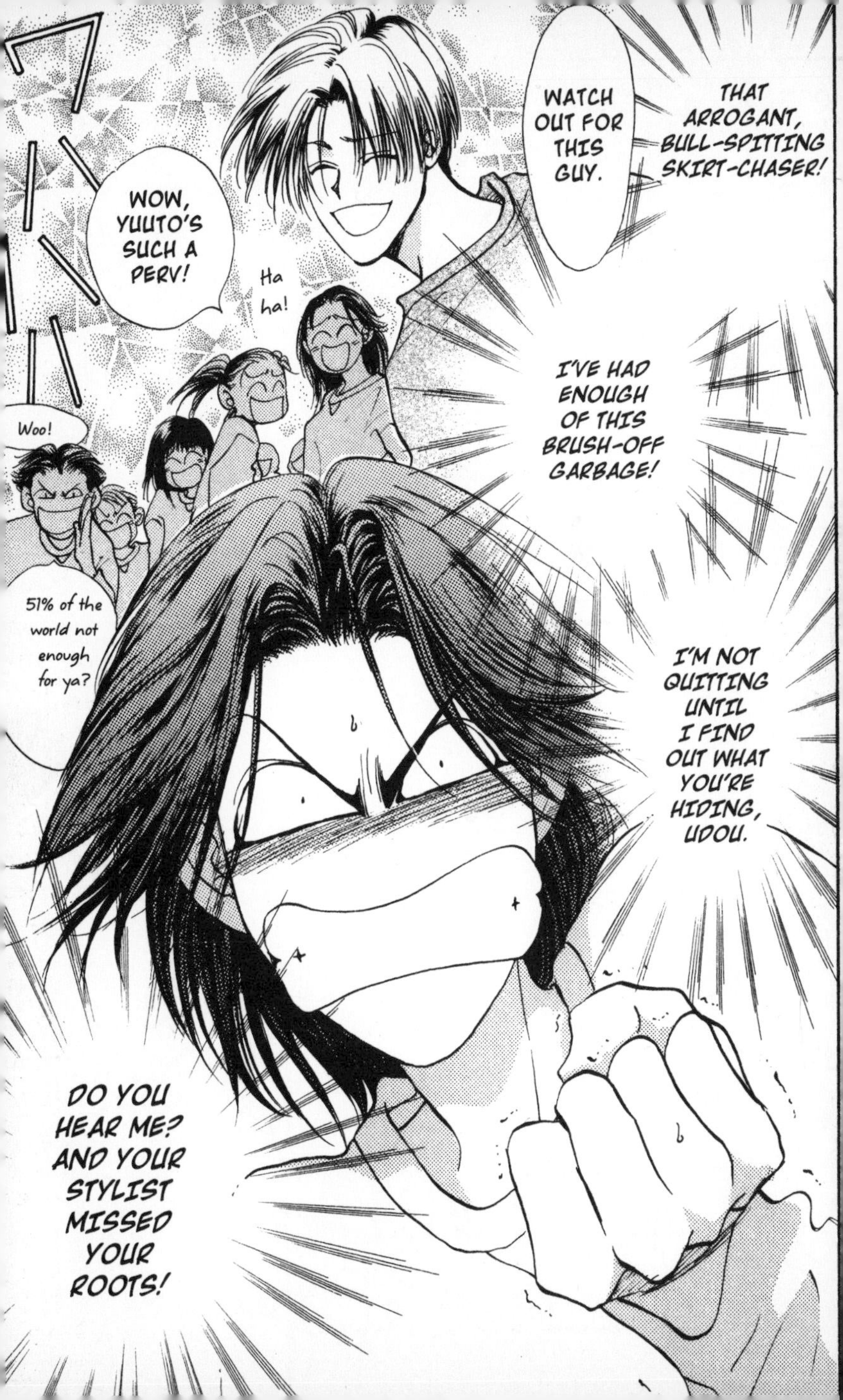
THAT ARROGANT, BULL-SPITTING SKIRT-CHASER!
WATCH OUT FOR THIS GUY.
WOW, YUUTO'S SUCH A PERV!
Ha ha!
I'VE HAD ENOUGH OF THIS BRUSH-OFF GARBAGE!
Woo!
51% of the world not enough for ya?
I'M NOT QUITTING UNTIL I FIND OUT WHAT YOU'RE HIDING, UDOU.
DO YOU HEAR ME? AND YOUR STYLIST MISSED YOUR ROOTS!

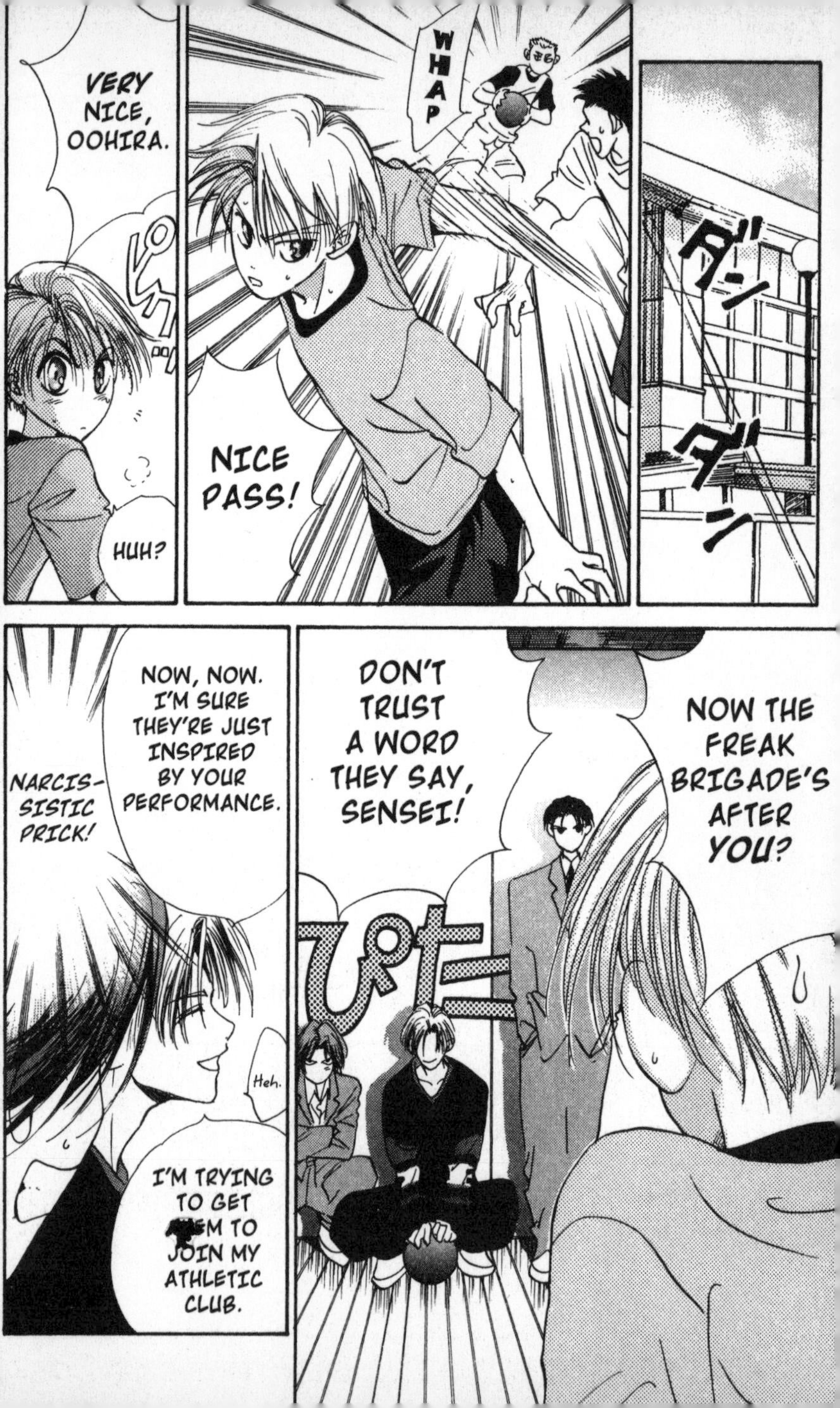
ダーン
ダーン
WHAP
NICE PASS!
VERY NICE, OOHIRA.
HUH?
NOW THE FREAK BRIGADE'S AFTER YOU?
DON'T TRUST A WORD THEY SAY, SENSEI!
NOW, NOW. I'M SURE THEY'RE JUST INSPIRED BY YOUR PERFORMANCE.
NARCISSISTIC PRICK!
Heh.
I'M TRYING TO GET THEM TO JOIN MY ATHLETIC CLUB.

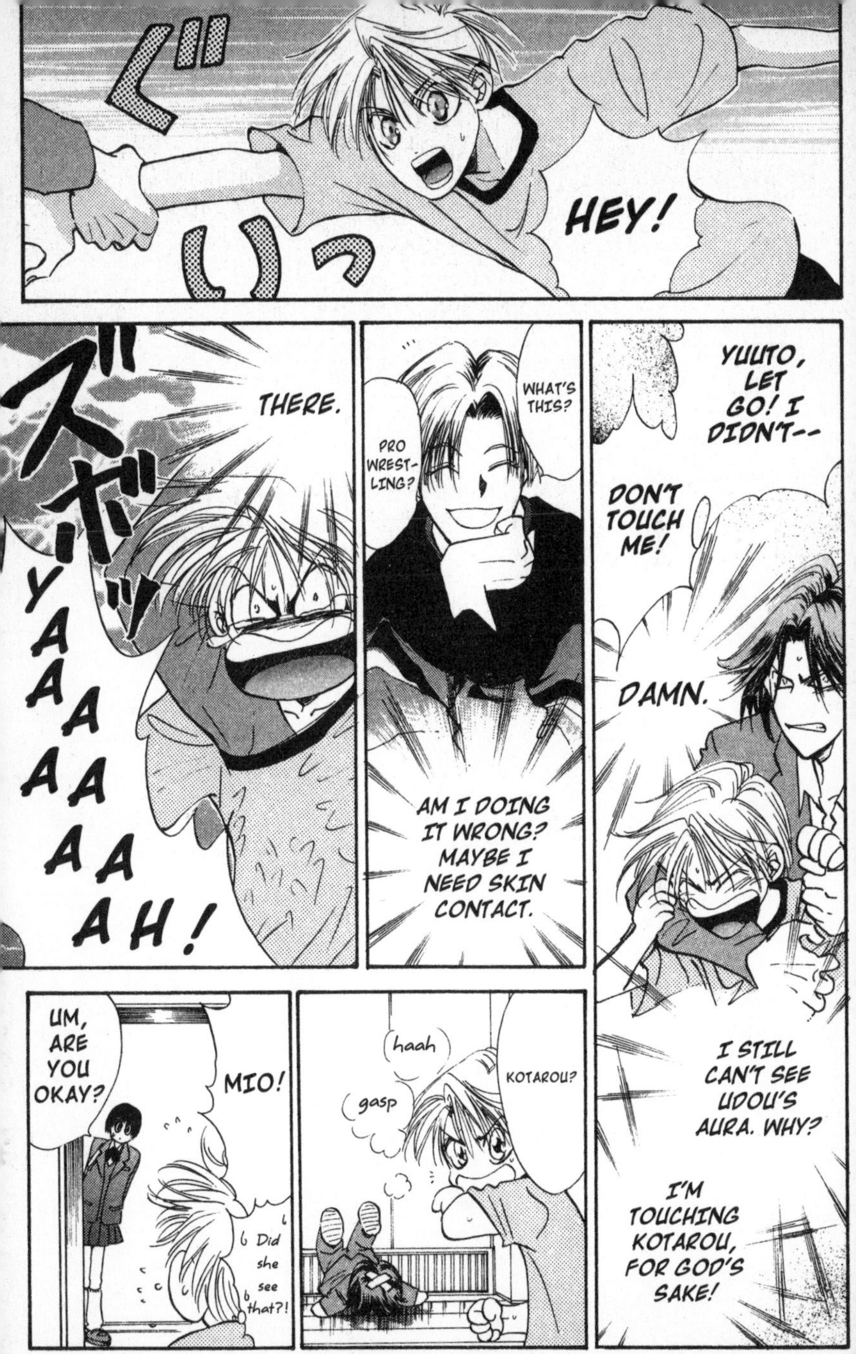
ぐいっ
HEY!
YUUTO, LET GO! I DIDN'T--
DON'T TOUCH ME!
DAMN.
I STILL CAN'T SEE UDOU'S AURA. WHY?
I'M TOUCHING KOTAROU, FOR GOD'S SAKE!
WHAT'S THIS?
PRO WRESTLING?
...
AM I DOING IT WRONG? MAYBE I NEED SKIN CONTACT.
ズボッ
THERE.
YAAAAAAAAAAH!
KOTAROU?
haah
gasp
UM, ARE YOU OKAY?
MIO!
Did she see that?!

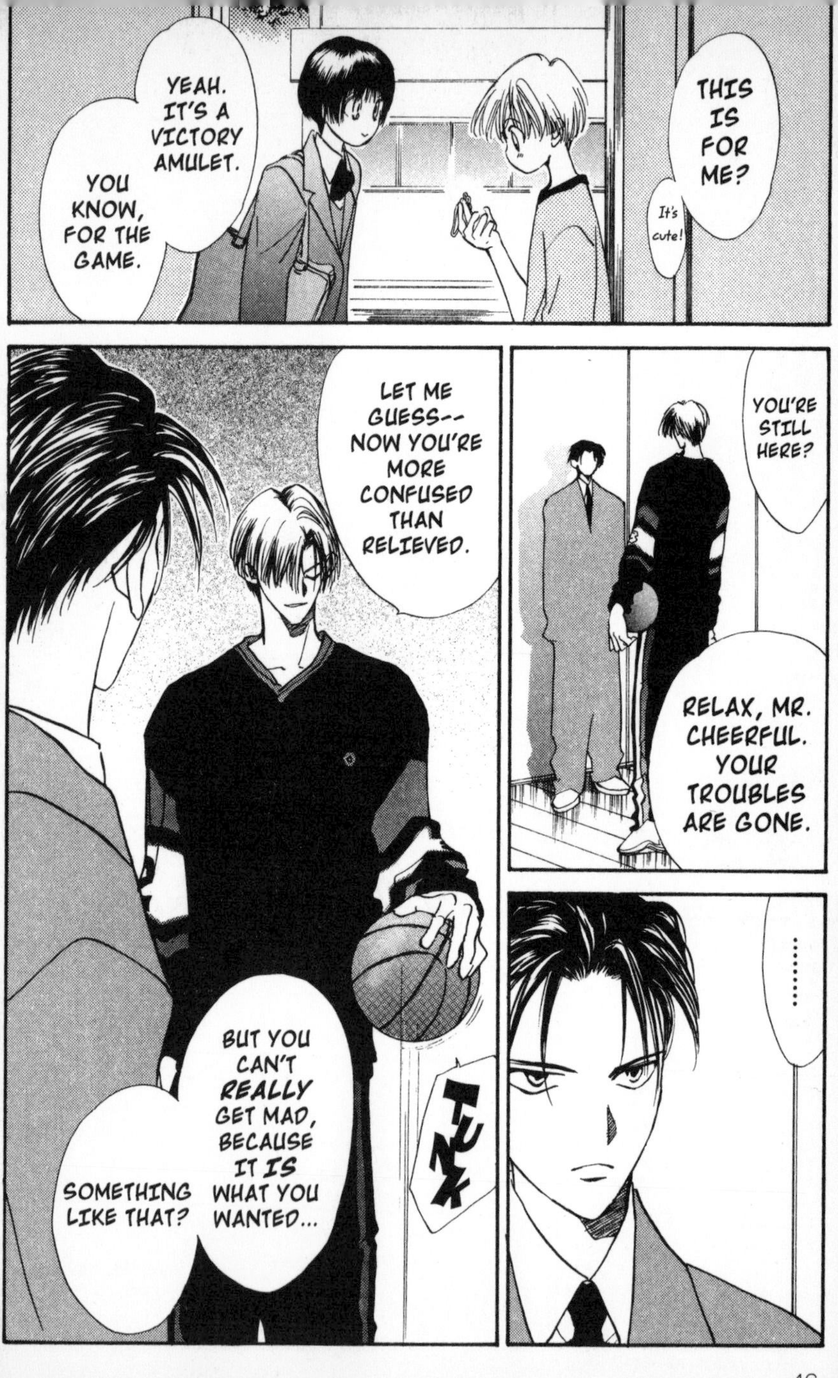
THIS IS FOR ME?
It's cute!
YEAH. IT'S A VICTORY AMULET.
YOU KNOW, FOR THE GAME.
YOU'RE STILL HERE?
RELAX, MR. CHEERFUL. YOUR TROUBLES ARE GONE.
....
LET ME GUESS-- NOW YOU'RE MORE CONFUSED THAN RELIEVED.
TUNK
BUT YOU CAN'T REALLY GET MAD, BECAUSE IT IS WHAT YOU WANTED...
SOMETHING LIKE THAT?

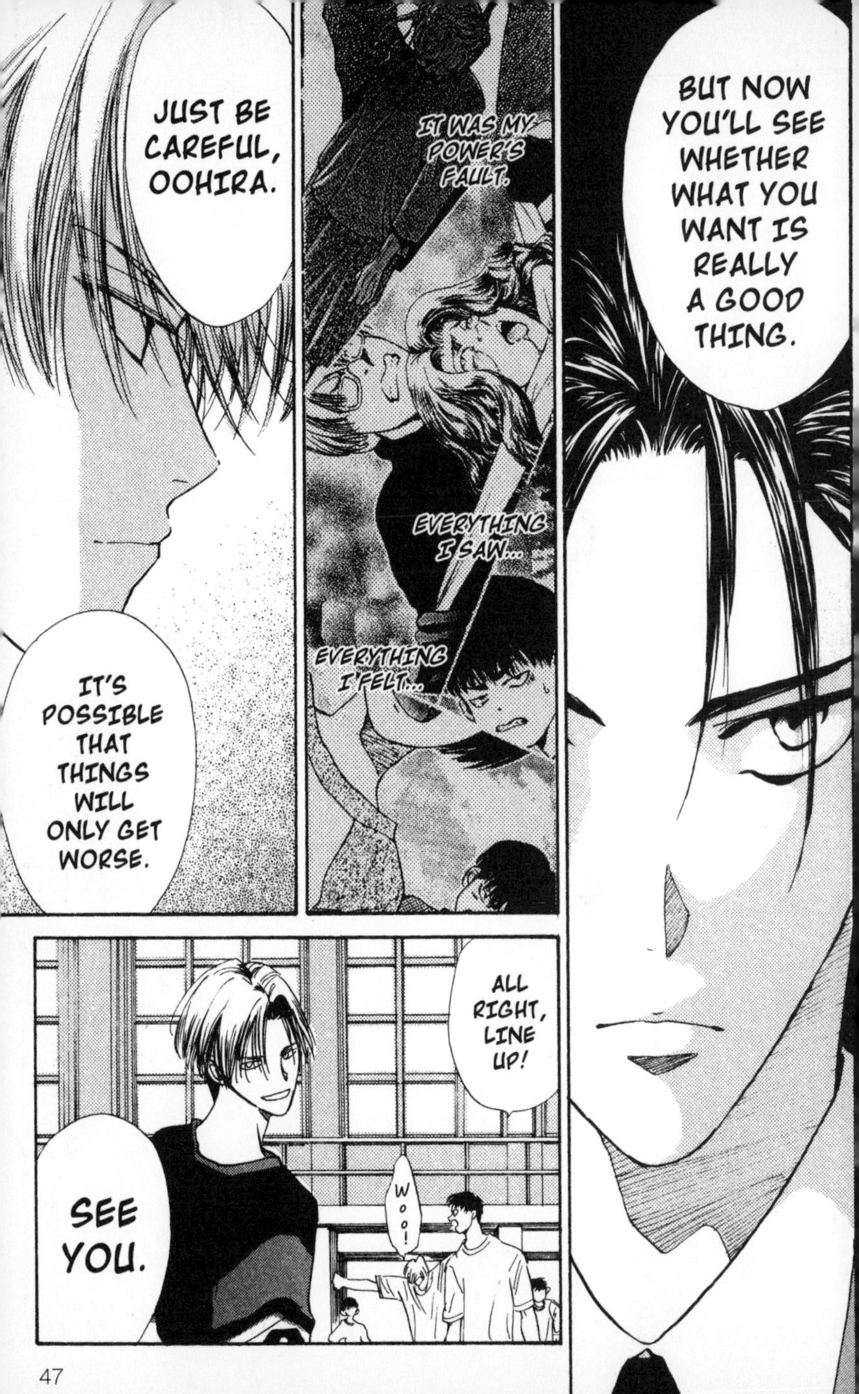
BUT NOW YOU'LL SEE WHETHER WHAT YOU WANT IS REALLY A GOOD THING.
IT WAS MY POWER'S FAULT.
EVERYTHING I SAW...
EVERYTHING I FELT...
JUST BE CAREFUL, OOHIRA.
IT'S POSSIBLE THAT THINGS WILL ONLY GET WORSE.
ALL RIGHT, LINE UP!
Woo!
SEE YOU.

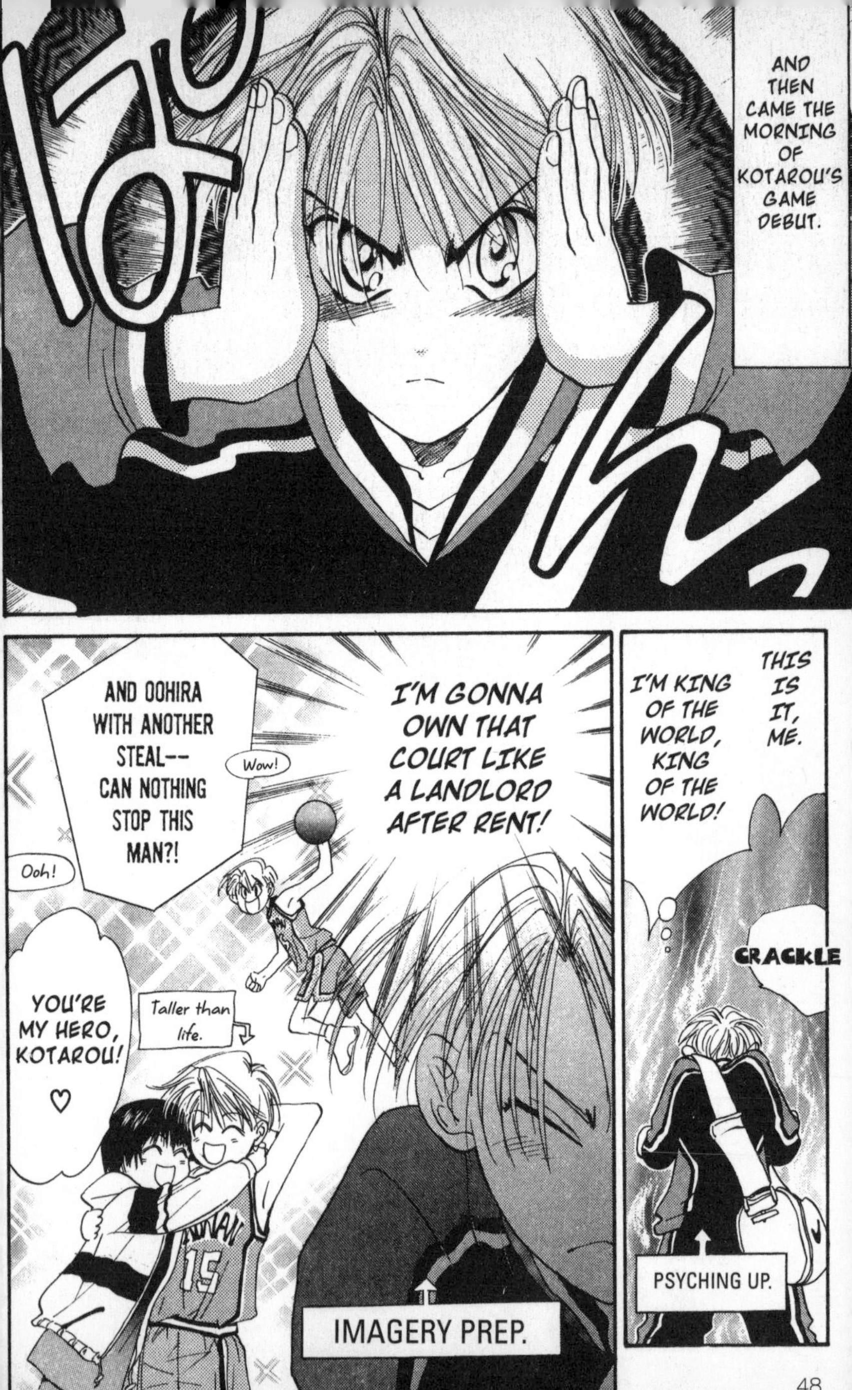
AND THEN CAME THE MORNING OF KOTAROU'S GAME DEBUT.
THIS IS IT, ME.
I'M KING OF THE WORLD, KING OF THE WORLD!
CRACKLE
PSYCHING UP.
I'M GONNA OWN THAT COURT LIKE A LANDLORD AFTER RENT!
AND OOHIRA WITH ANOTHER STEAL-- CAN NOTHING STOP THIS MAN?!
Wow!
Ooh!
YOU'RE MY HERO, KOTAROU! ♡
Taller than life.
IMAGERY PREP.

ACT 8

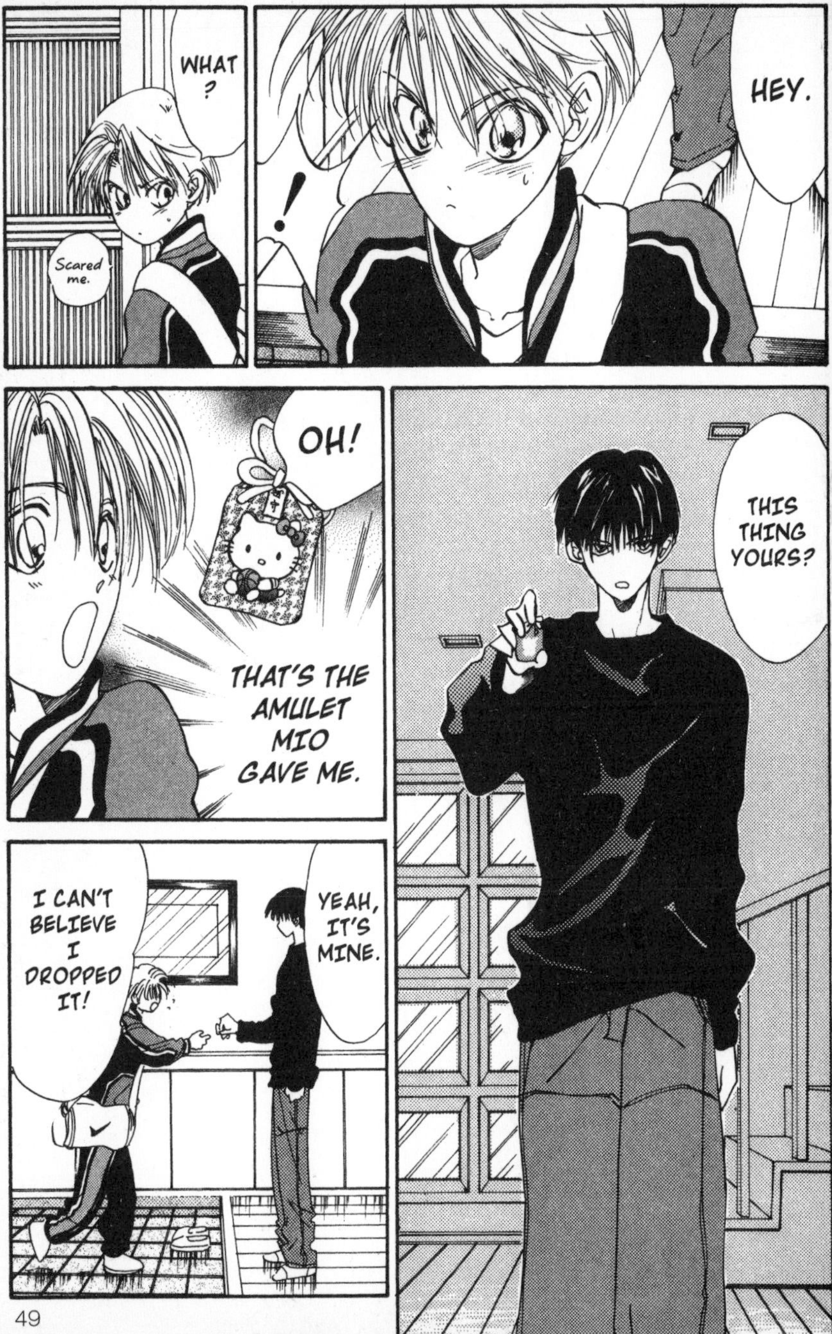
HEY.
!
WHAT?
Scared me.
THIS THING YOURS?
OH!
THAT'S THE AMULET MIO GAVE ME.
YEAH, IT'S MINE.
I CAN'T BELIEVE I DROPPED IT!

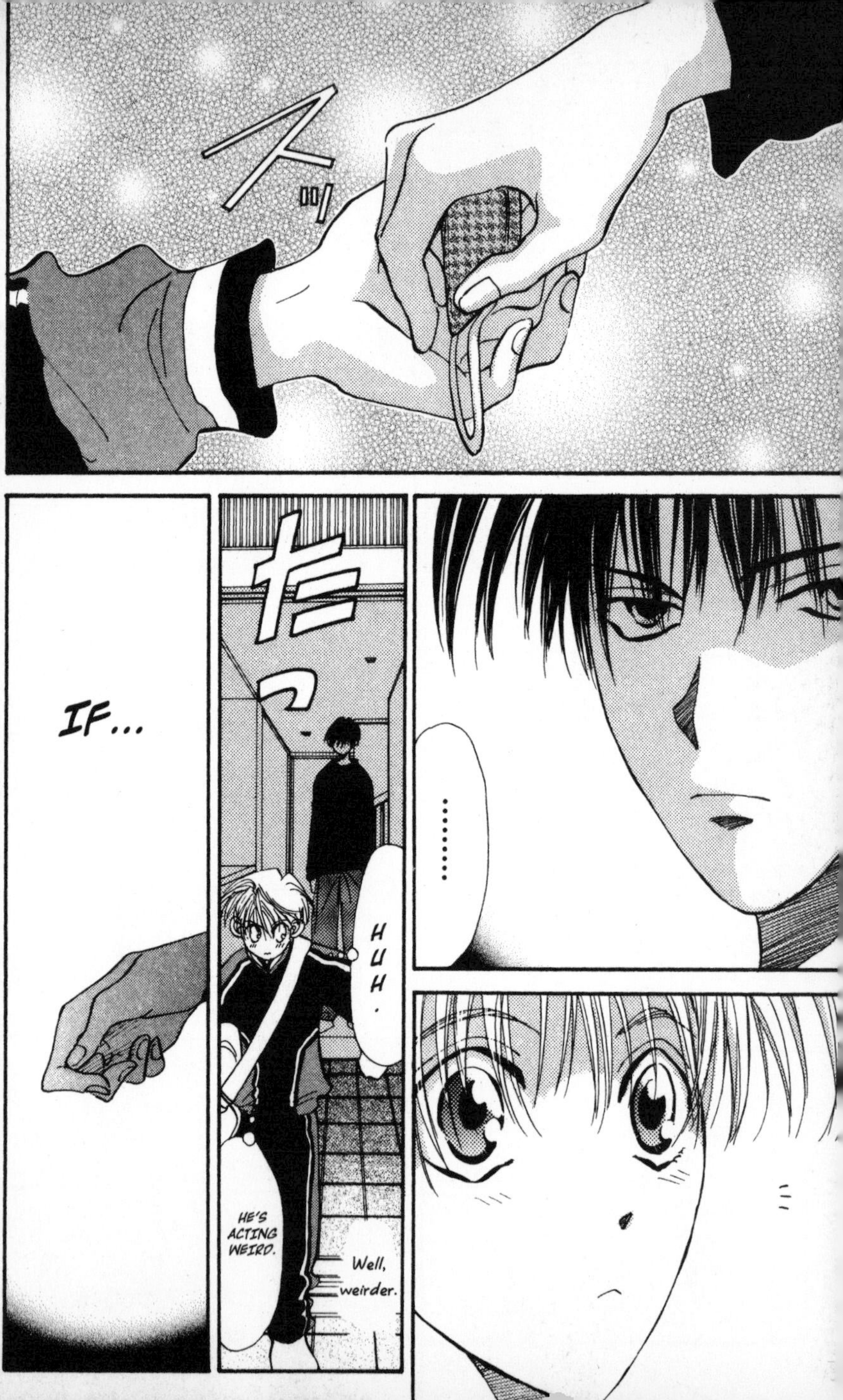
スッ
......
たっ
HUH.
HE'S ACTING WEIRD.
Well, weirder.
IF...

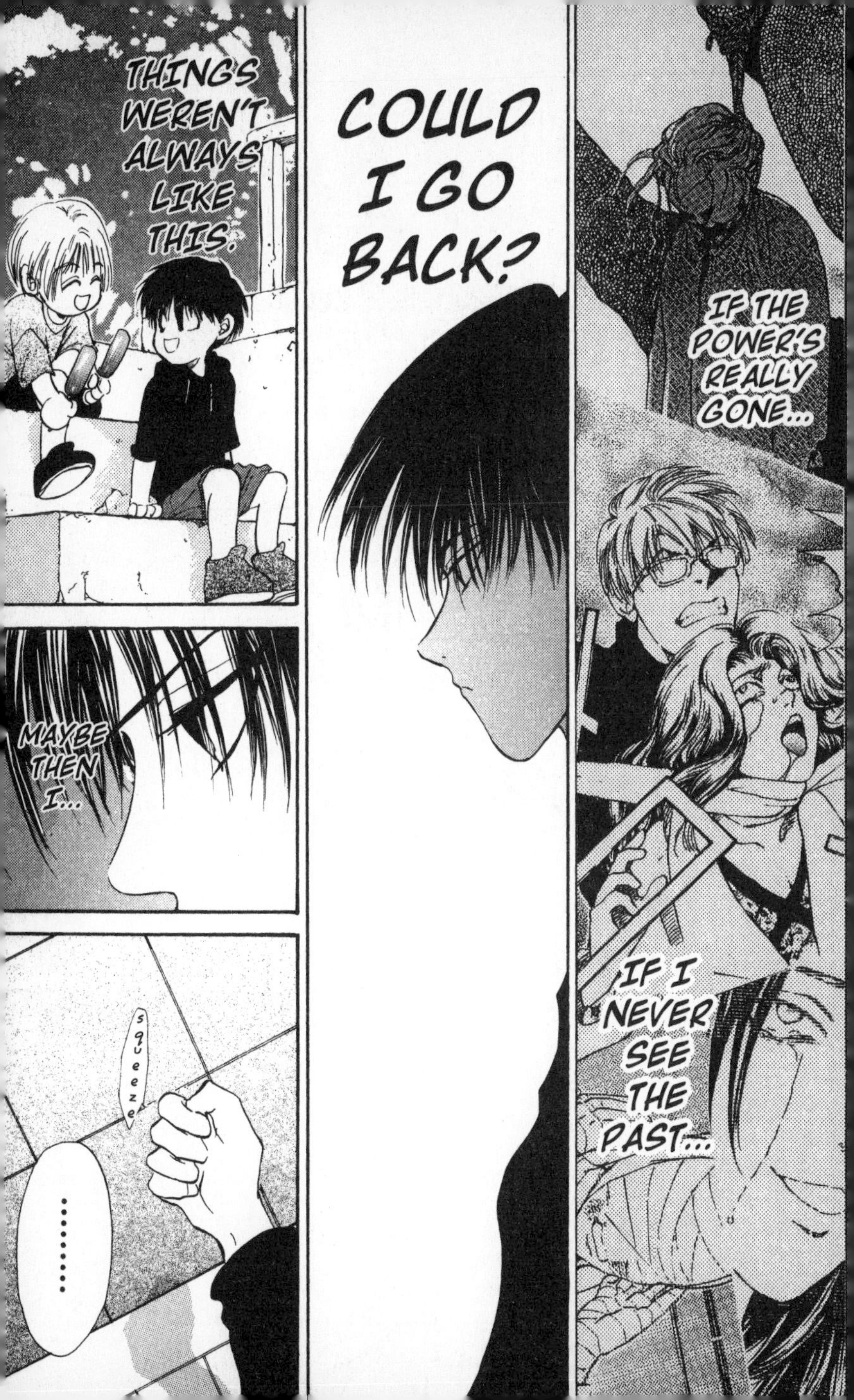
IF THE POWER'S REALLY GONE...
IF I NEVER SEE THE PAST...
COULD I GO BACK?
THINGS WEREN'T ALWAYS LIKE THIS.
MAYBE THEN I...
squeeze
....

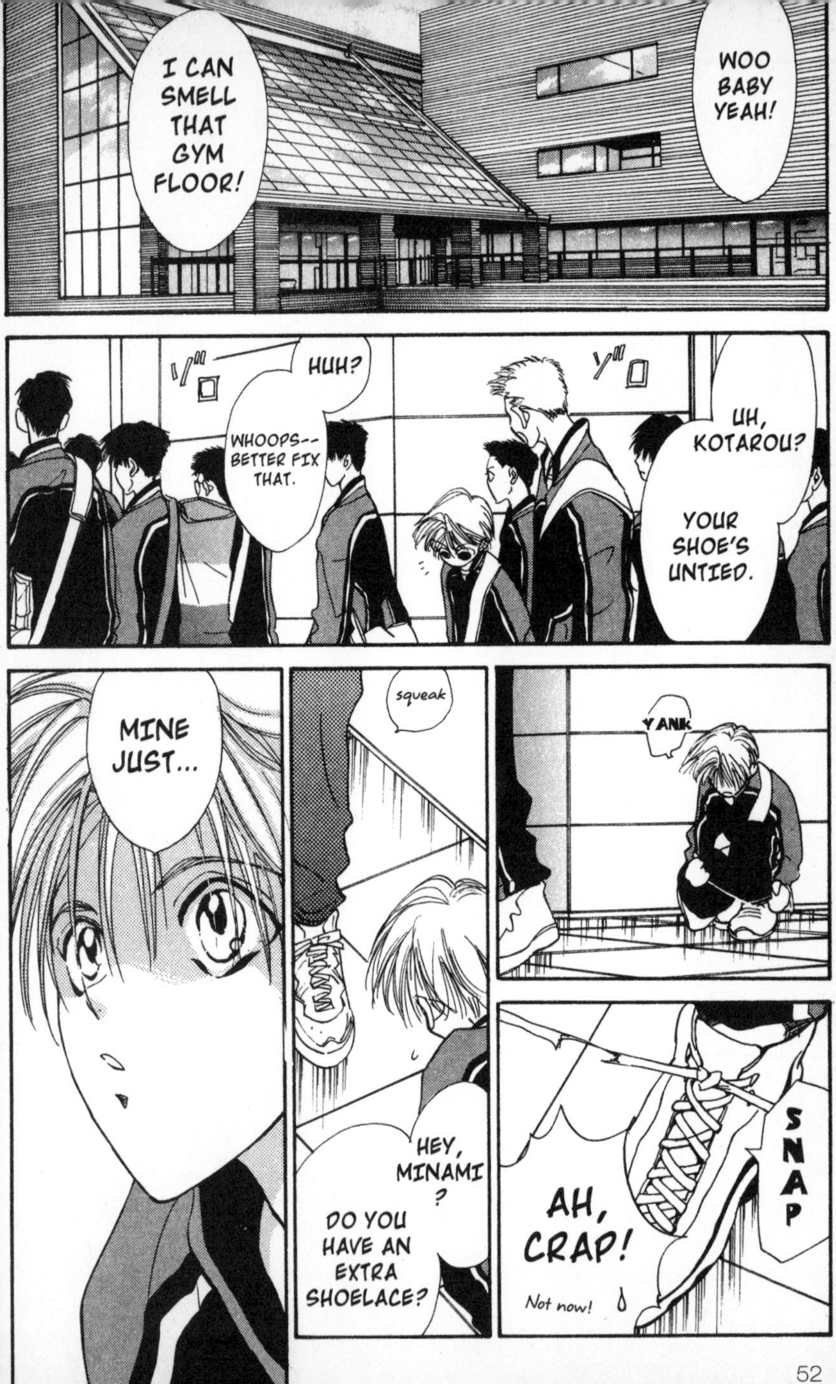
WOO BABY YEAH!
I CAN SMELL THAT GYM FLOOR!
UH, KOTAROU?
YOUR SHOE'S UNTIED.
HUH?
WHOOPS-- BETTER FIX THAT.
YANK
SNAP
AH, CRAP!
Not now!
squeak
HEY, MINAMI?
DO YOU HAVE AN EXTRA SHOELACE?
MINE JUST...

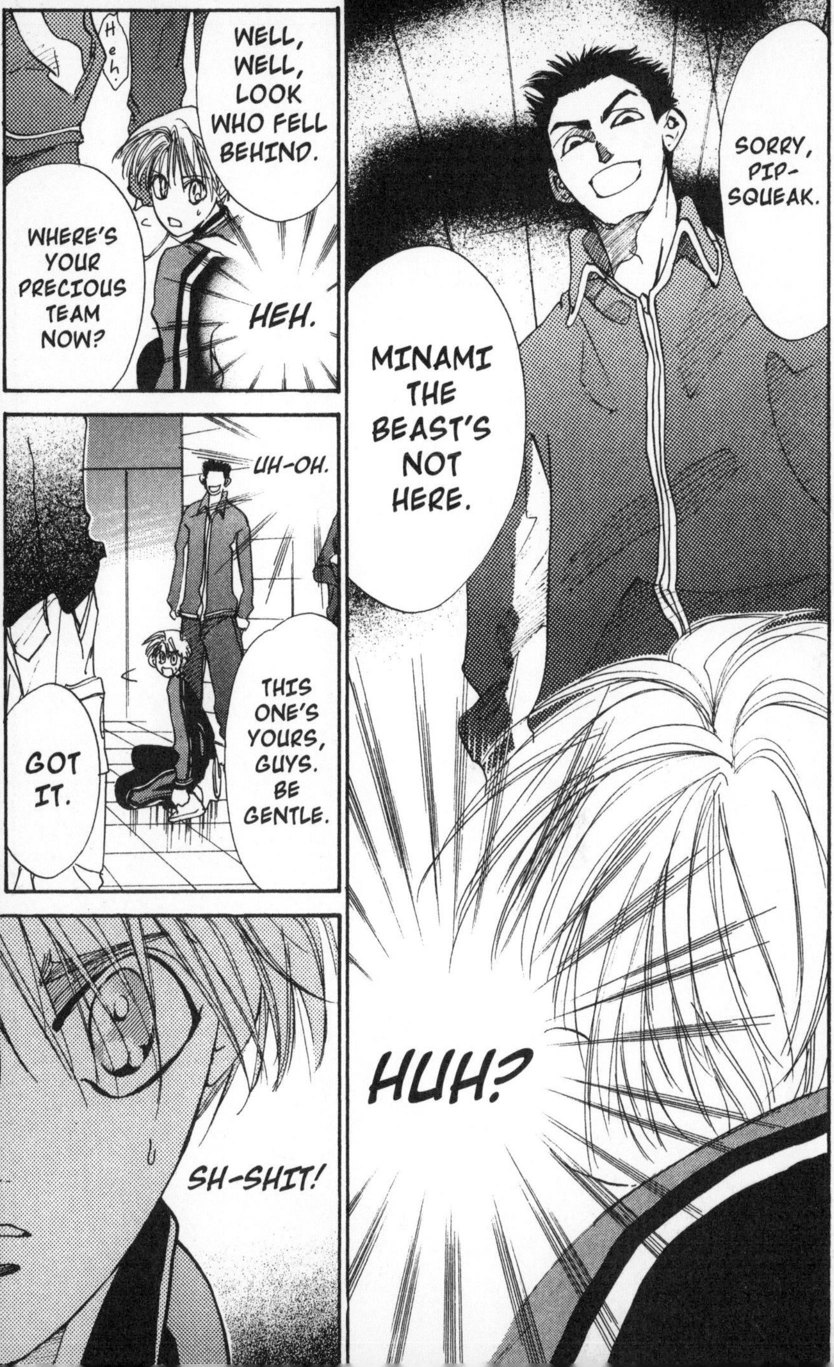
SORRY, PIP-SQUEAK.
MINAMI THE BEAST'S NOT HERE.
HUH?
WELL, WELL, LOOK WHO FELL BEHIND.
Heh.
WHERE'S YOUR PRECIOUS TEAM NOW?
HEH.
UH-OH.
THIS ONE'S YOURS, GUYS. BE GENTLE.
GOT IT.
SH-SHIT!

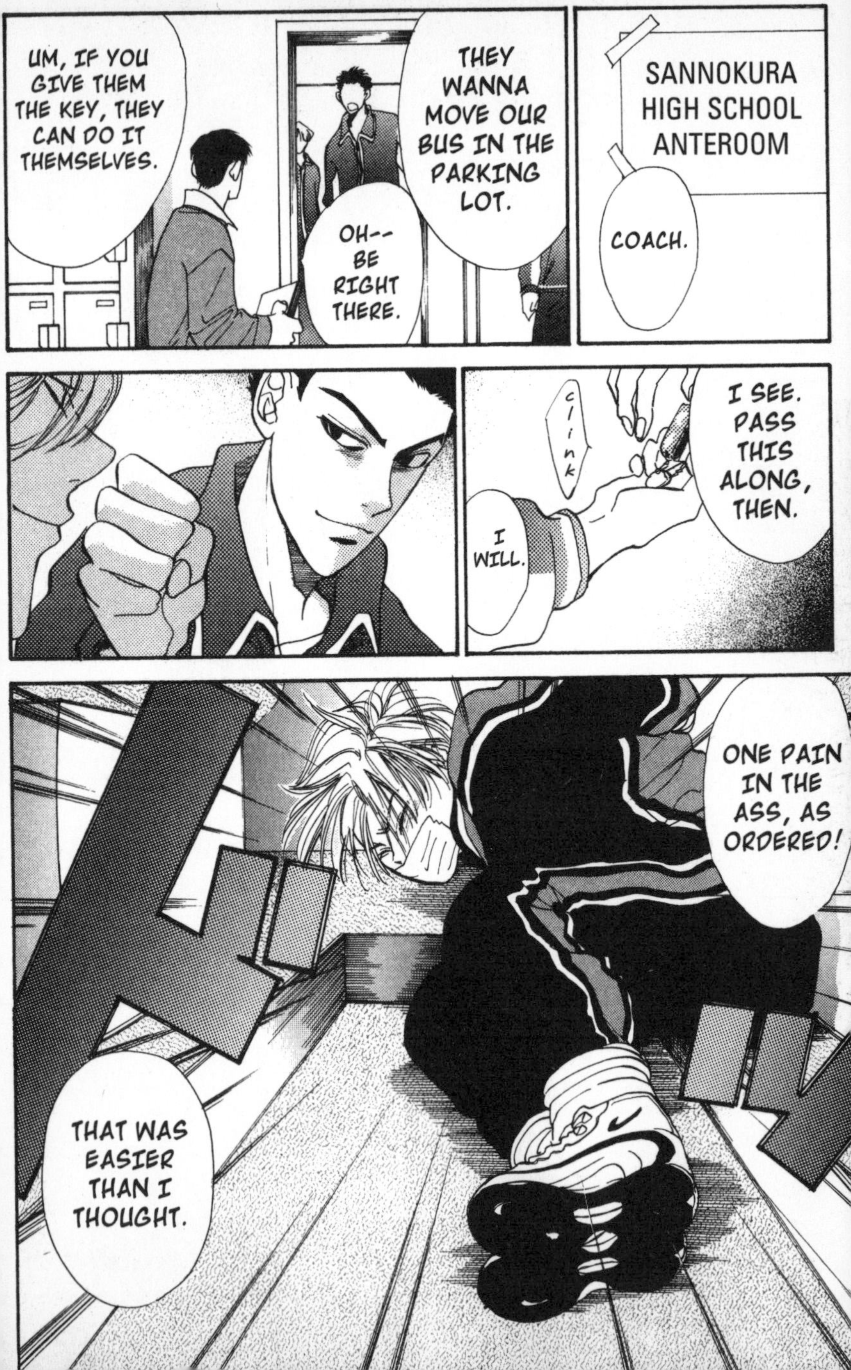
SANNOKURA HIGH SCHOOL ANTEROOM
COACH.
THEY WANNA MOVE OUR BUS IN THE PARKING LOT.
OH-- BE RIGHT THERE.
UM, IF YOU GIVE THEM THE KEY, THEY CAN DO IT THEMSELVES.
I SEE. PASS THIS ALONG, THEN.
clink
I WILL.
ONE PAIN IN THE ASS, AS ORDERED!
THAT WAS EASIER THAN I THOUGHT.

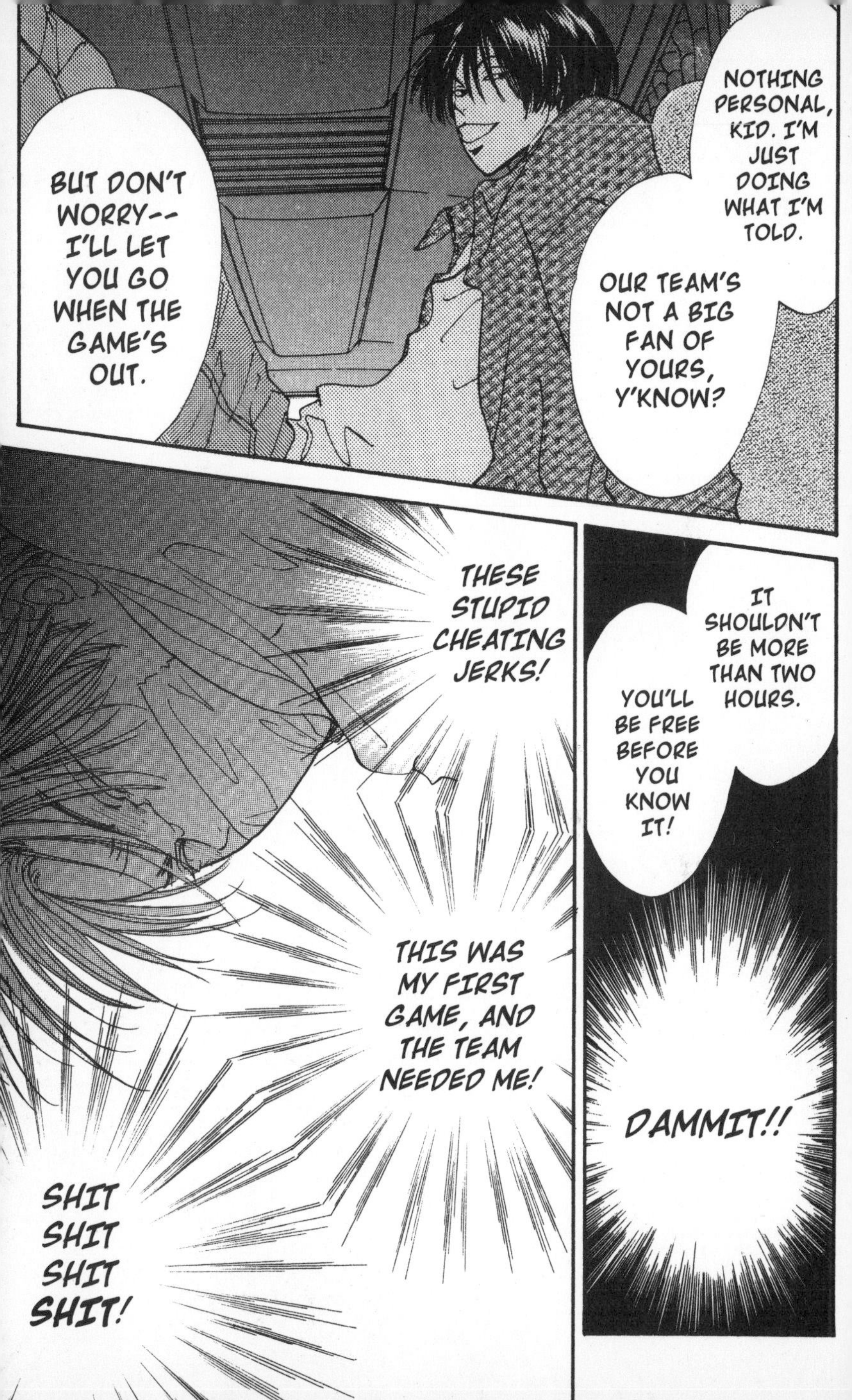
NOTHING PERSONAL, KID. I'M JUST DOING WHAT I'M TOLD.
OUR TEAM'S NOT A BIG FAN OF YOURS, Y'KNOW?
BUT DON'T WORRY-- I'LL LET YOU GO WHEN THE GAME'S OUT.
IT SHOULDN'T BE MORE THAN TWO HOURS.
YOU'LL BE FREE BEFORE YOU KNOW IT!
DAMMIT!!
THESE STUPID CHEATING JERKS!
THIS WAS MY FIRST GAME, AND THE TEAM NEEDED ME!
SHIT SHIT SHIT SHIT!

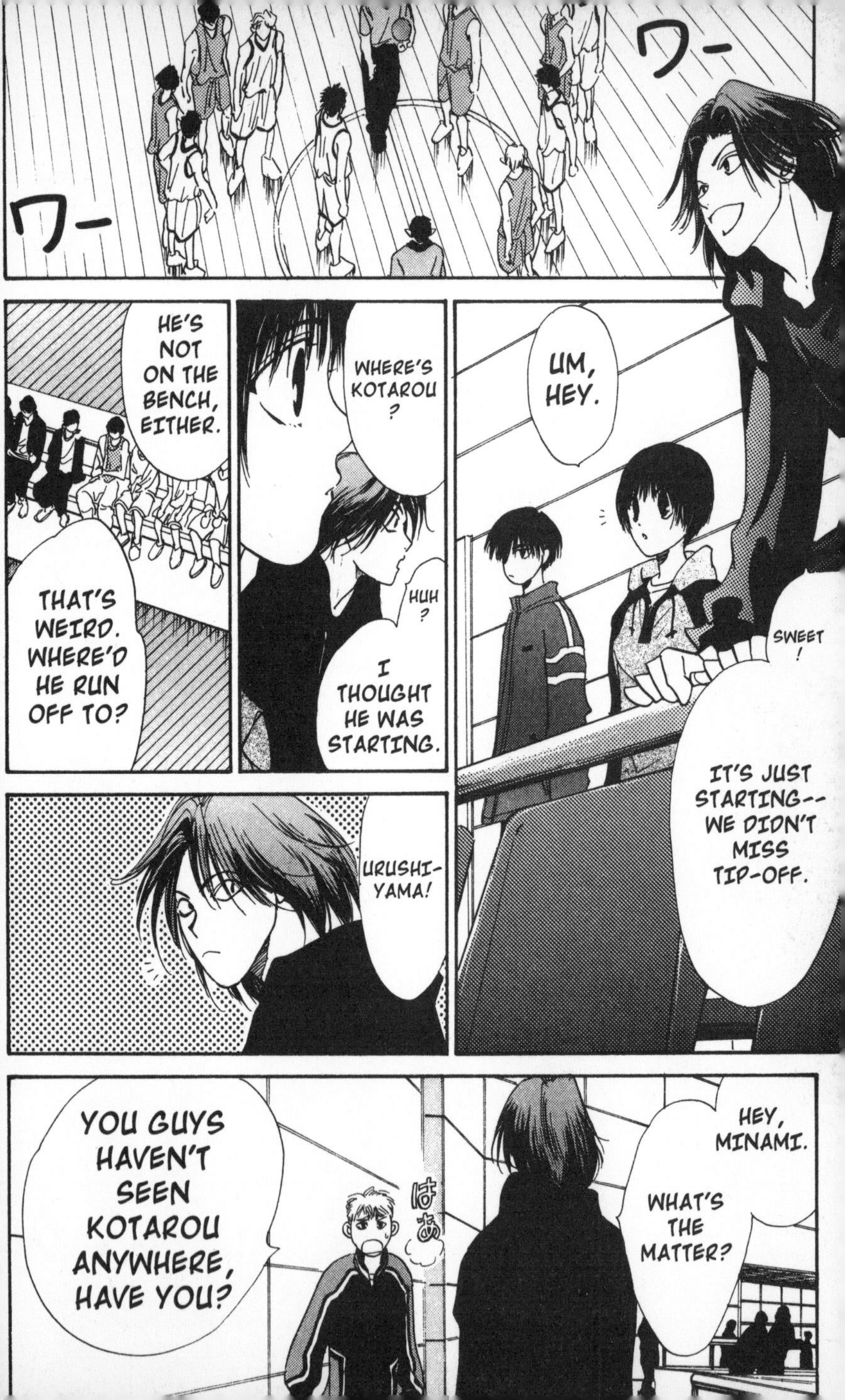
ワー
ワー
UM, HEY.
SWEET!
IT'S JUST STARTING--WE DIDN'T MISS TIP-OFF.
WHERE'S KOTAROU?
HUH?
I THOUGHT HE WAS STARTING.
HE'S NOT ON THE BENCH, EITHER.
THAT'S WEIRD. WHERE'D HE RUN OFF TO?
URUSHI-YAMA!
HEY, MINAMI.
WHAT'S THE MATTER?
はぁ
YOU GUYS HAVEN'T SEEN KOTAROU ANYWHERE, HAVE YOU?

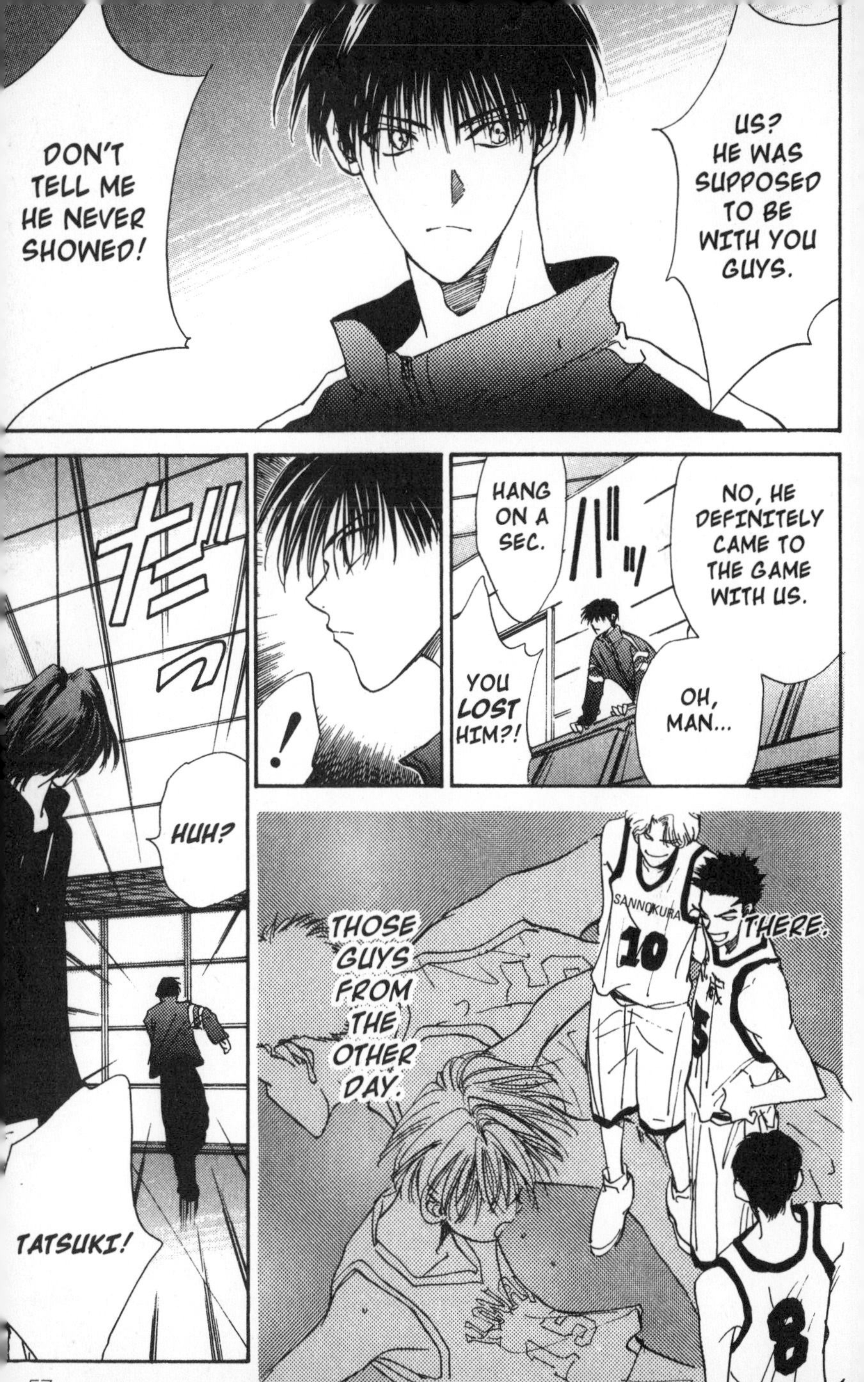
US? HE WAS SUPPOSED TO BE WITH YOU GUYS.
DON'T TELL ME HE NEVER SHOWED!
NO, HE DEFINITELY CAME TO THE GAME WITH US.
バッ
HANG ON A SEC.
OH, MAN...
YOU LOST HIM?!
!
ダッ
HUH?
TATSUKI!
THOSE GUYS FROM THE OTHER DAY.
THERE.

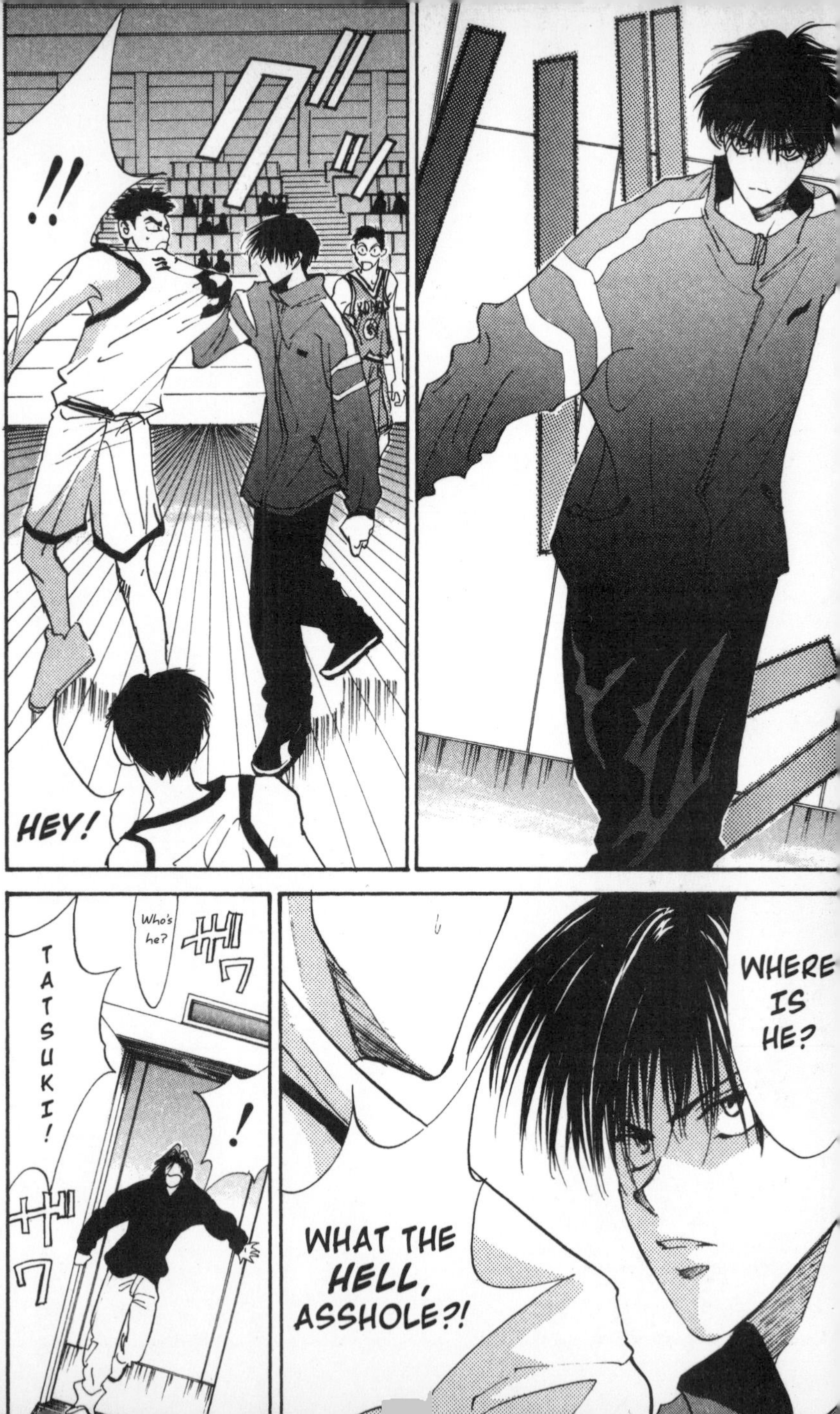

!!
HEY!
WHERE IS HE?
WHAT THE HELL, ASSHOLE?!
Who's he?
TATSUKI!
!

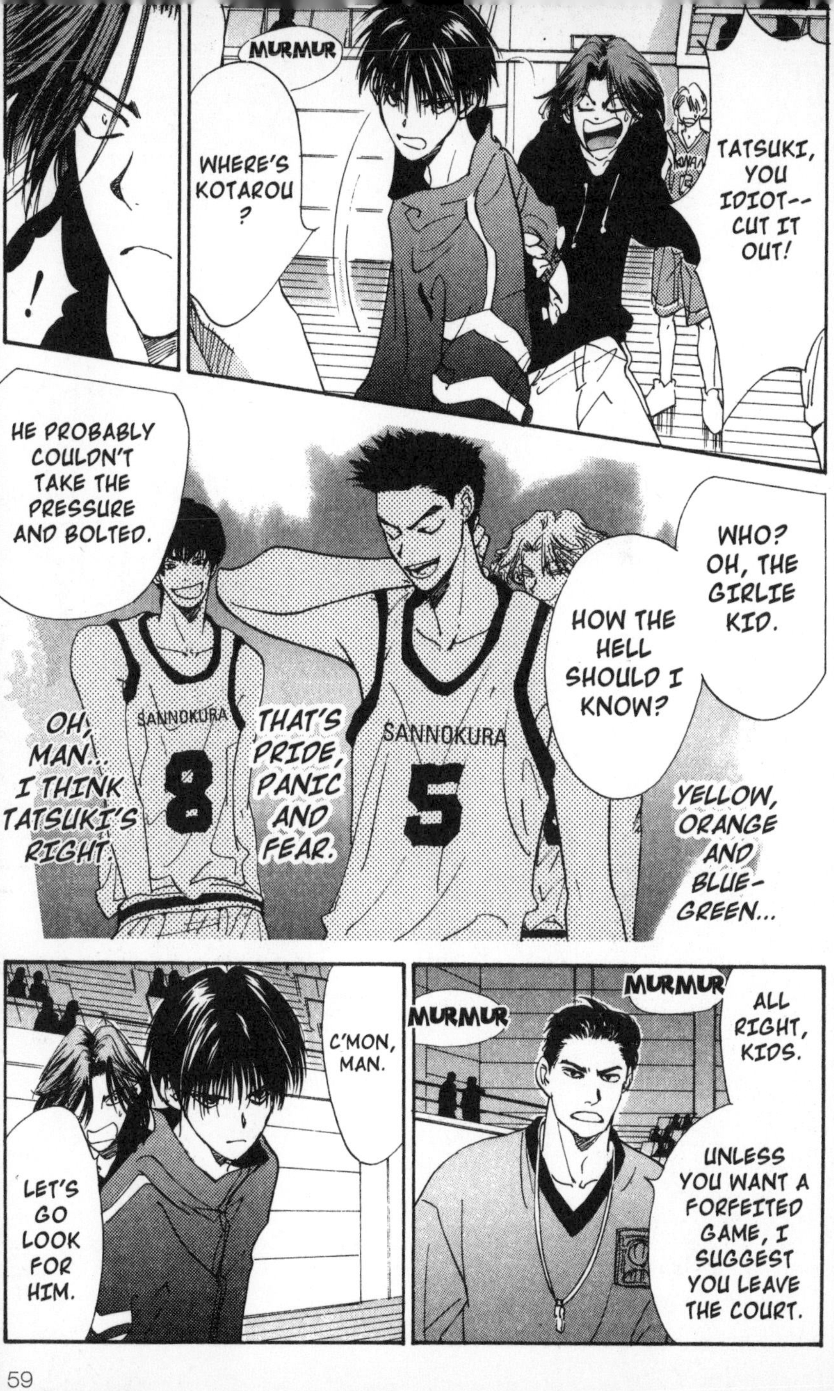
MURMUR
WHERE'S KOTAROU?
TATSUKI, YOU IDIOT-- CUT IT OUT!
!
WHO? OH, THE GIRLIE KID.
HOW THE HELL SHOULD I KNOW?
HE PROBABLY COULDN'T TAKE THE PRESSURE AND BOLTED.
YELLOW, ORANGE AND BLUE-GREEN...
SANNOKURA 5
THAT'S PRIDE, PANIC AND FEAR.
SANNOKURA 8
OH, MAN... I THINK TATSUKI'S RIGHT.
MURMUR
ALL RIGHT, KIDS.
MURMUR
UNLESS YOU WANT A FORFEITED GAME, I SUGGEST YOU LEAVE THE COURT.
C'MON, MAN.
LET'S GO LOOK FOR HIM.

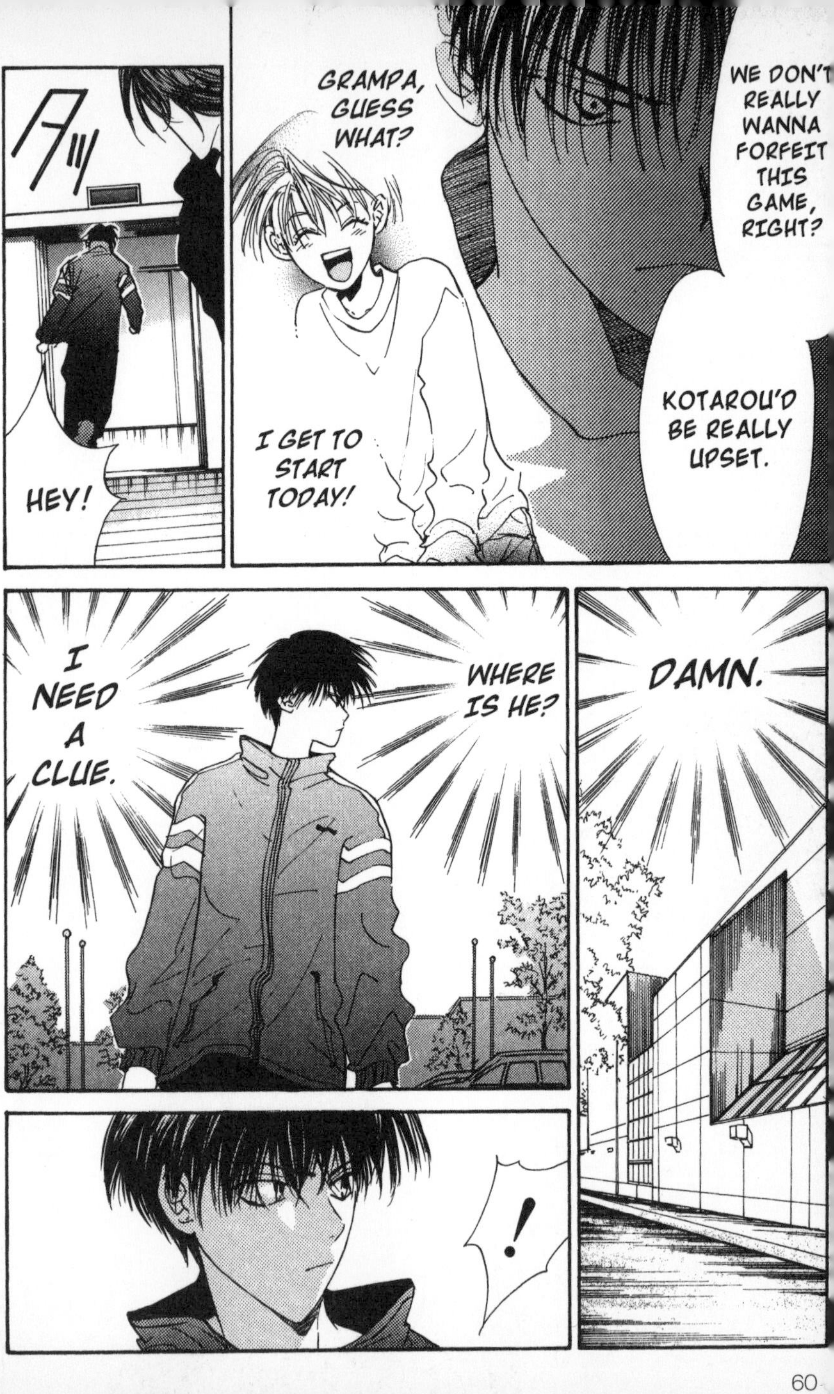
WE DON'T REALLY WANNA FORFEIT THIS GAME, RIGHT?
KOTAROU'D BE REALLY UPSET.
GRAMPA, GUESS WHAT?
I GET TO START TODAY!
HEY!
DAMN.
WHERE IS HE?
I NEED A CLUE.
!

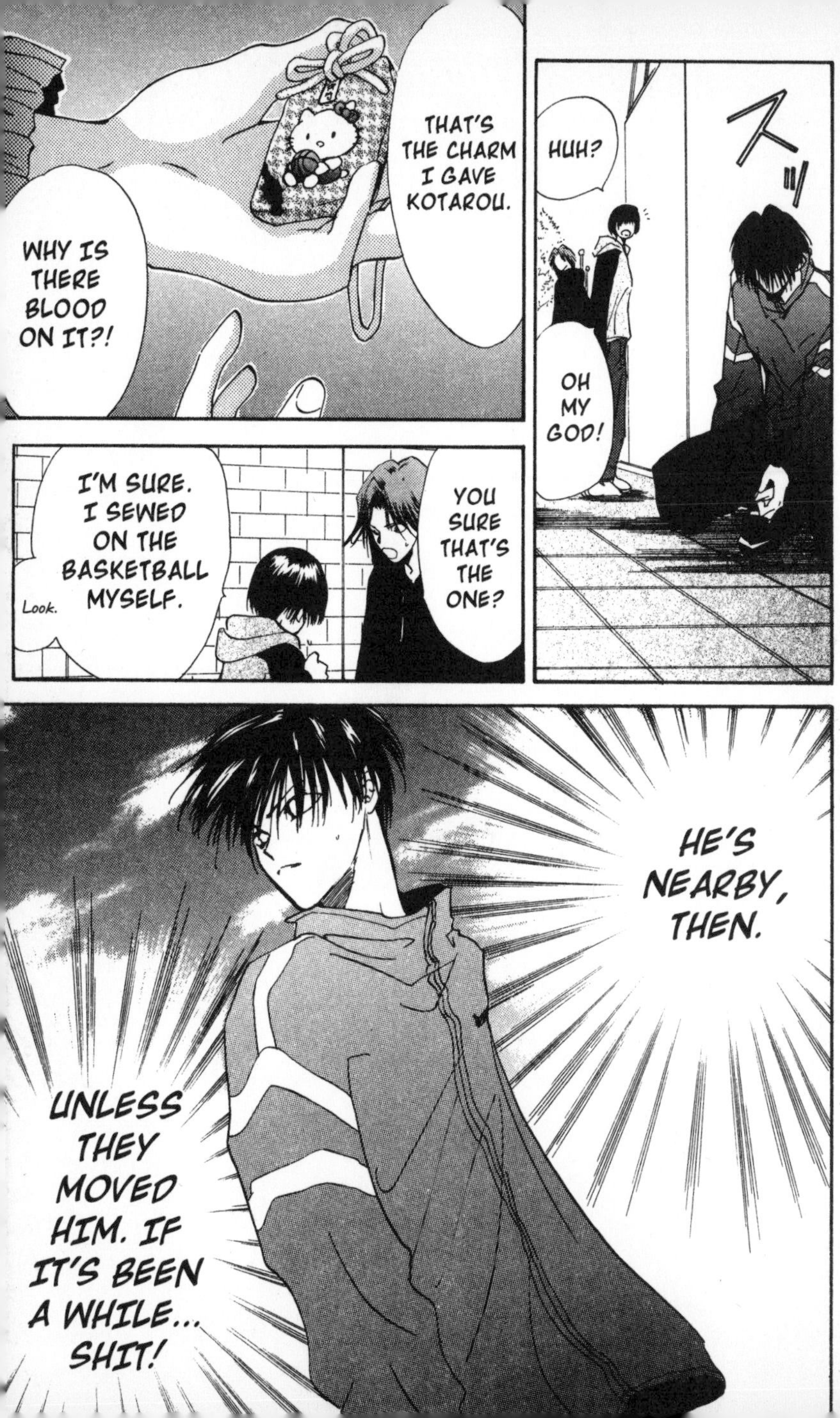
HUH?
OH MY GOD!
THAT'S THE CHARM I GAVE KOTAROU.
WHY IS THERE BLOOD ON IT?!
YOU SURE THAT'S THE ONE?
I'M SURE. I SEWED ON THE BASKETBALL MYSELF.
Look.
HE'S NEARBY, THEN.
UNLESS THEY MOVED HIM. IF IT'S BEEN A WHILE... SHIT!

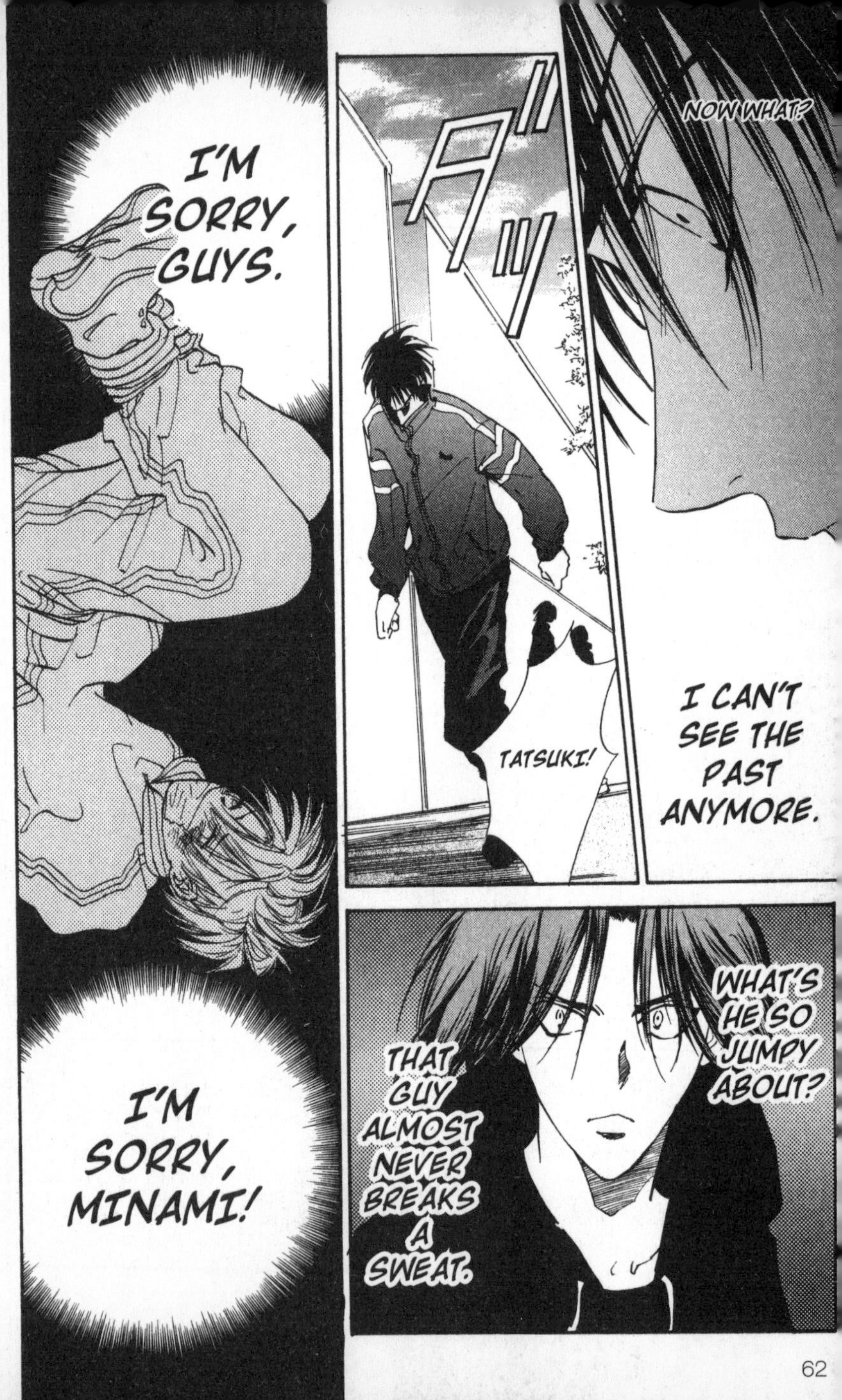
NOW WHAT?
I CAN'T SEE THE PAST ANYMORE.
TATSUKI!
WHAT'S HE SO JUMPY ABOUT?
THAT GUY ALMOST NEVER BREAKS A SWEAT.
I'M SORRY, GUYS.
I'M SORRY, MINAMI!

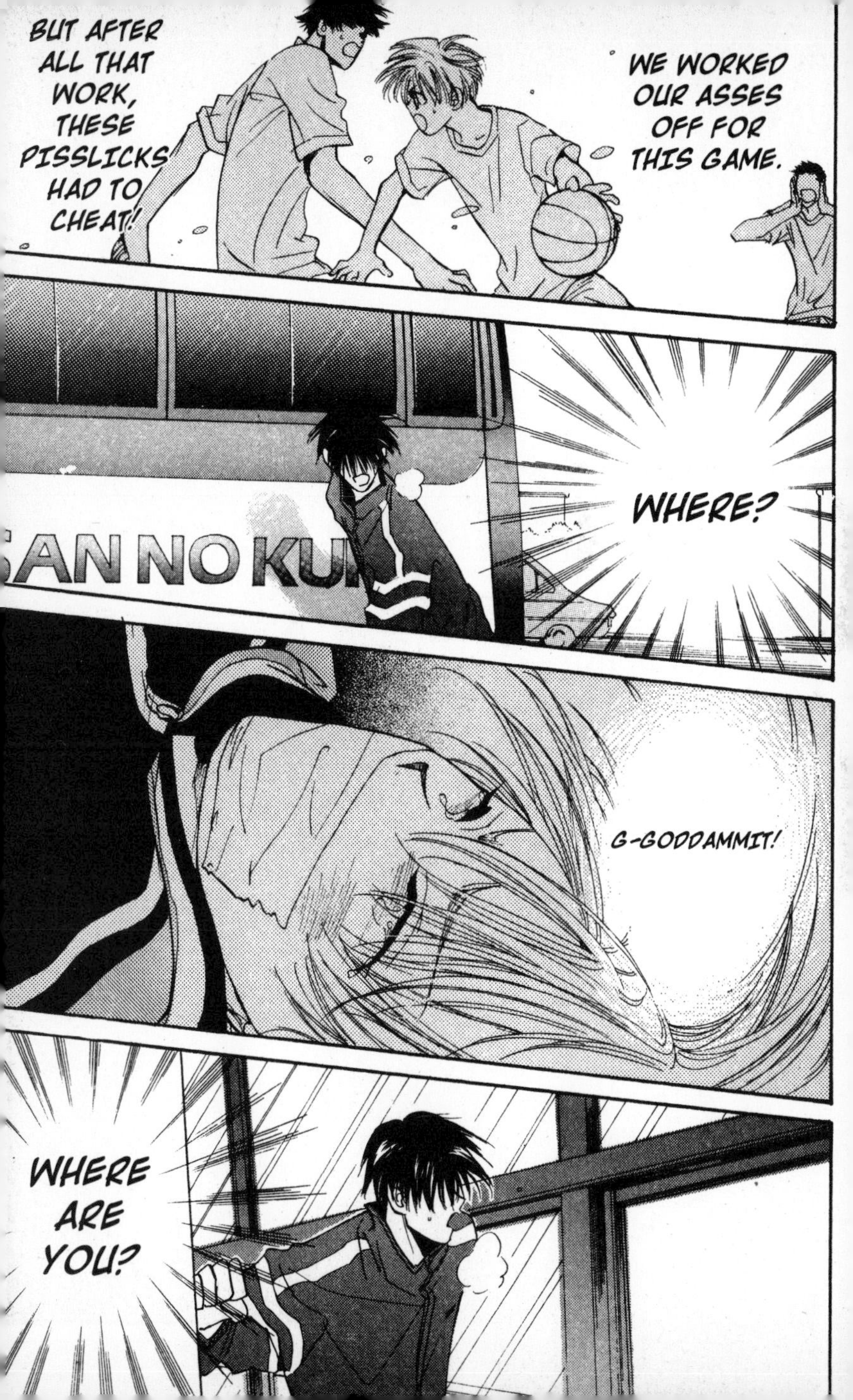
WE WORKED OUR ASSES OFF FOR THIS GAME.
BUT AFTER ALL THAT WORK, THESE PISSLICKS HAD TO CHEAT!
WHERE?
SAN NO KU
G-GODDAMMIT!
WHERE ARE YOU?

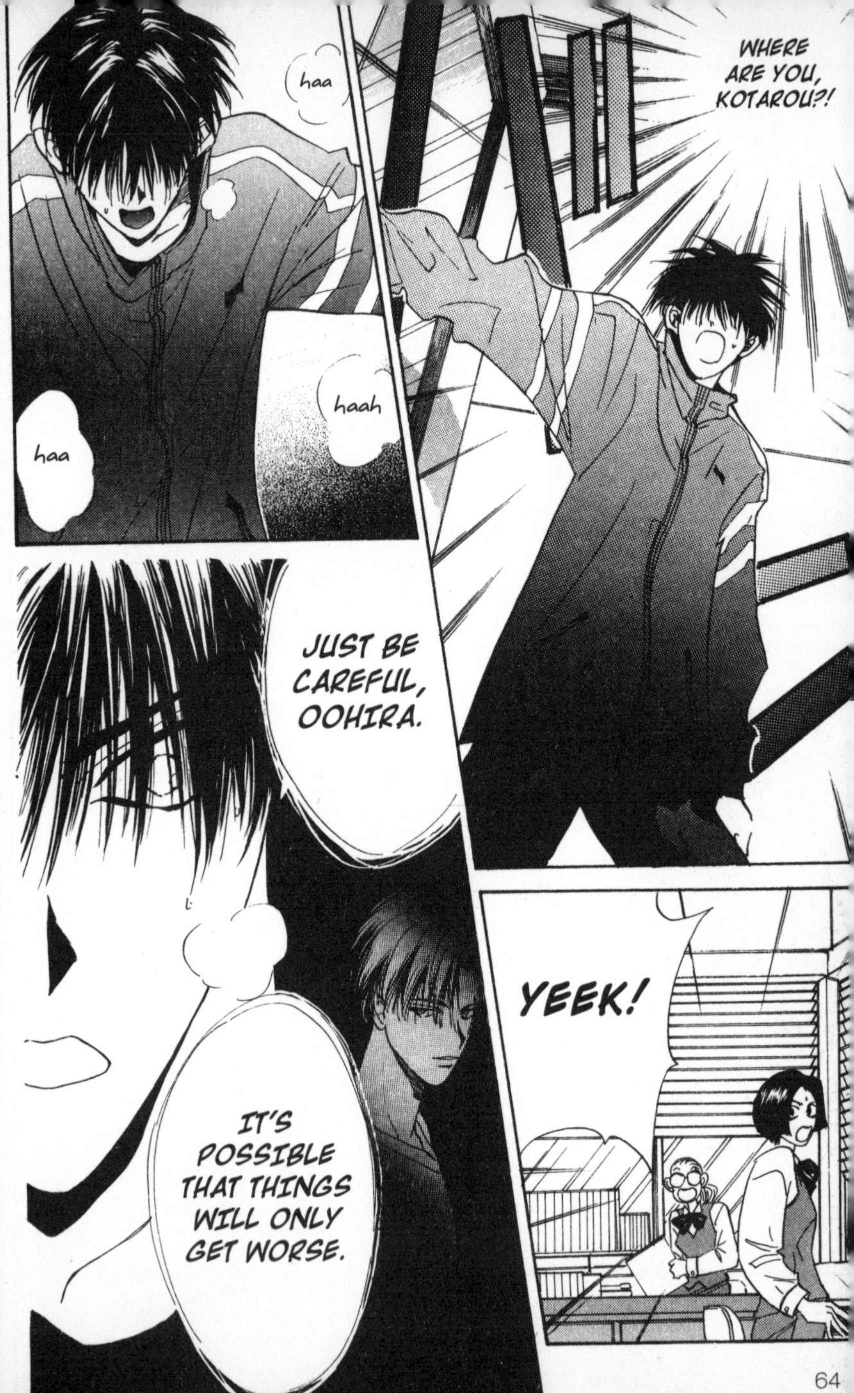

WHERE ARE YOU, KOTAROU?!
haa
haah
haa
YEEK!
JUST BE CAREFUL, OOHIRA.
IT'S POSSIBLE THAT THINGS WILL ONLY GET WORSE.

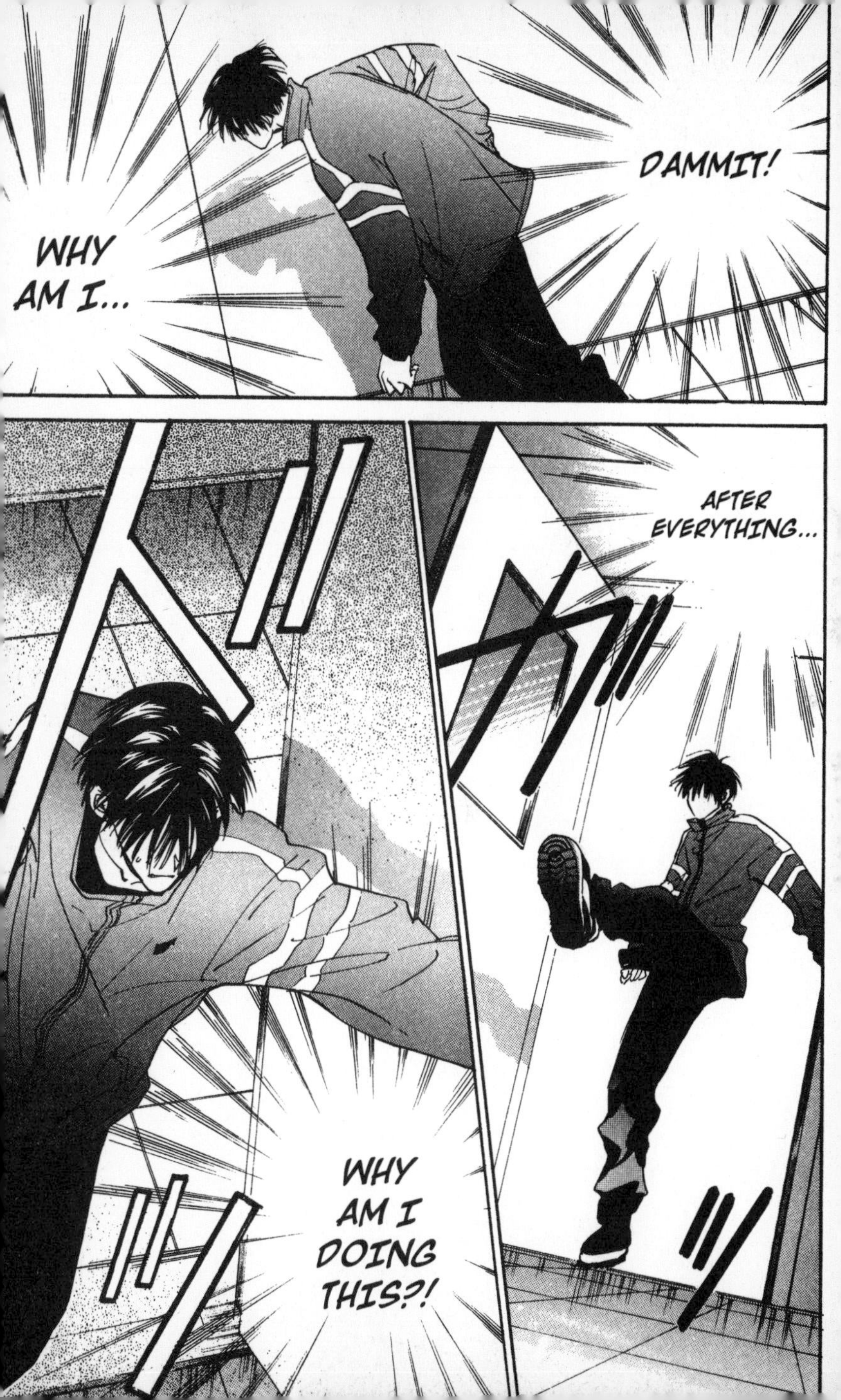
DAMMIT!
WHY AM I...
AFTER EVERYTHING...
WHY AM I DOING THIS?!

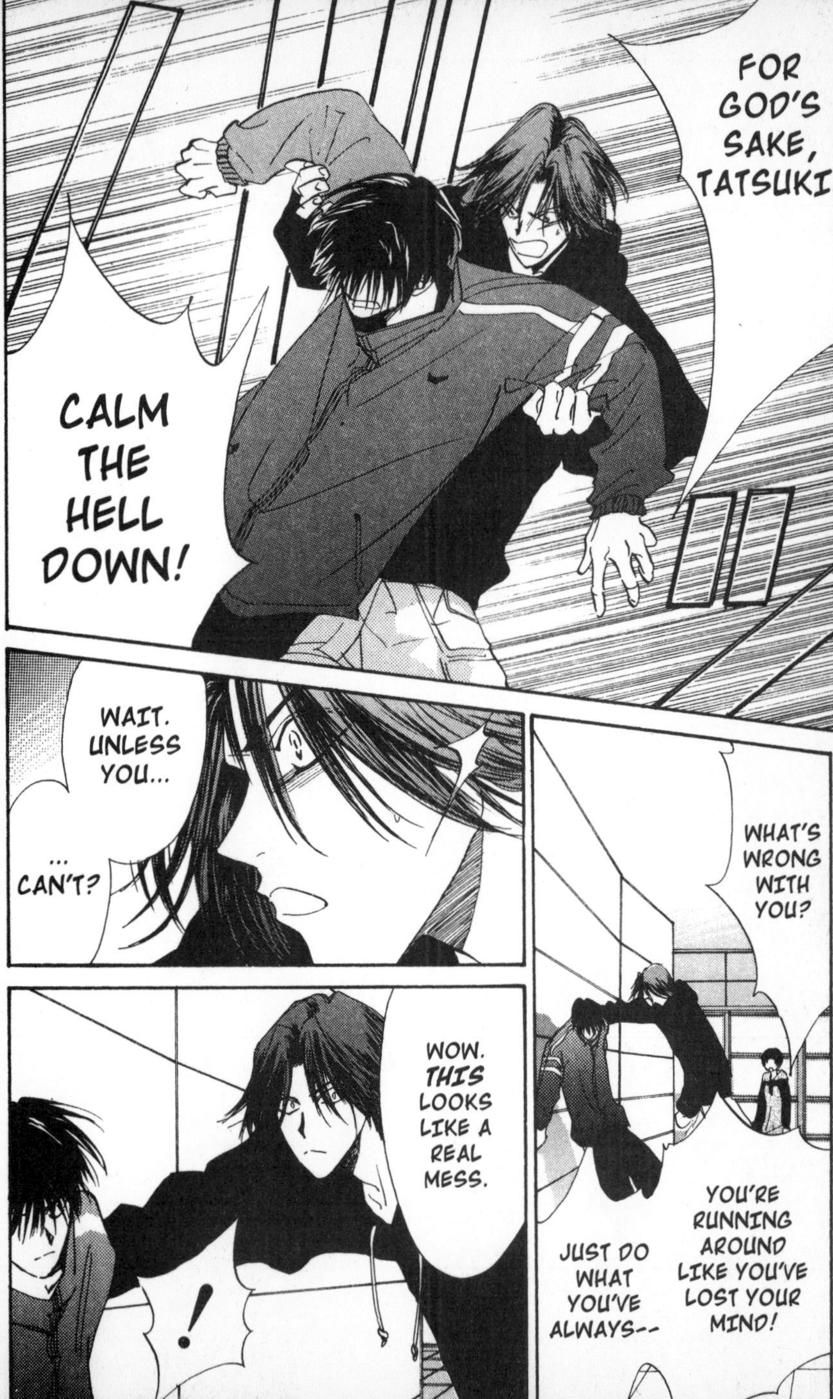
FOR GOD'S SAKE, TATSUKI!
CALM THE HELL DOWN!
WHAT'S WRONG WITH YOU?
YOU'RE RUNNING AROUND LIKE YOU'VE LOST YOUR MIND!
JUST DO WHAT YOU'VE ALWAYS--
WAIT. UNLESS YOU...
...CAN'T?
WOW. *THIS* LOOKS LIKE A REAL MESS.
!

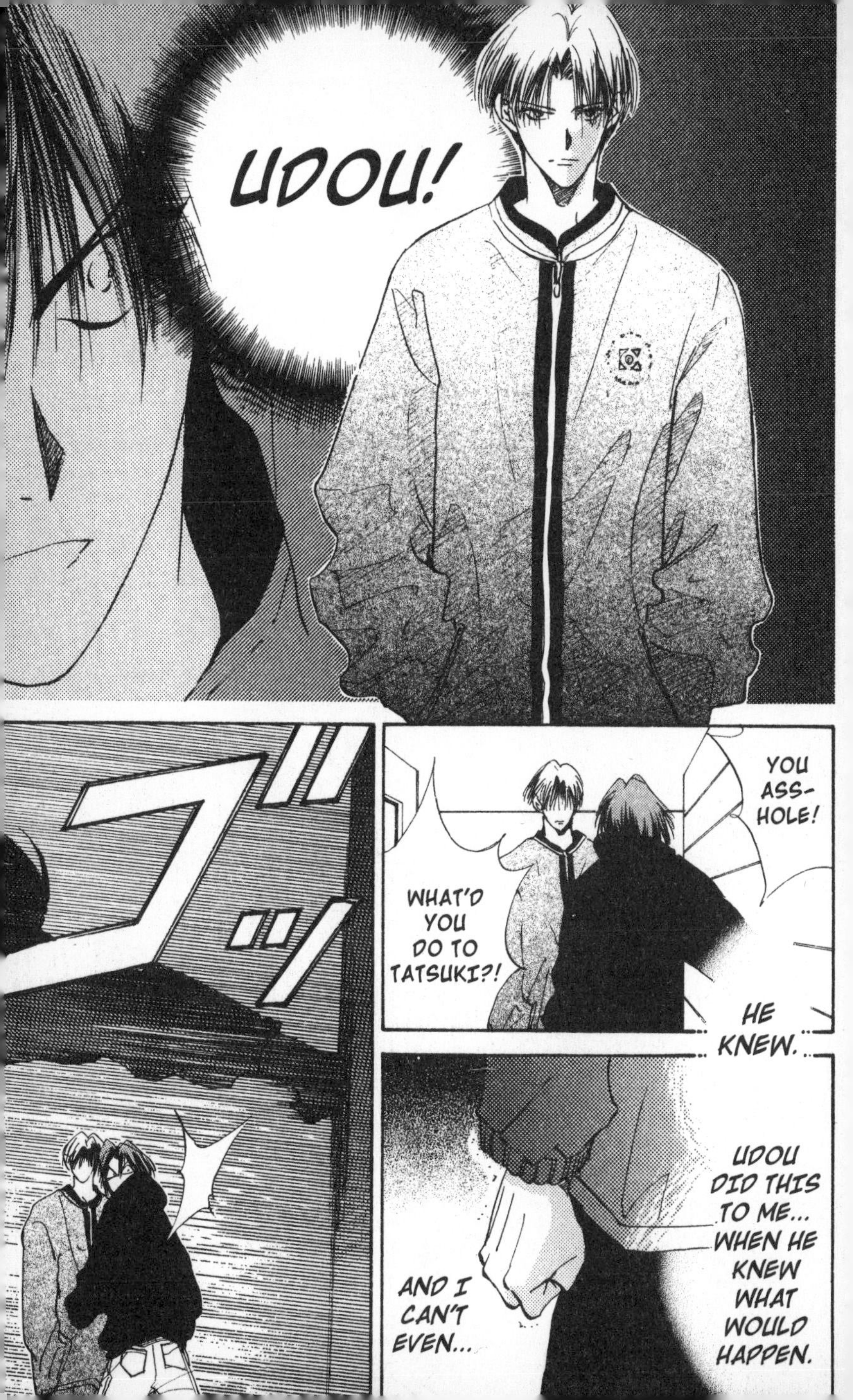
UDOU!
YOU ASS-HOLE!
WHAT'D YOU DO TO TATSUKI?!
HE KNEW.
UDOU DID THIS TO ME... WHEN HE KNEW WHAT WOULD HAPPEN.
AND I CAN'T EVEN...

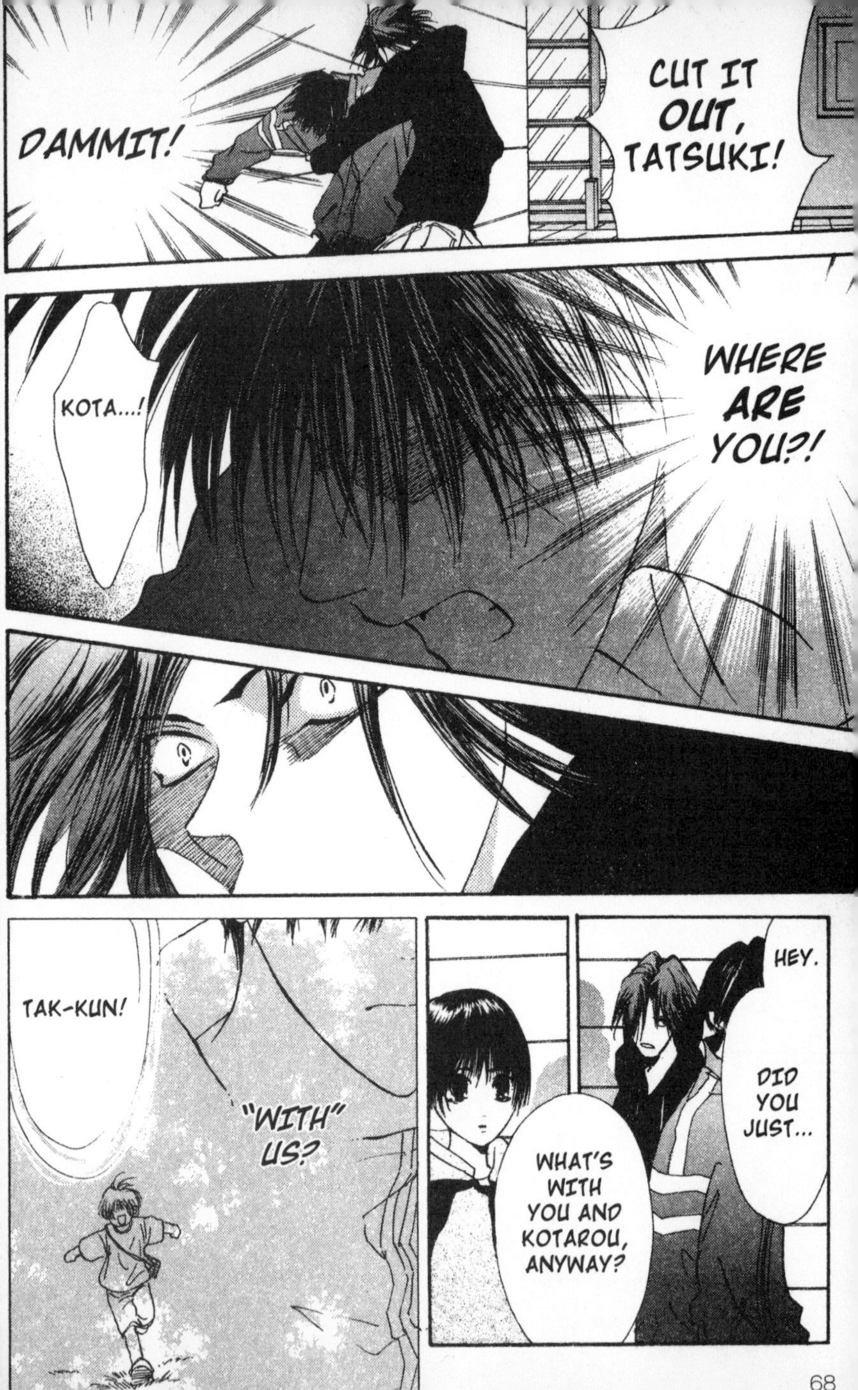
CUT IT OUT, TATSUKI!
DAMMIT!
WHERE ARE YOU?!
KOTA...!
HEY.
DID YOU JUST...
WHAT'S WITH YOU AND KOTAROU, ANYWAY?
TAK-KUN!
"WITH" US?

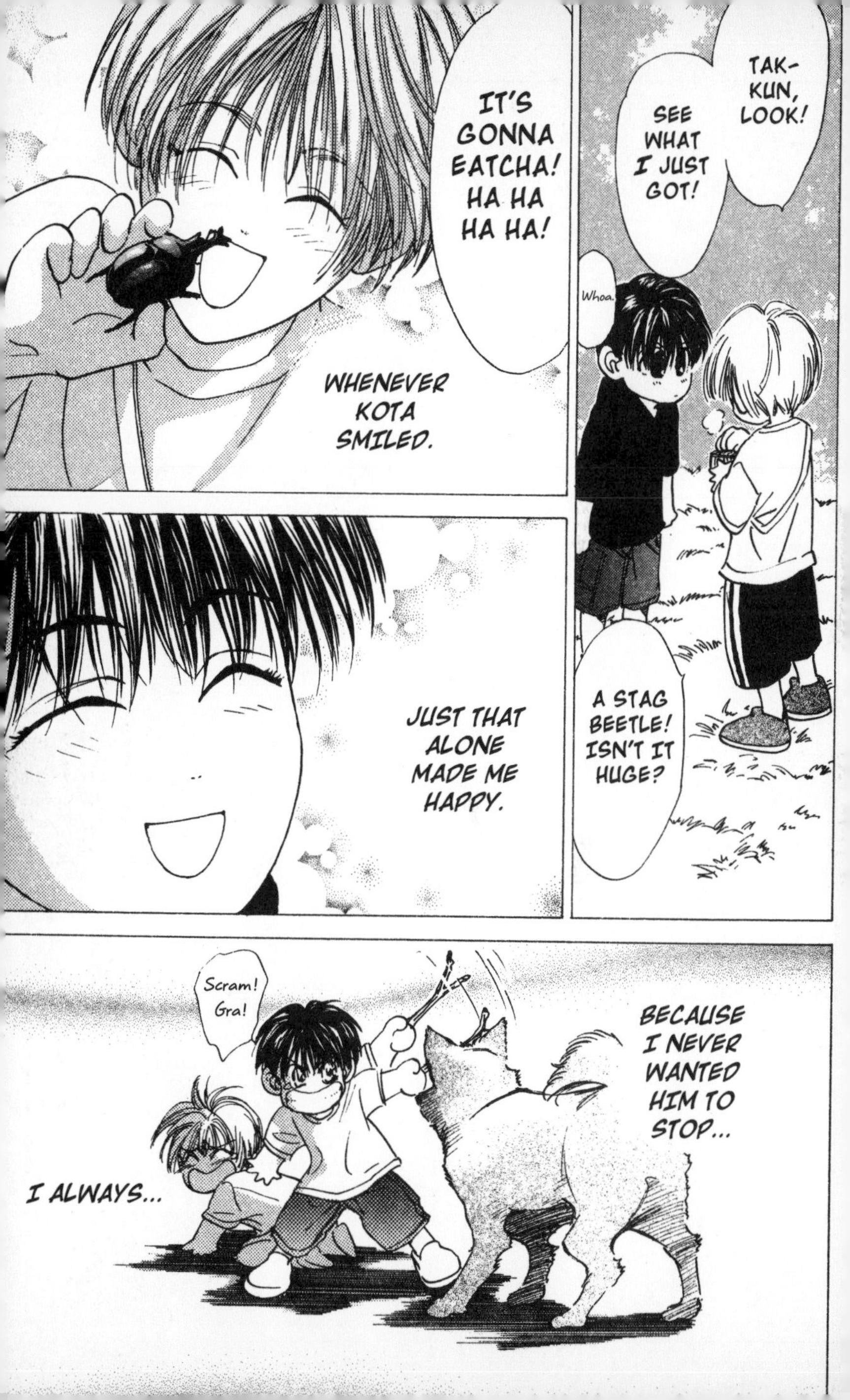
TAK-KUN, LOOK!
SEE WHAT I JUST GOT!
Whoa.
A STAG BEETLE! ISN'T IT HUGE?
IT'S GONNA EATCHA! HA HA HA HA!
WHENEVER KOTA SMILED.
JUST THAT ALONE MADE ME HAPPY.
BECAUSE I NEVER WANTED HIM TO STOP...
Scram! Gra!
I ALWAYS...

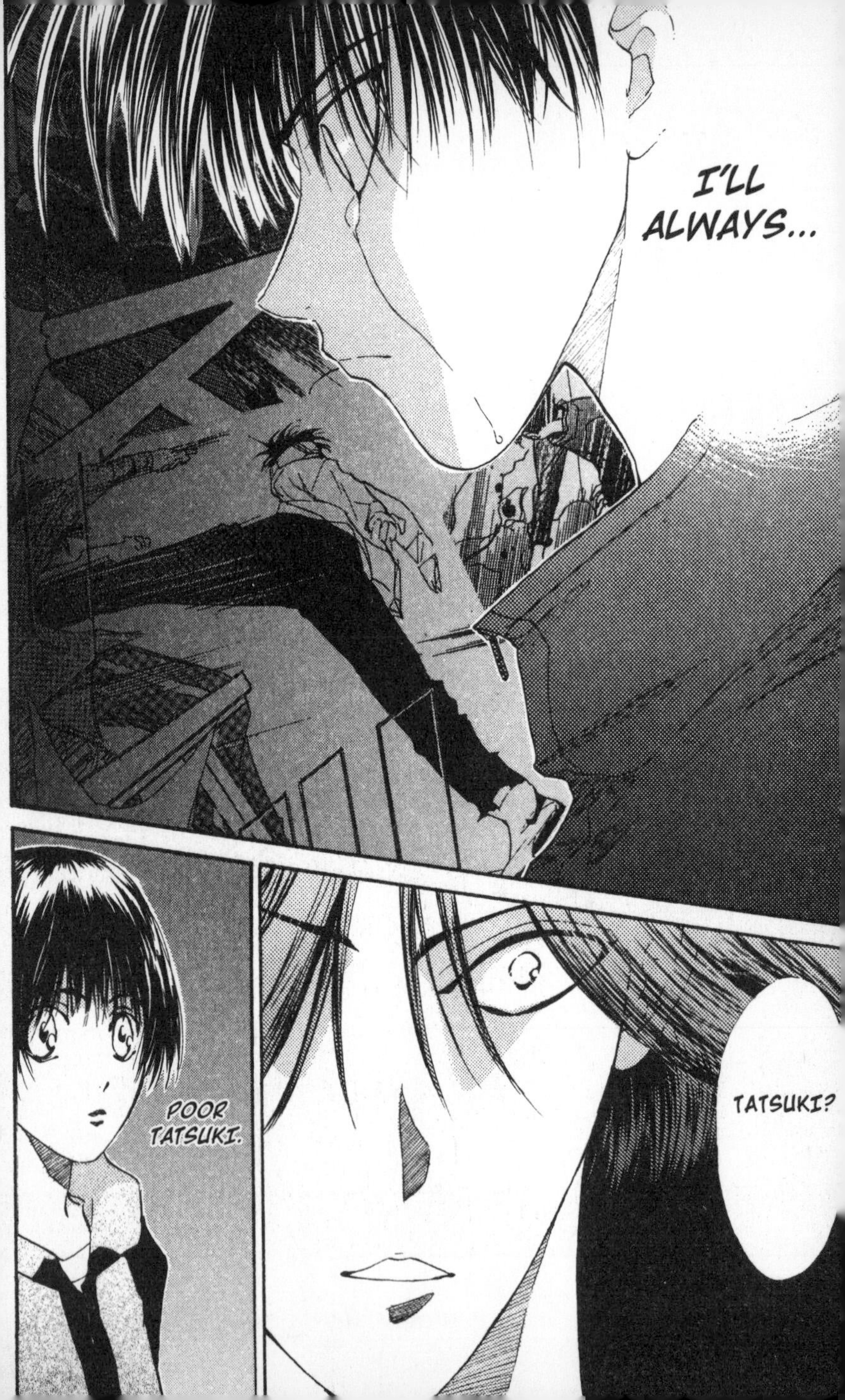
I'LL ALWAYS...
TATSUKI?
POOR TATSUKI.

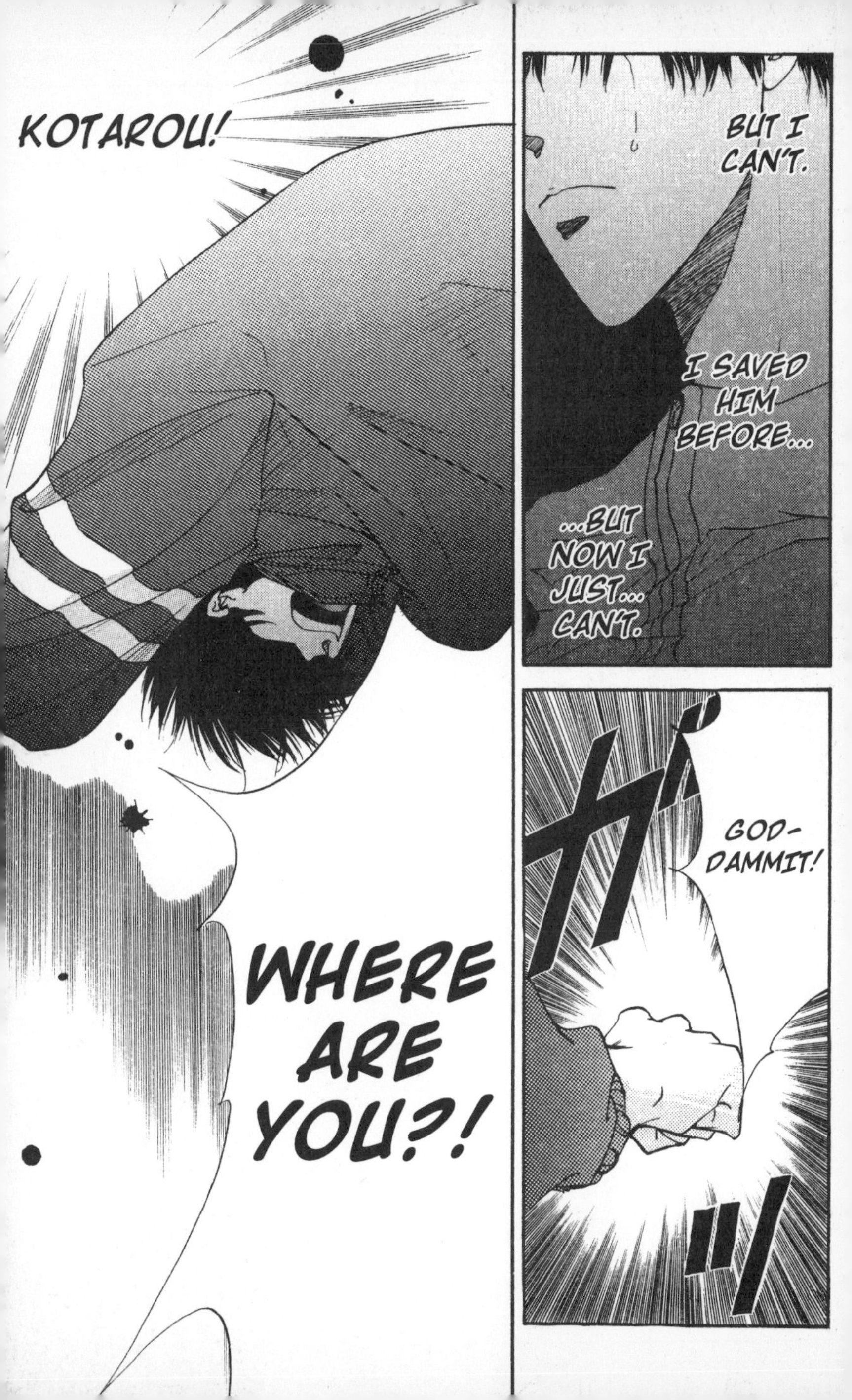
BUT I CAN'T.
I SAVED HIM BEFORE...
...BUT NOW I JUST... CAN'T.
GOD-DAMMIT!
KOTAROU!
WHERE ARE YOU?!

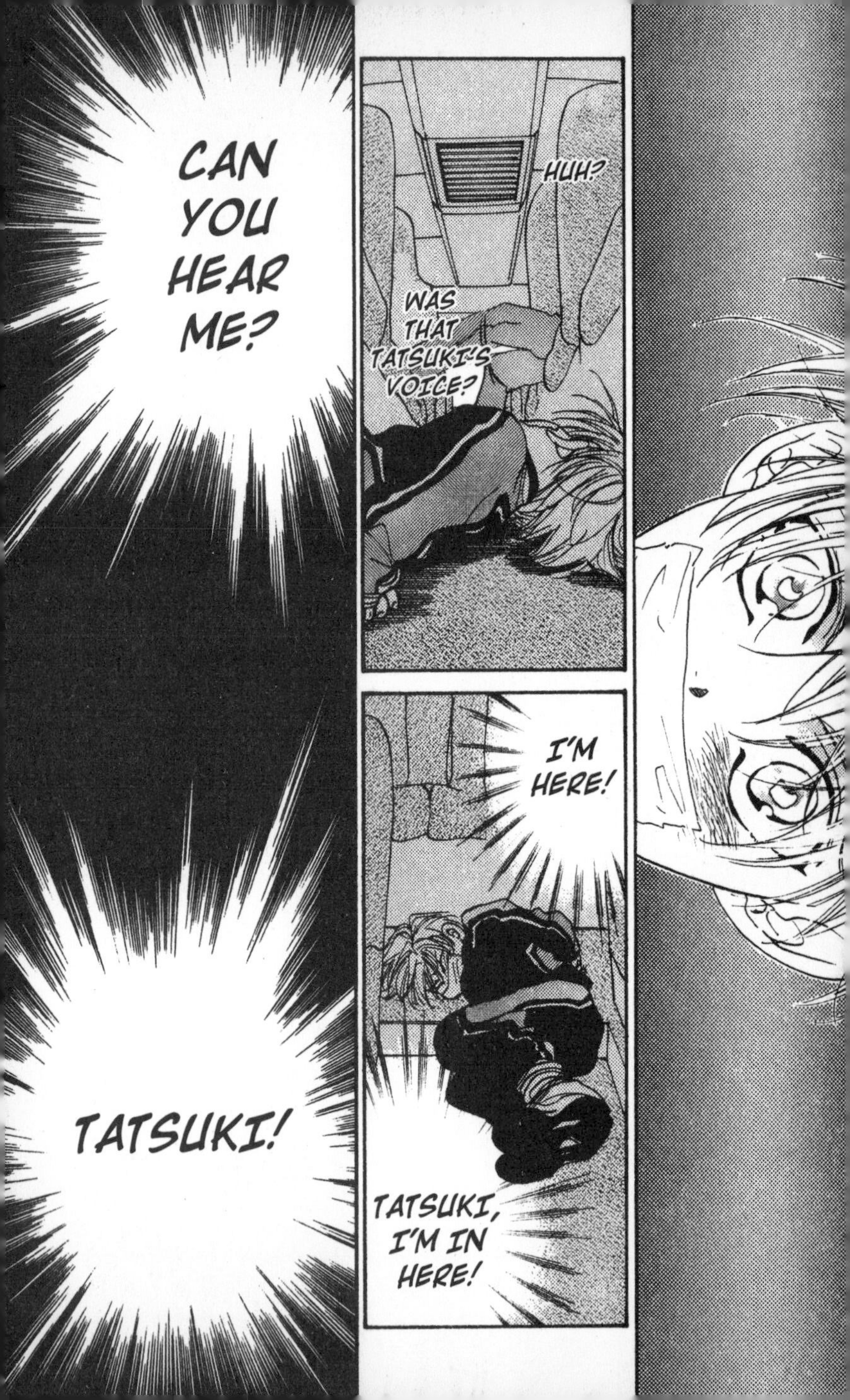
HUH?
WAS THAT TATSUKI'S VOICE?
I'M HERE!
TATSUKI, I'M IN HERE!
CAN YOU HEAR ME?
TATSUKI!

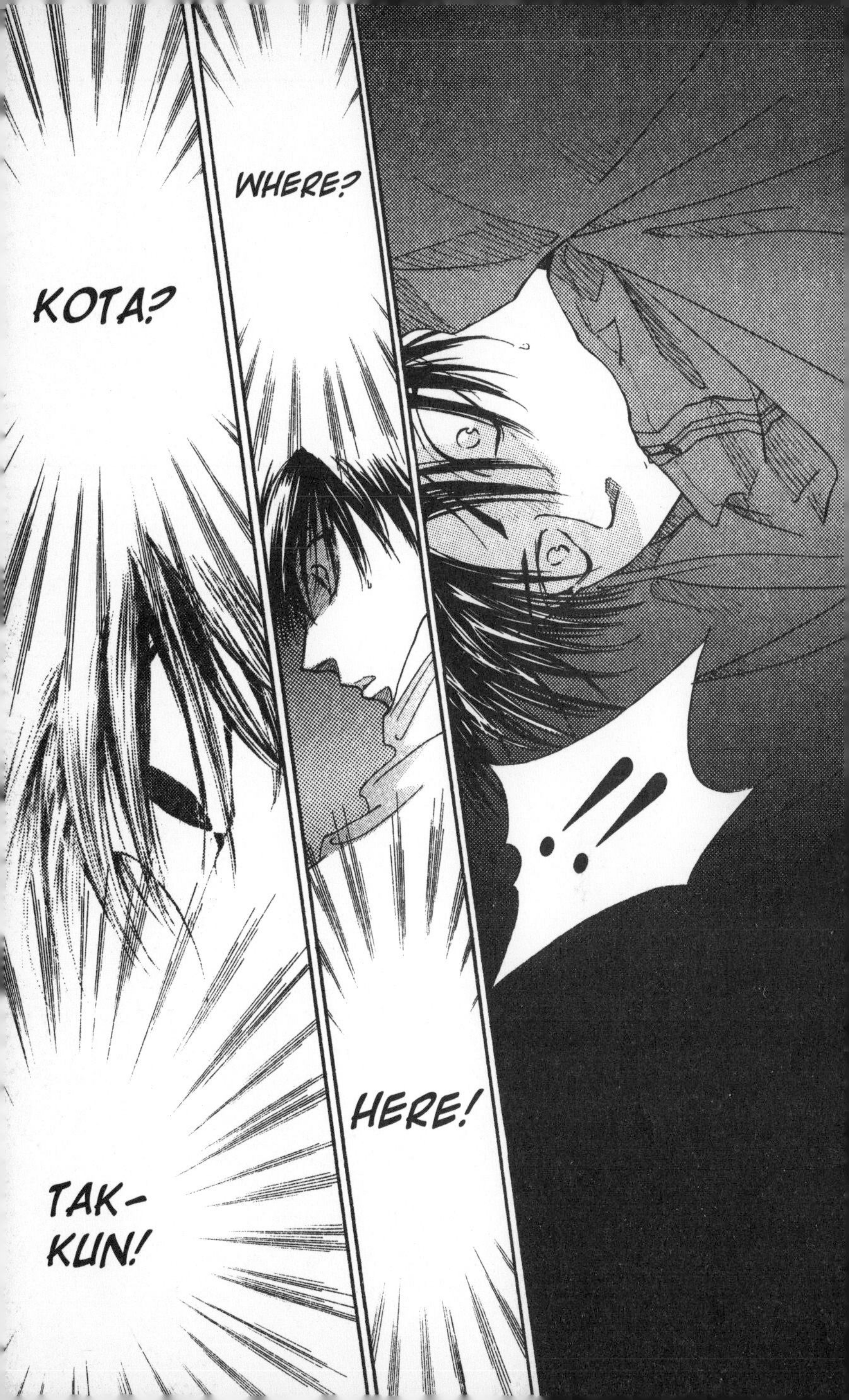
..!!
WHERE?
HERE!
KOTA?
TAK-
KUN!

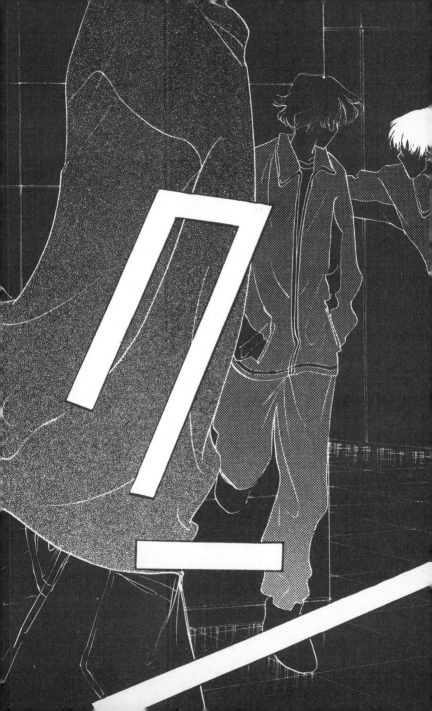

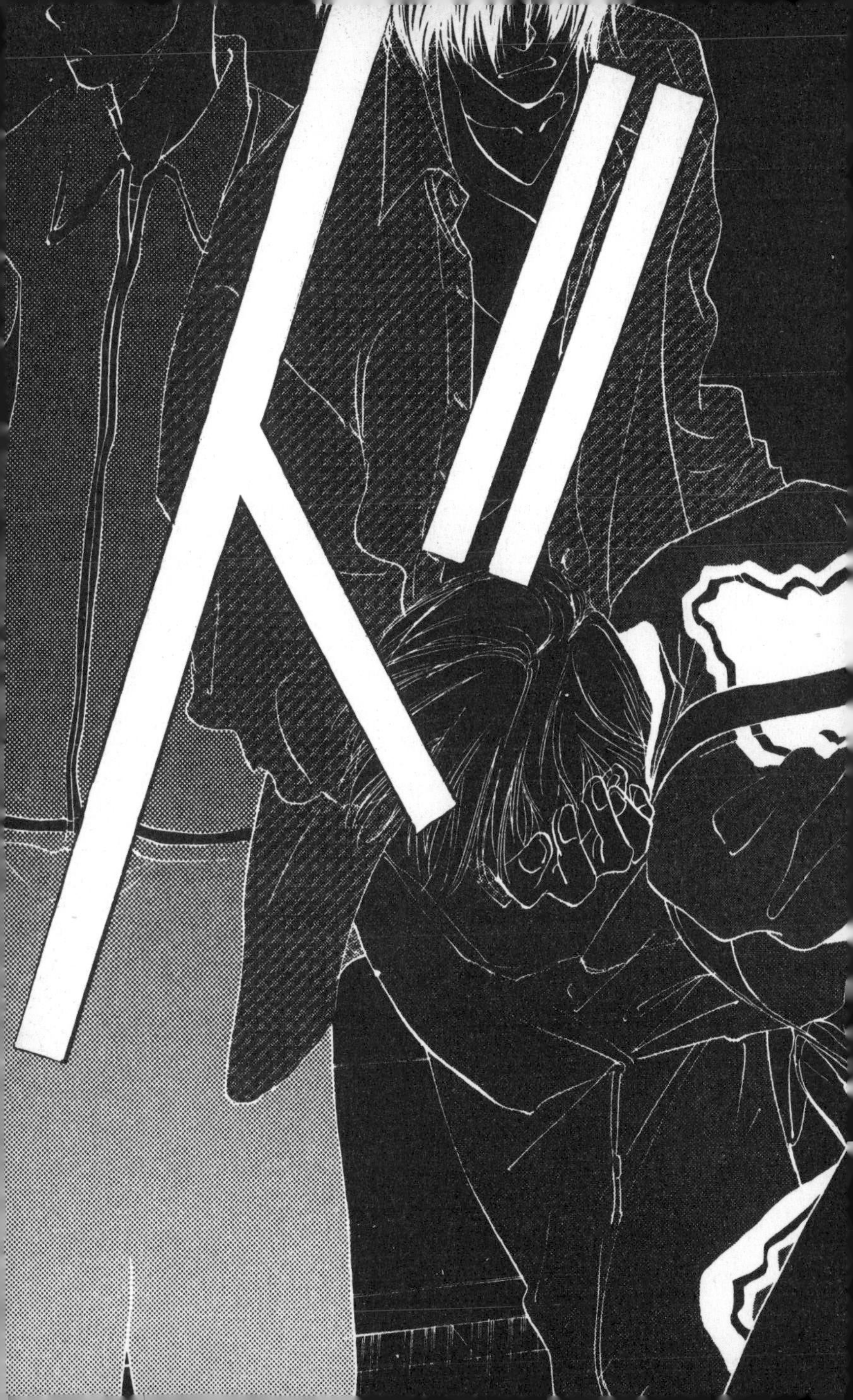

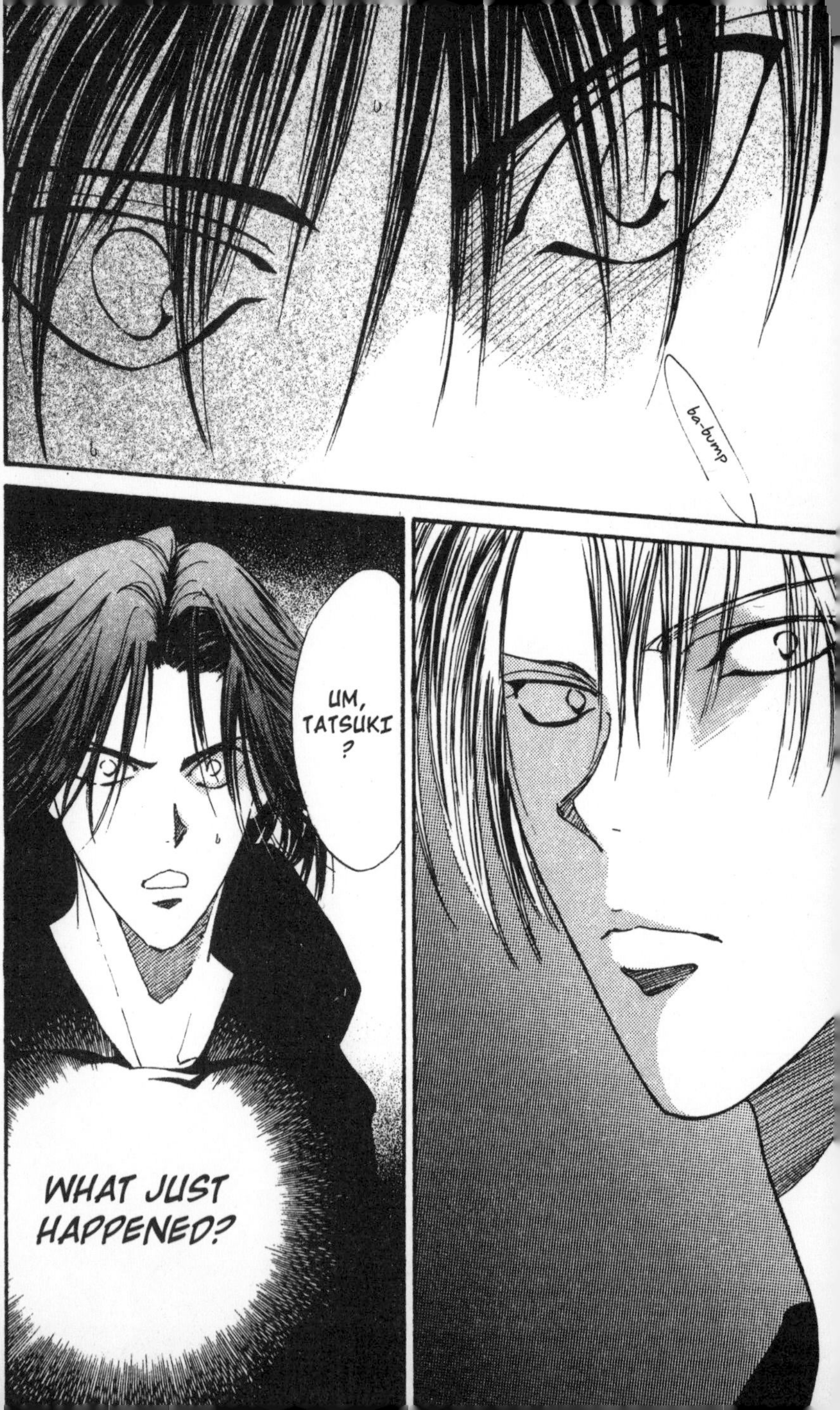
ba-bump
UM, TATSUKI ?
WHAT JUST HAPPENED?

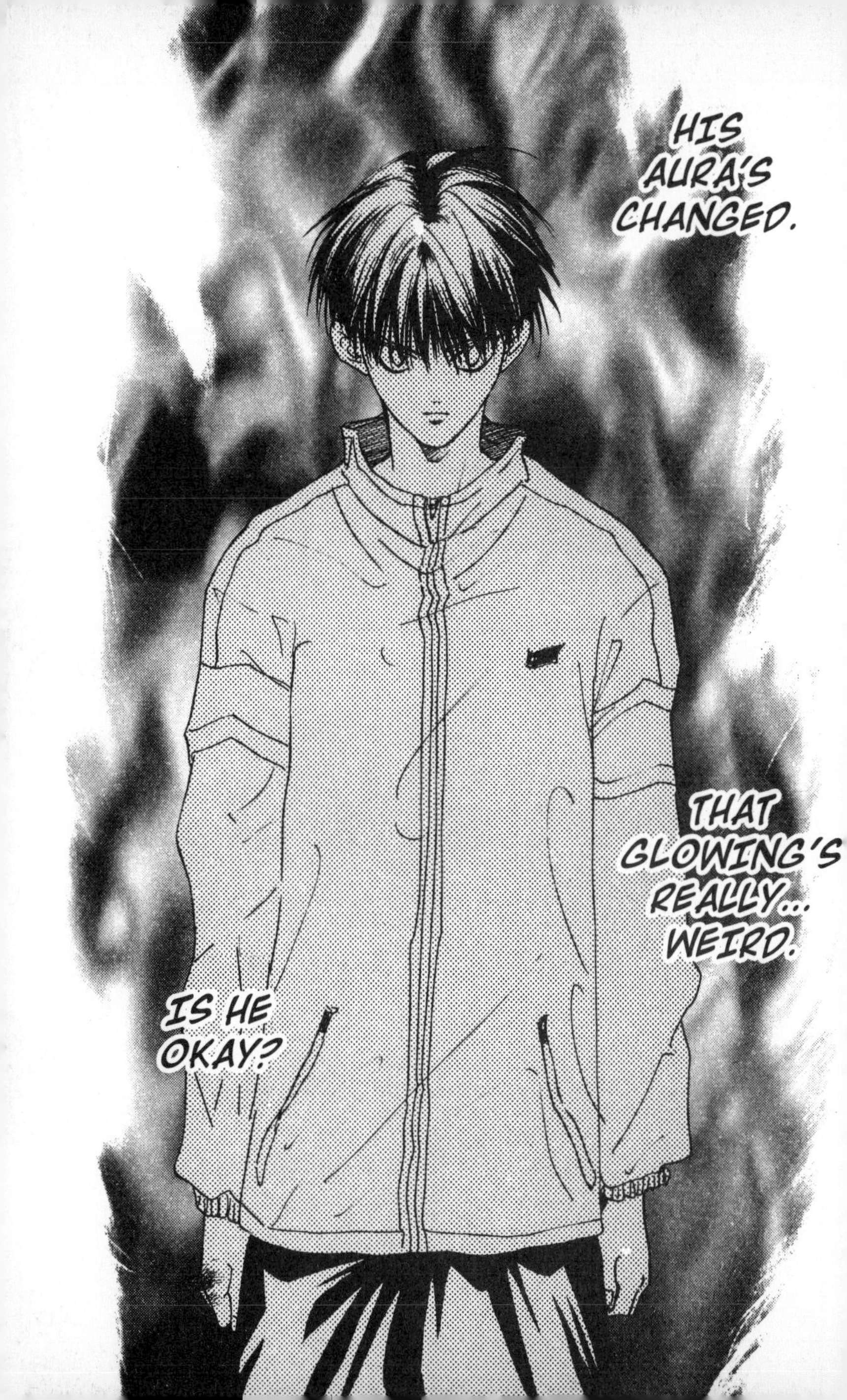
HIS AURA'S CHANGED.
THAT GLOWING'S REALLY... WEIRD.
IS HE OKAY?

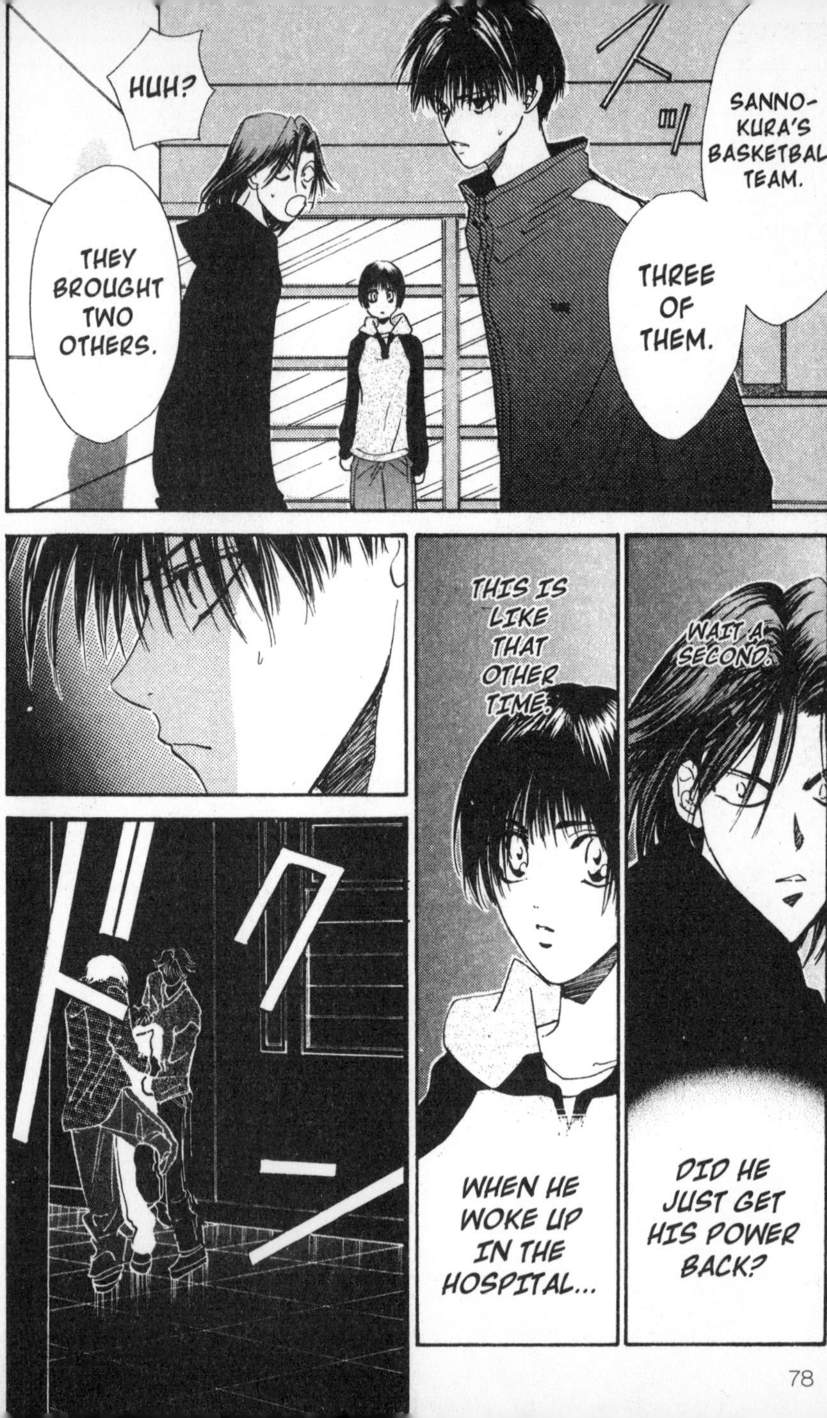
SANNO-KURA'S BASKETBALL TEAM.
HUH?
THREE OF THEM.
THEY BROUGHT TWO OTHERS.
WAIT A SECOND.
DID HE JUST GET HIS POWER BACK?
THIS IS LIKE THAT OTHER TIME.
WHEN HE WOKE UP IN THE HOSPITAL...

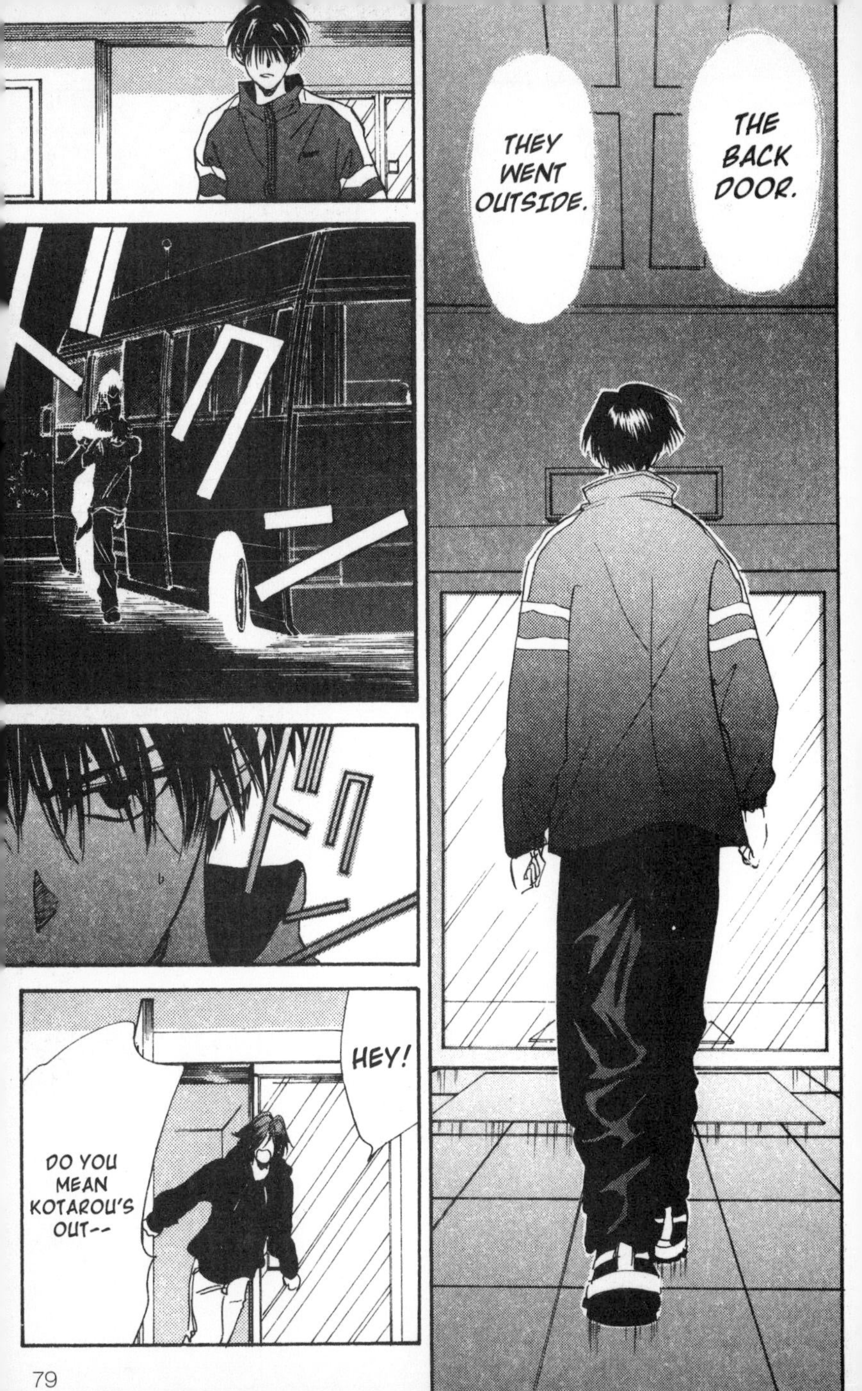
THE BACK DOOR.
THEY WENT OUTSIDE.
HEY!
DO YOU MEAN KOTAROU'S OUT--

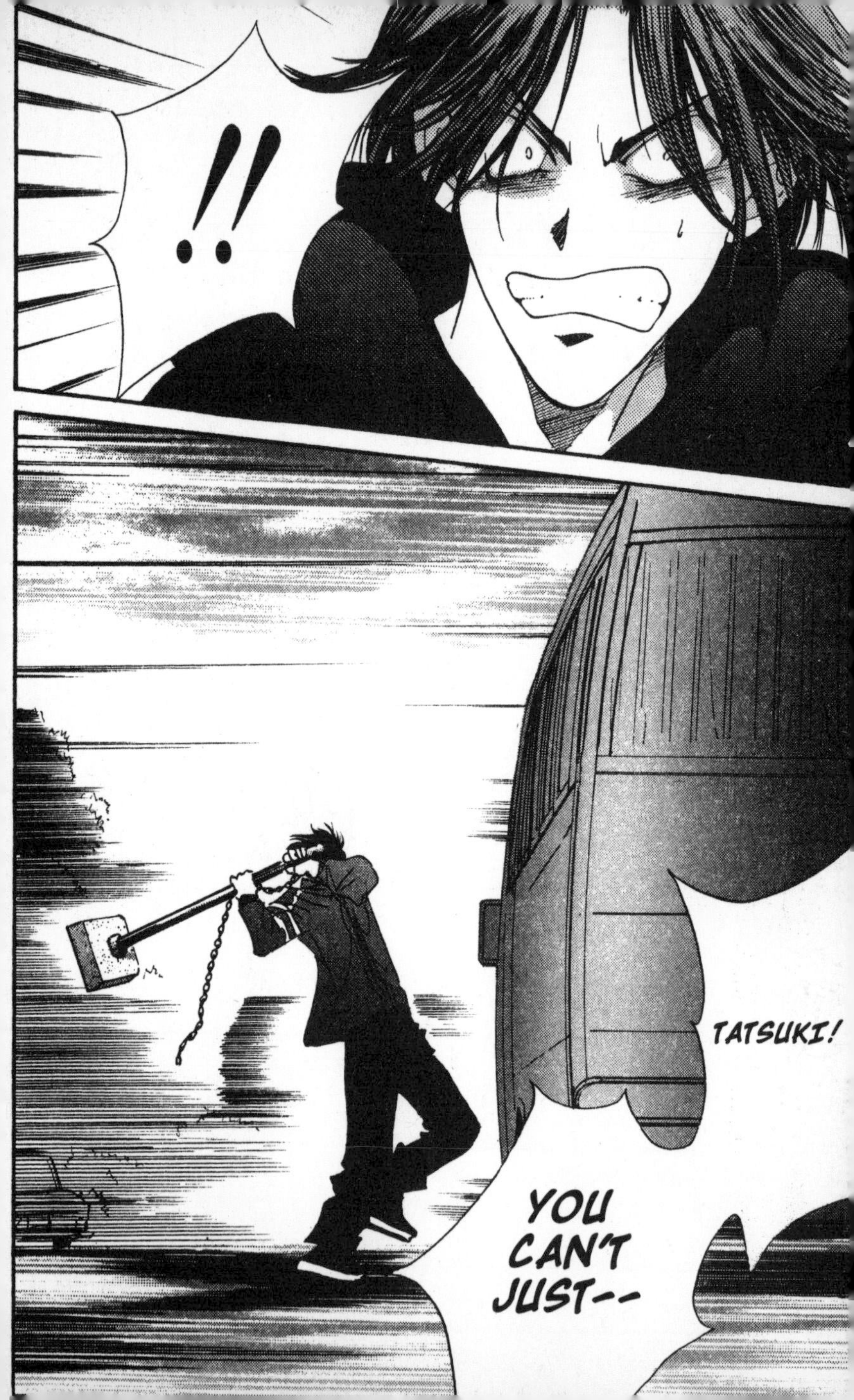
!!
TATSUKI!
YOU CAN'T JUST--

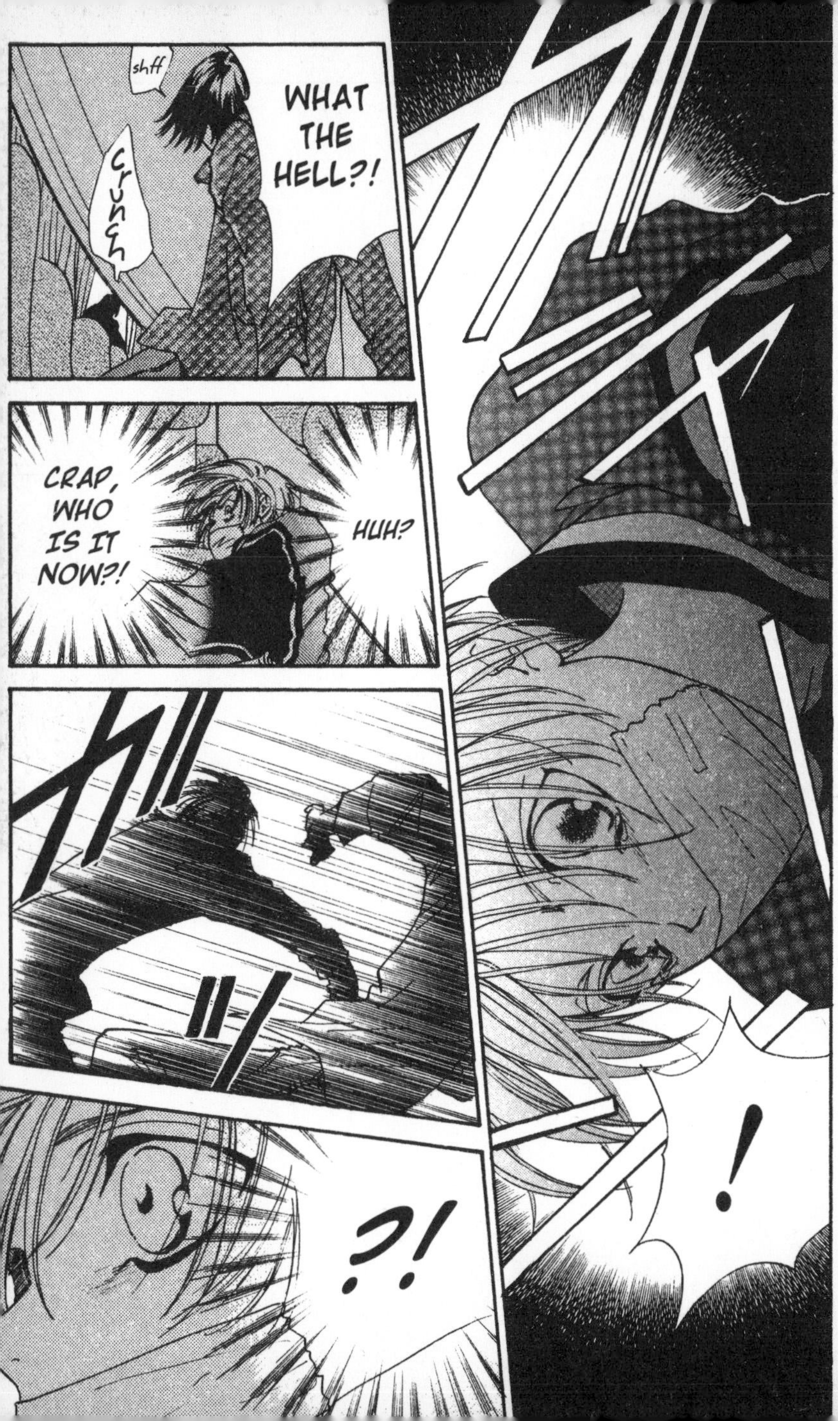
!
WHAT THE HELL?!
shff
crunch
HUH?
CRAP, WHO IS IT NOW?!
?!

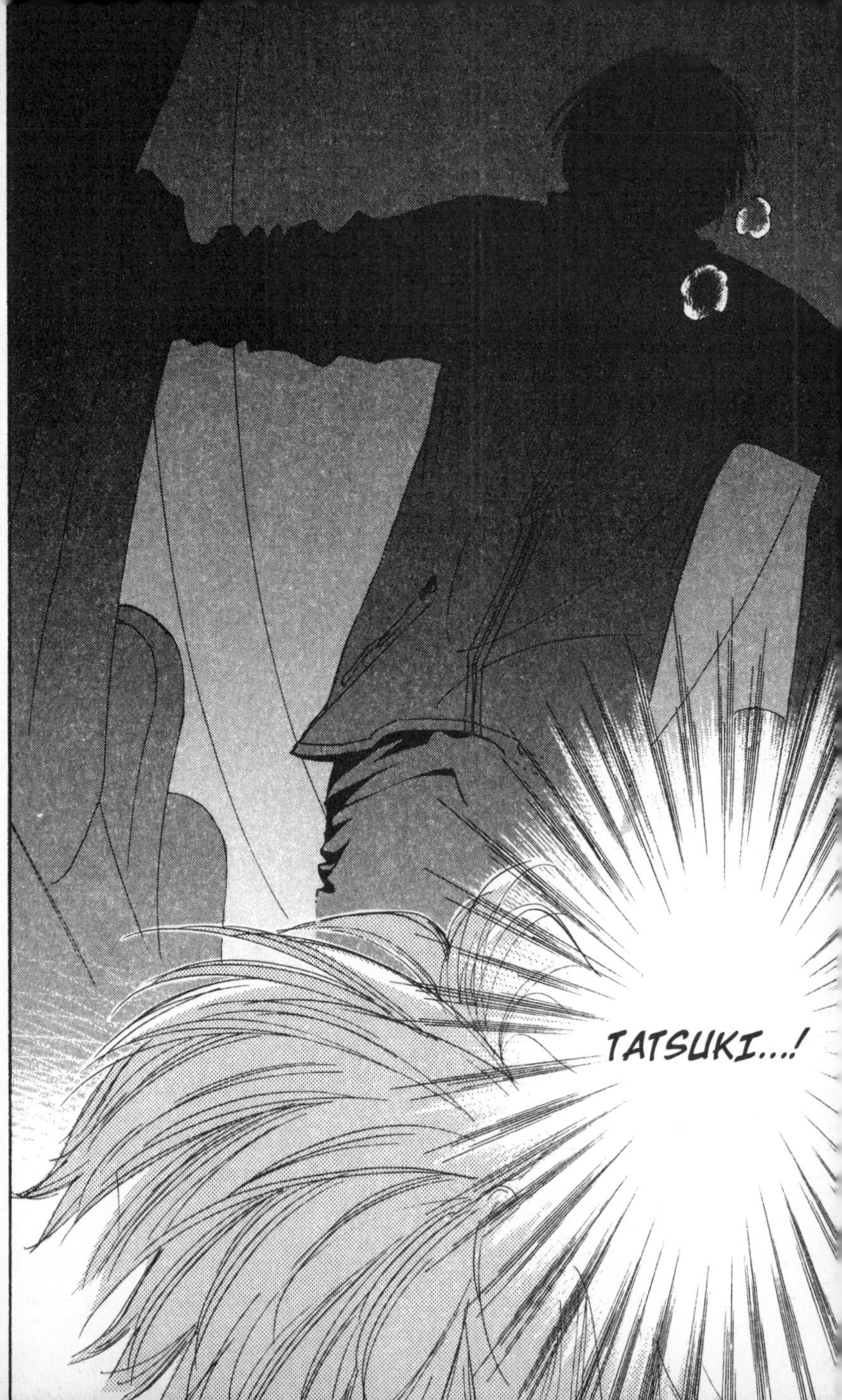
TATSUKI...!

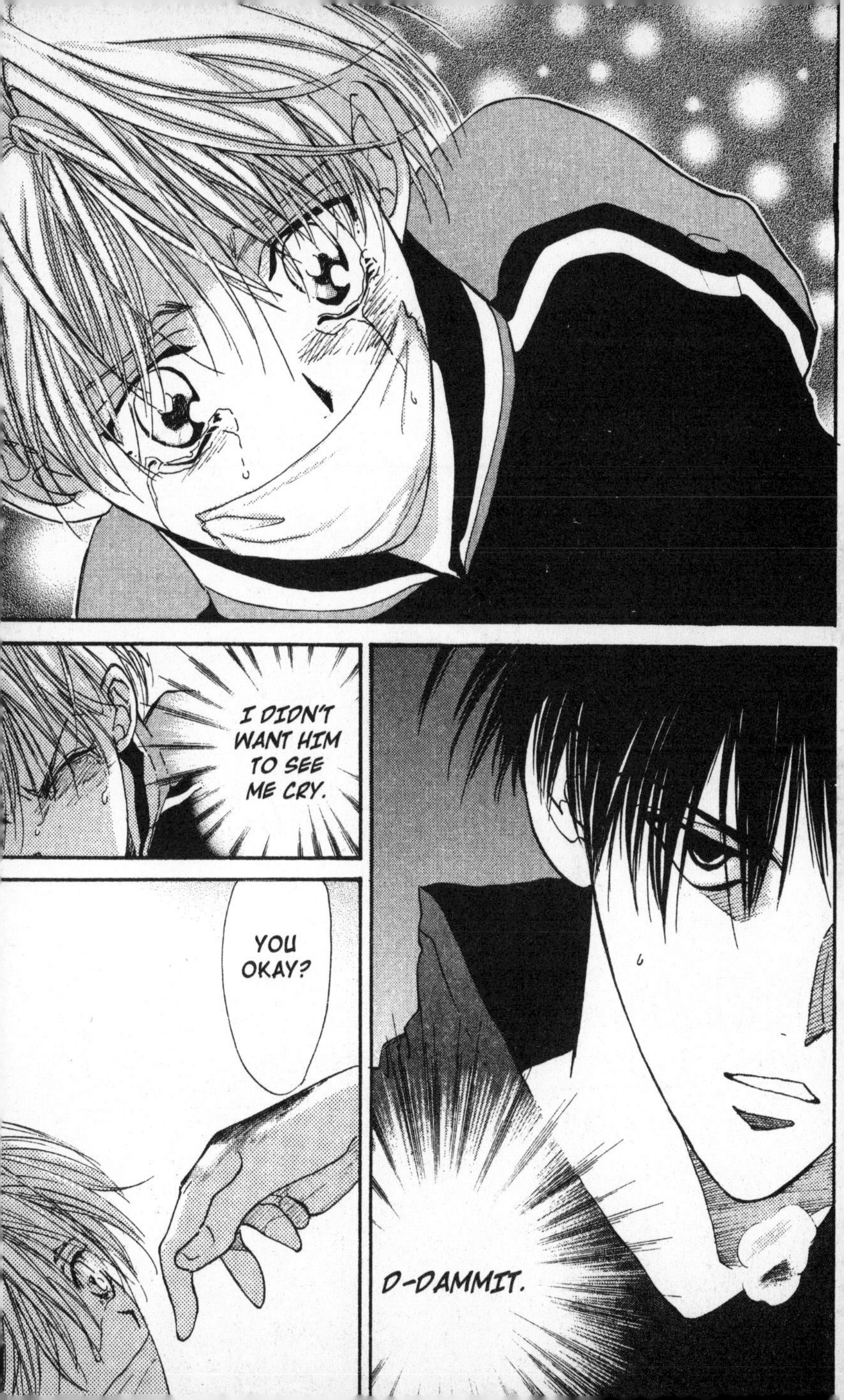
D-DAMMIT.
I DIDN'T WANT HIM TO SEE ME CRY.
YOU OKAY?

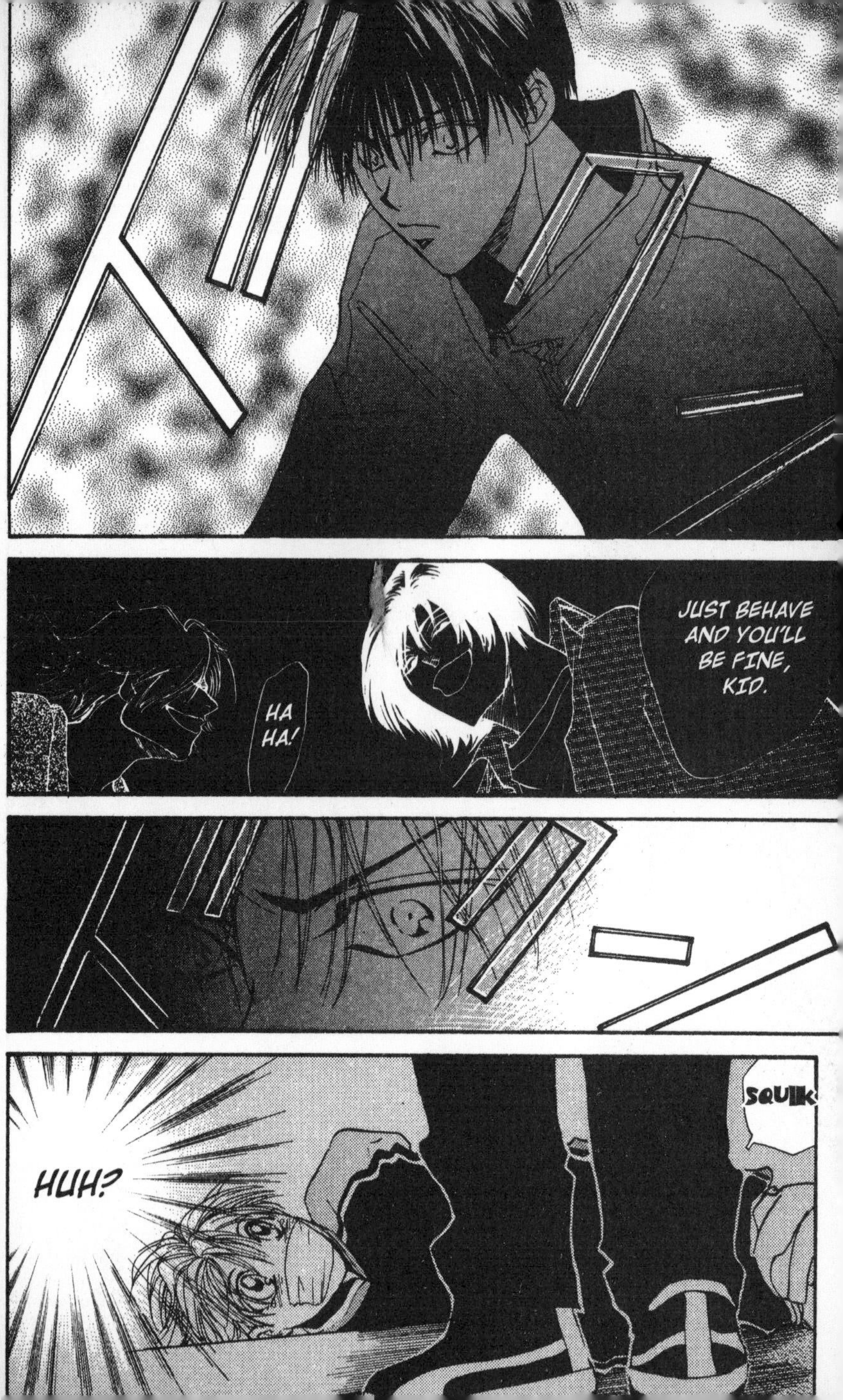
JUST BEHAVE AND YOU'LL BE FINE, KID.
HA HA!
SQUIK
HUH?

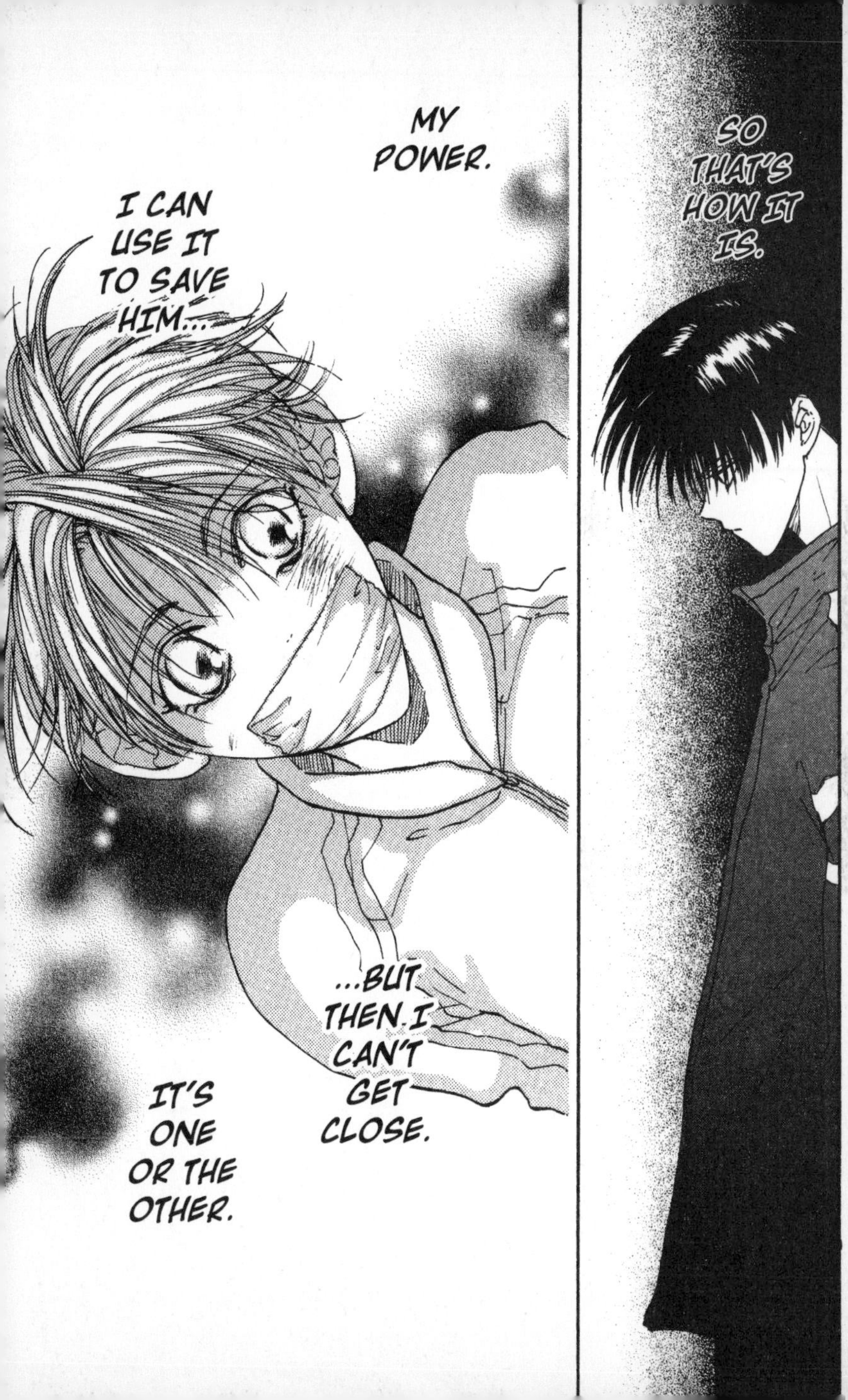
SO THAT'S HOW IT IS.
MY POWER.
I CAN USE IT TO SAVE HIM...
...BUT THEN I CAN'T GET CLOSE.
IT'S ONE OR THE OTHER.

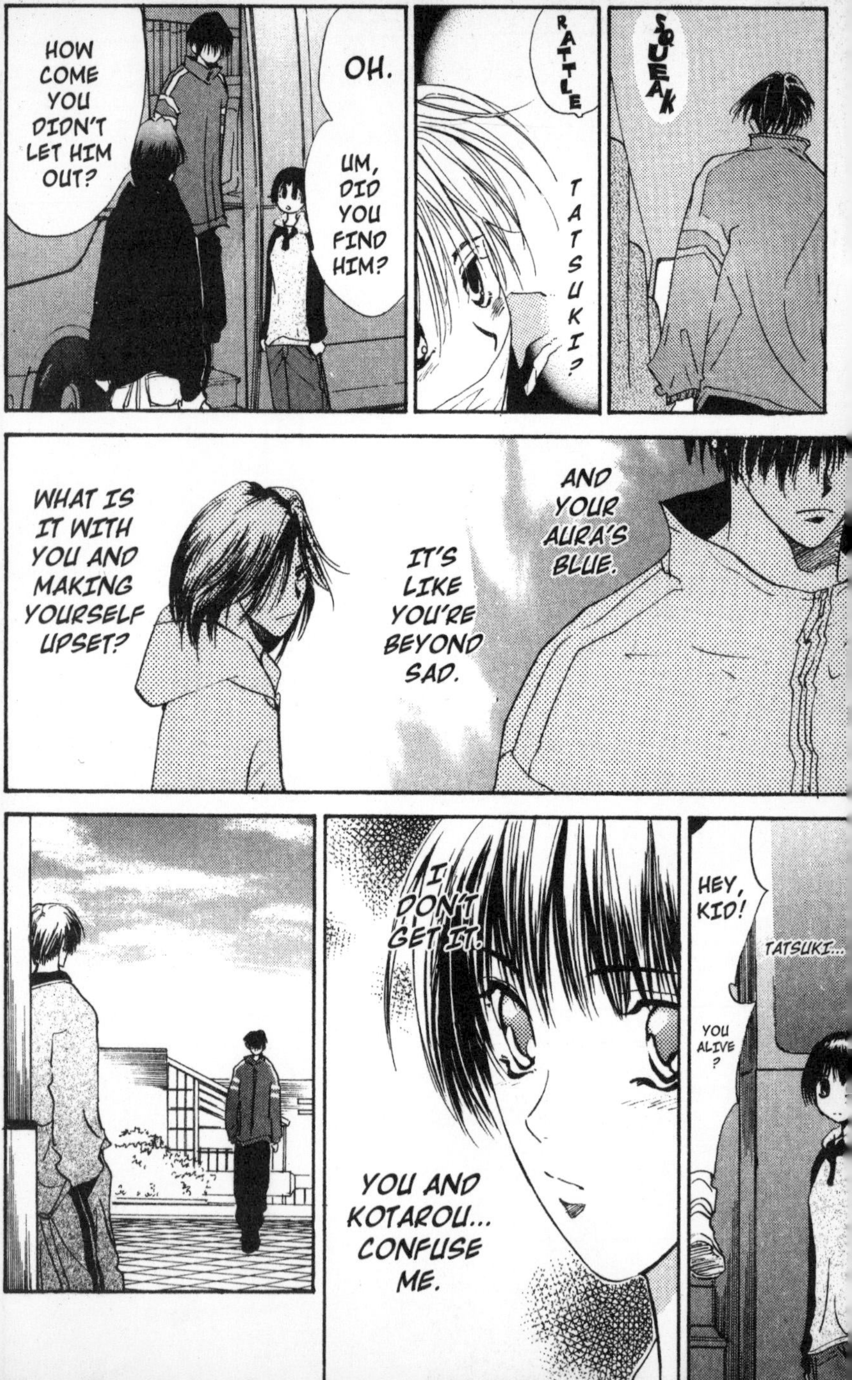
SQUEAK
RATTLE
TATSUKI?
OH.
UM, DID YOU FIND HIM?
HOW COME YOU DIDN'T LET HIM OUT?
AND YOUR AURA'S BLUE.
IT'S LIKE YOU'RE BEYOND SAD.
WHAT IS IT WITH YOU AND MAKING YOURSELF UPSET?
HEY, KID!
TATSUKI...
YOU ALIVE?
I DON'T GET IT.
YOU AND KOTAROU... CONFUSE ME.

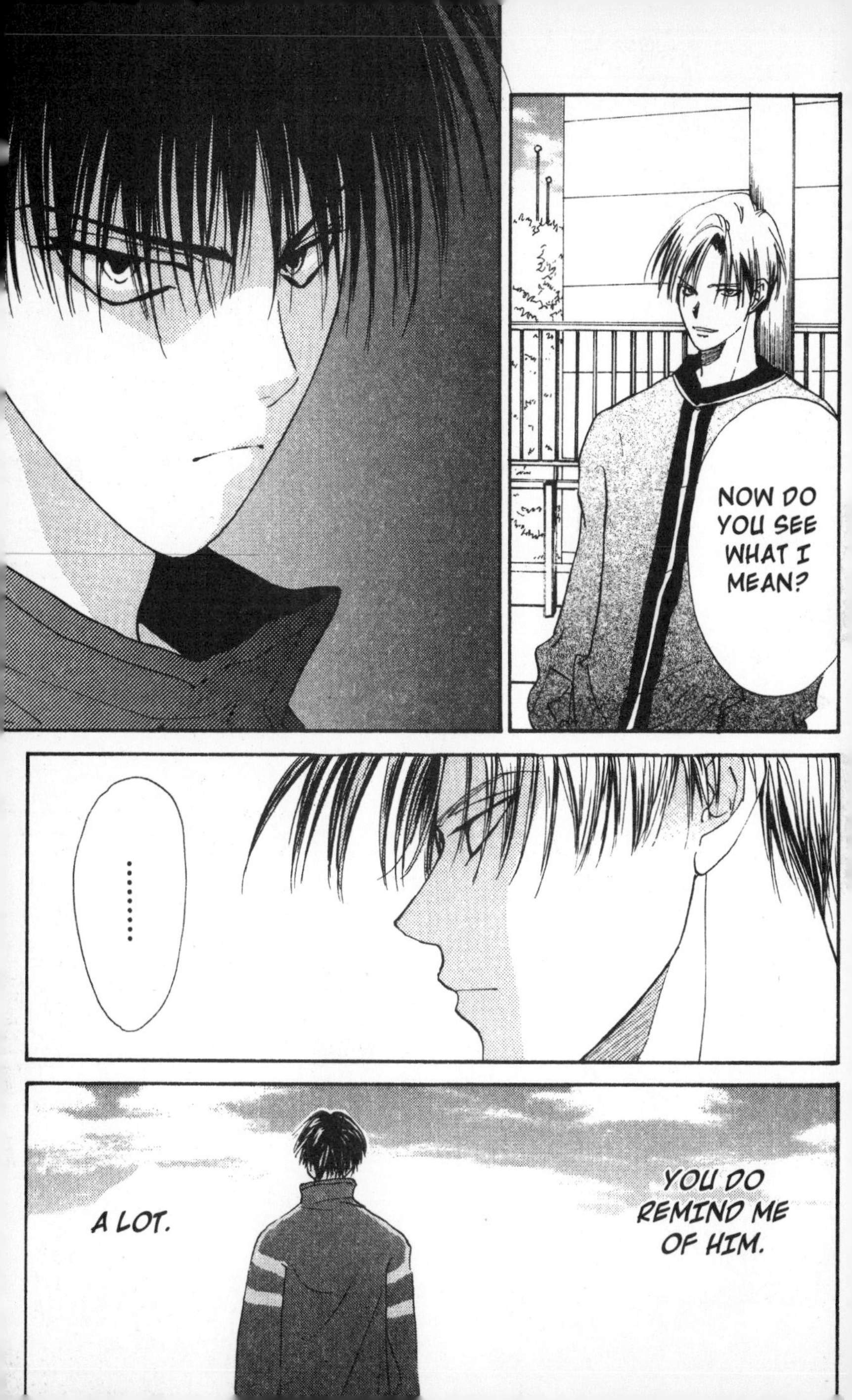
NOW DO YOU SEE WHAT I MEAN?
....
YOU DO REMIND ME OF HIM.
A LOT.

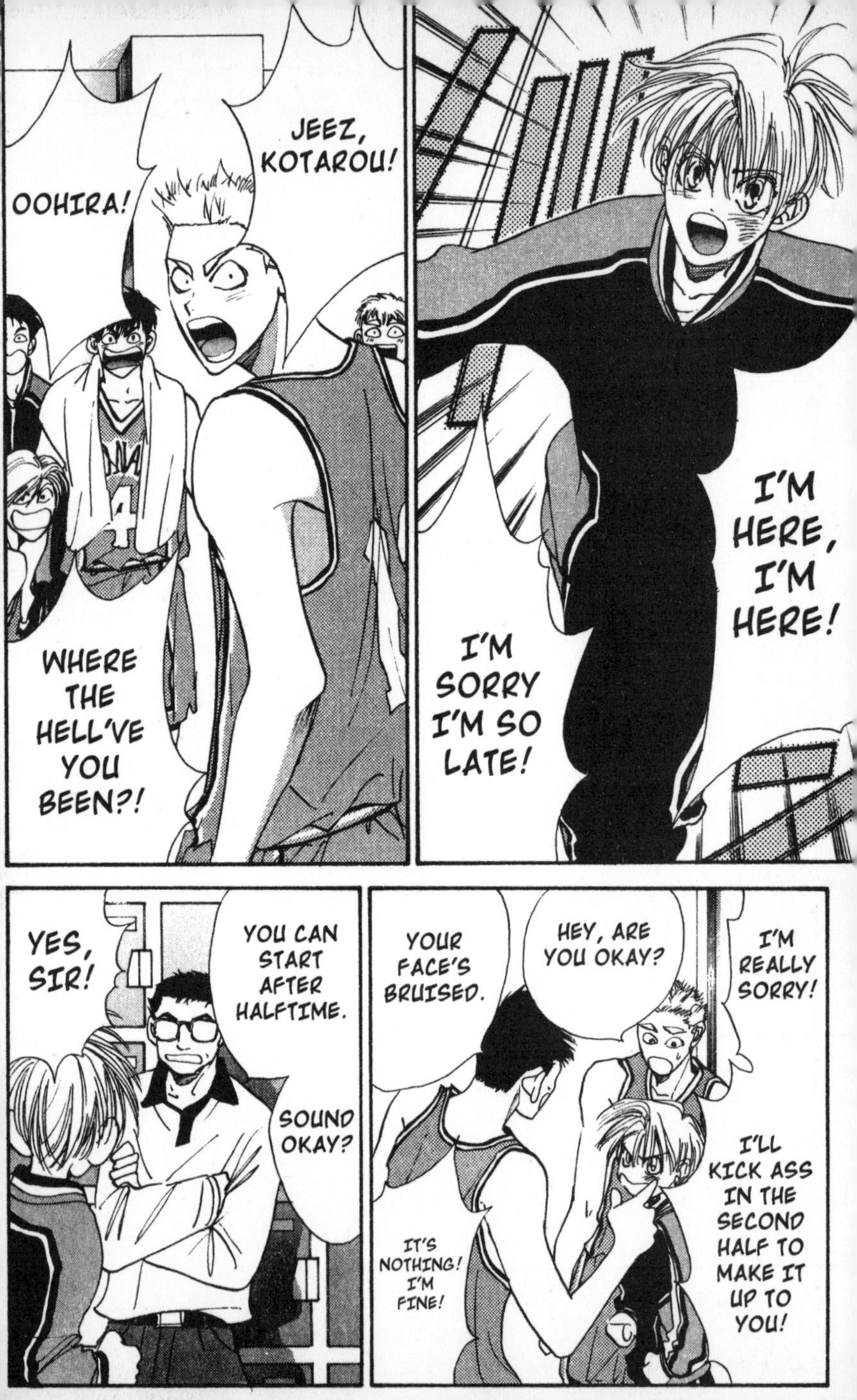
I'M HERE, I'M HERE!
I'M SORRY I'M SO LATE!
JEEZ, KOTAROU!
OOHIRA!
WHERE THE HELL'VE YOU BEEN?!
I'M REALLY SORRY!
HEY, ARE YOU OKAY?
YOUR FACE'S BRUISED.
I'LL KICK ASS IN THE SECOND HALF TO MAKE IT UP TO YOU!
IT'S NOTHING! I'M FINE!
YOU CAN START AFTER HALFTIME.
SOUND OKAY?
YES, SIR!

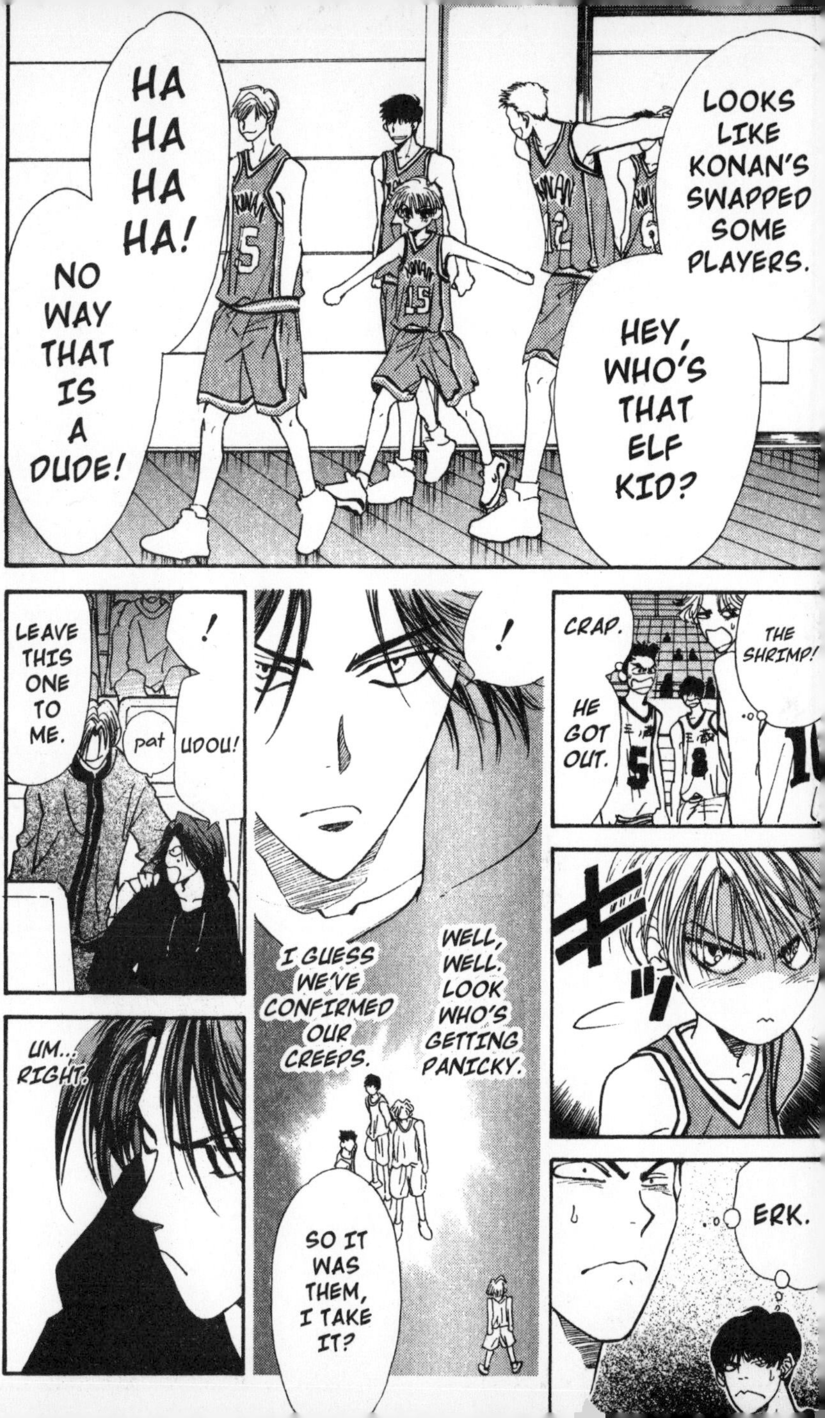
LOOKS LIKE KONAN'S SWAPPED SOME PLAYERS.
HEY, WHO'S THAT ELF KID?
HA HA HA HA!
NO WAY THAT IS A DUDE!
THE SHRIMP!
CRAP.
HE GOT OUT.
ERK.
!
WELL, WELL. LOOK WHO'S GETTING PANICKY.
I GUESS WE'VE CONFIRMED OUR CREEPS.
SO IT WAS THEM, I TAKE IT?
!
UDOU!
pat
LEAVE THIS ONE TO ME.
UM... RIGHT.

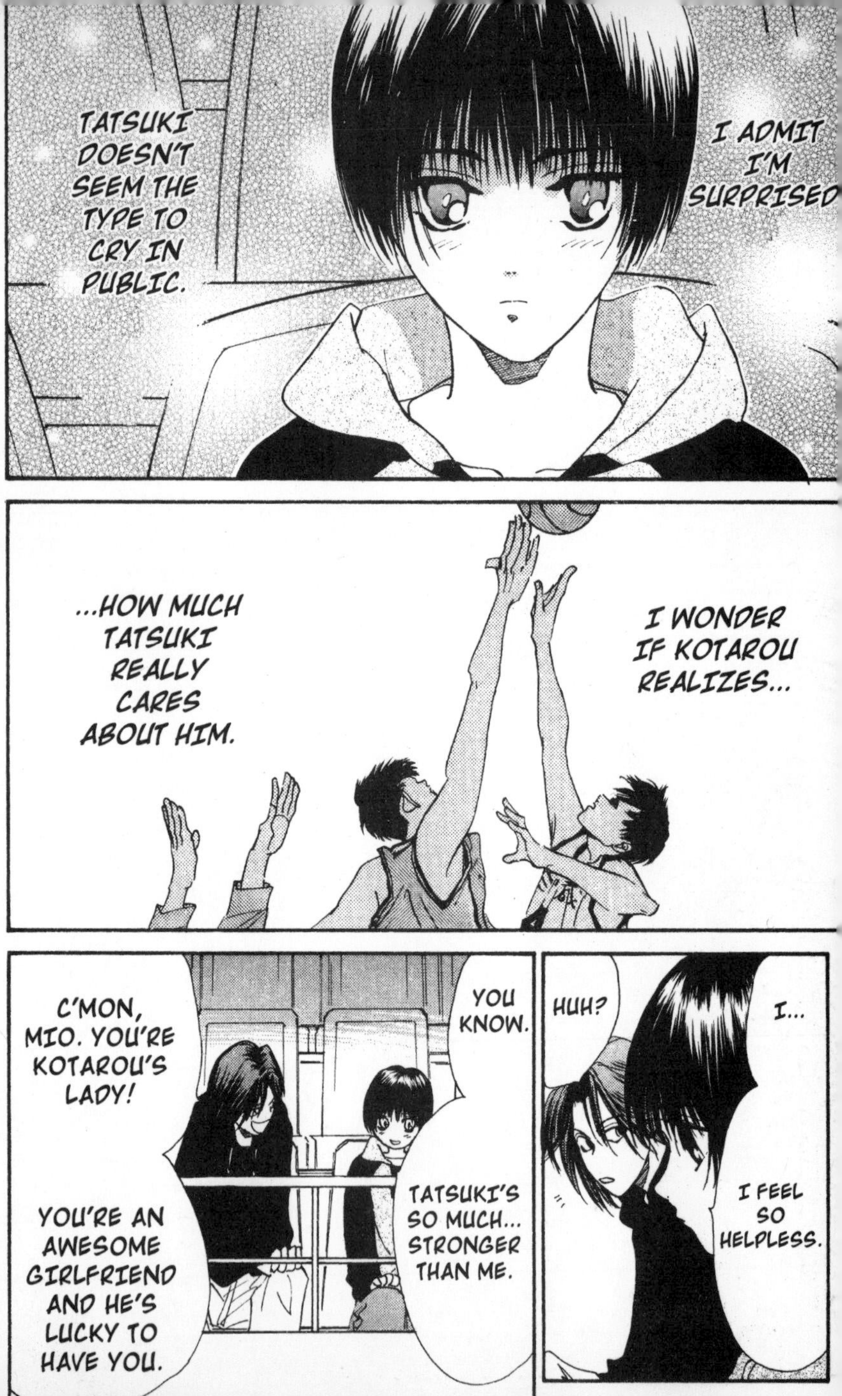
I ADMIT I'M SURPRISED
TATSUKI DOESN'T SEEM THE TYPE TO CRY IN PUBLIC.
I WONDER IF KOTAROU REALIZES...
...HOW MUCH TATSUKI REALLY CARES ABOUT HIM.
I...
HUH?
I FEEL SO HELPLESS.
YOU KNOW.
TATSUKI'S SO MUCH... STRONGER THAN ME.
C'MON, MIO. YOU'RE KOTAROU'S LADY!
YOU'RE AN AWESOME GIRLFRIEND AND HE'S LUCKY TO HAVE YOU.

ACT 8

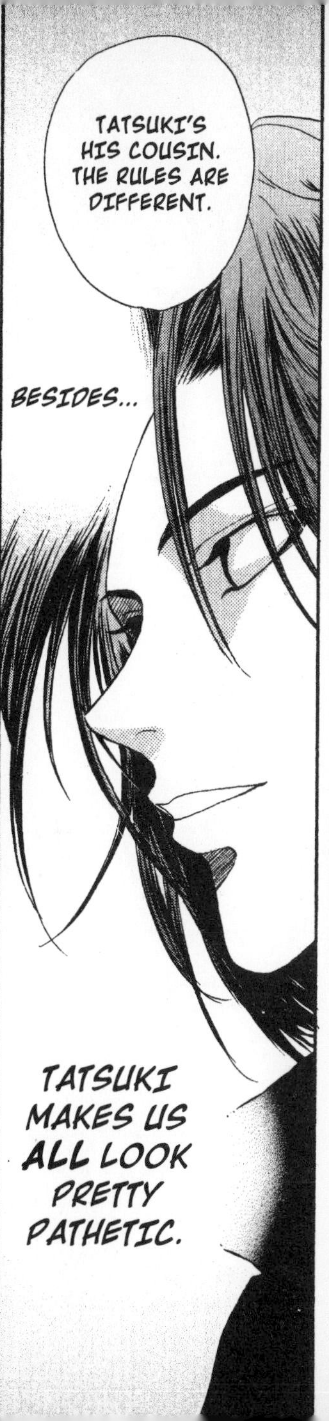
TATSUKI'S HIS COUSIN. THE RULES ARE DIFFERENT.
BESIDES...
TATSUKI MAKES US **ALL** LOOK PRETTY PATHETIC.

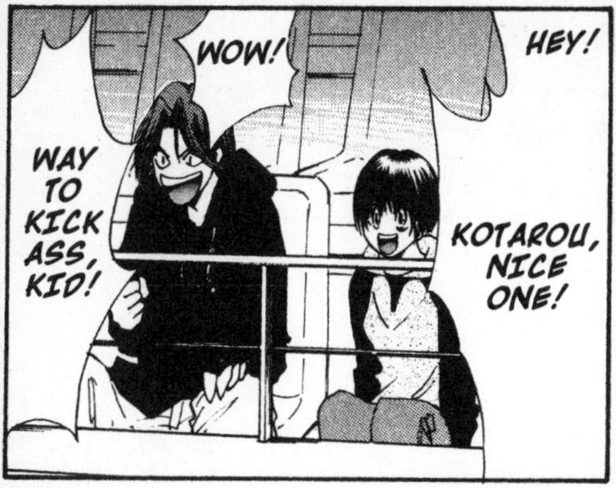
HEY!
KOTAROU, NICE ONE!
WOW!
WAY TO KICK ASS, KID!

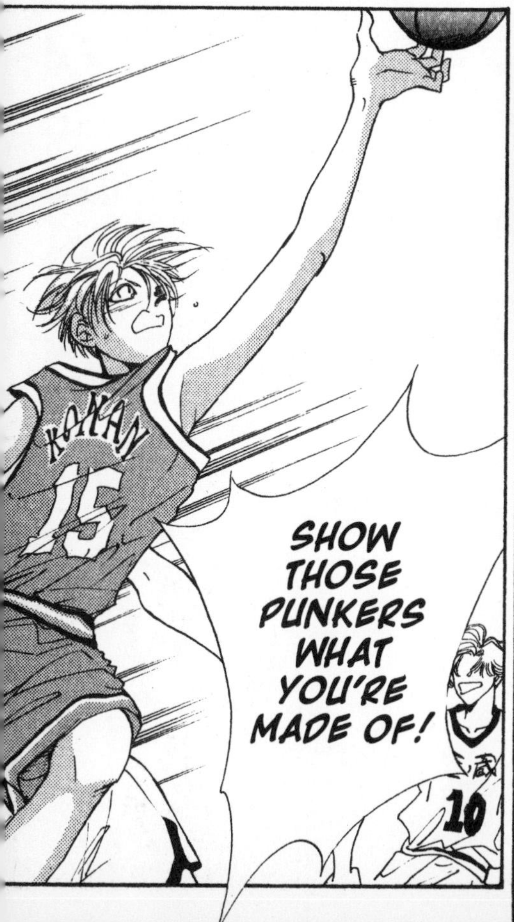
KONAN
15
SHOW THOSE PUNKERS WHAT YOU'RE MADE OF!
10

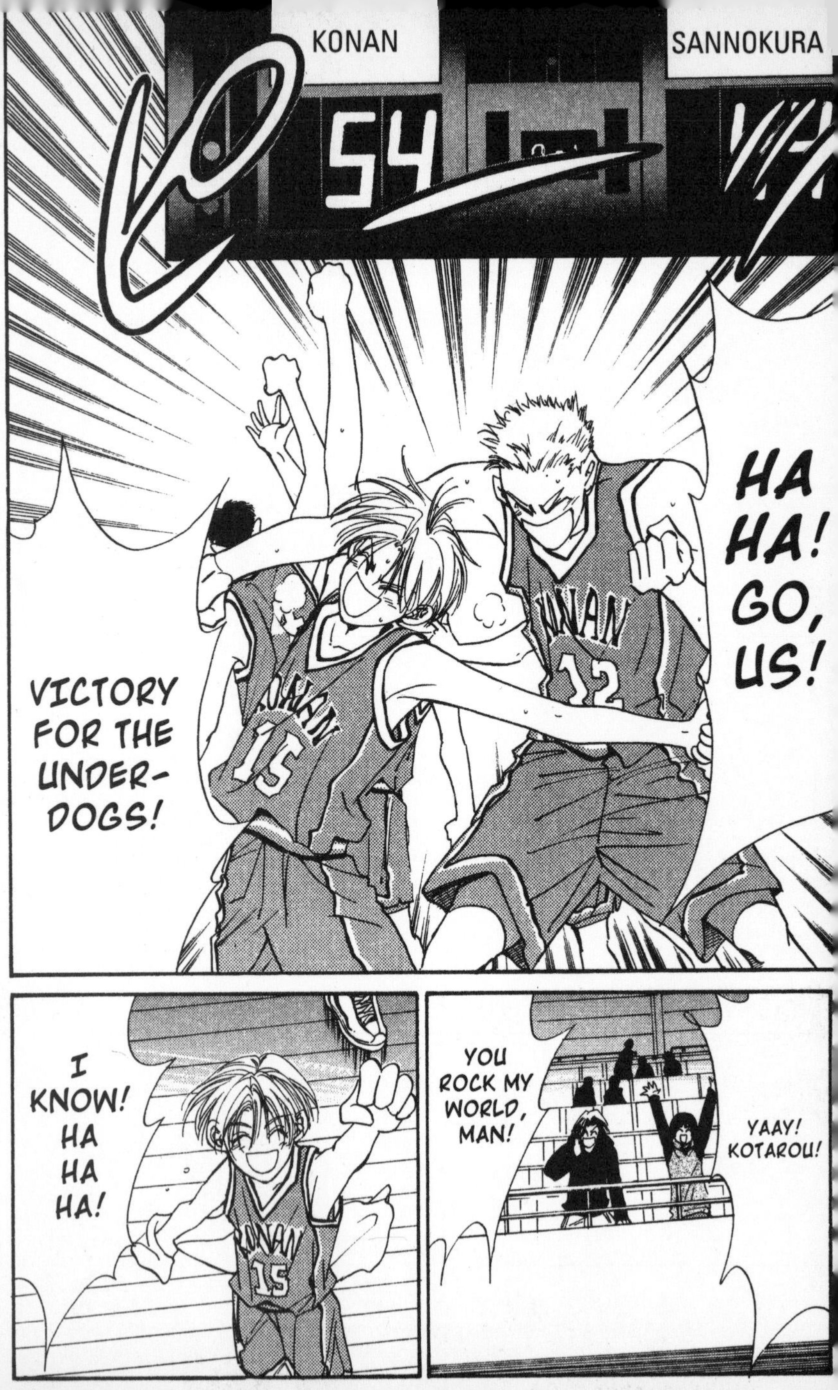
KONAN
SANNOKURA
54
HA HA! GO, US!
VICTORY FOR THE UNDER-DOGS!
YAAY! KOTAROU!
YOU ROCK MY WORLD, MAN!
I KNOW! HA HA HA!

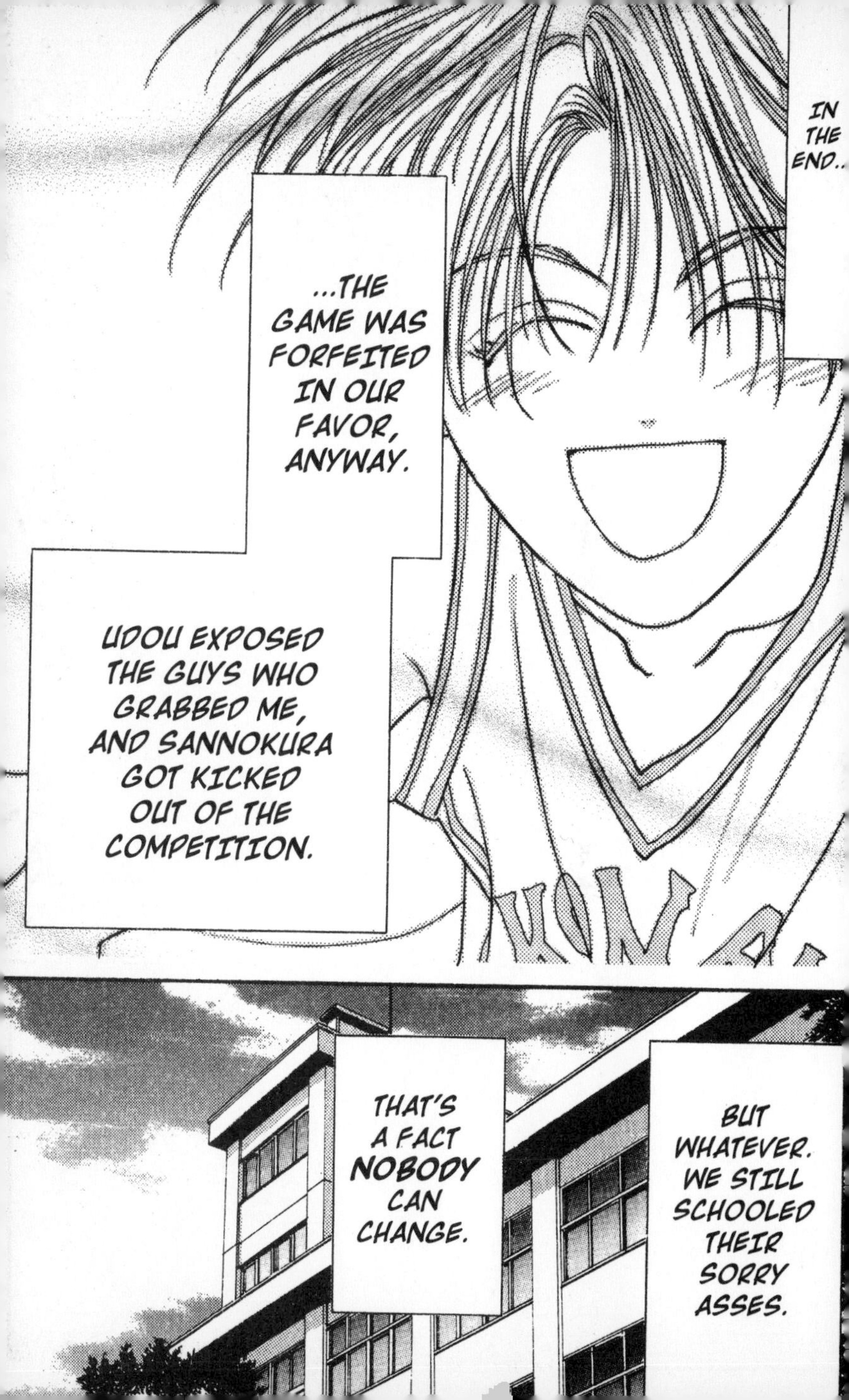
IN THE END...
...THE GAME WAS FORFEITED IN OUR FAVOR, ANYWAY.
UDOU EXPOSED THE GUYS WHO GRABBED ME, AND SANNOKURA GOT KICKED OUT OF THE COMPETITION.
BUT WHATEVER. WE STILL SCHOOLED THEIR SORRY ASSES.
THAT'S A FACT NOBODY CAN CHANGE.

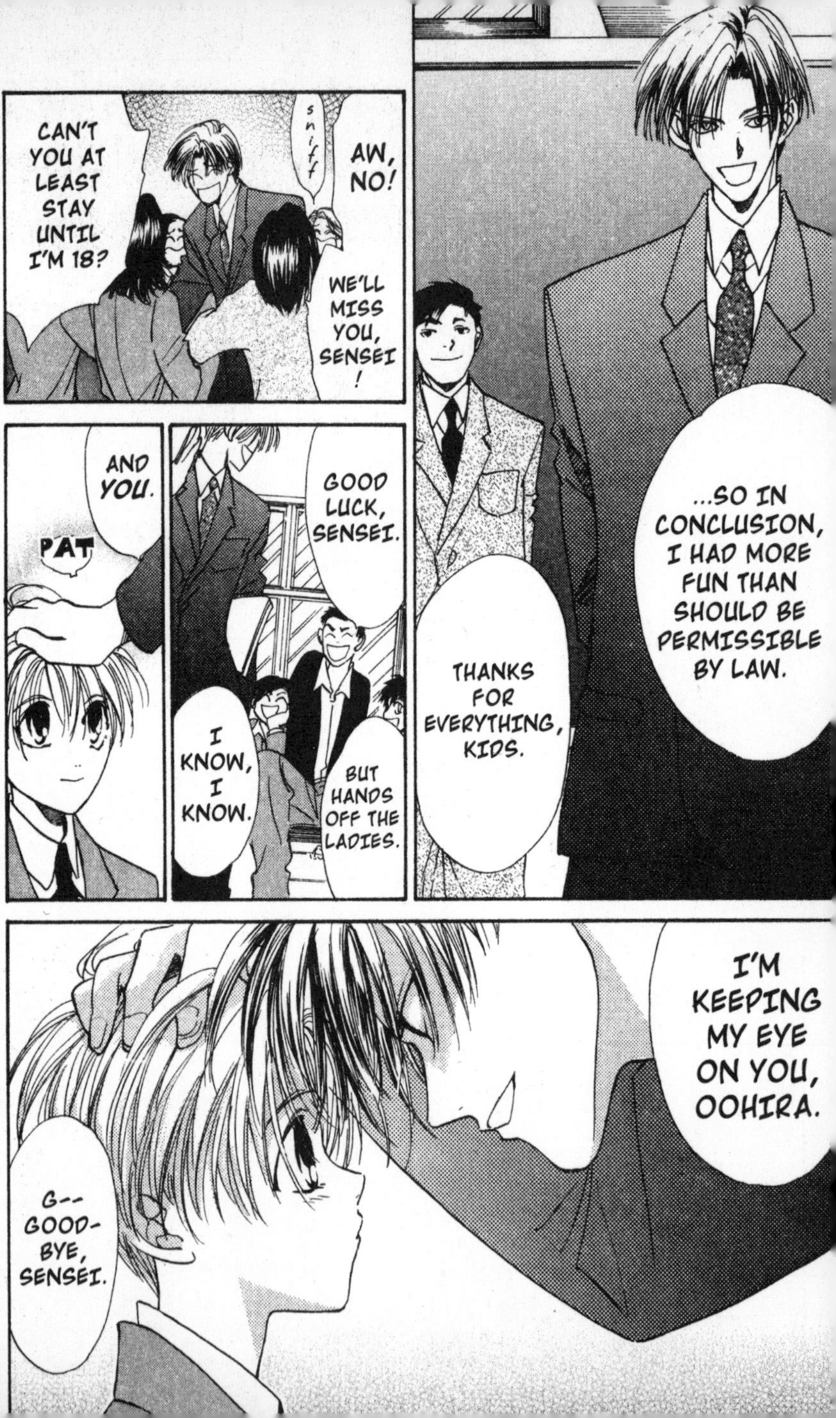
...SO IN CONCLUSION, I HAD MORE FUN THAN SHOULD BE PERMISSIBLE BY LAW.
THANKS FOR EVERYTHING, KIDS.
AW, NO!
sniff
WE'LL MISS YOU, SENSEI!
CAN'T YOU AT LEAST STAY UNTIL I'M 18?
GOOD LUCK, SENSEI.
BUT HANDS OFF THE LADIES.
I KNOW, I KNOW.
AND YOU.
PAT
I'M KEEPING MY EYE ON YOU, OOHIRA.
G-- GOOD-BYE, SENSEI.

ACT 8

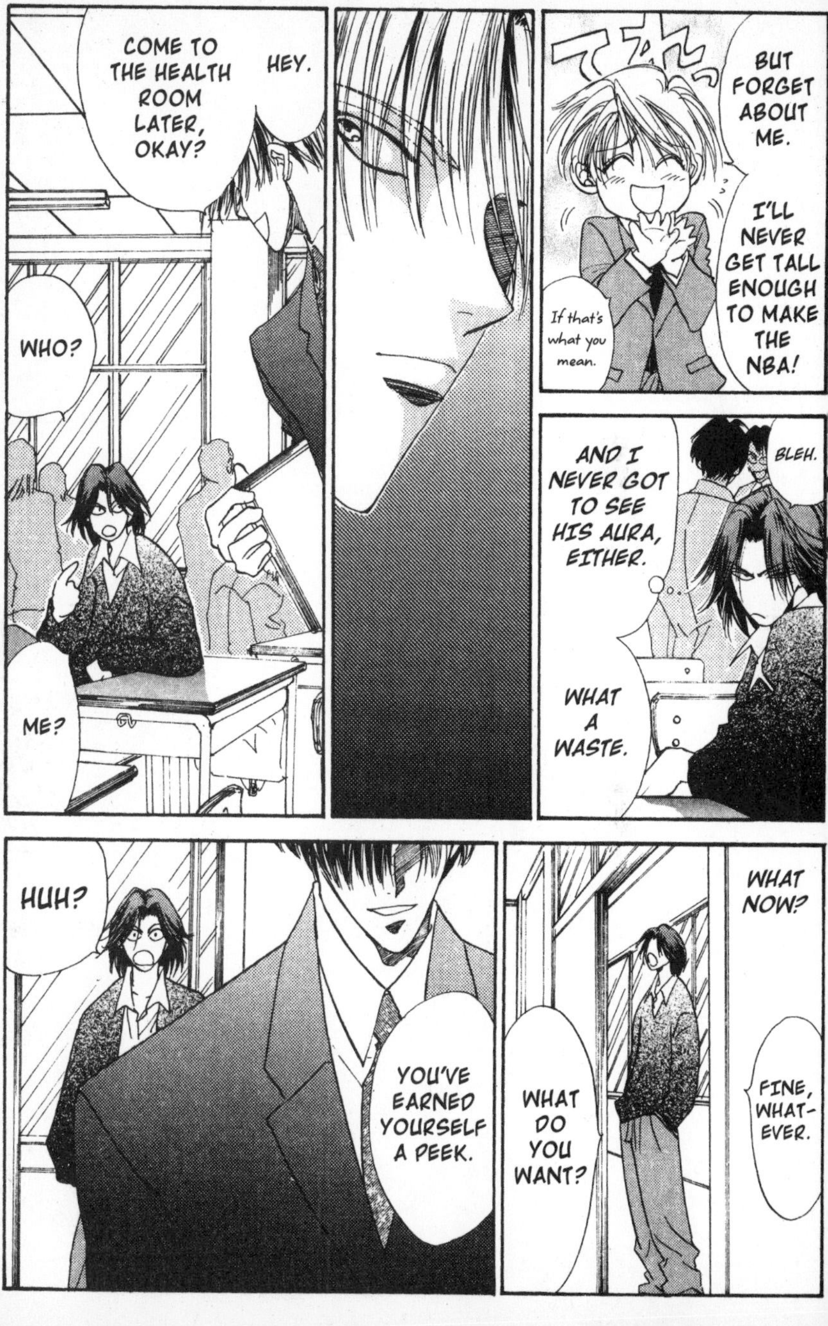
てへっ
BUT FORGET ABOUT ME.
I'LL NEVER GET TALL ENOUGH TO MAKE THE NBA!
If that's what you mean.
BLEH.
AND I NEVER GOT TO SEE HIS AURA, EITHER.
WHAT A WASTE.
HEY.
COME TO THE HEALTH ROOM LATER, OKAY?
WHO?
ME?
WHAT NOW?
FINE, WHATEVER.
WHAT DO YOU WANT?
YOU'VE EARNED YOURSELF A PEEK.
HUH?

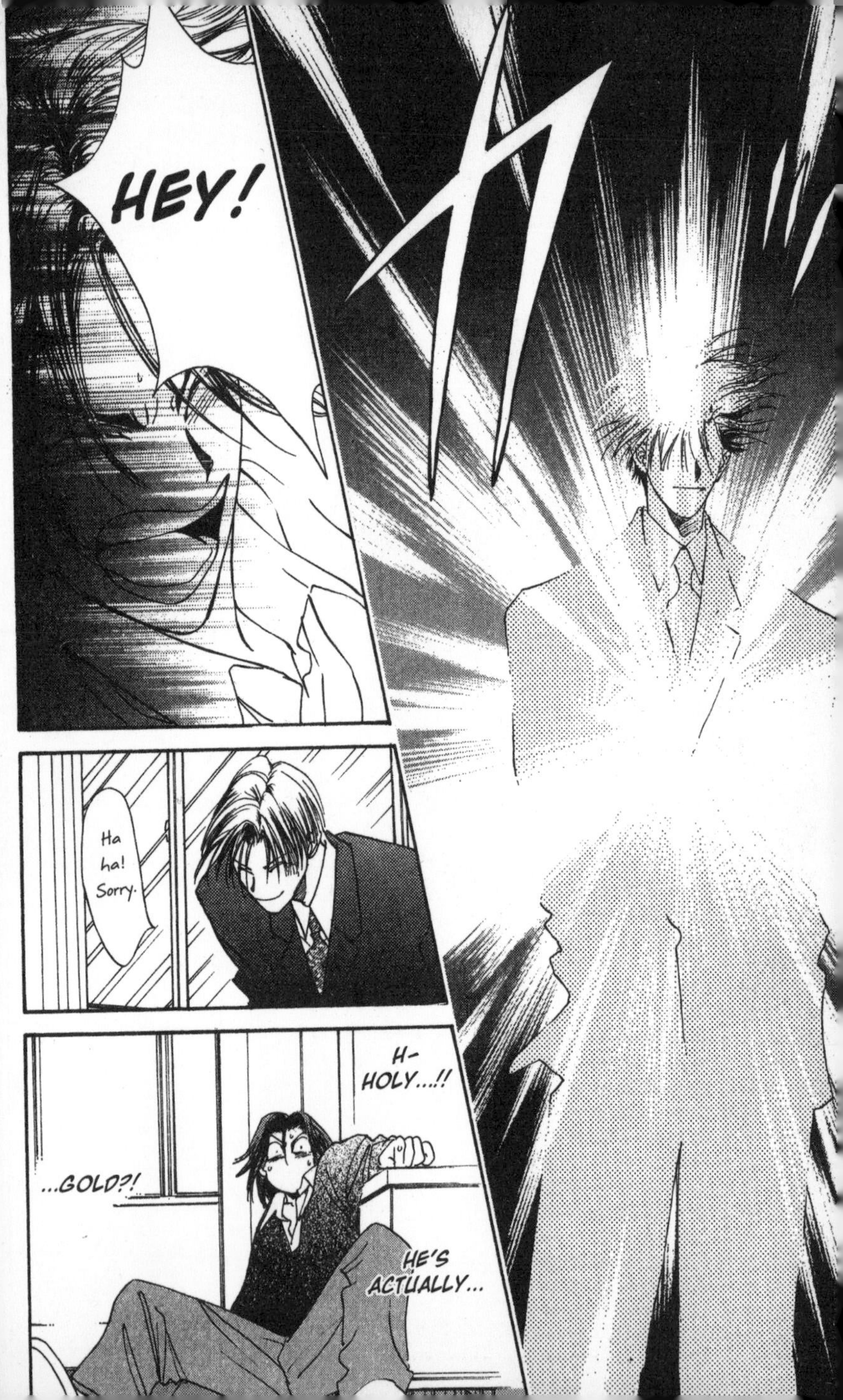
HEY!
Ha ha! Sorry.
H-HOLY...!!
HE'S ACTUALLY...
...GOLD?!

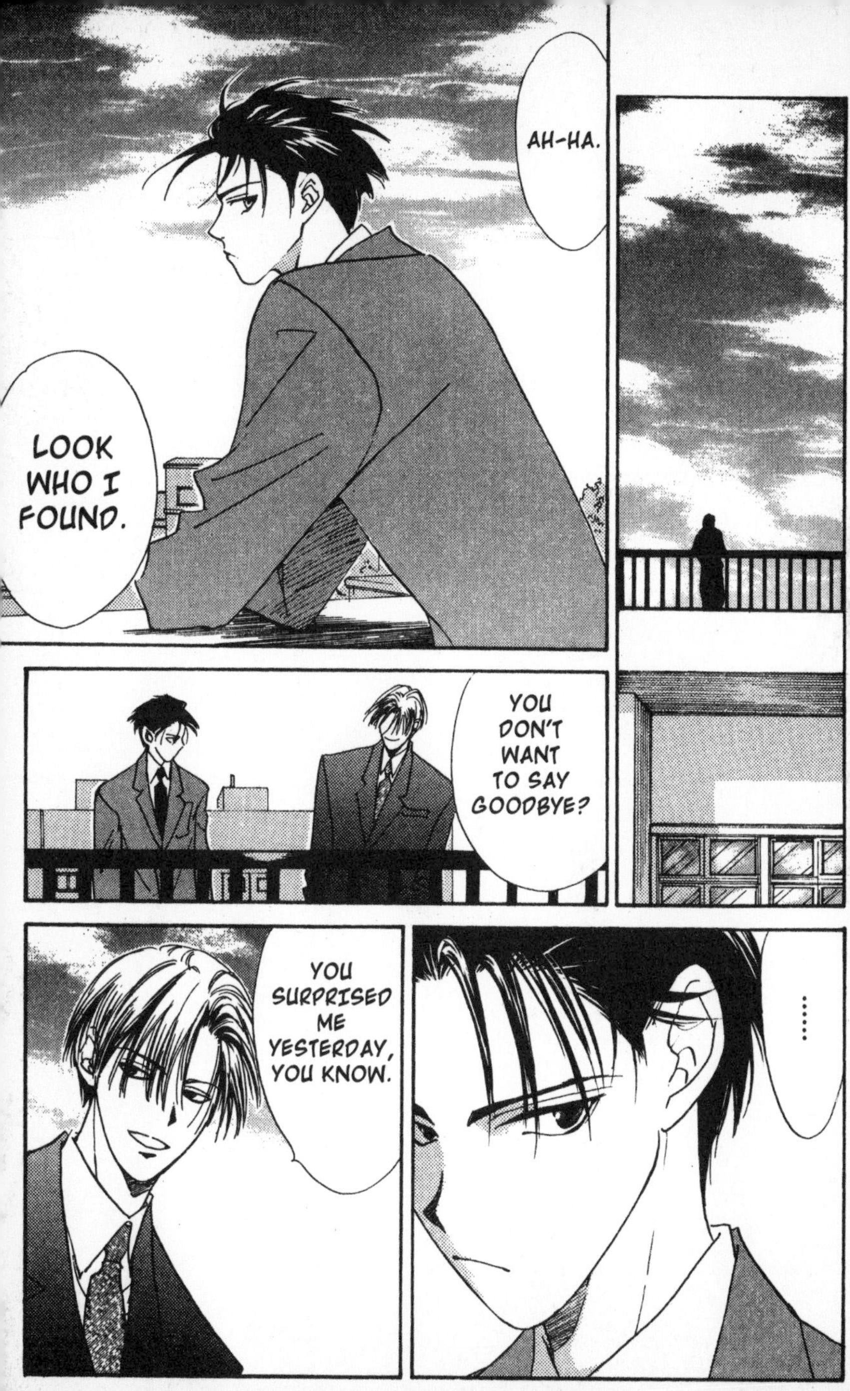
AH-HA.
LOOK WHO I FOUND.
YOU DON'T WANT TO SAY GOODBYE?
......
YOU SURPRISED ME YESTERDAY, YOU KNOW.

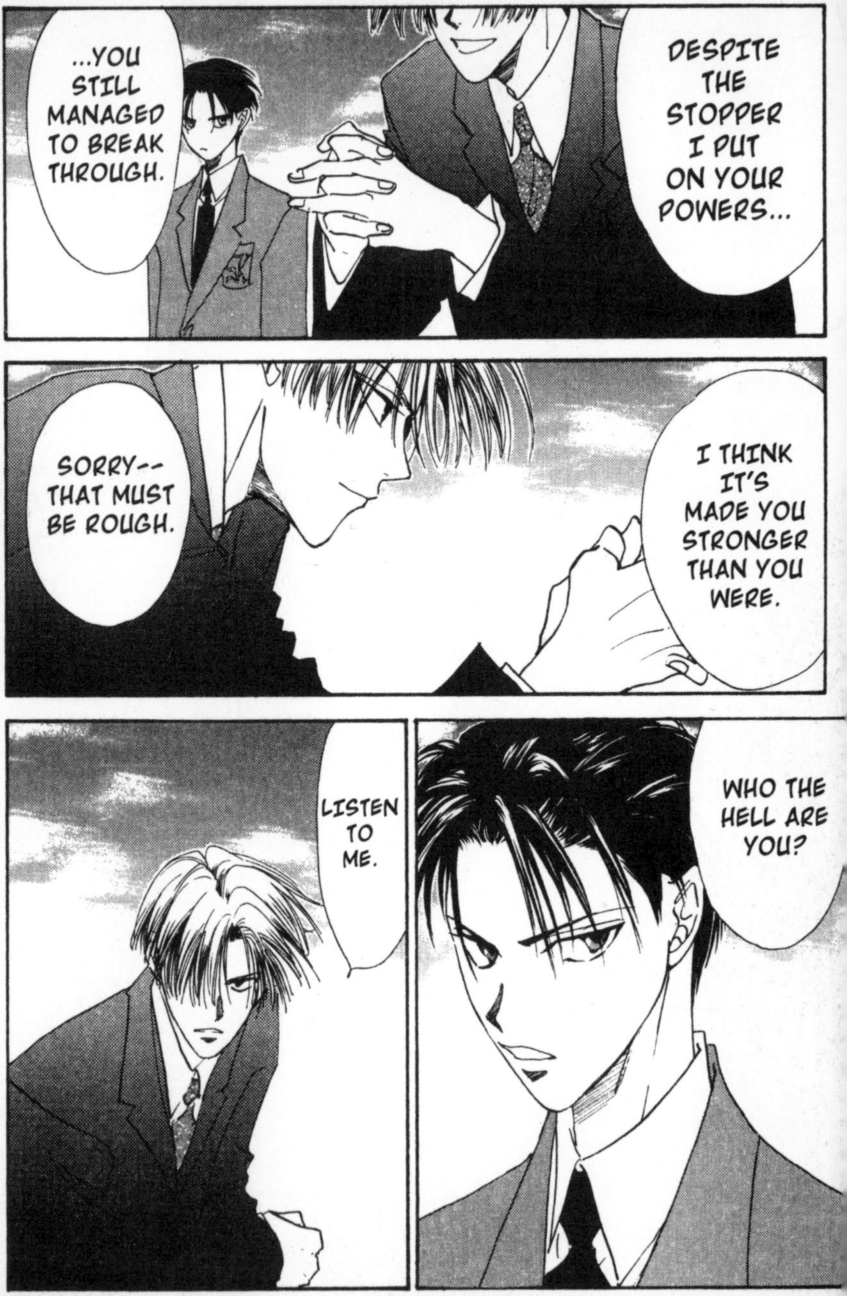
DESPITE THE STOPPER I PUT ON YOUR POWERS...
...YOU STILL MANAGED TO BREAK THROUGH.
I THINK IT'S MADE YOU STRONGER THAN YOU WERE.
SORRY-- THAT MUST BE ROUGH.
WHO THE HELL ARE YOU?
LISTEN TO ME.

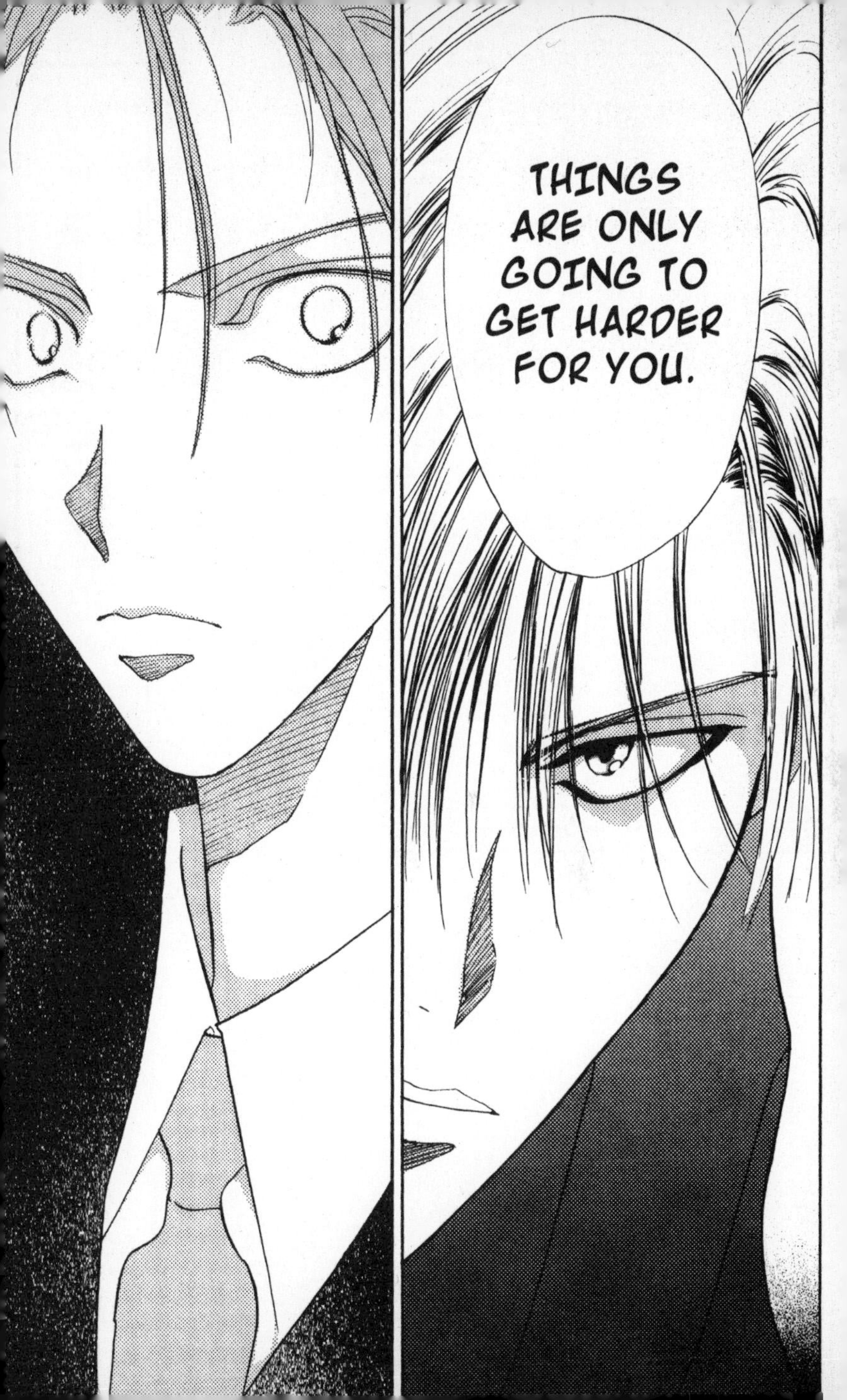
THINGS ARE ONLY GOING TO GET HARDER FOR YOU.

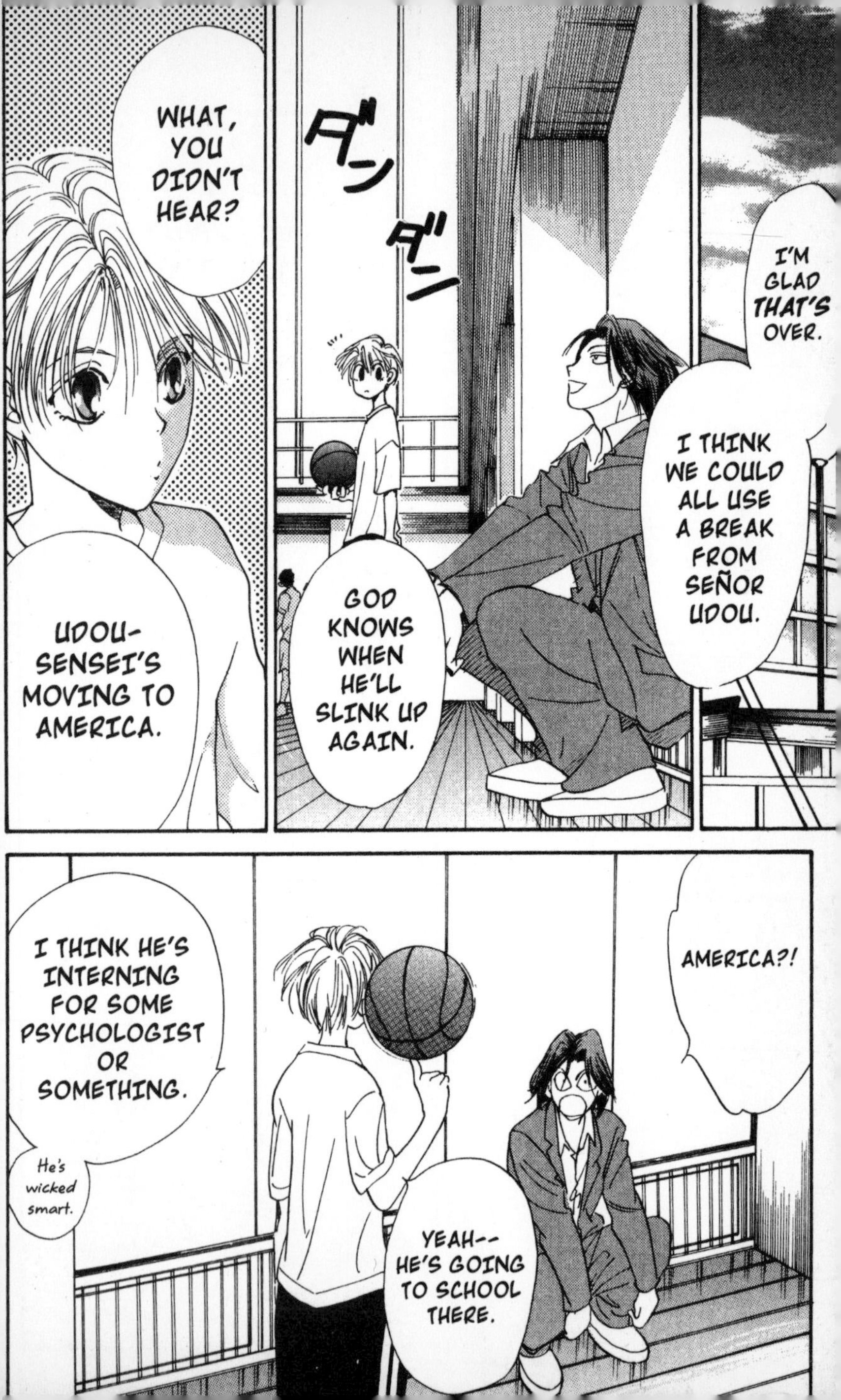
I'M GLAD THAT'S OVER.
I THINK WE COULD ALL USE A BREAK FROM SEÑOR UDOU.
ダン
ダン
GOD KNOWS WHEN HE'LL SLINK UP AGAIN.
WHAT, YOU DIDN'T HEAR?
UDOU-SENSEI'S MOVING TO AMERICA.
AMERICA?!
YEAH-- HE'S GOING TO SCHOOL THERE.
I THINK HE'S INTERNING FOR SOME PSYCHOLOGIST OR SOMETHING.
He's wicked smart.

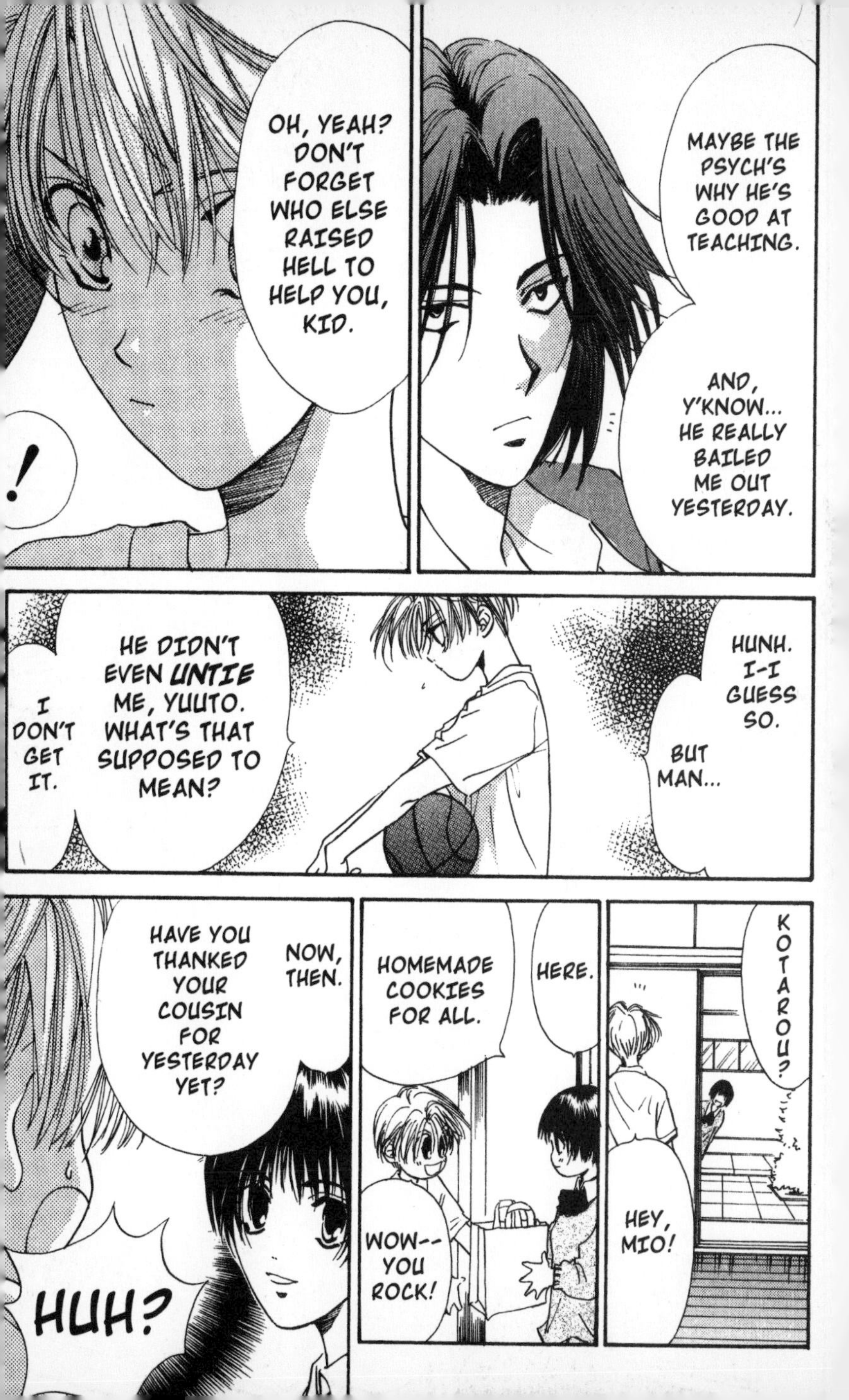
MAYBE THE PSYCH'S WHY HE'S GOOD AT TEACHING.
AND, Y'KNOW... HE REALLY BAILED ME OUT YESTERDAY.
OH, YEAH? DON'T FORGET WHO ELSE RAISED HELL TO HELP YOU, KID.
!
HUNH. I-I GUESS SO.
BUT MAN...
HE DIDN'T EVEN *UNTIE* ME, YUUTO. WHAT'S THAT SUPPOSED TO MEAN?
I DON'T GET IT.
KOTAROU?
HEY, MIO!
HERE.
HOMEMADE COOKIES FOR ALL.
WOW--YOU ROCK!
NOW, THEN.
HAVE YOU THANKED YOUR COUSIN FOR YESTERDAY YET?
HUH?

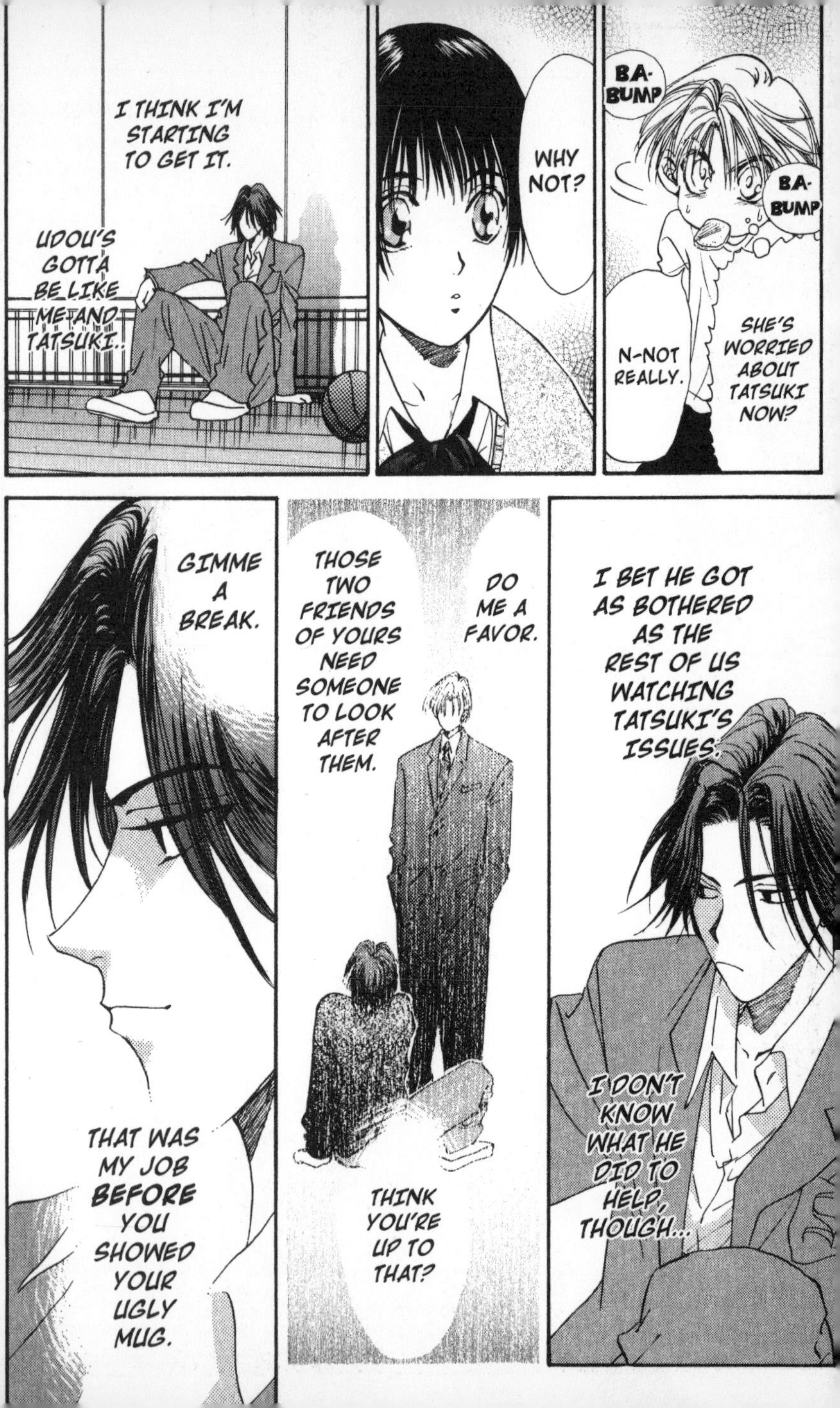
BA-BUMP
BA-BUMP
SHE'S WORRIED ABOUT TATSUKI NOW?
N-NOT REALLY.
WHY NOT?
I THINK I'M STARTING TO GET IT.
UDOU'S GOTTA BE LIKE ME AND TATSUKI...
I BET HE GOT AS BOTHERED AS THE REST OF US WATCHING TATSUKI'S ISSUES.
I DON'T KNOW WHAT HE DID TO HELP, THOUGH...
DO ME A FAVOR.
THOSE TWO FRIENDS OF YOURS NEED SOMEONE TO LOOK AFTER THEM.
THINK YOU'RE UP TO THAT?
GIMME A BREAK.
THAT WAS MY JOB BEFORE YOU SHOWED YOUR UGLY MUG.

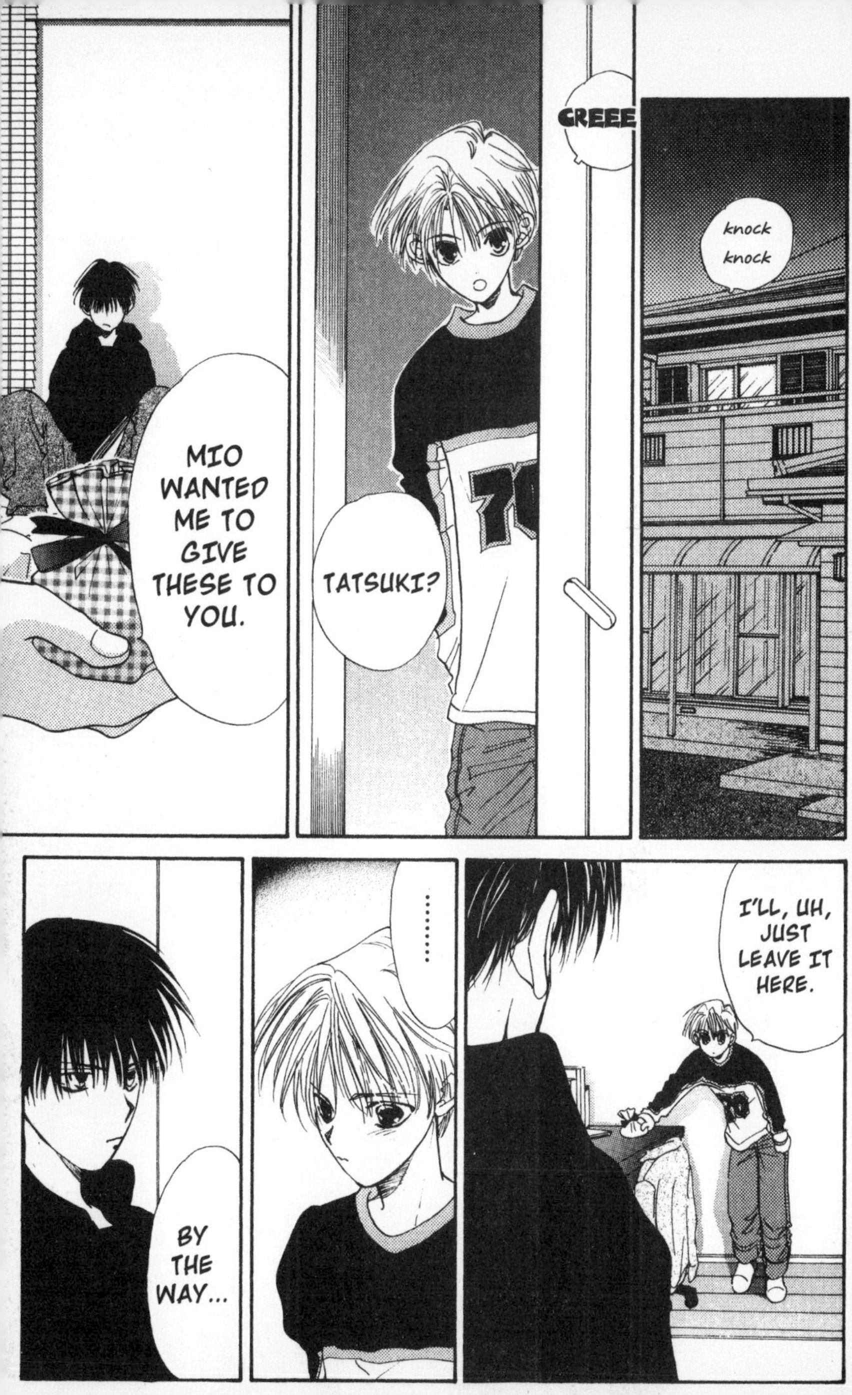
knock knock
CREEE
TATSUKI?
MIO WANTED ME TO GIVE THESE TO YOU.
I'LL, UH, JUST LEAVE IT HERE.
......
BY THE WAY...

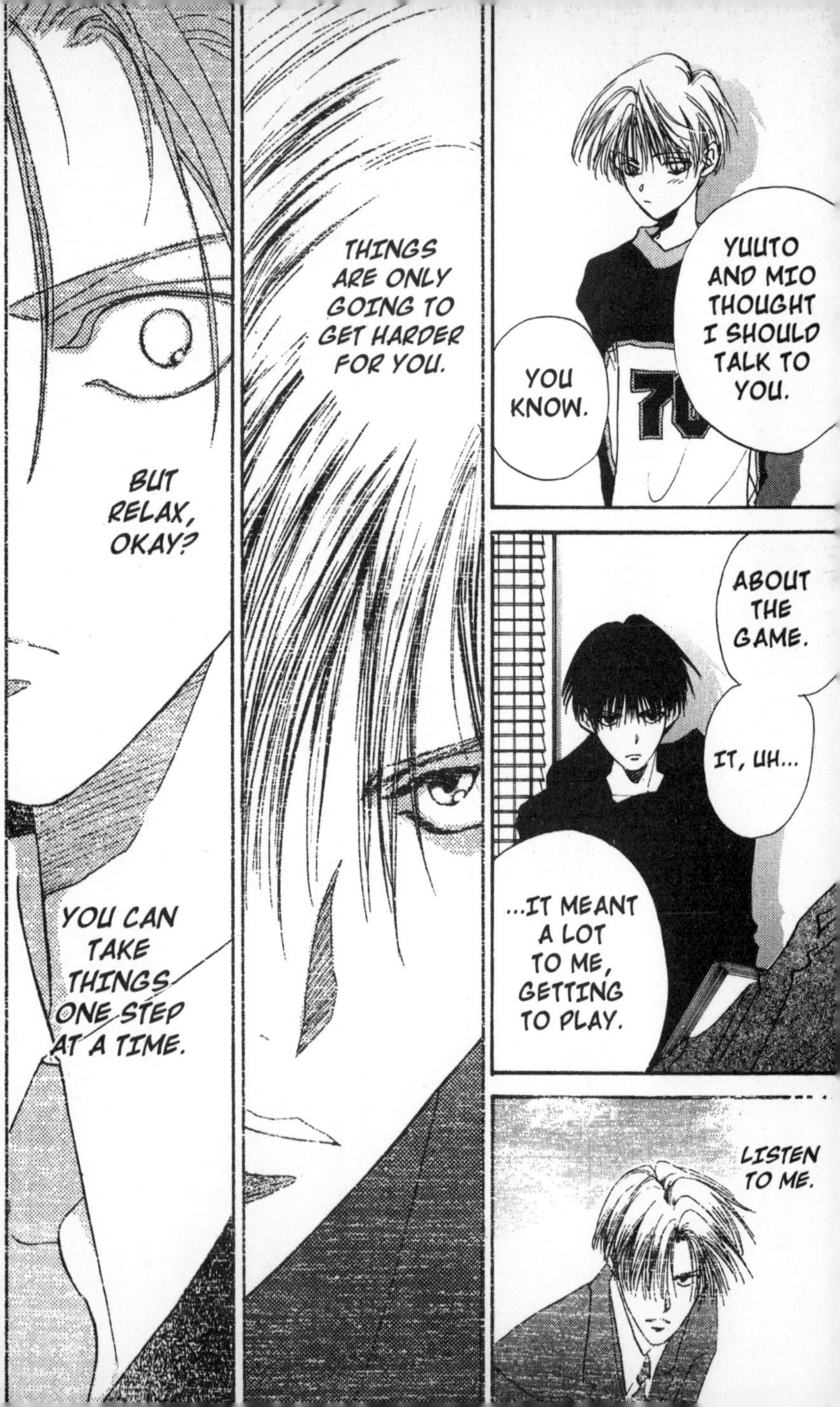
YUUTO AND MIO THOUGHT I SHOULD TALK TO YOU.
YOU KNOW.
ABOUT THE GAME.
IT, UH...
...IT MEANT A LOT TO ME, GETTING TO PLAY.
LISTEN TO ME.
THINGS ARE ONLY GOING TO GET HARDER FOR YOU.
BUT RELAX, OKAY?
YOU CAN TAKE THINGS ONE STEP AT A TIME.

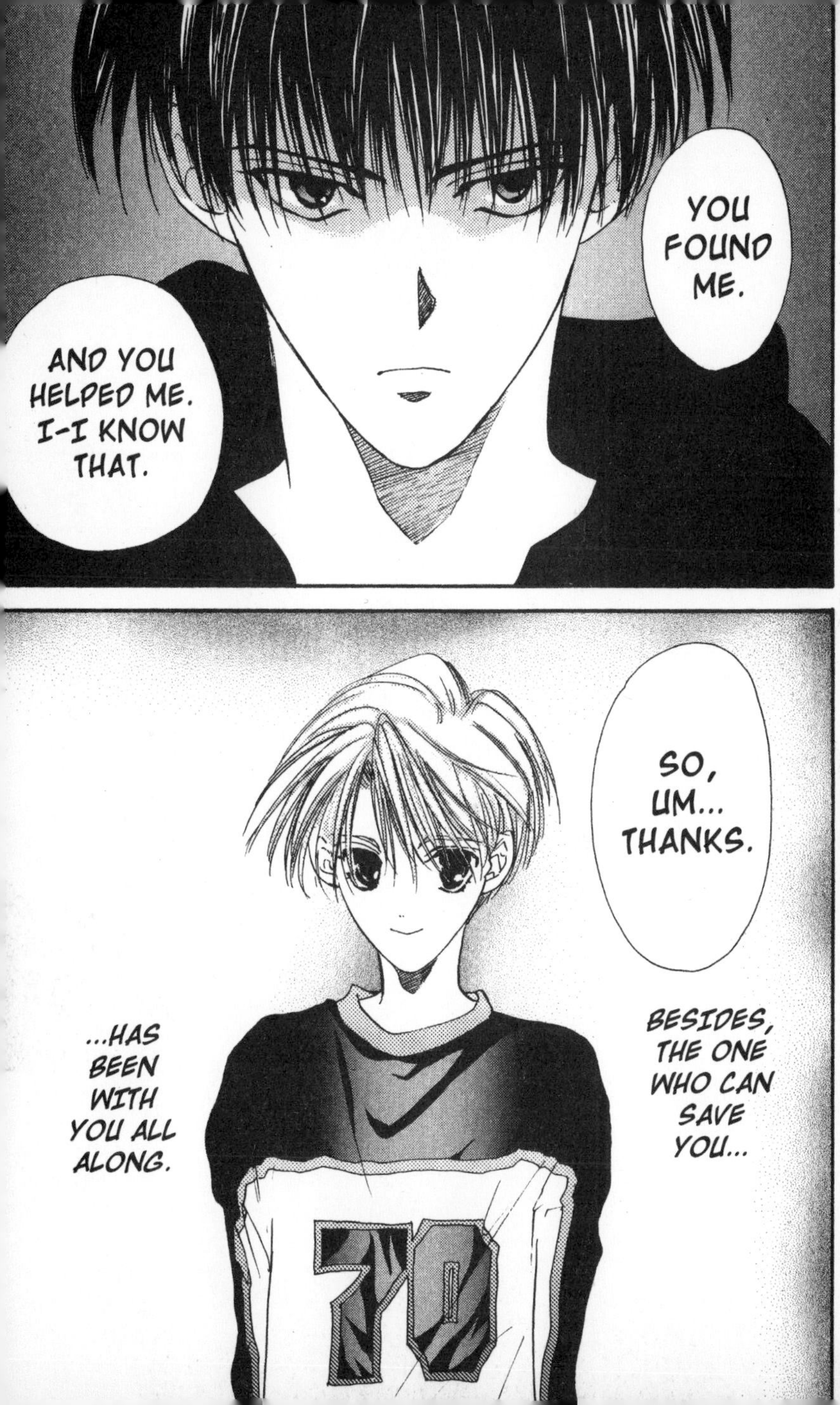
YOU FOUND ME.
AND YOU HELPED ME. I-I KNOW THAT.
SO, UM... THANKS.
BESIDES, THE ONE WHO CAN SAVE YOU...
...HAS BEEN WITH YOU ALL ALONG.

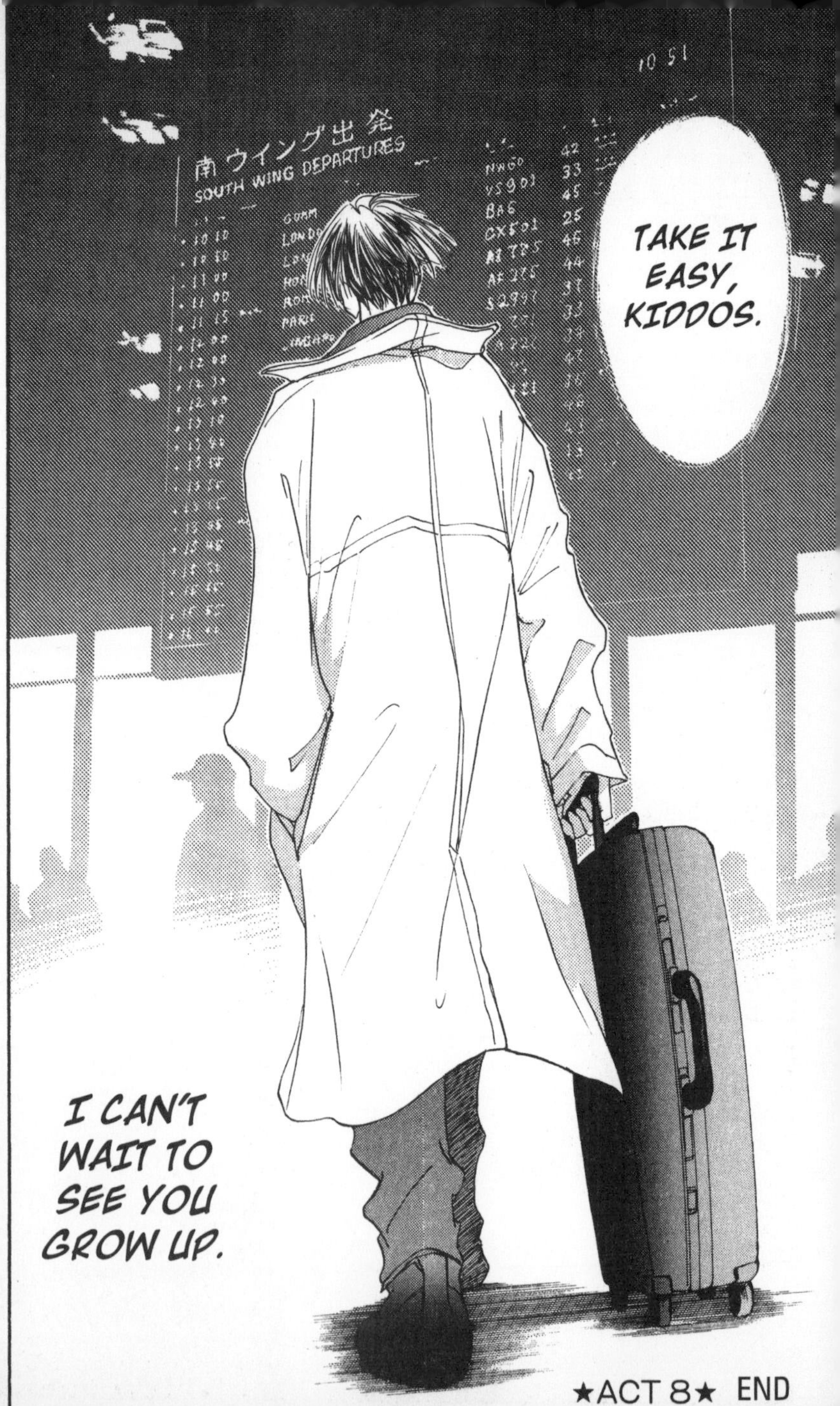
南ウイング出発
SOUTH WING DEPARTURES
TAKE IT EASY, KIDDOS.
I CAN'T WAIT TO SEE YOU GROW UP.

★ACT 8★ END

ACT 9

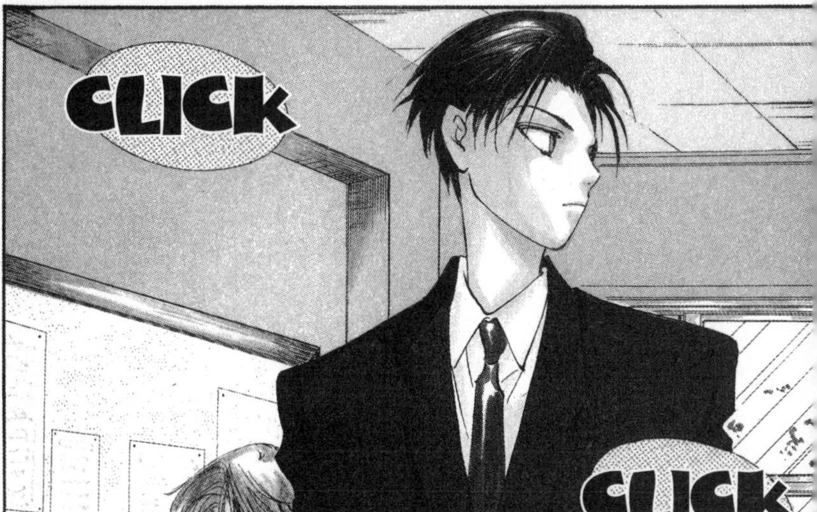
CLICK
CLICK

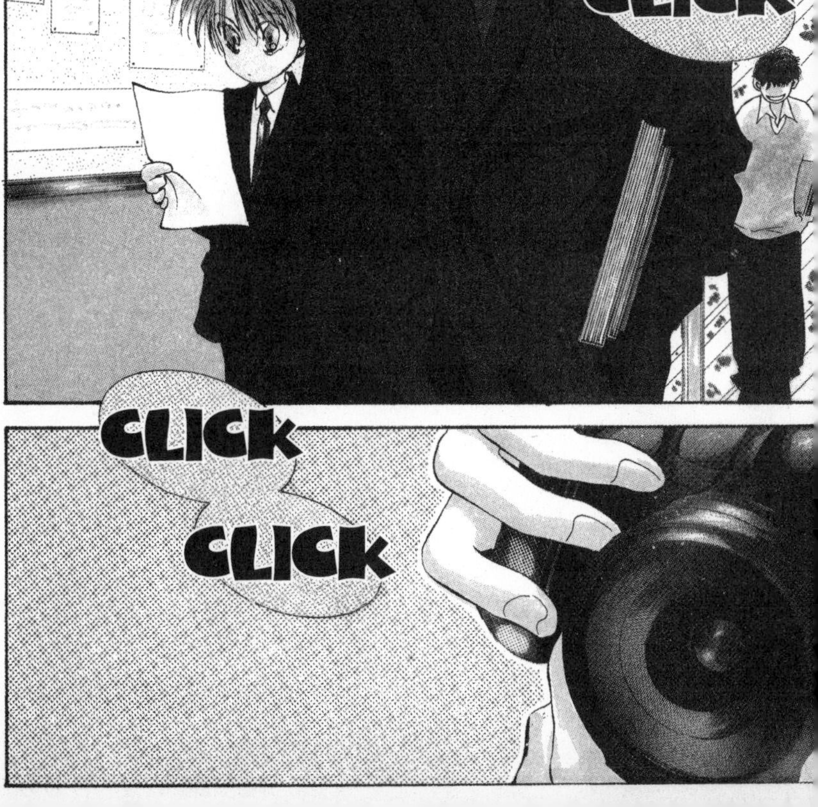
CLICK
CLICK

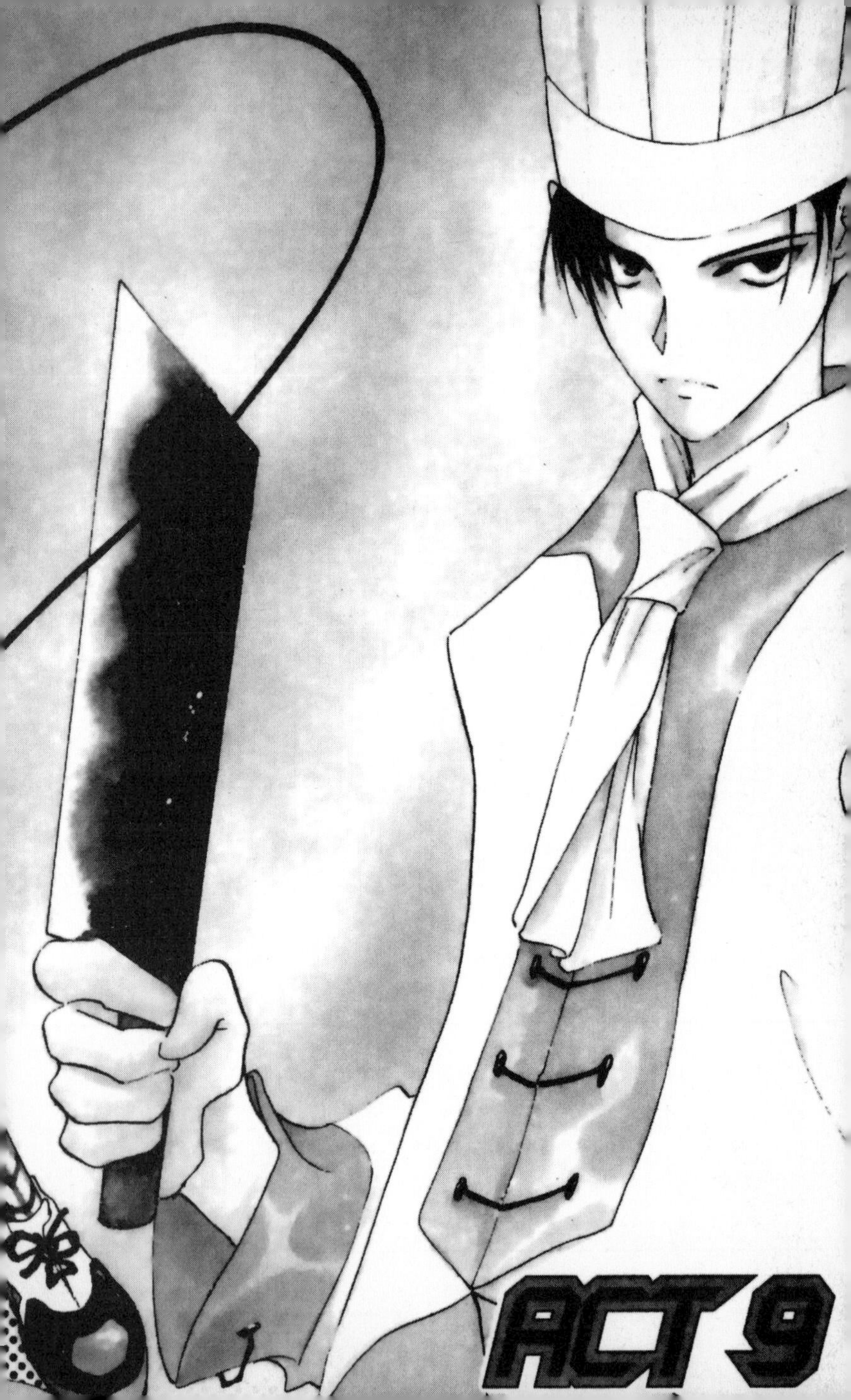
ACT 9

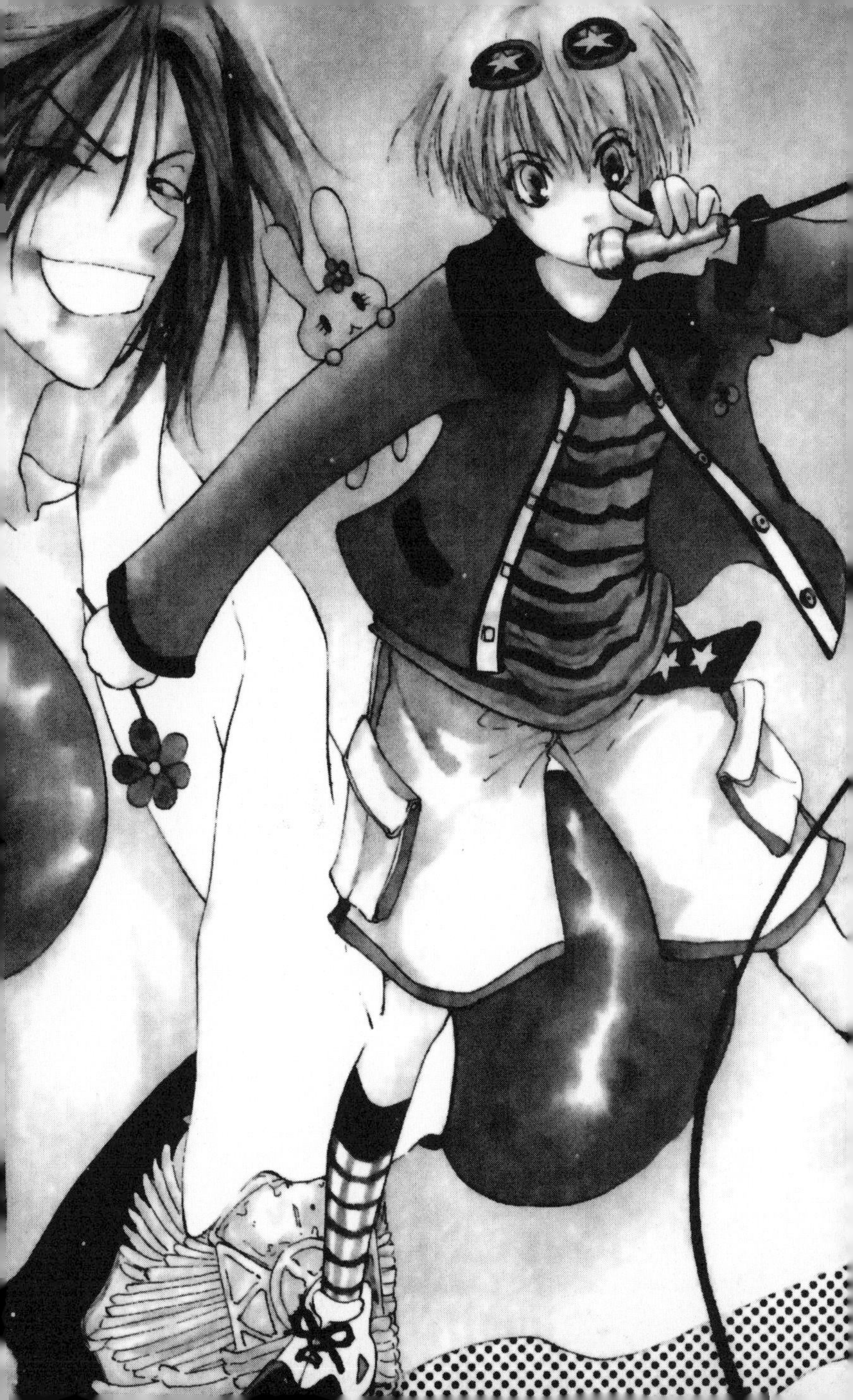

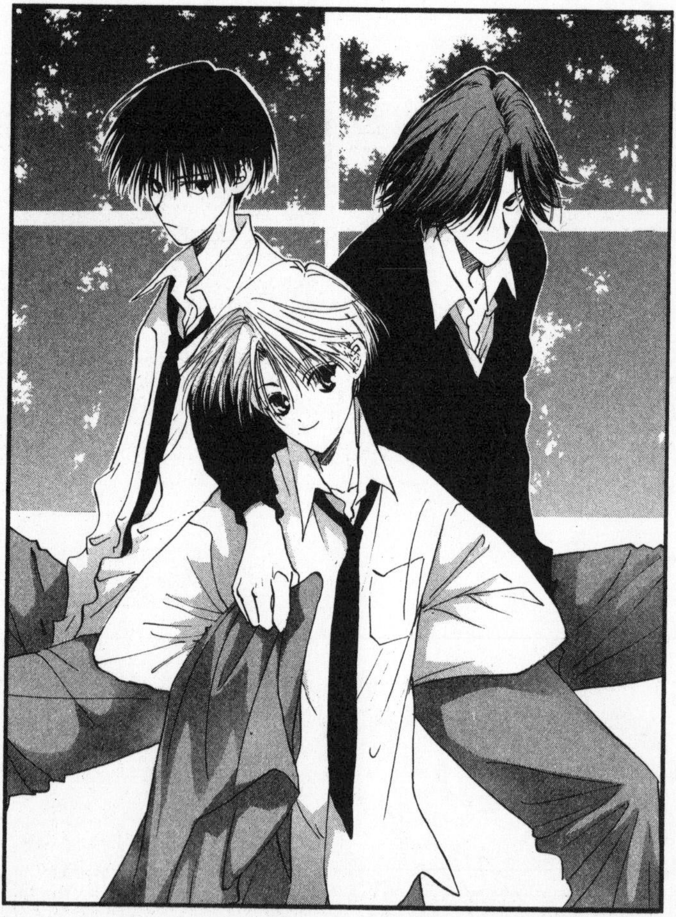

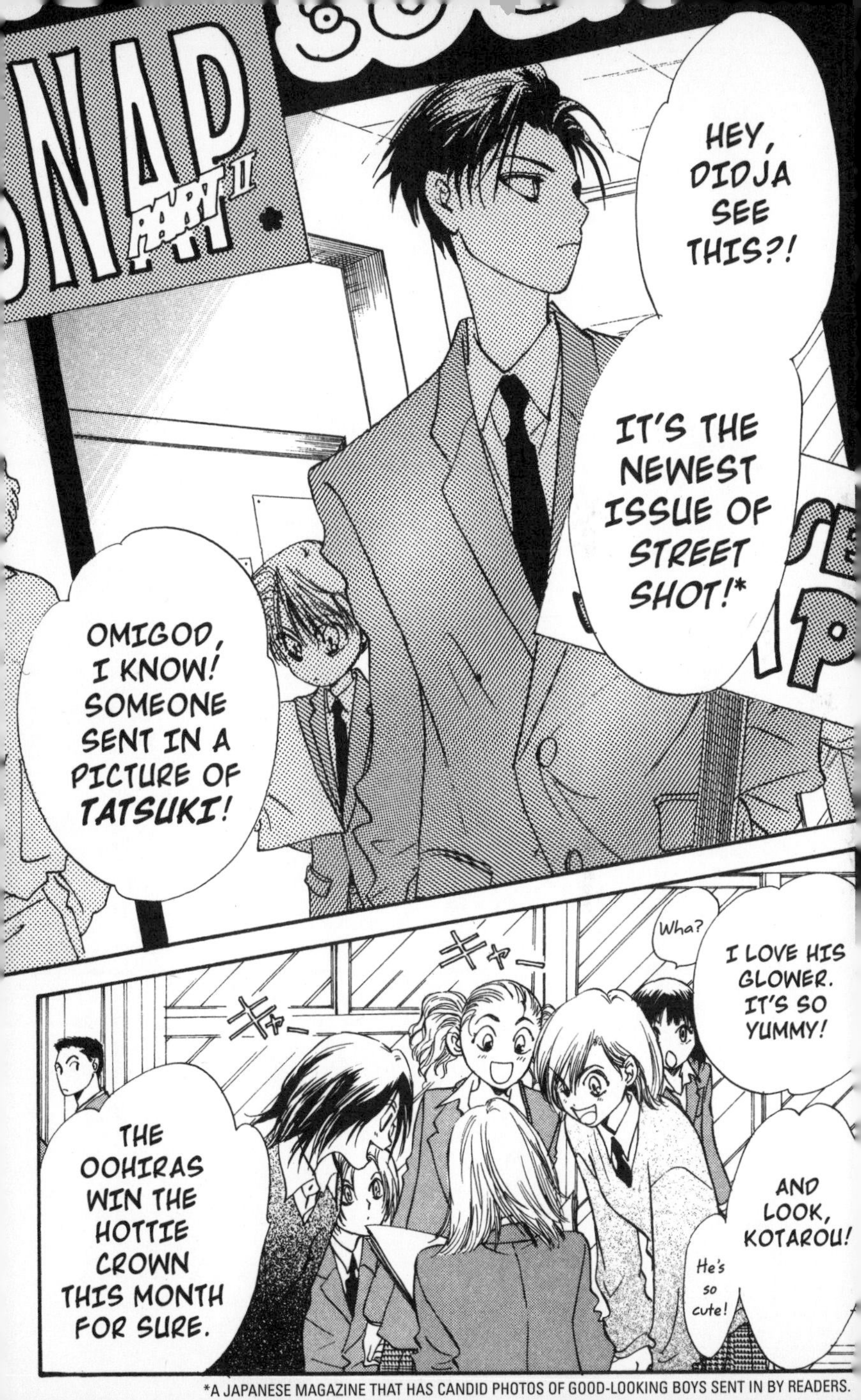
HEY, DIDJA SEE THIS?!
IT'S THE NEWEST ISSUE OF STREET SHOT!*
OMIGOD, I KNOW! SOMEONE SENT IN A PICTURE OF TATSUKI!
Wha?
I LOVE HIS GLOWER. IT'S SO YUMMY!
キャー
キャー
AND LOOK, KOTAROU!
He's so cute!
THE OOHIRAS WIN THE HOTTIE CROWN THIS MONTH FOR SURE.

*A JAPANESE MAGAZINE THAT HAS CANDID PHOTOS OF GOOD-LOOKING BOYS SENT IN BY READERS.

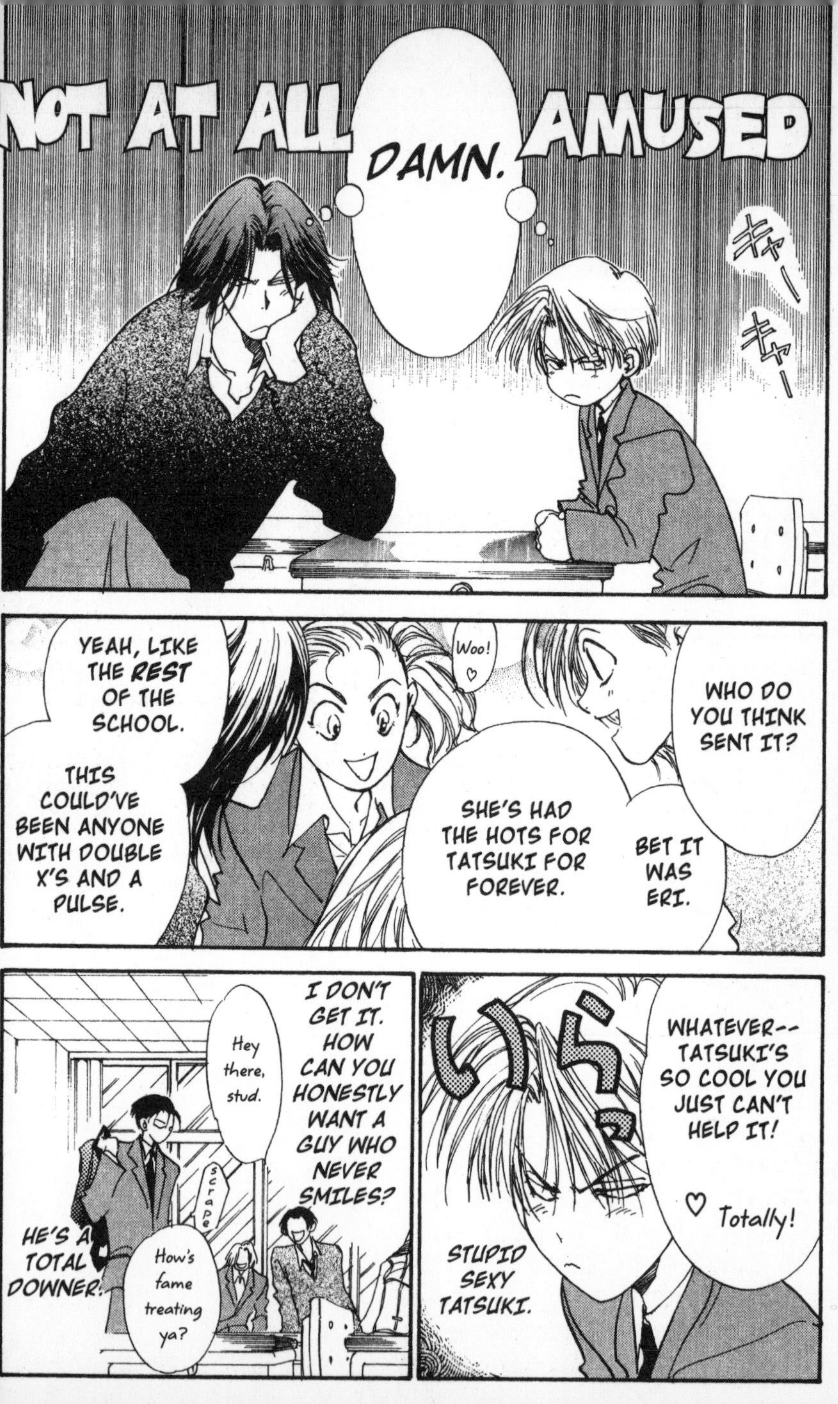
NOT AT ALL AMUSED
DAMN.
キャーキャー
WHO DO YOU THINK SENT IT?
Woo! ♡
BET IT WAS ERI.
SHE'S HAD THE HOTS FOR TATSUKI FOR FOREVER.
YEAH, LIKE THE REST OF THE SCHOOL.
THIS COULD'VE BEEN ANYONE WITH DOUBLE X'S AND A PULSE.
WHATEVER--TATSUKI'S SO COOL YOU JUST CAN'T HELP IT!
♡ Totally!
いら
STUPID SEXY TATSUKI.
I DON'T GET IT. HOW CAN YOU HONESTLY WANT A GUY WHO NEVER SMILES?
Hey there, stud.
scrape
How's fame treating ya?
HE'S A TOTAL DOWNER.

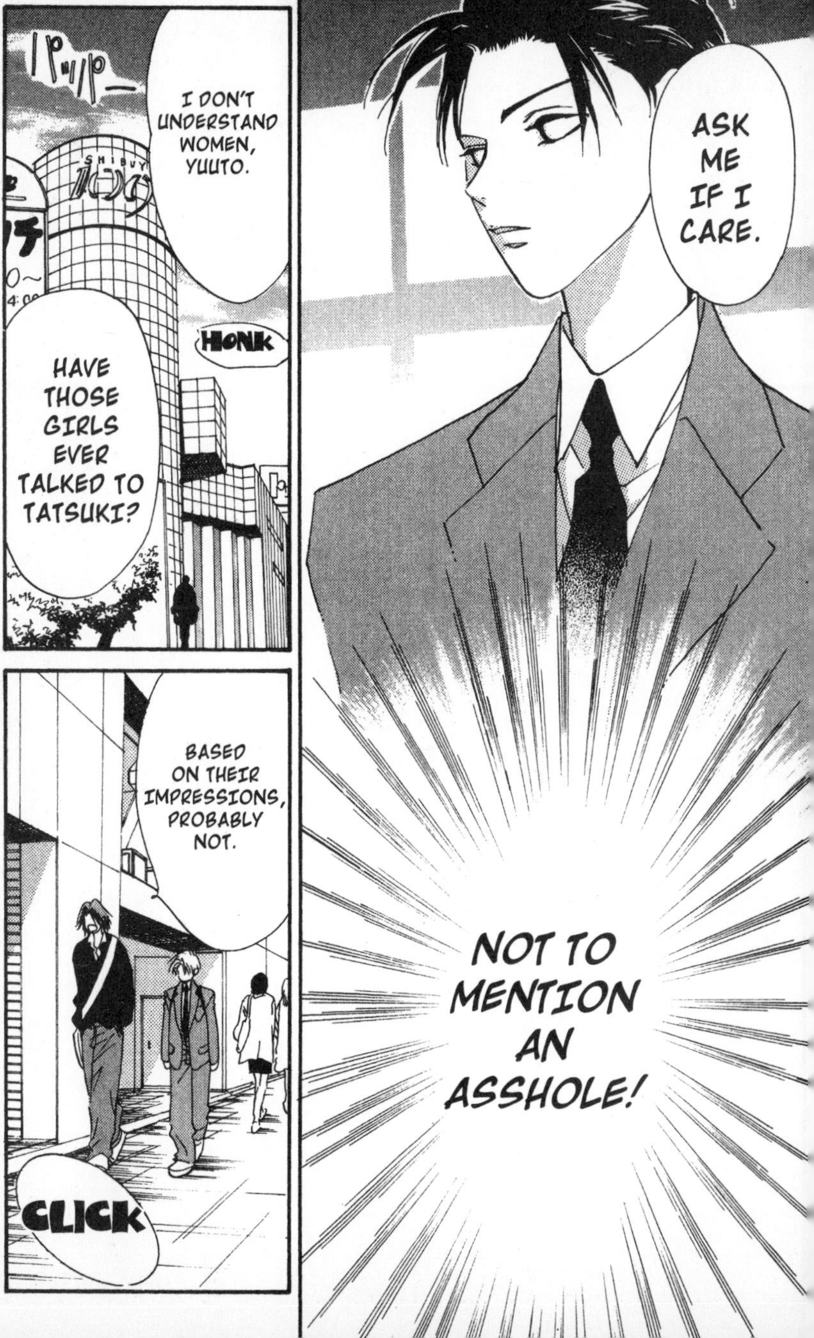
I DON'T UNDERSTAND WOMEN, YUUTO.
HONK
HAVE THOSE GIRLS EVER TALKED TO TATSUKI?
BASED ON THEIR IMPRESSIONS, PROBABLY NOT.
CLICK
ASK ME IF I CARE.
NOT TO MENTION AN ASSHOLE!

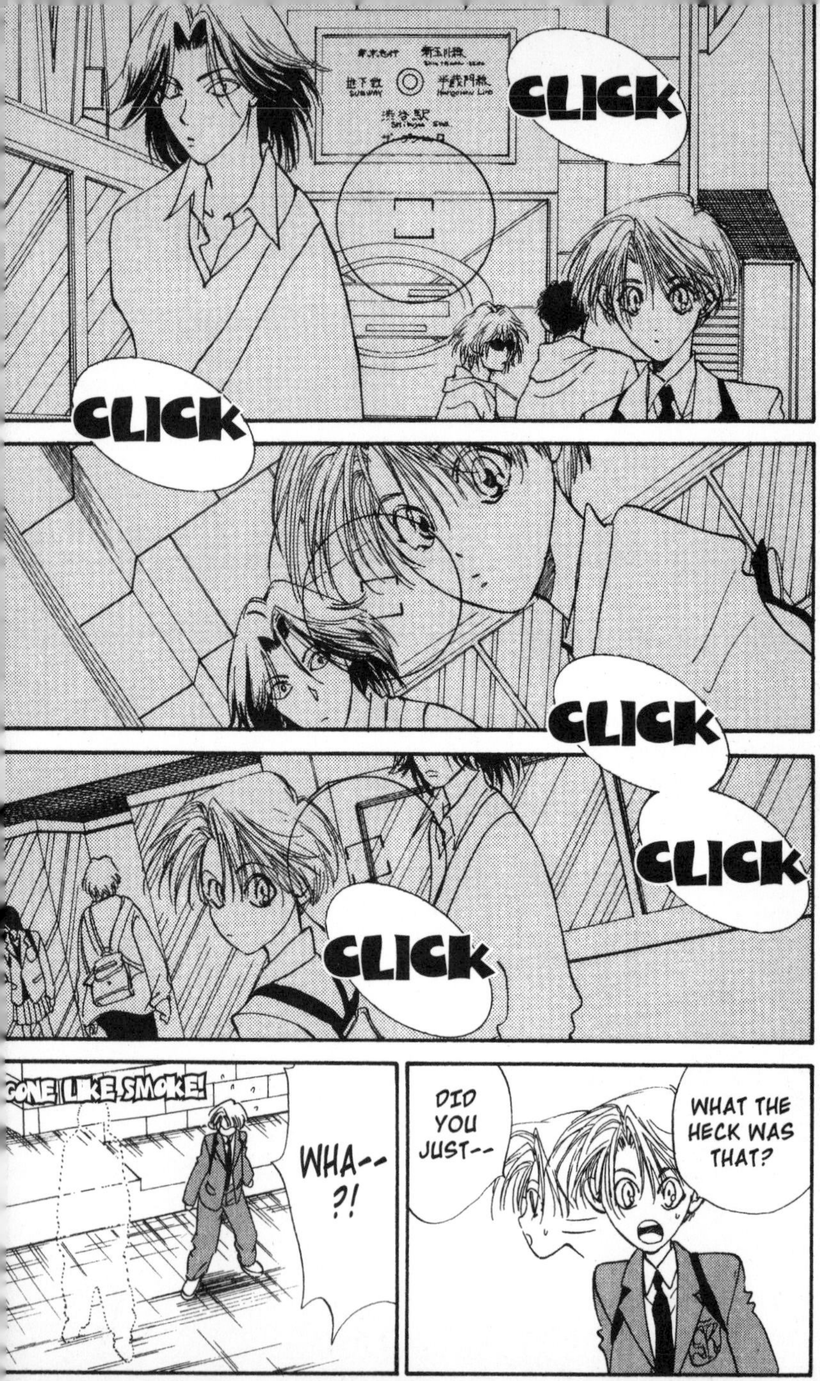
CLICK
CLICK
CLICK
CLICK
CLICK
CLICK
WHAT THE HECK WAS THAT?
DID YOU JUST--
WHA-- ?!
GONE LIKE SMOKE!

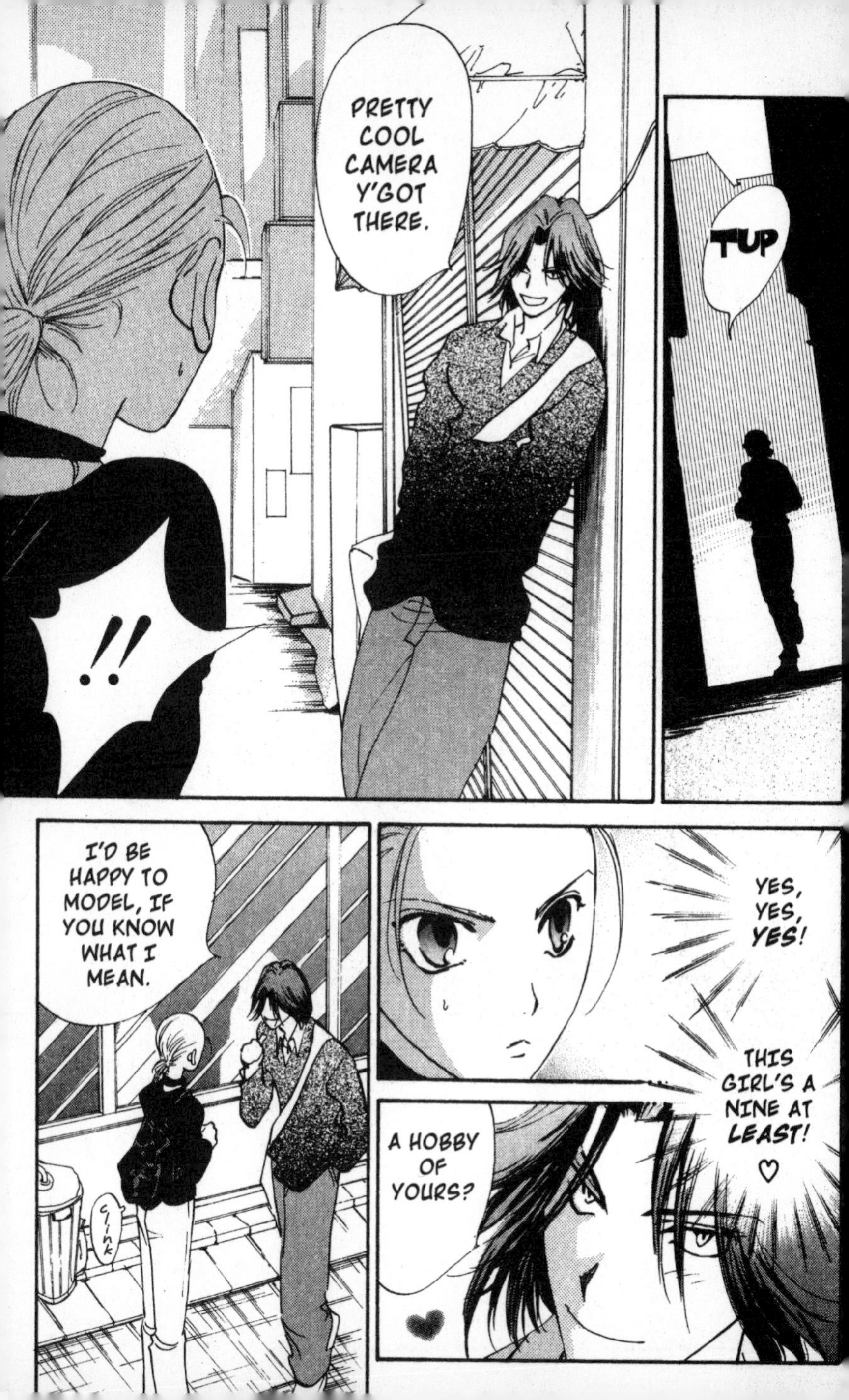
TUP
PRETTY COOL CAMERA Y'GOT THERE.
!!
YES, YES, YES!
THIS GIRL'S A NINE AT LEAST! ♡
A HOBBY OF YOURS?
I'D BE HAPPY TO MODEL, IF YOU KNOW WHAT I MEAN.
clink

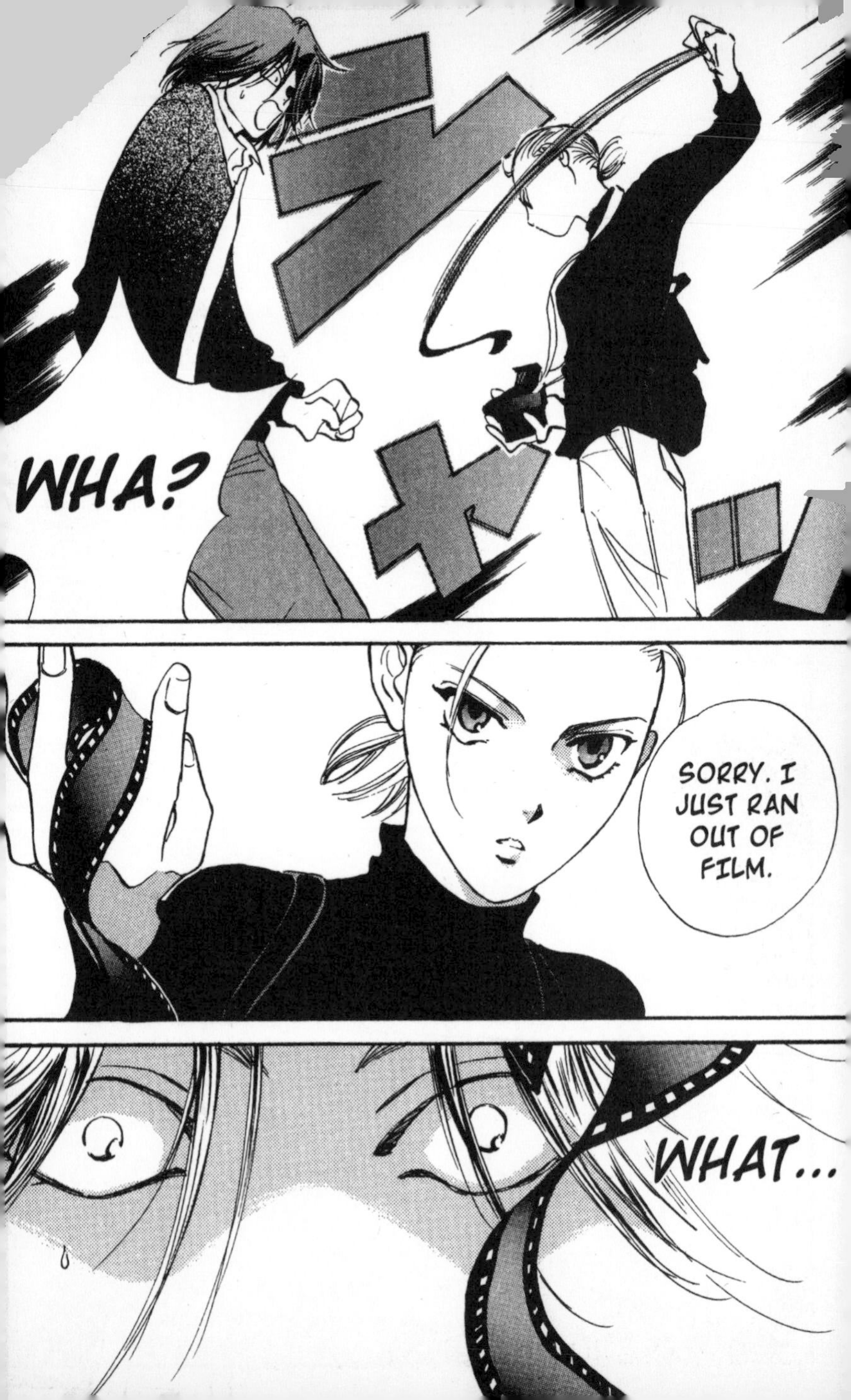
WHA?
SORRY. I JUST RAN OUT OF FILM.
WHAT...

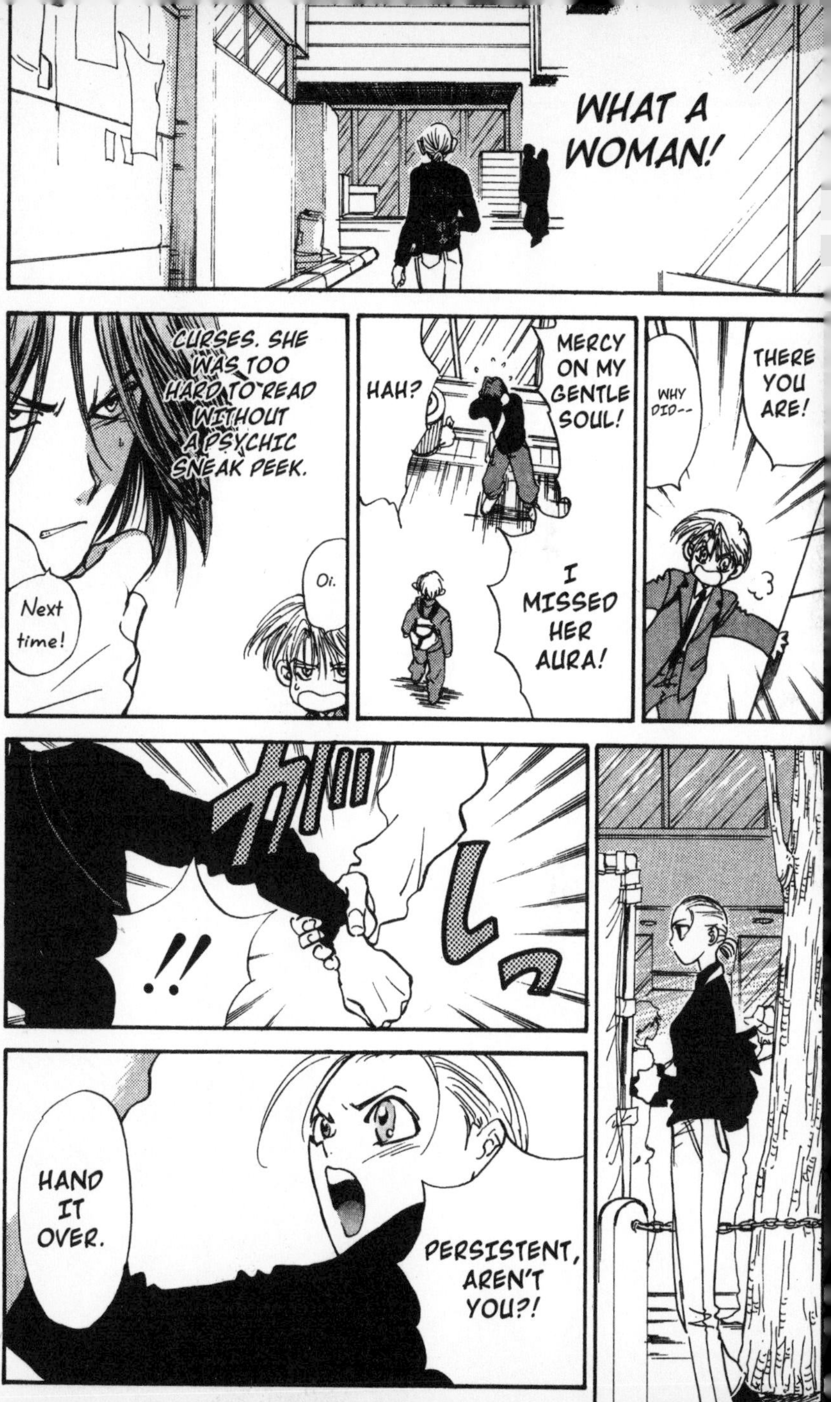
WHAT A WOMAN!
THERE YOU ARE!
WHY DID--
MERCY ON MY GENTLE SOUL!
HAH?
I MISSED HER AURA!
CURSES. SHE WAS TOO HARD TO READ WITHOUT A PSYCHIC SNEAK PEEK.
Oi.
Next time!
ガシッ
!!
PERSISTENT, AREN'T YOU?!
HAND IT OVER.

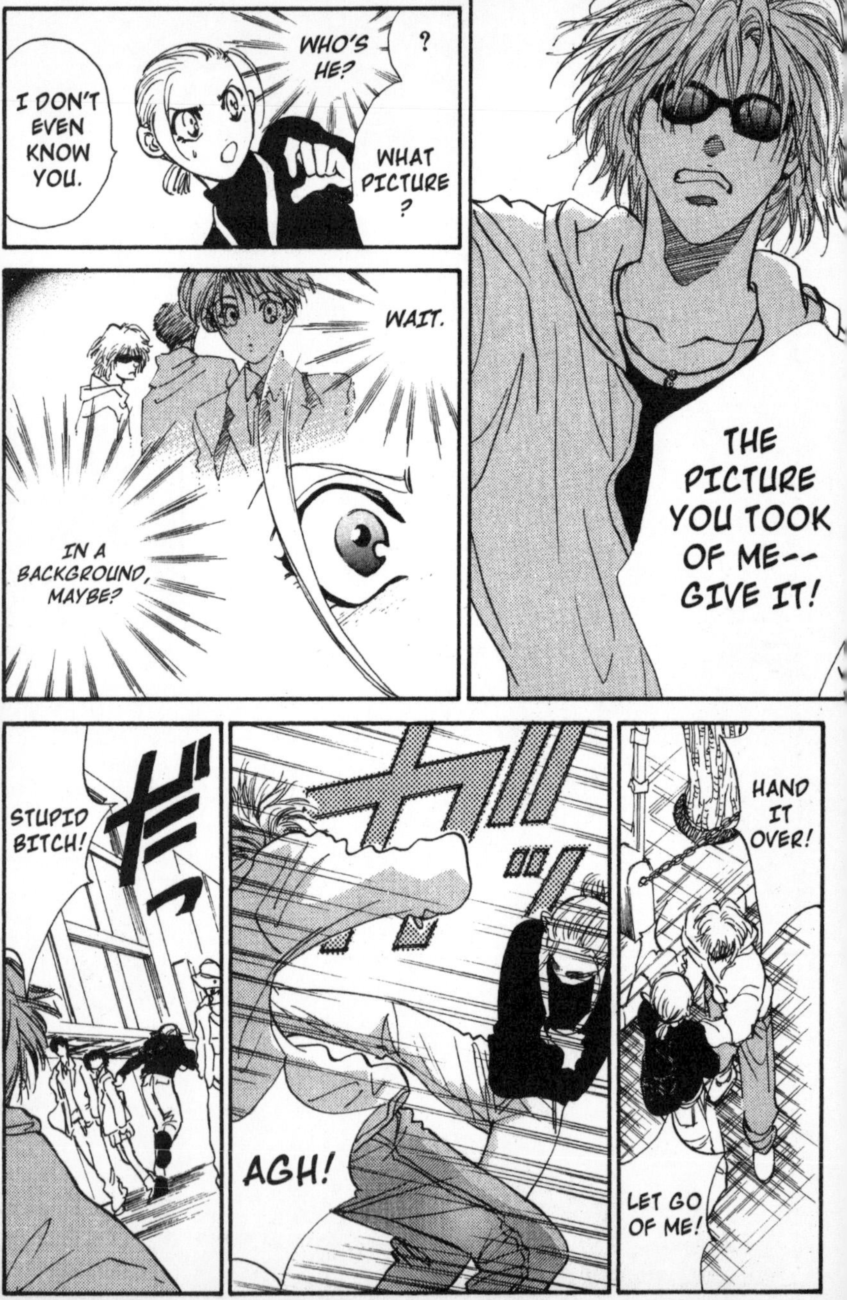
THE PICTURE YOU TOOK OF ME-- GIVE IT!
?
WHO'S HE?
WHAT PICTURE ?
I DON'T EVEN KNOW YOU.
WAIT.
IN A BACKGROUND, MAYBE?
HAND IT OVER!
LET GO OF ME!
AGH!
STUPID BITCH!

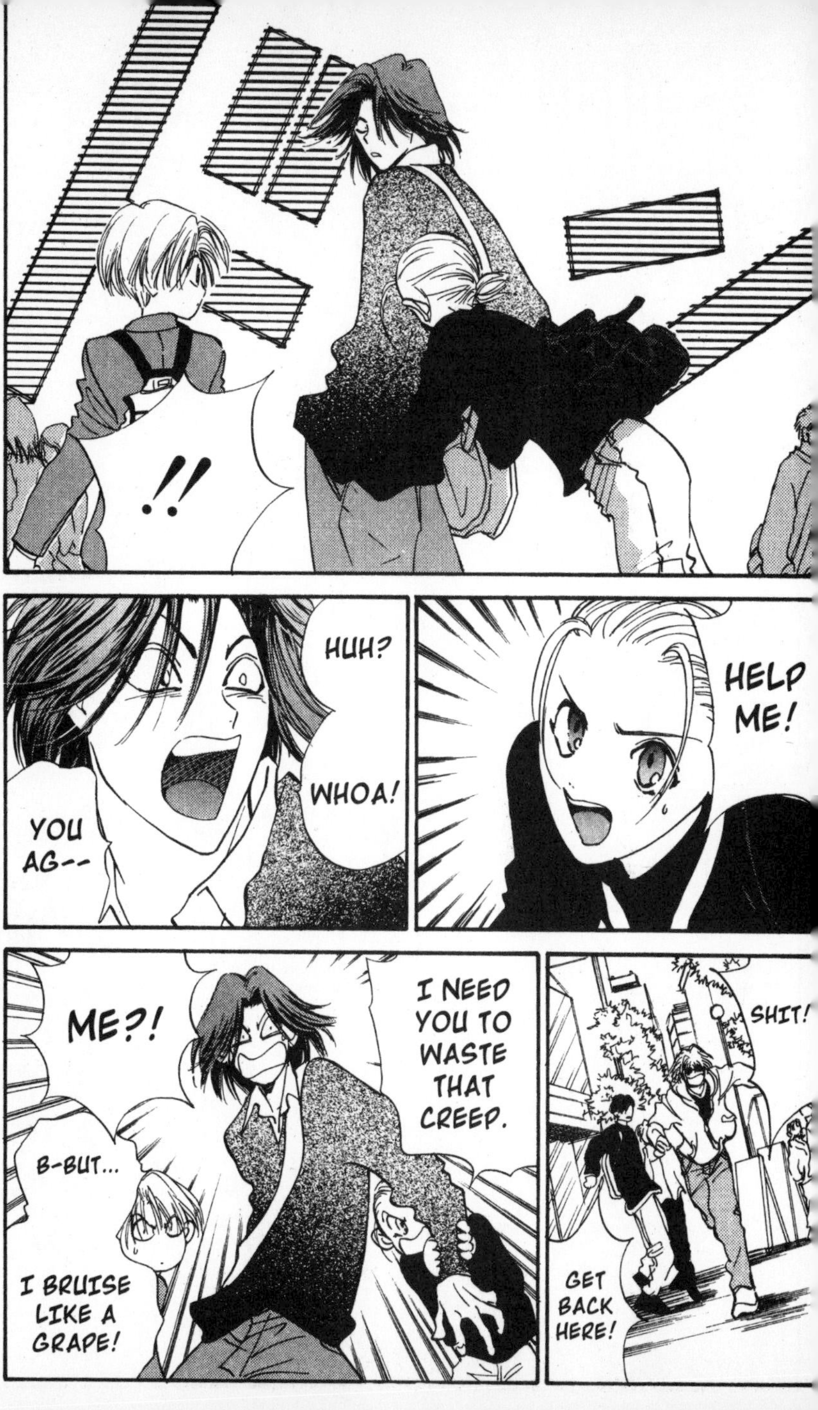
!!
HELP ME!
HUH?
WHOA!
YOU AG--
SHIT!
GET BACK HERE!
I NEED YOU TO WASTE THAT CREEP.
ME?!
B-BUT...
I BRUISE LIKE A GRAPE!

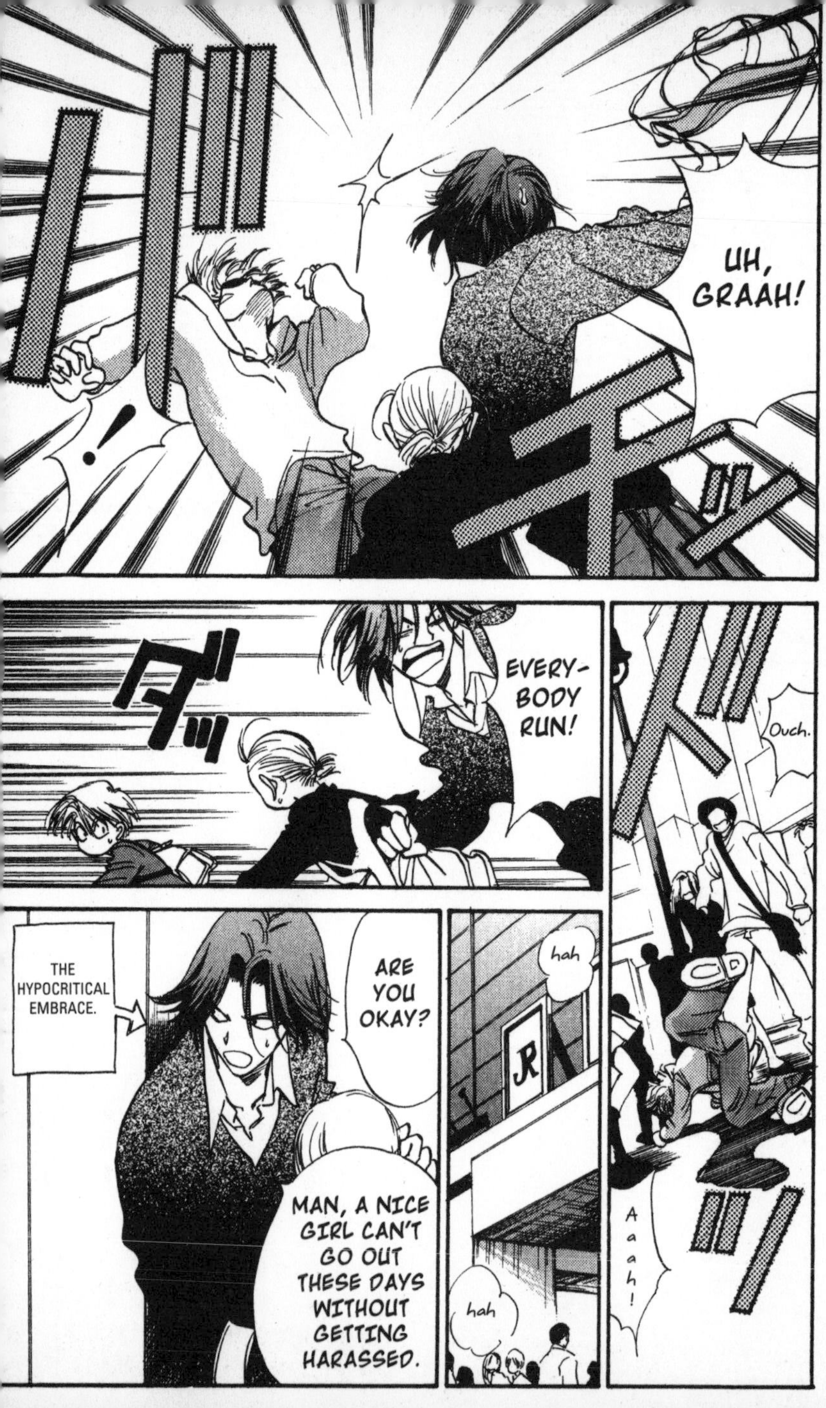
UH, GRAAH!
!
Ouch.
Aaah!
EVERY-BODY RUN!
hah
hah
ARE YOU OKAY?
THE HYPOCRITICAL EMBRACE.
MAN, A NICE GIRL CAN'T GO OUT THESE DAYS WITHOUT GETTING HARASSED.

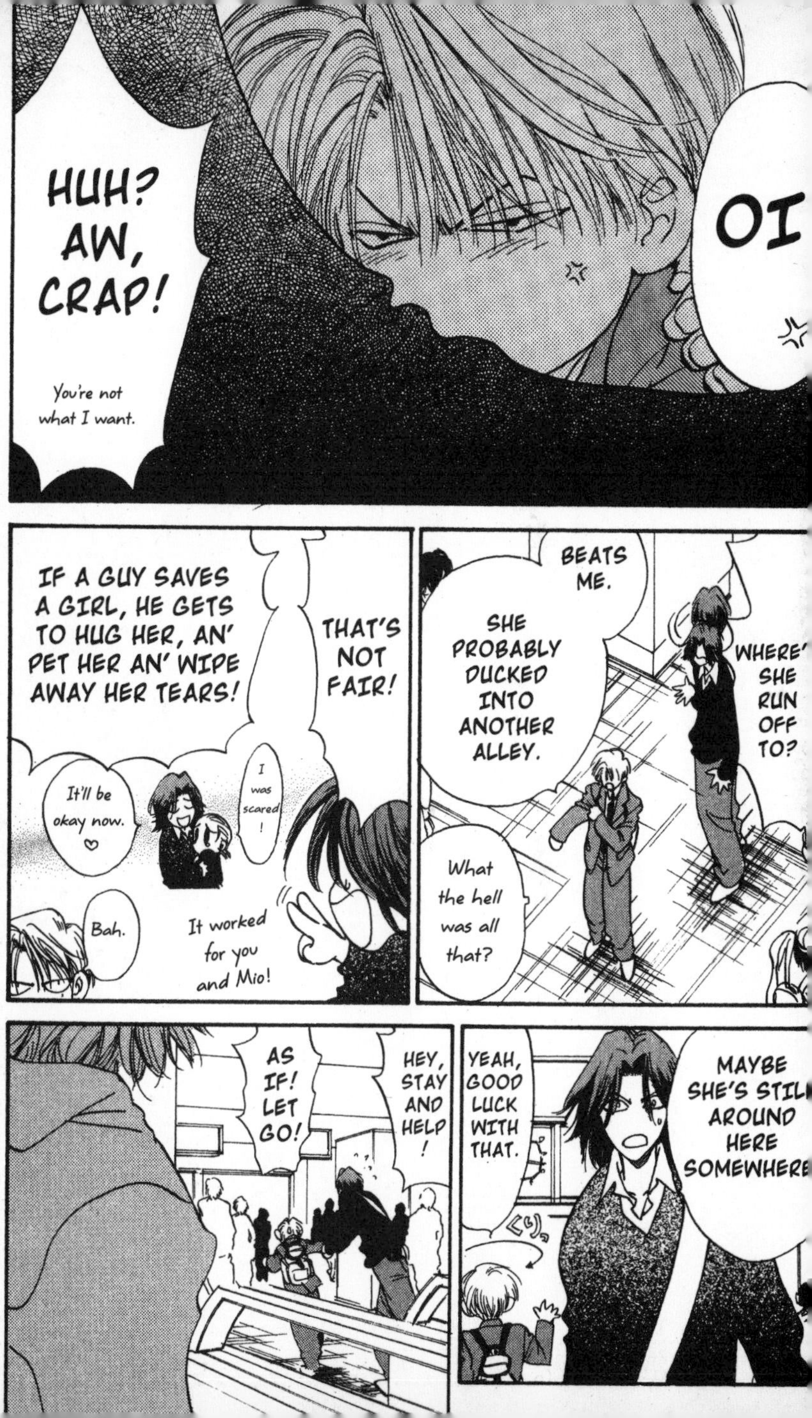
OI
HUH? AW, CRAP!
You're not what I want.
WHERE' SHE RUN OFF TO?
BEATS ME.
SHE PROBABLY DUCKED INTO ANOTHER ALLEY.
What the hell was all that?
THAT'S NOT FAIR!
IF A GUY SAVES A GIRL, HE GETS TO HUG HER, AN' PET HER AN' WIPE AWAY HER TEARS!
I was scared!
It'll be okay now. ♡
It worked for you and Mio!
Bah.
MAYBE SHE'S STIL AROUND HERE SOMEWHERE
YEAH, GOOD LUCK WITH THAT.
HEY, STAY AND HELP!
AS IF! LET GO!

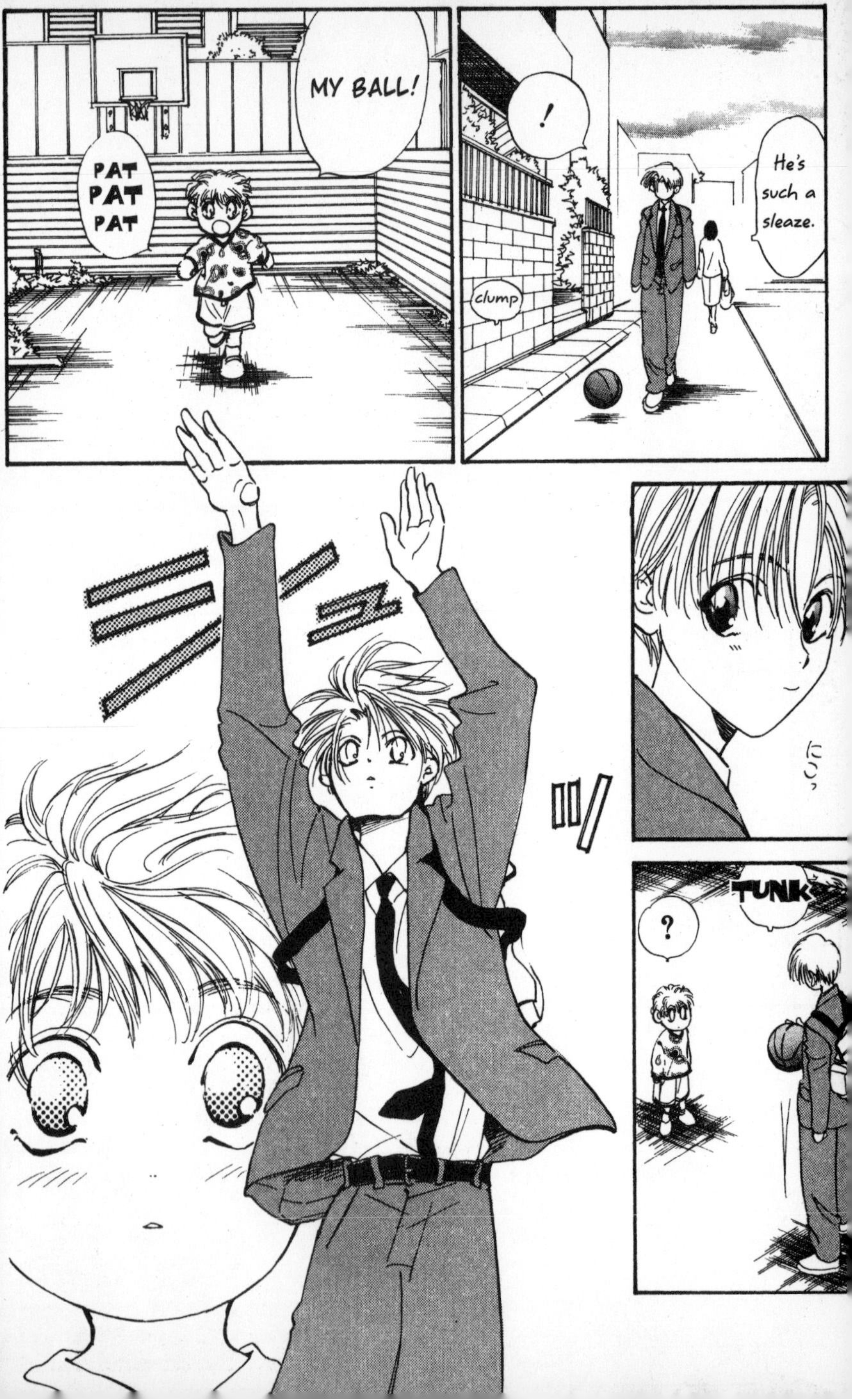
He's such a sleaze.
!
clump
MY BALL!
PAT PAT PAT
にこっ
TUNK
?

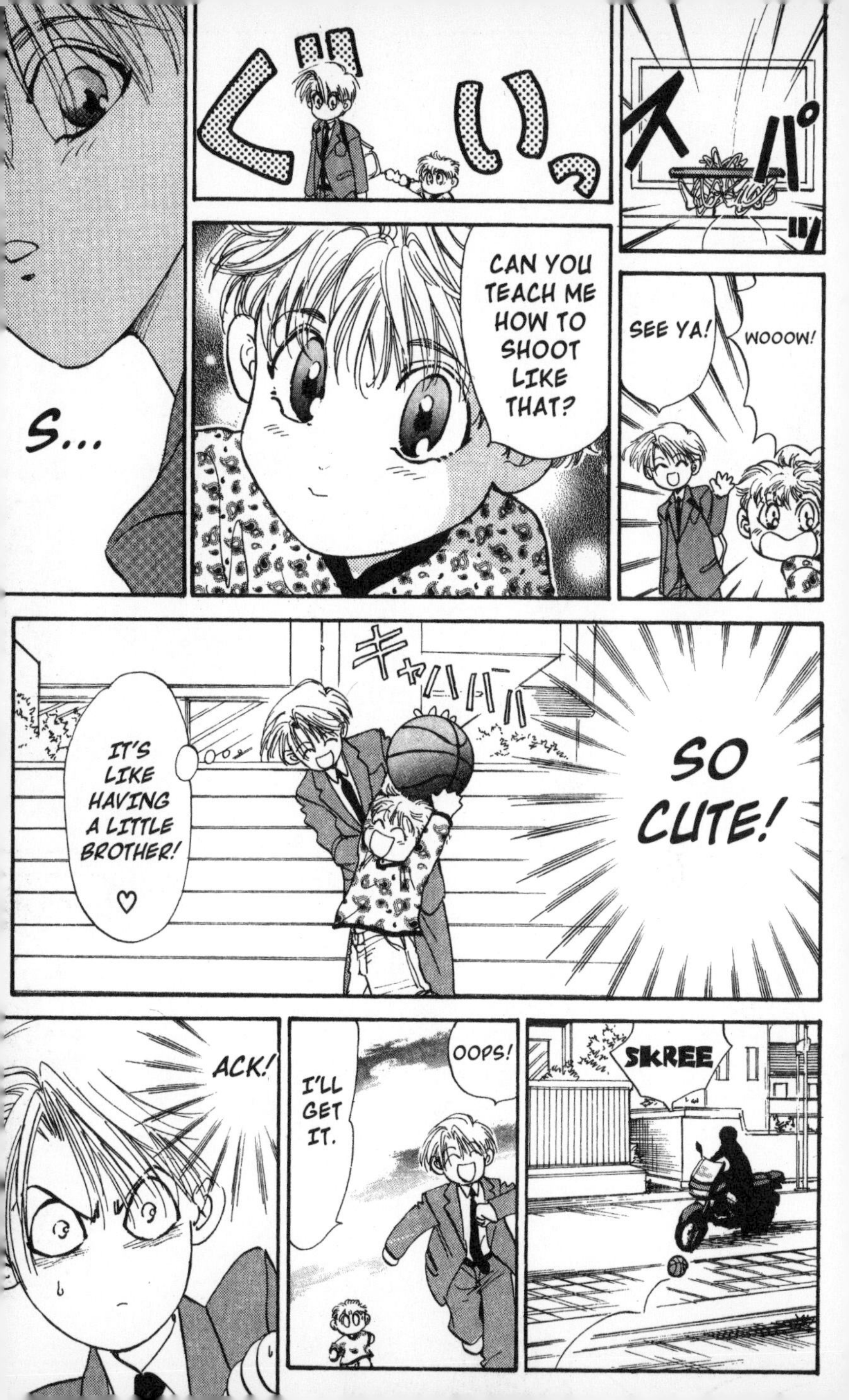

スパッ
ぐいっ
WOOOW!
SEE YA!
CAN YOU TEACH ME HOW TO SHOOT LIKE THAT?
S...
SO CUTE!
キャハハハハ
IT'S LIKE HAVING A LITTLE BROTHER! ♡
SKREE
OOPS!
I'LL GET IT.
ACK!

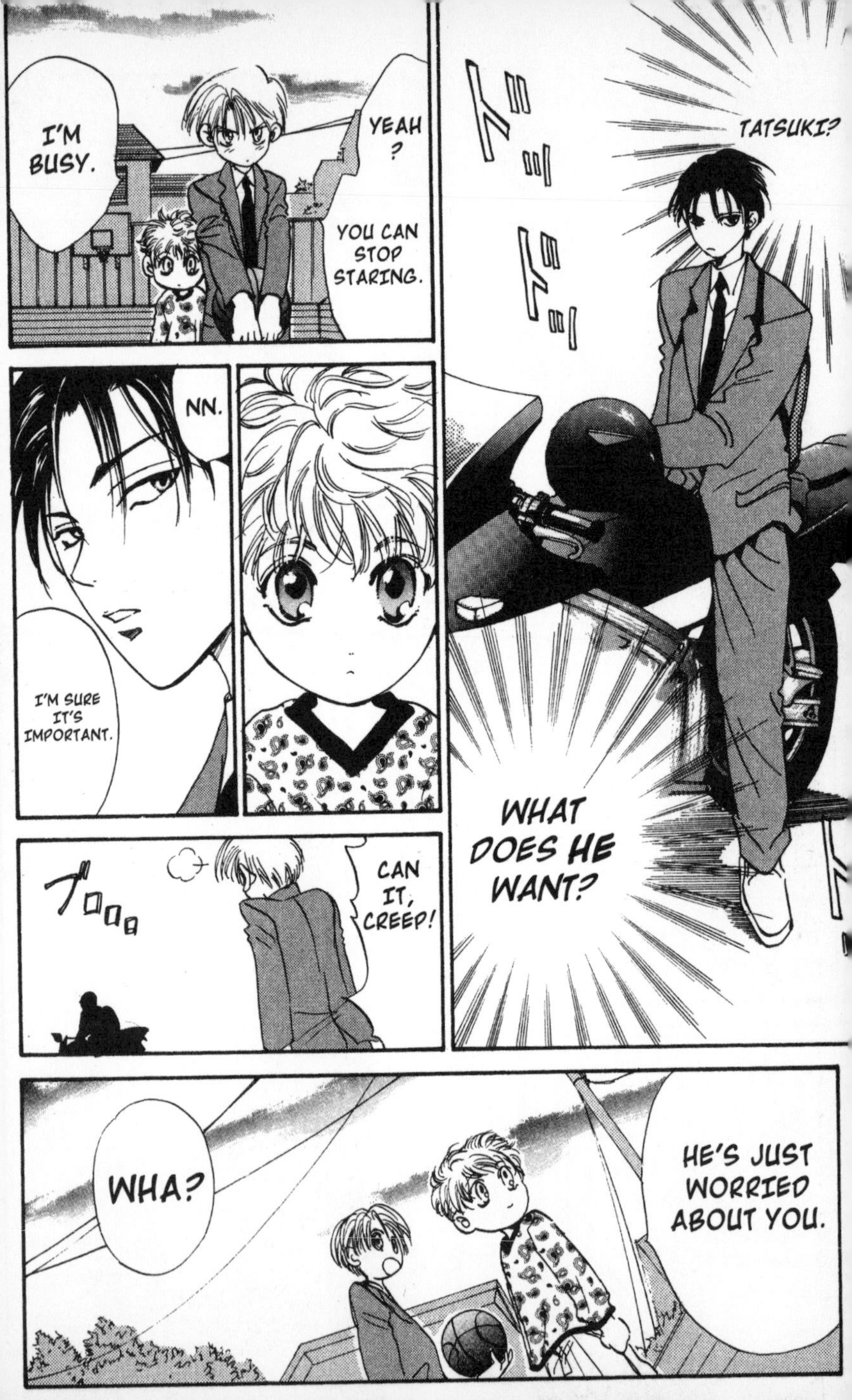
TATSUKI?
WHAT DOES HE WANT?
YEAH?
YOU CAN STOP STARING.
I'M BUSY.
NN.
I'M SURE IT'S IMPORTANT.
CAN IT, CREEP!
ブロロロ
HE'S JUST WORRIED ABOUT YOU.
WHA?

ACT 9

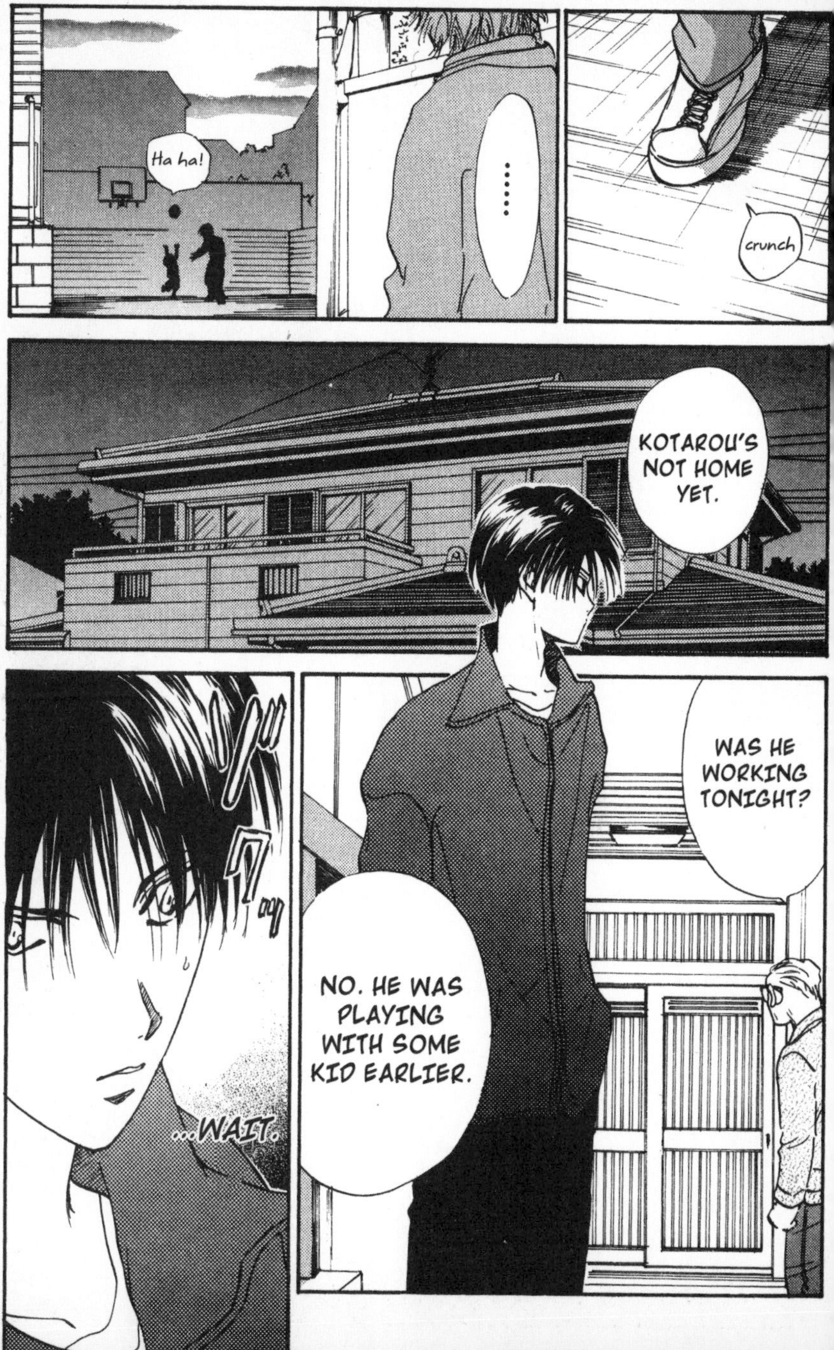
crunch
......
Ha ha!
KOTAROU'S NOT HOME YET.
WAS HE WORKING TONIGHT?
NO. HE WAS PLAYING WITH SOME KID EARLIER.
...WAIT.

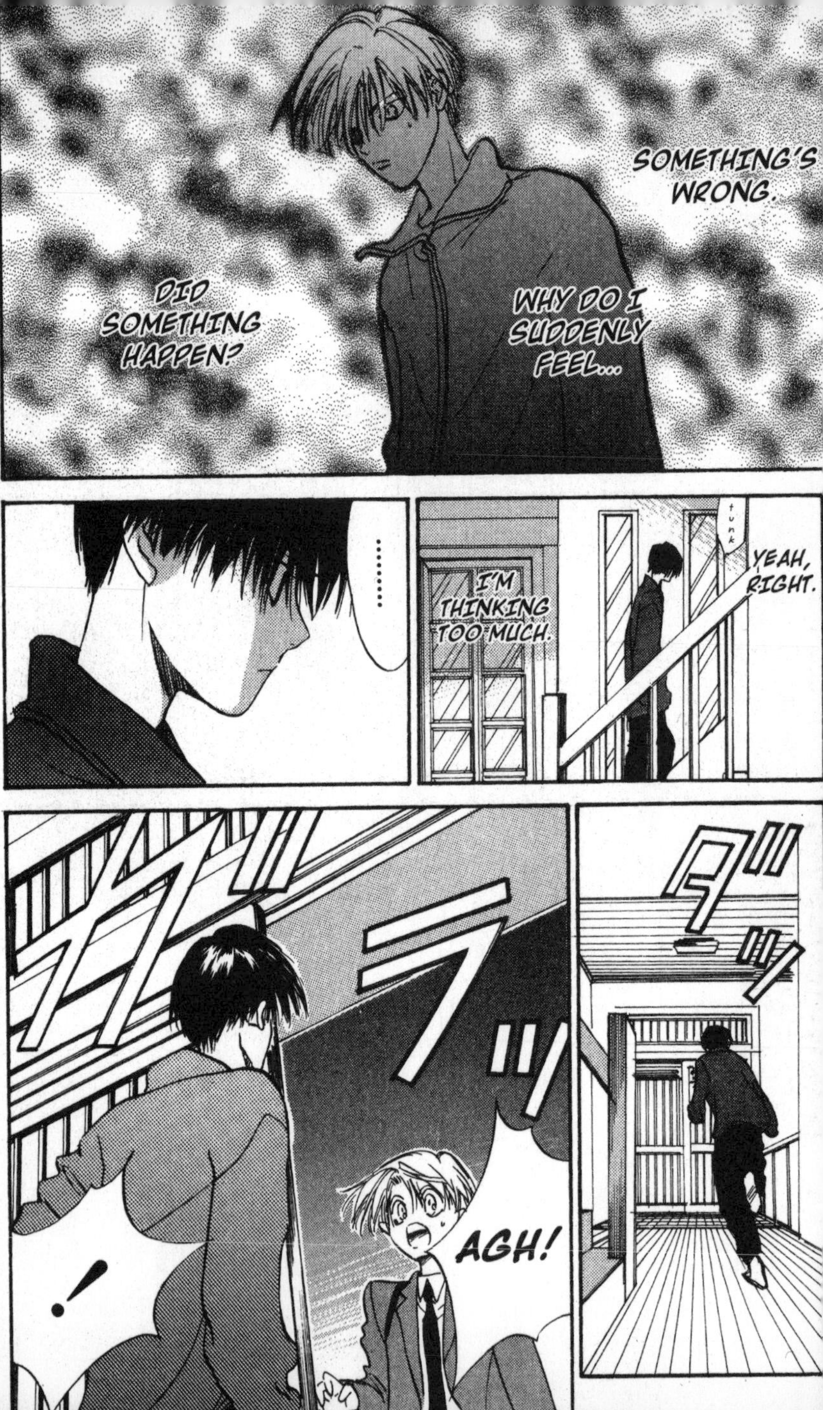
SOMETHING'S WRONG.
WHY DO I SUDDENLY FEEL...
DID SOMETHING HAPPEN?
tunk
YEAH, RIGHT.
I'M THINKING TOO MUCH.
......
AGH!
!

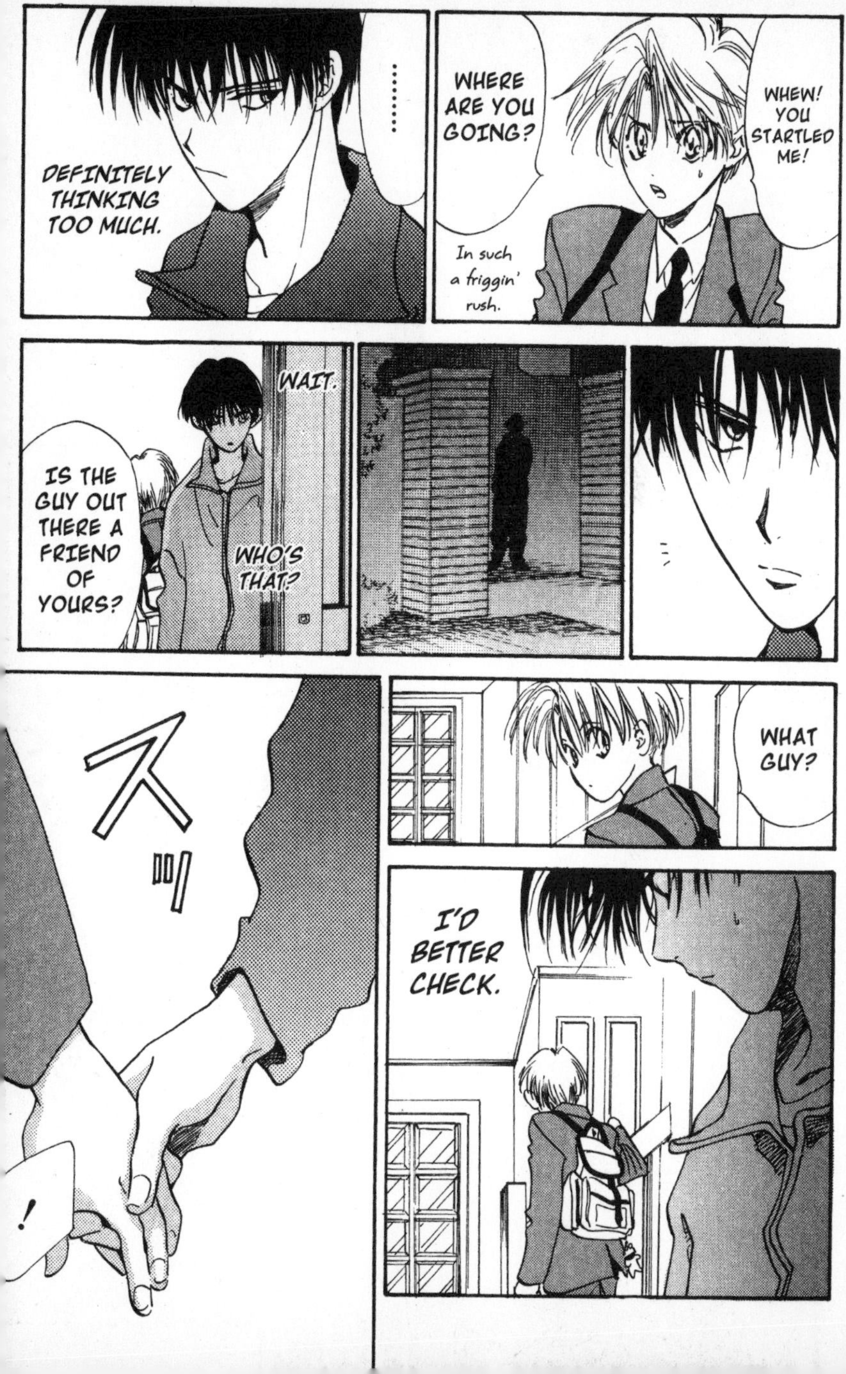
WHEW! YOU STARTLED ME!
WHERE ARE YOU GOING?
In such a friggin' rush.
......
DEFINITELY THINKING TOO MUCH.
WAIT.
WHO'S THAT?
IS THE GUY OUT THERE A FRIEND OF YOURS?
WHAT GUY?
I'D BETTER CHECK.
スッ
!

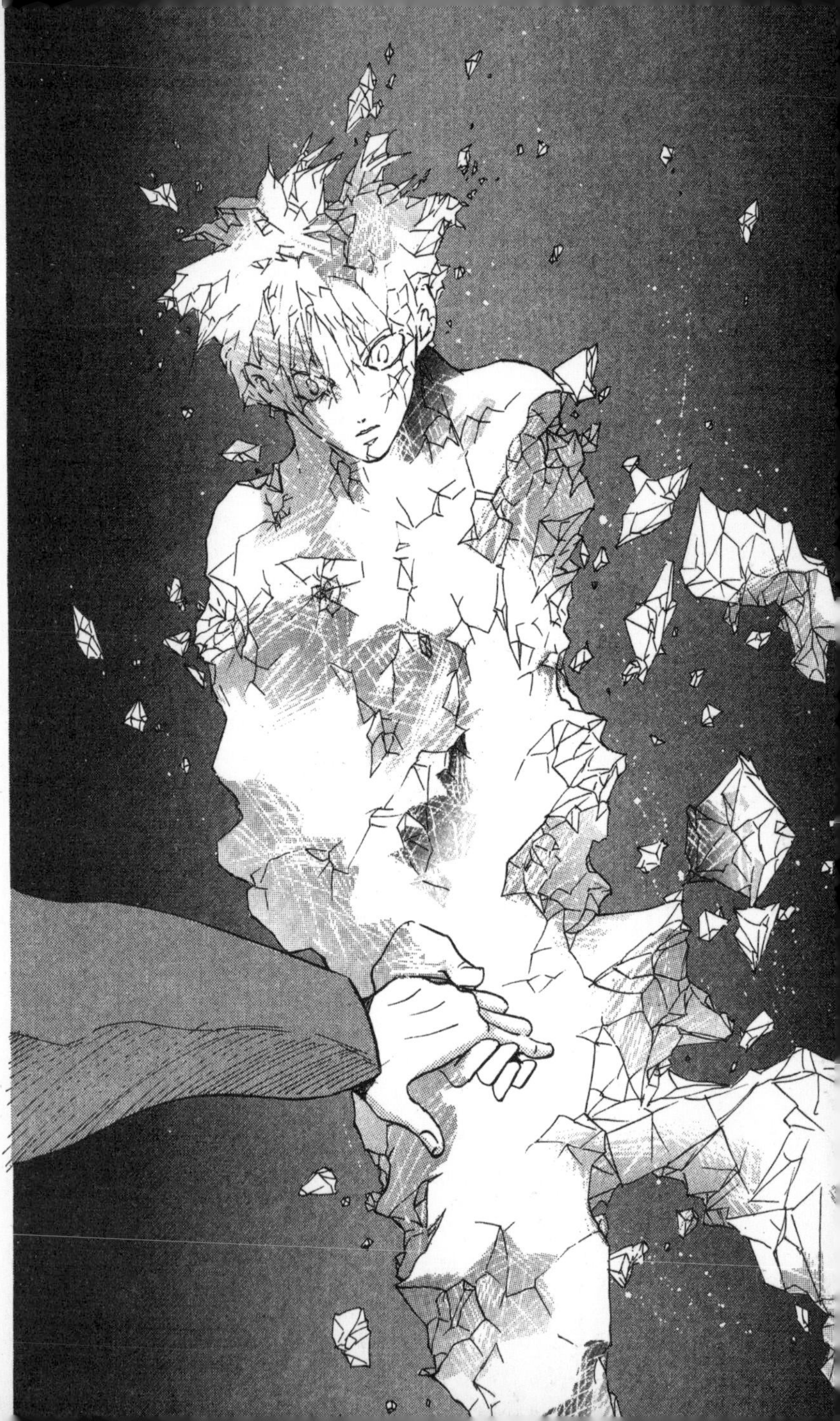

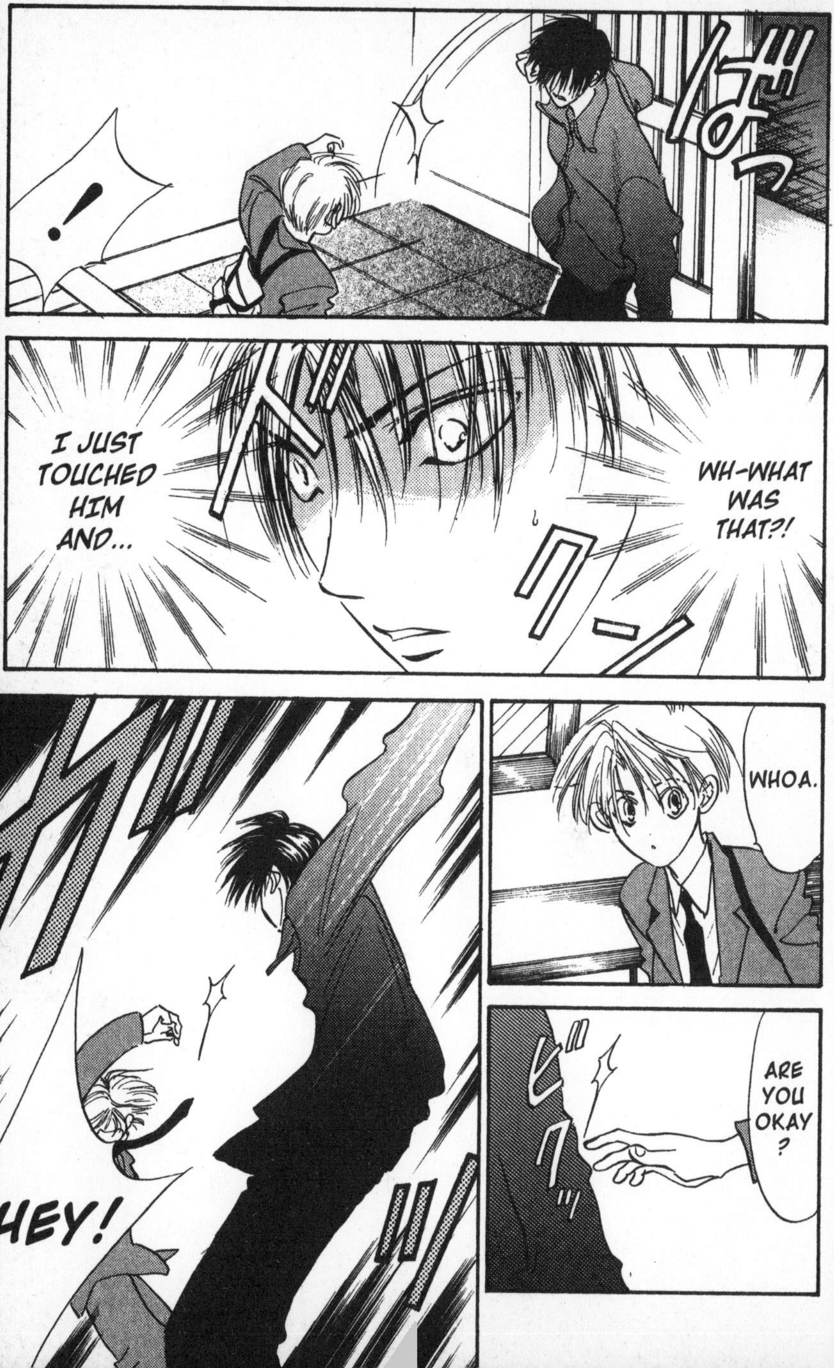
ばっ
!
WH-WHAT WAS THAT?!
I JUST TOUCHED HIM AND...
WHOA.
ARE YOU OKAY?
HEY!

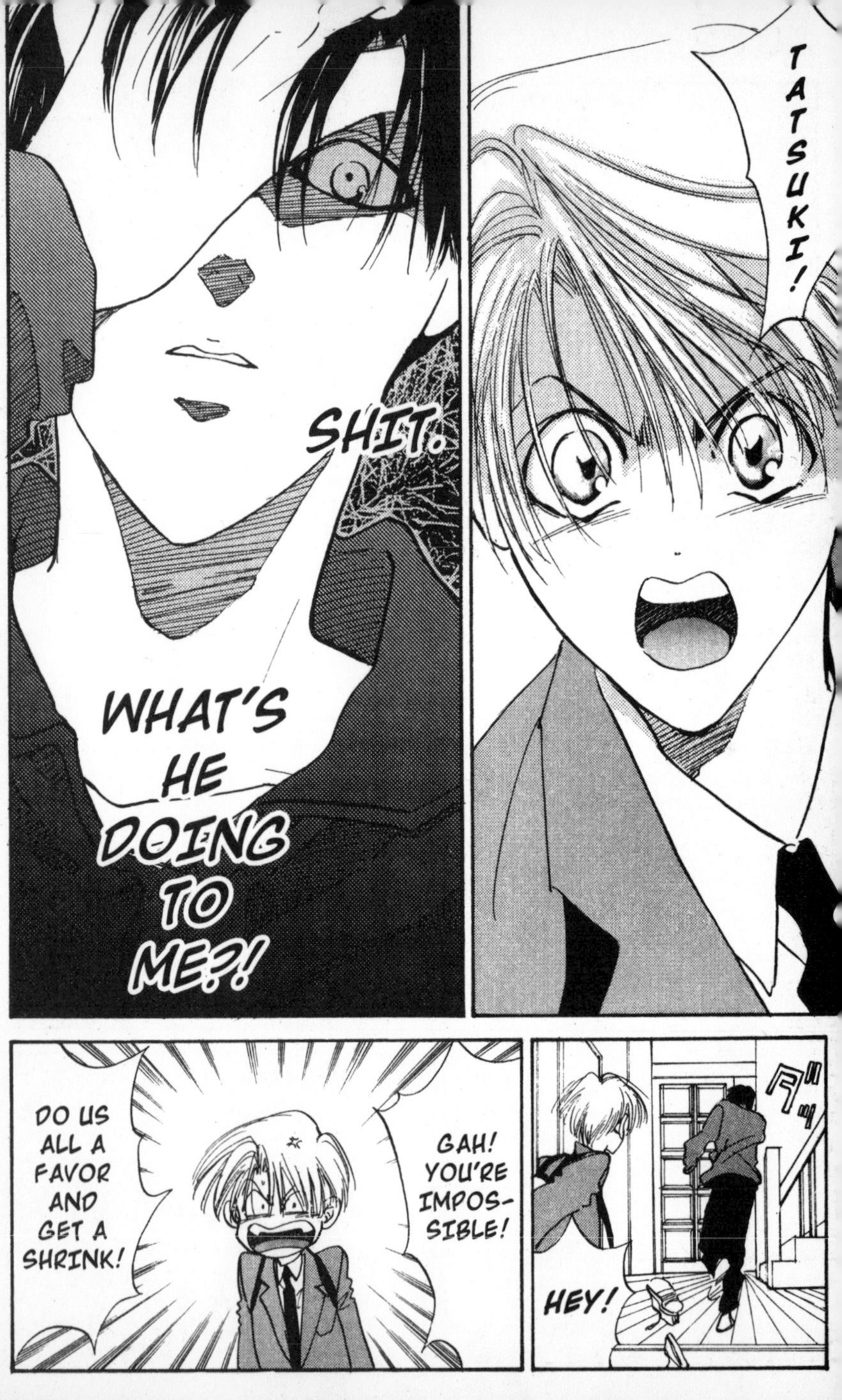
TATSUKI!
SHIT.
WHAT'S HE DOING TO ME?!
HEY!
GAH! YOU'RE IMPOSSIBLE!
DO US ALL A FAVOR AND GET A SHRINK!

ACT 9

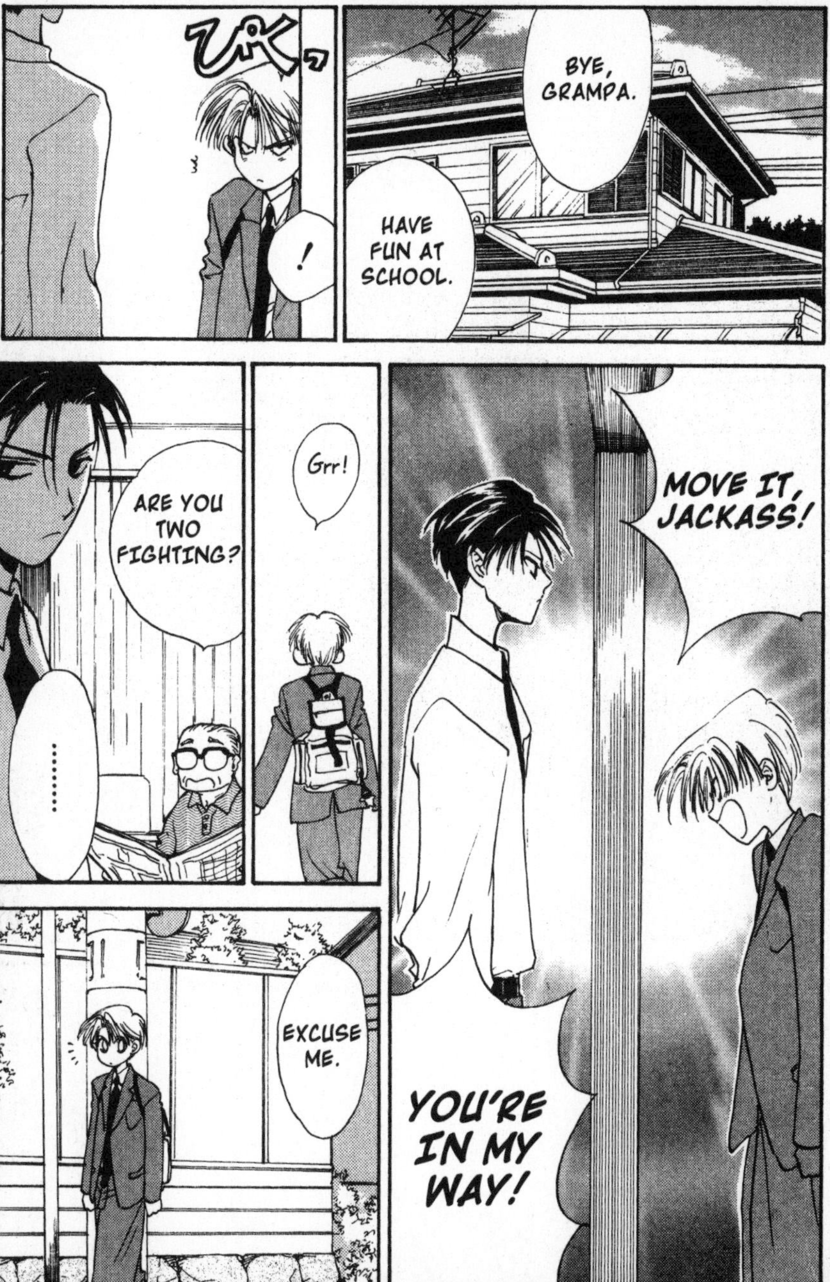
BYE, GRAMPA.
HAVE FUN AT SCHOOL.
ぴくっ
!
MOVE IT, JACKASS!
YOU'RE IN MY WAY!
Grr!
ARE YOU TWO FIGHTING?
....
EXCUSE ME.

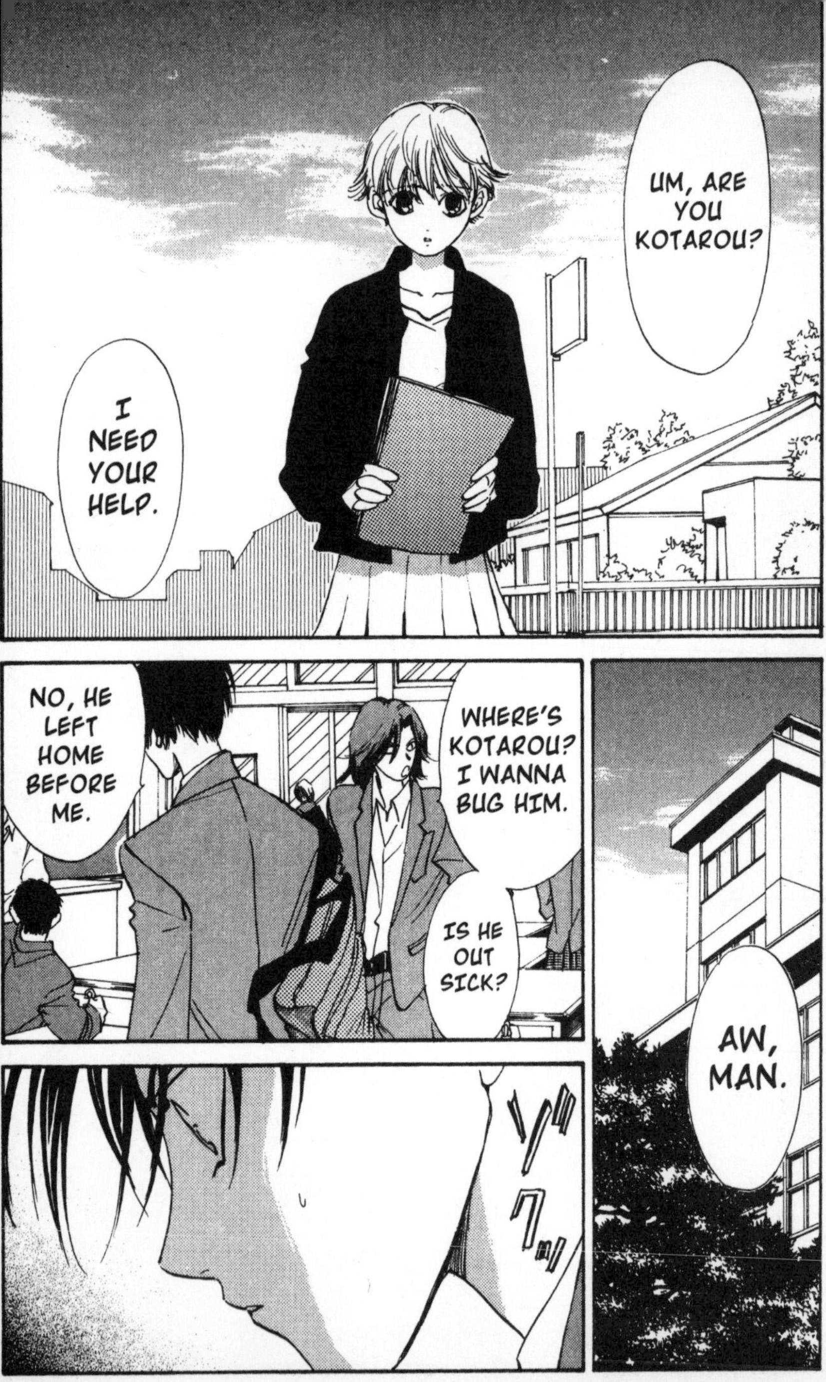
UM, ARE YOU KOTAROU?
I NEED YOUR HELP.
AW, MAN.
WHERE'S KOTAROU? I WANNA BUG HIM.
IS HE OUT SICK?
NO, HE LEFT HOME BEFORE ME.

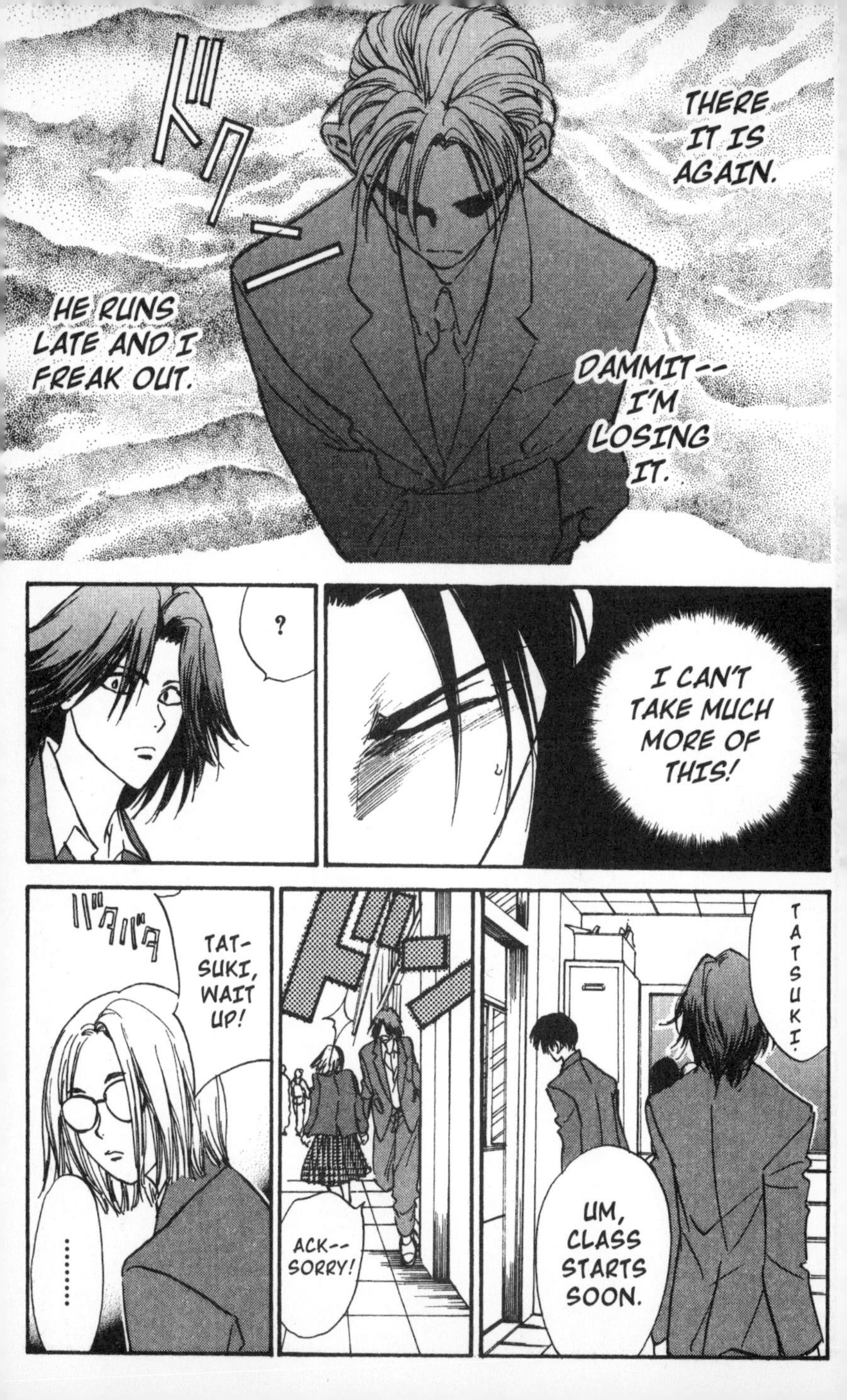
THERE IT IS AGAIN.
ドク
DAMMIT-- I'M LOSING IT.
HE RUNS LATE AND I FREAK OUT.
I CAN'T TAKE MUCH MORE OF THIS!
?
TATSUKI.
UM, CLASS STARTS SOON.
ACK-- SORRY!
バタバタ
TAT-SUKI, WAIT UP!
....

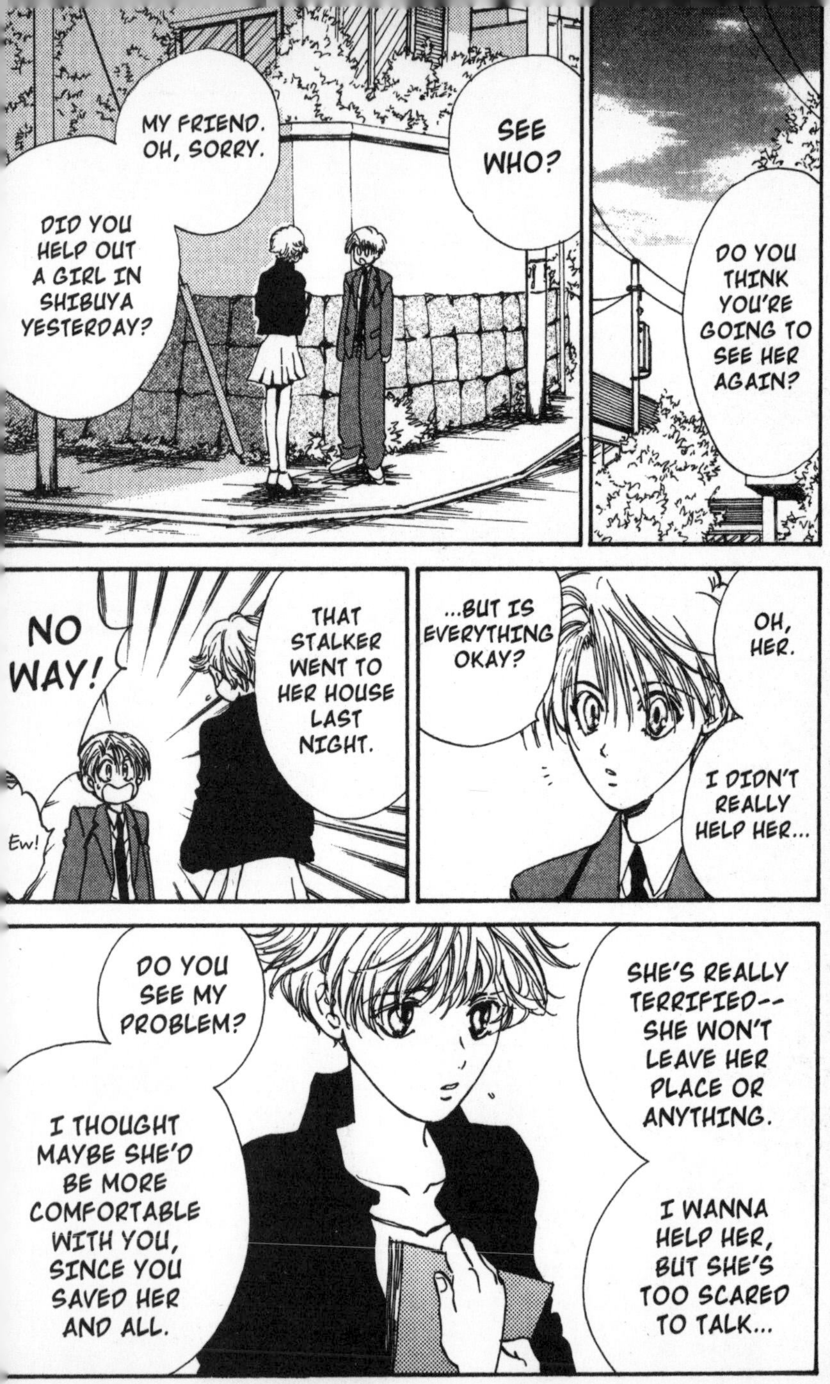
DO YOU THINK YOU'RE GOING TO SEE HER AGAIN?
SEE WHO?
MY FRIEND. OH, SORRY.
DID YOU HELP OUT A GIRL IN SHIBUYA YESTERDAY?
OH, HER.
I DIDN'T REALLY HELP HER...
...BUT IS EVERYTHING OKAY?
THAT STALKER WENT TO HER HOUSE LAST NIGHT.
NO WAY!
Ew!
SHE'S REALLY TERRIFIED--SHE WON'T LEAVE HER PLACE OR ANYTHING.
I WANNA HELP HER, BUT SHE'S TOO SCARED TO TALK...
I THOUGHT MAYBE SHE'D BE MORE COMFORTABLE WITH YOU, SINCE YOU SAVED HER AND ALL.
DO YOU SEE MY PROBLEM?

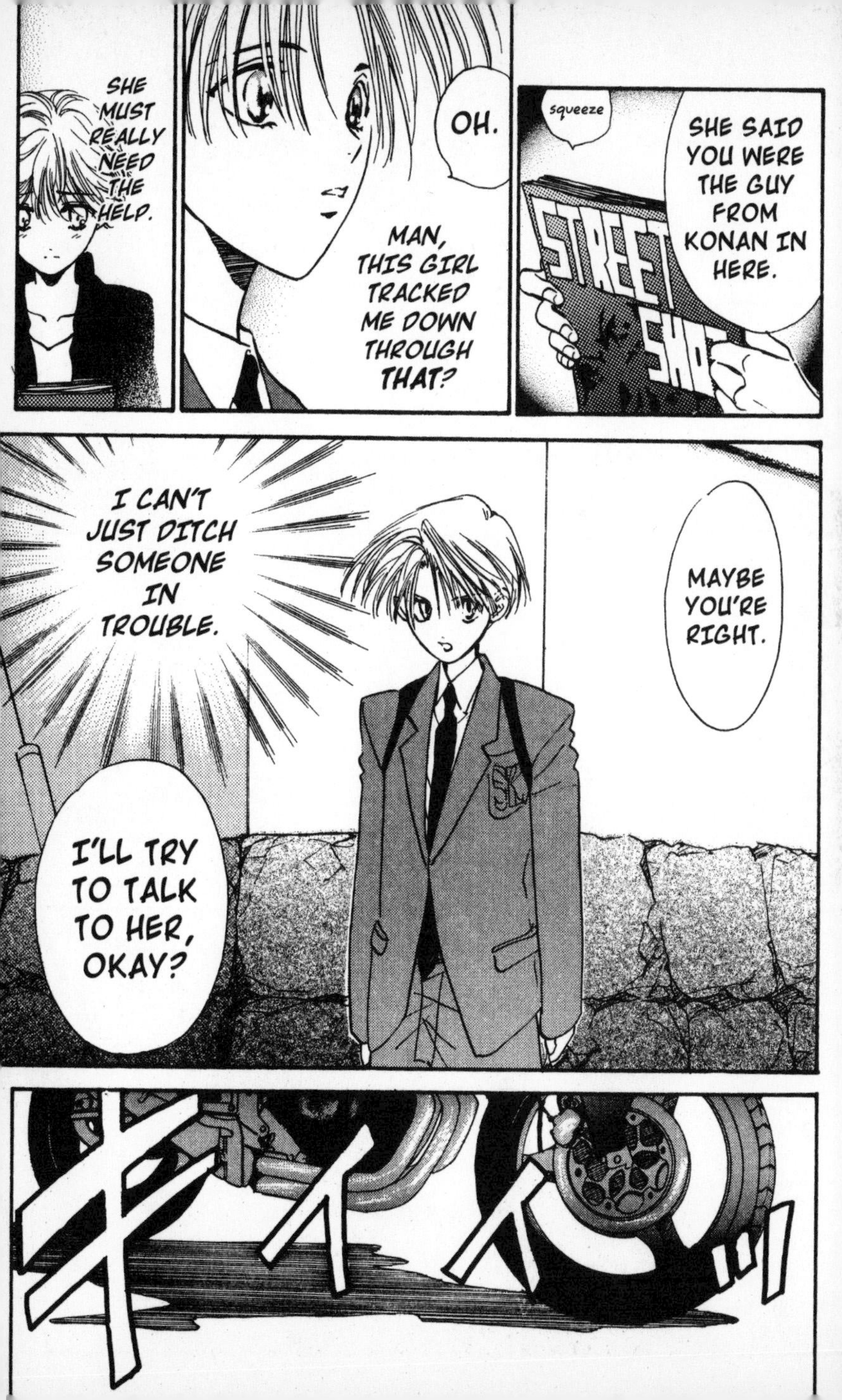
squeeze
SHE SAID YOU WERE THE GUY FROM KONAN IN HERE.
OH.
MAN, THIS GIRL TRACKED ME DOWN THROUGH THAT?
SHE MUST REALLY NEED THE HELP.
MAYBE YOU'RE RIGHT.
I CAN'T JUST DITCH SOMEONE IN TROUBLE.
I'LL TRY TO TALK TO HER, OKAY?
キイイ

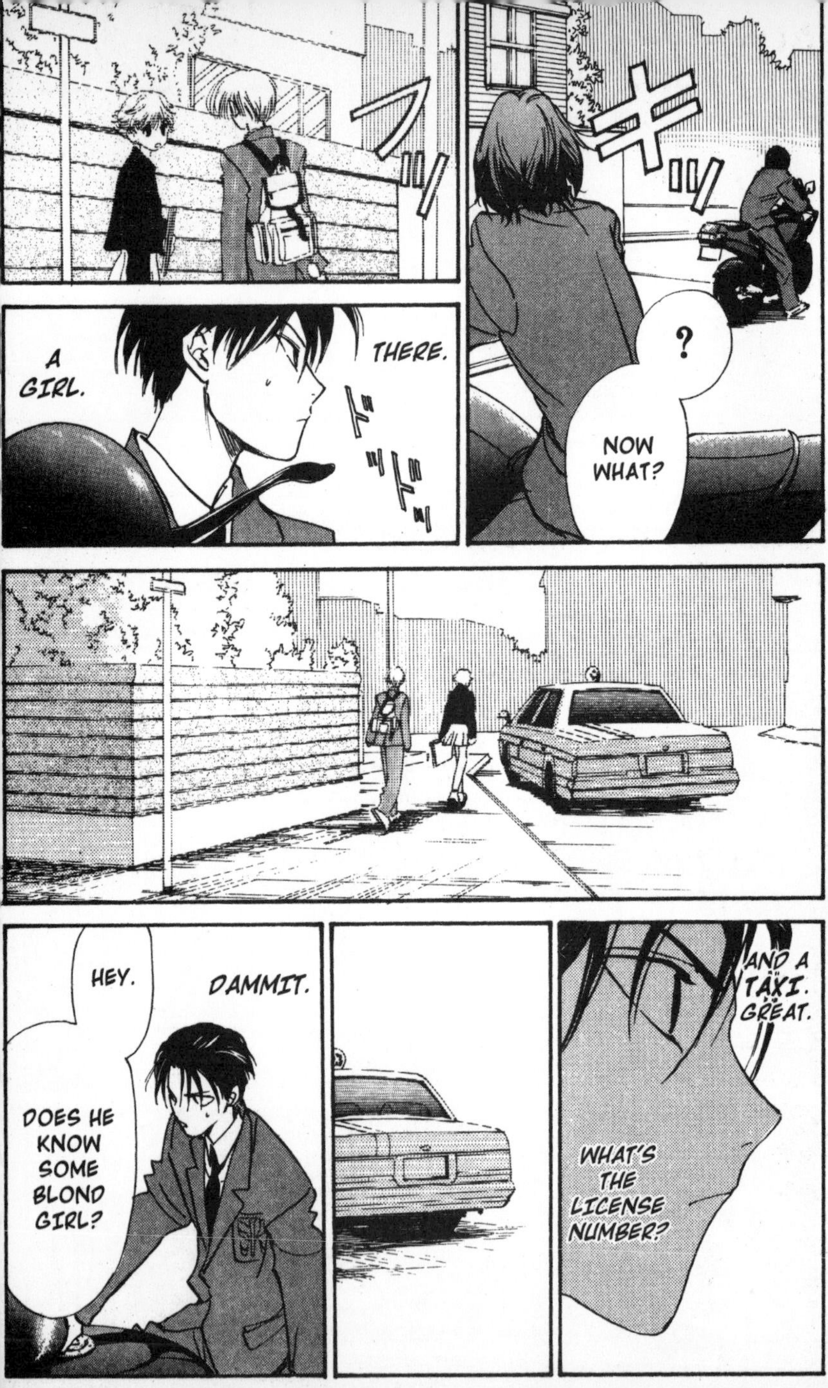
?
NOW WHAT?
THERE.
A GIRL.
AND A TAXI. GREAT.
WHAT'S THE LICENSE NUMBER?
DAMMIT.
HEY.
DOES HE KNOW SOME BLOND GIRL?

ACT 9

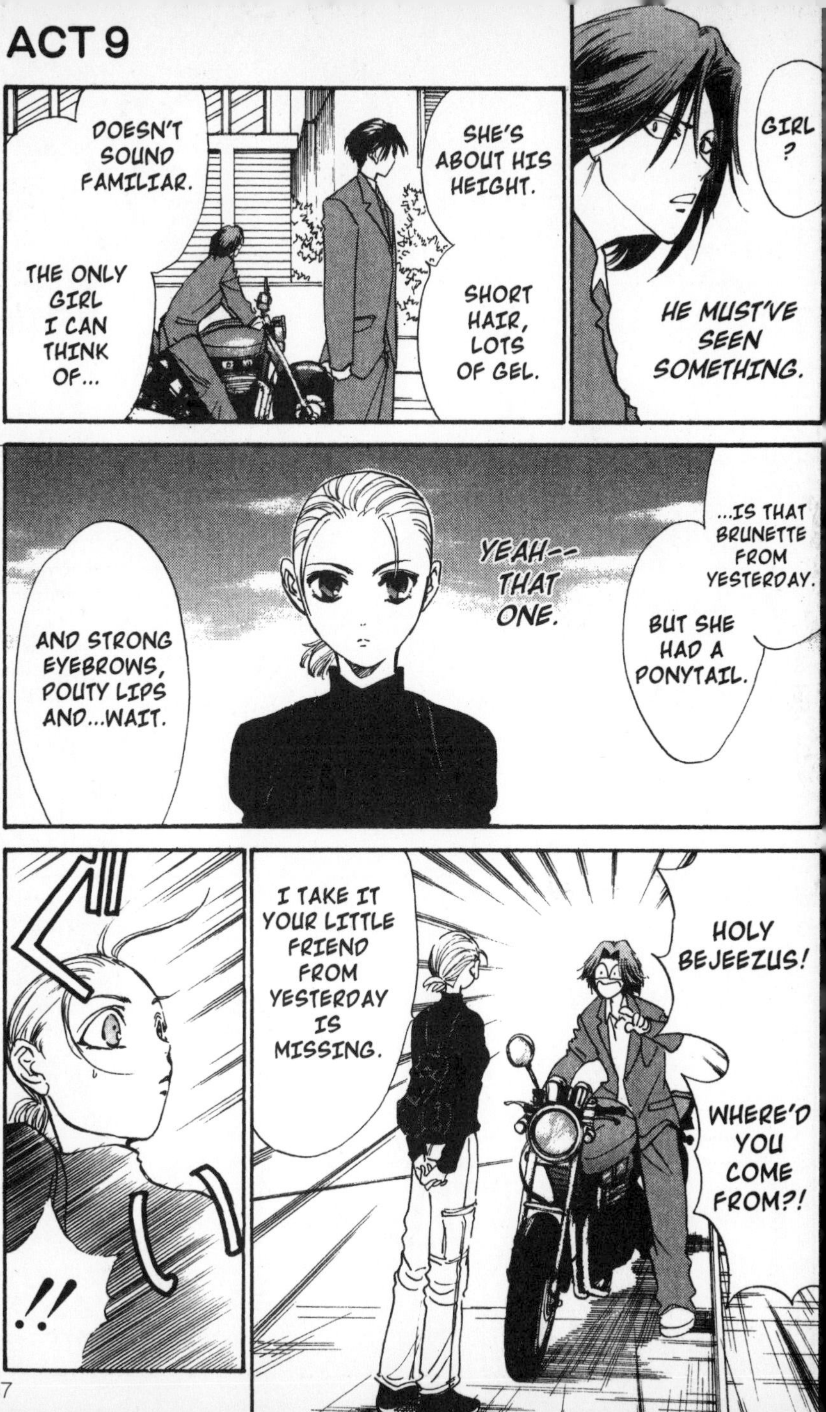
GIRL?
HE MUST'VE SEEN SOMETHING.
SHE'S ABOUT HIS HEIGHT.
SHORT HAIR, LOTS OF GEL.
DOESN'T SOUND FAMILIAR.
THE ONLY GIRL I CAN THINK OF...
...IS THAT BRUNETTE FROM YESTERDAY.
BUT SHE HAD A PONYTAIL.
YEAH--THAT ONE.
AND STRONG EYEBROWS, POUTY LIPS AND...WAIT.
HOLY BEJEEZUS!
WHERE'D YOU COME FROM?!
I TAKE IT YOUR LITTLE FRIEND FROM YESTERDAY IS MISSING.
!!

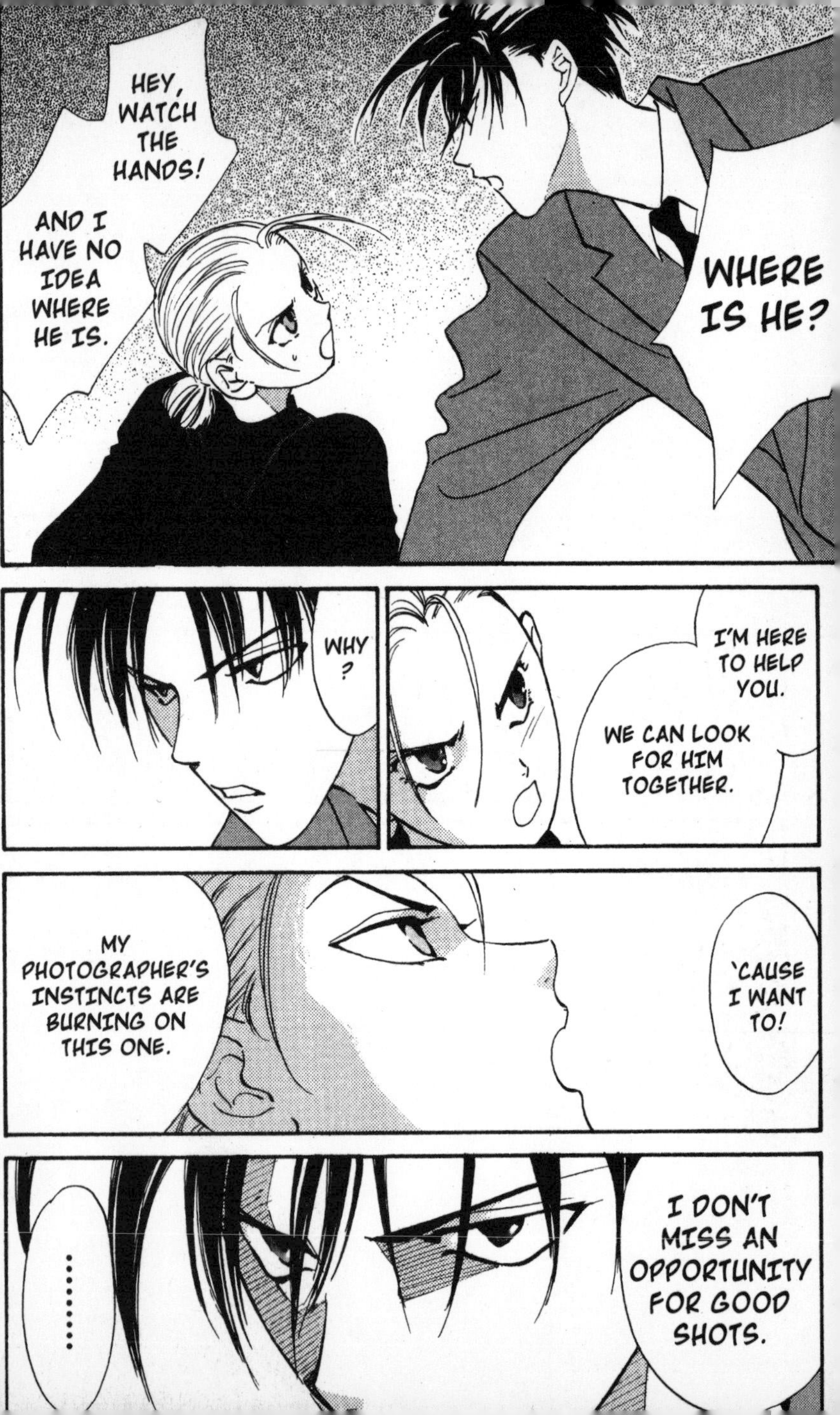
WHERE IS HE?
HEY, WATCH THE HANDS!
AND I HAVE NO IDEA WHERE HE IS.
I'M HERE TO HELP YOU.
WE CAN LOOK FOR HIM TOGETHER.
WHY?
'CAUSE I WANT TO!
MY PHOTOGRAPHER'S INSTINCTS ARE BURNING ON THIS ONE.
I DON'T MISS AN OPPORTUNITY FOR GOOD SHOTS.
....

ACT 9

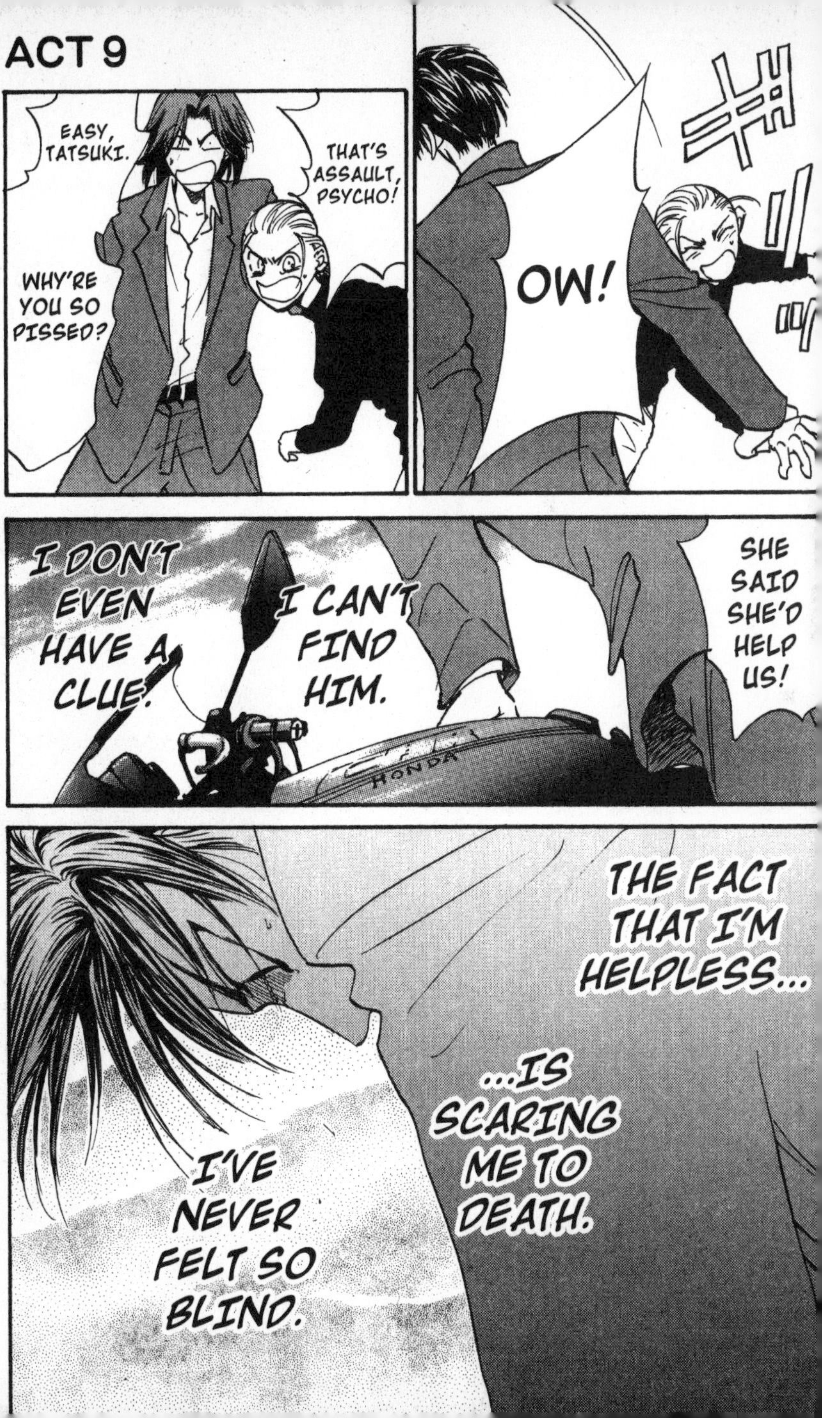
OW!
THAT'S ASSAULT, PSYCHO!
EASY, TATSUKI.
WHY'RE YOU SO PISSED?
SHE SAID SHE'D HELP US!
I CAN'T FIND HIM.
I DON'T EVEN HAVE A CLUE.
HONDA
THE FACT THAT I'M HELPLESS...
...IS SCARING ME TO DEATH.
I'VE NEVER FELT SO BLIND.

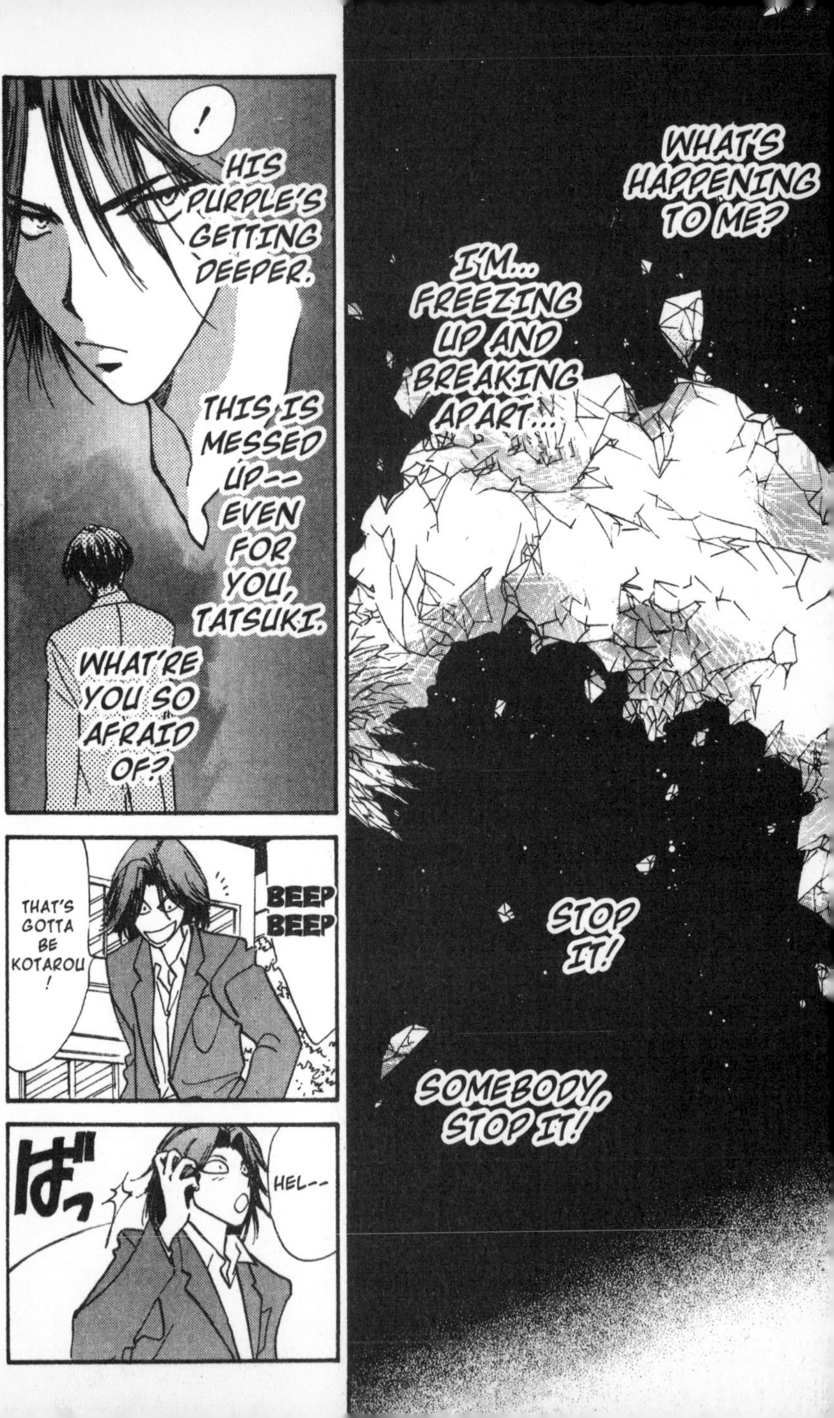
WHAT'S HAPPENING TO ME?
I'M... FREEZING UP AND BREAKING APART...
STOP IT!
SOMEBODY, STOP IT!
!
HIS PURPLE'S GETTING DEEPER.
THIS IS MESSED UP-- EVEN FOR YOU, TATSUKI.
WHAT'RE YOU SO AFRAID OF?
BEEP BEEP
THAT'S GOTTA BE KOTAROU!
ばっ
HEL--

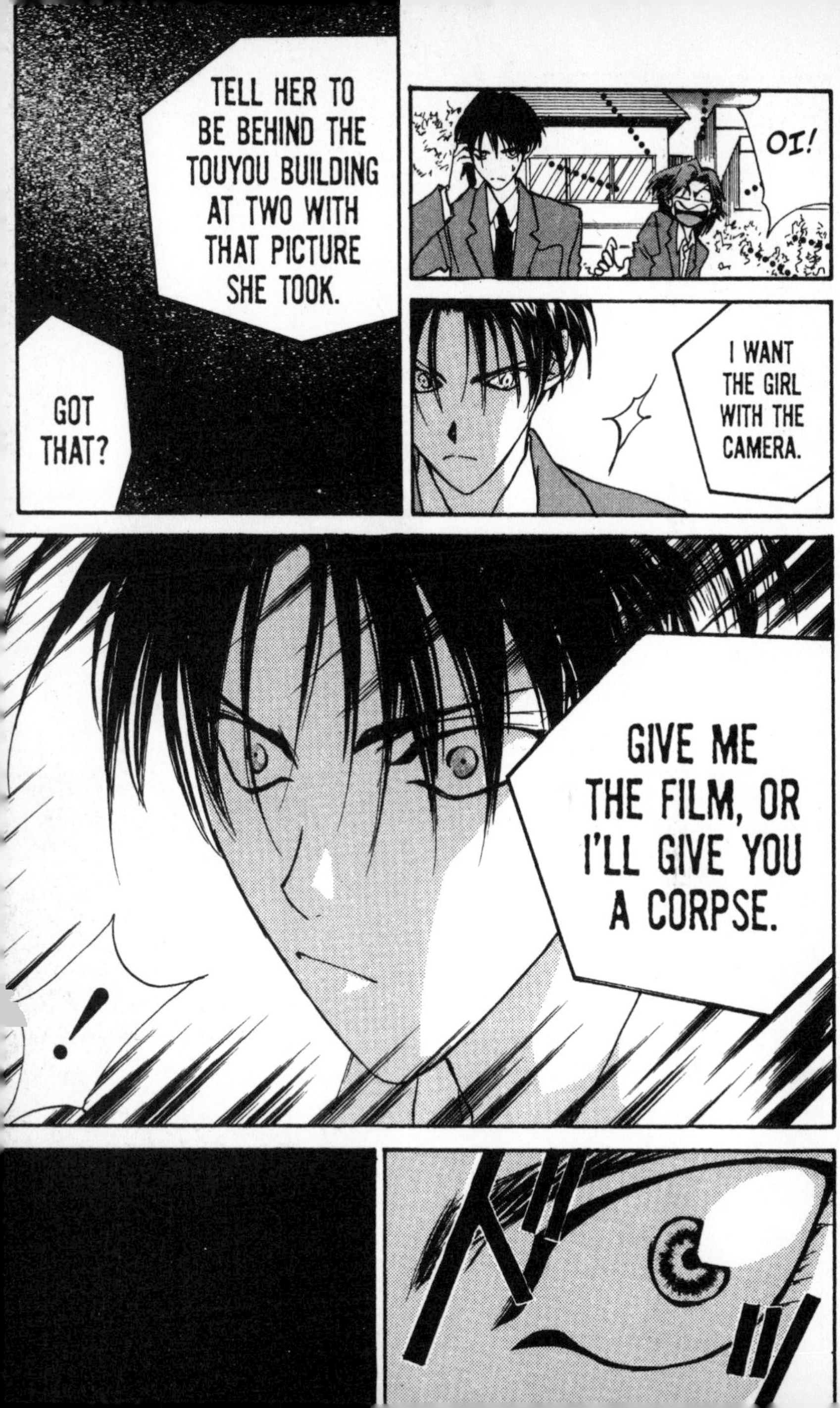
OI!
I WANT THE GIRL WITH THE CAMERA.
TELL HER TO BE BEHIND THE TOUYOU BUILDING AT TWO WITH THAT PICTURE SHE TOOK.
GOT THAT?
GIVE ME THE FILM, OR I'LL GIVE YOU A CORPSE.
!

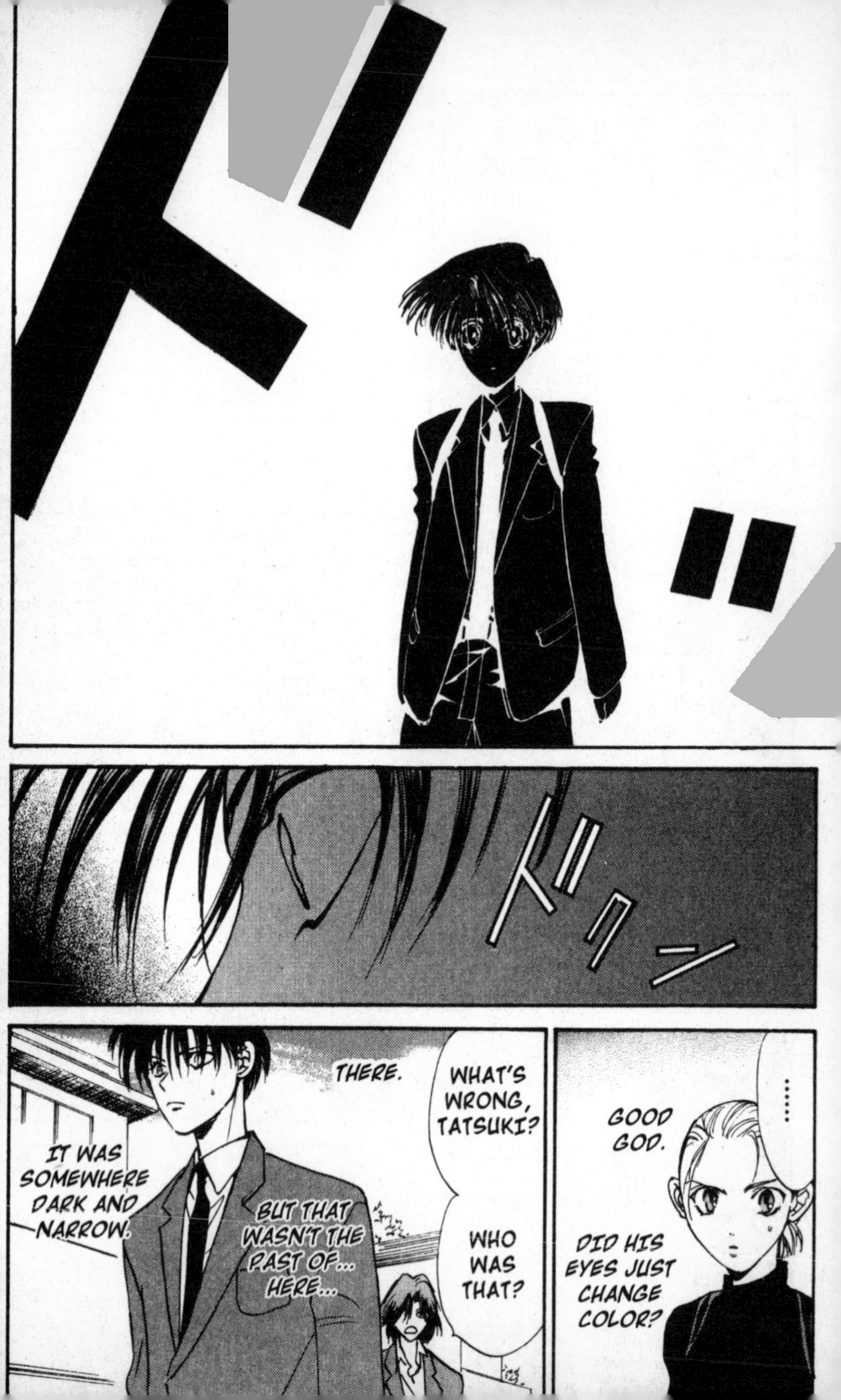

ドクン
......
GOOD GOD.
DID HIS EYES JUST CHANGE COLOR?
WHAT'S WRONG, TATSUKI?
WHO WAS THAT?
THERE.
IT WAS SOMEWHERE DARK AND NARROW.
BUT THAT WASN'T THE PAST OF... HERE...

ACT 9

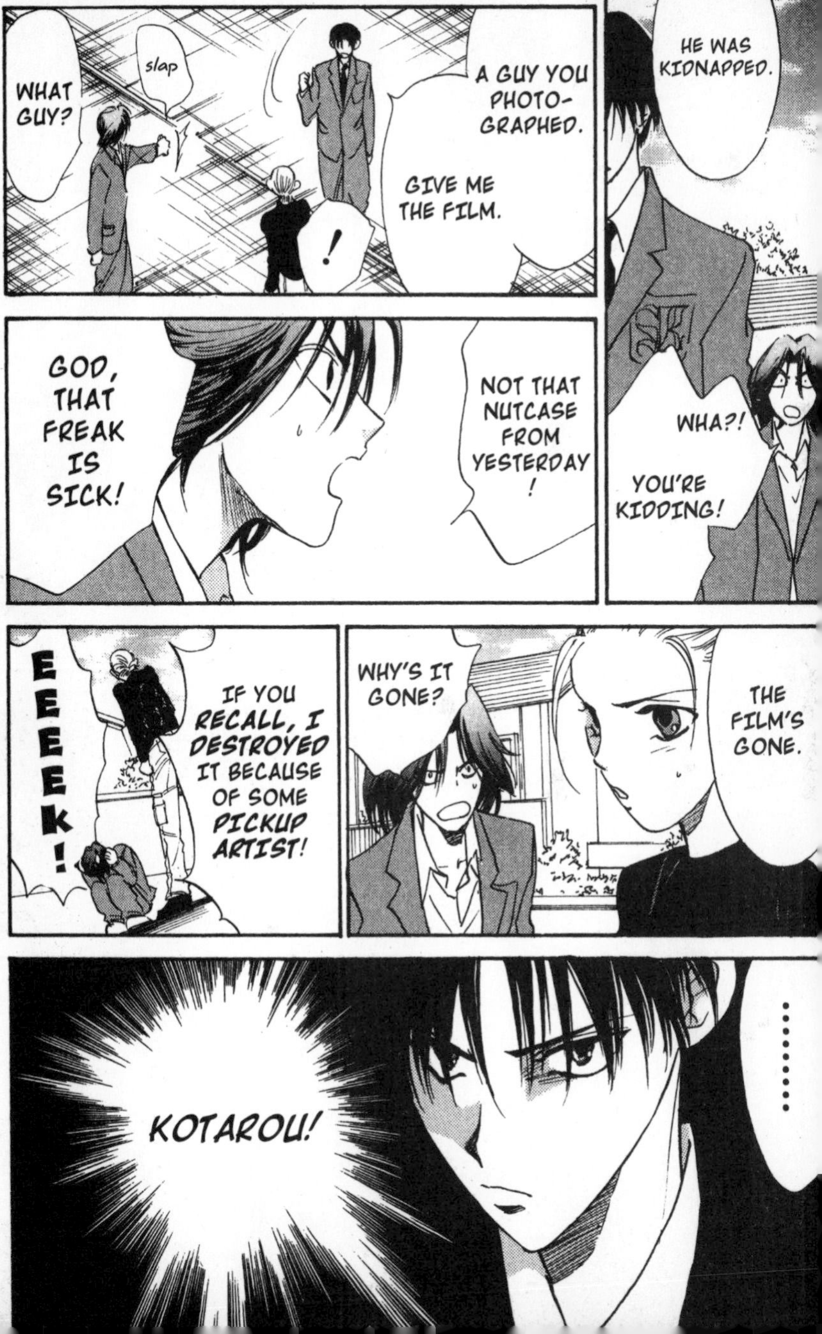
HE WAS KIDNAPPED.
WHA?!
YOU'RE KIDDING!
A GUY YOU PHOTOGRAPHED.
GIVE ME THE FILM.
!
slap
WHAT GUY?
NOT THAT NUTCASE FROM YESTERDAY!
GOD, THAT FREAK IS SICK!
THE FILM'S GONE.
WHY'S IT GONE?
IF YOU RECALL, I DESTROYED IT BECAUSE OF SOME PICKUP ARTIST!
EEEEK!
....
KOTAROU!

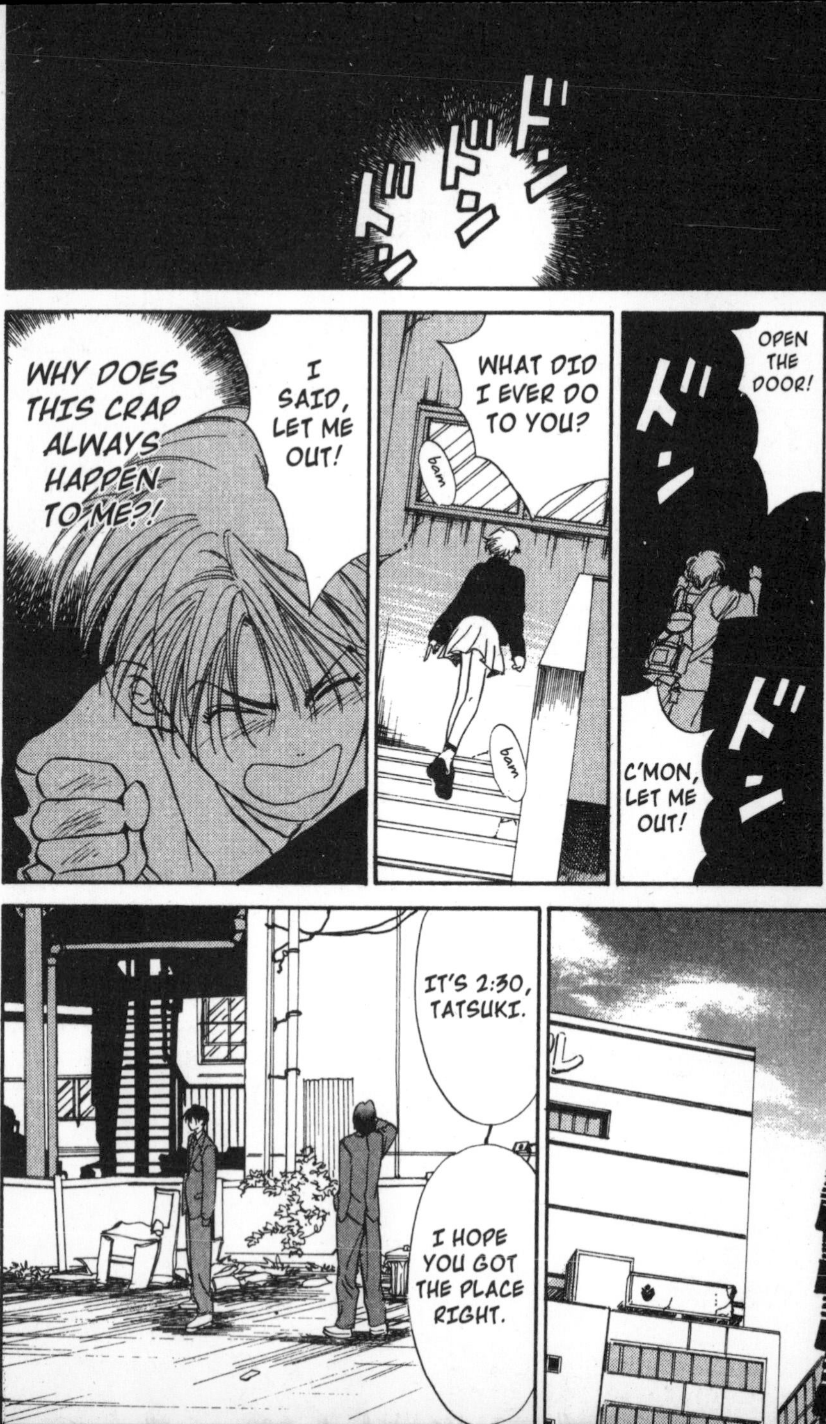
OPEN THE DOOR!
C'MON, LET ME OUT!
WHAT DID I EVER DO TO YOU?
bam
bam
I SAID, LET ME OUT!
WHY DOES THIS CRAP ALWAYS HAPPEN TO ME?!
IT'S 2:30, TATSUKI.
I HOPE YOU GOT THE PLACE RIGHT.

ACT 9

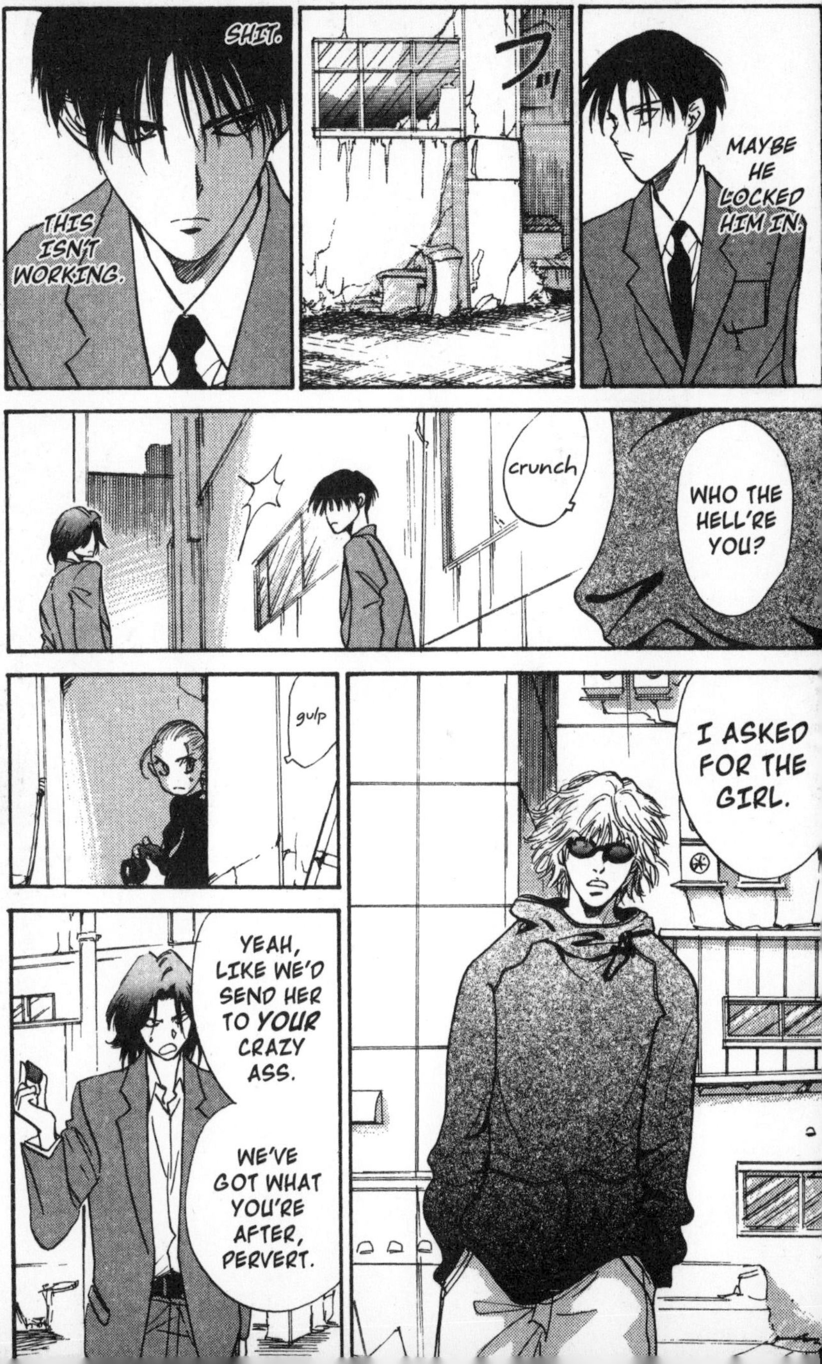
MAYBE HE LOCKED HIM IN.
SHIT.
THIS ISN'T WORKING.
WHO THE HELL'RE YOU?
crunch
I ASKED FOR THE GIRL.
gulp
YEAH, LIKE WE'D SEND HER TO YOUR CRAZY ASS.
WE'VE GOT WHAT YOU'RE AFTER, PERVERT.

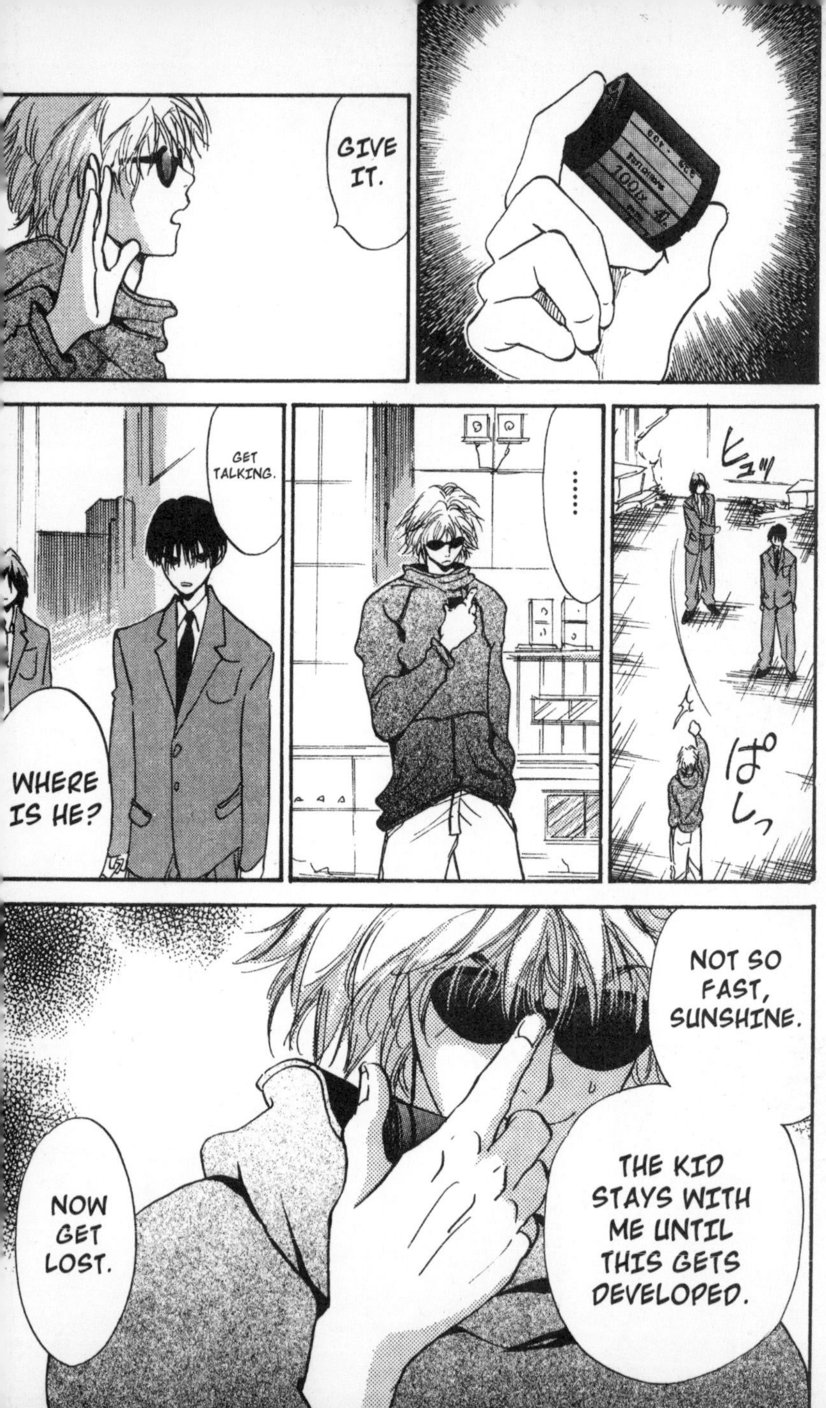
GIVE IT.
ヒュッ
ぱしっ
......
GET TALKING.
WHERE IS HE?
NOT SO FAST, SUNSHINE.
THE KID STAYS WITH ME UNTIL THIS GETS DEVELOPED.
NOW GET LOST.

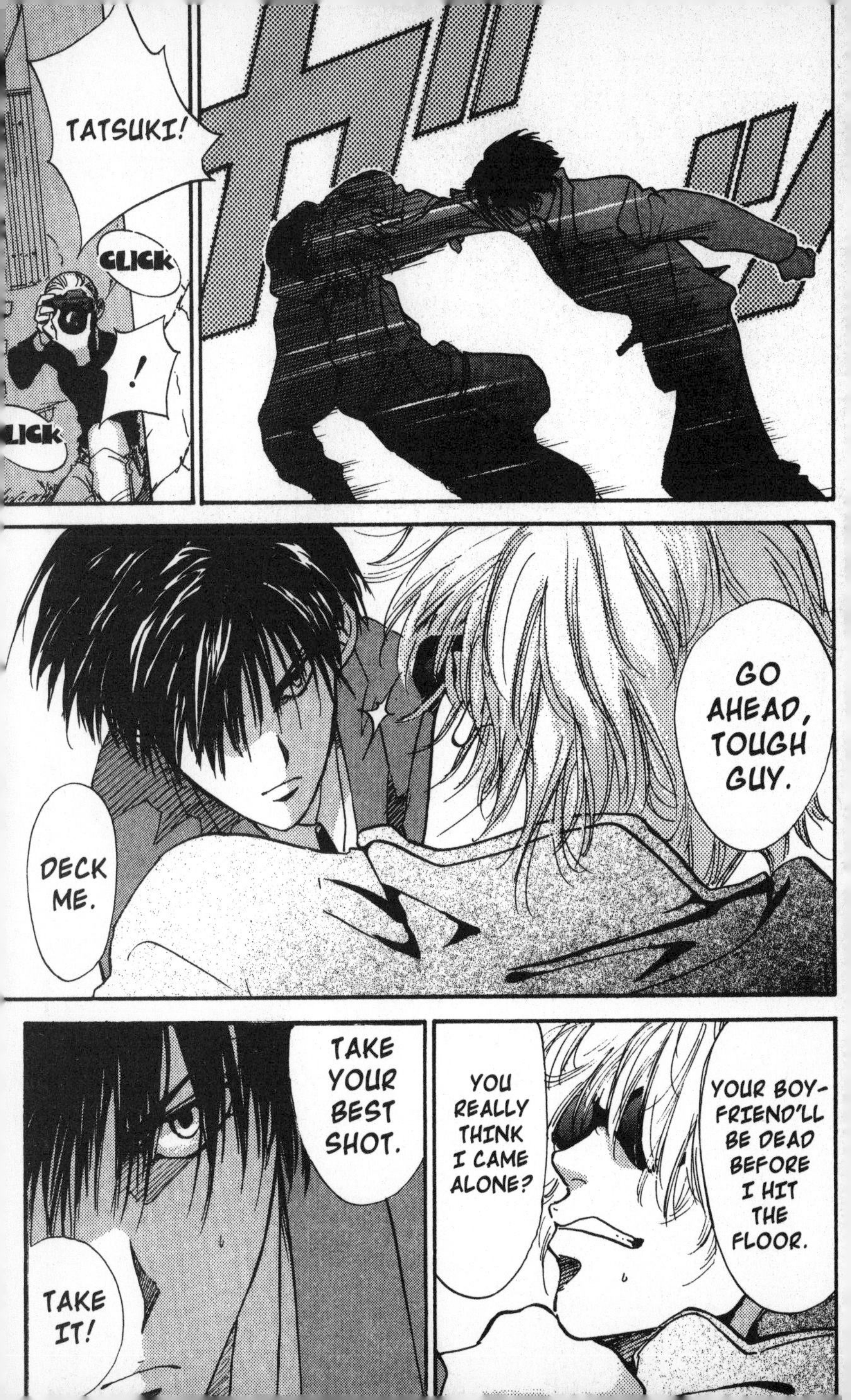
TATSUKI!
CLICK
!
LICK
GO AHEAD, TOUGH GUY.
DECK ME.
YOUR BOY-FRIEND'LL BE DEAD BEFORE I HIT THE FLOOR.
YOU REALLY THINK I CAME ALONE?
TAKE YOUR BEST SHOT.
TAKE IT!

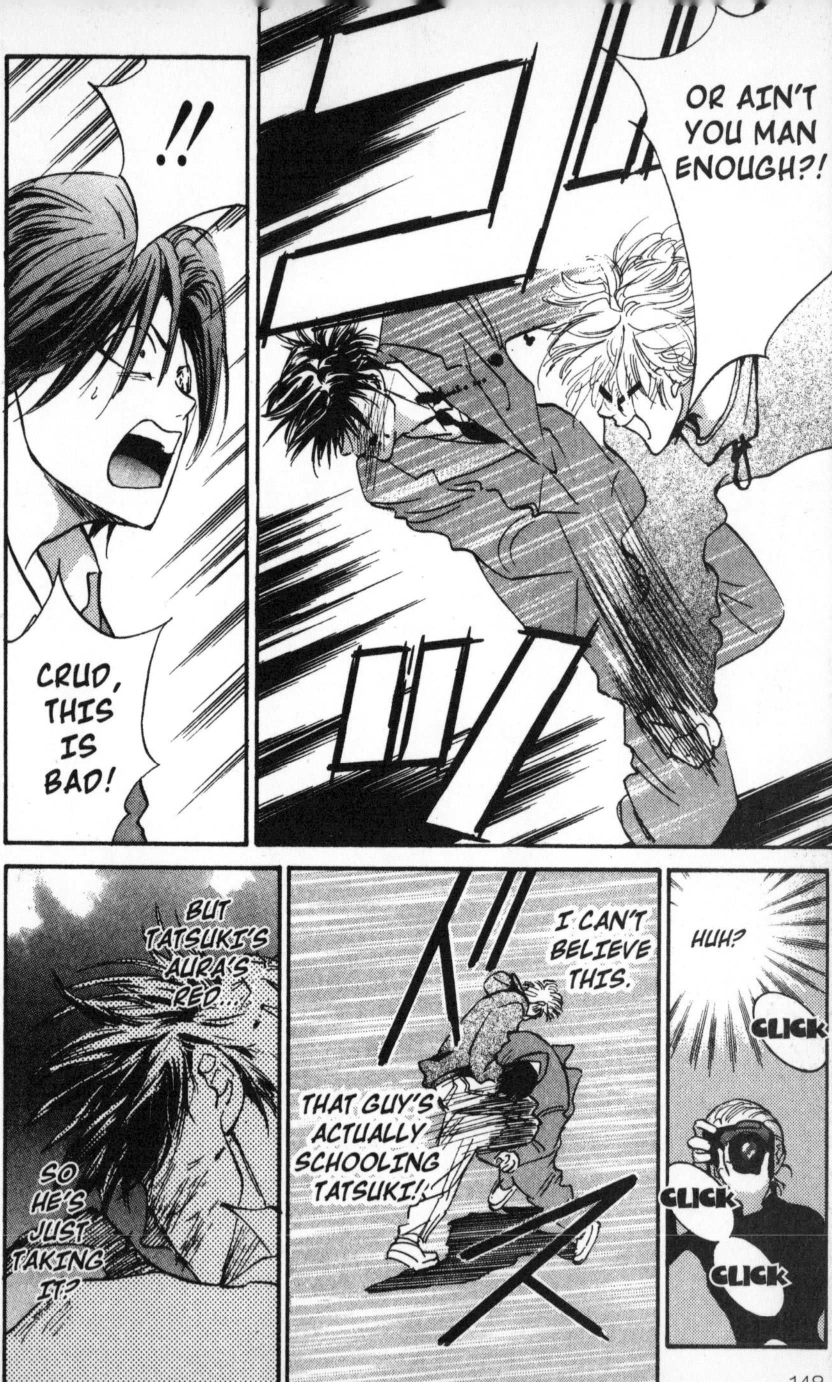
OR AIN'T YOU MAN ENOUGH?!
!!
CRUD, THIS IS BAD!
HUH?
CLICK
CLICK
CLICK
I CAN'T BELIEVE THIS.
THAT GUY'S ACTUALLY SCHOOLING TATSUKI!
BUT TATSUKI'S AURA'S RED...
SO HE'S JUST TAKING IT?

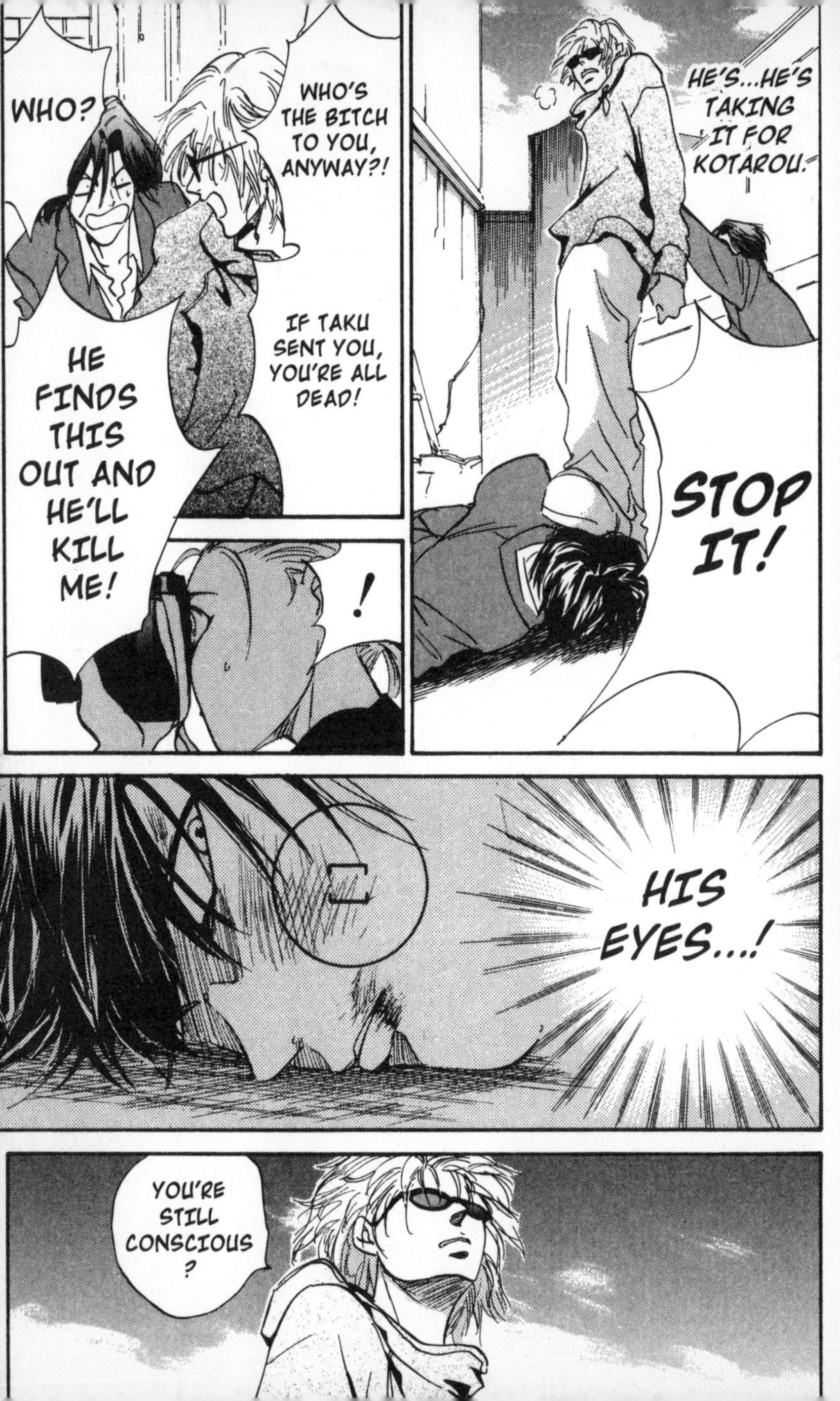
HE'S...HE'S TAKING IT FOR KOTAROU.
STOP IT!
WHO'S THE BITCH TO YOU, ANYWAY?!
WHO?
IF TAKU SENT YOU, YOU'RE ALL DEAD!
HE FINDS THIS OUT AND HE'LL KILL ME!
!
HIS EYES...!
YOU'RE STILL CONSCIOUS?

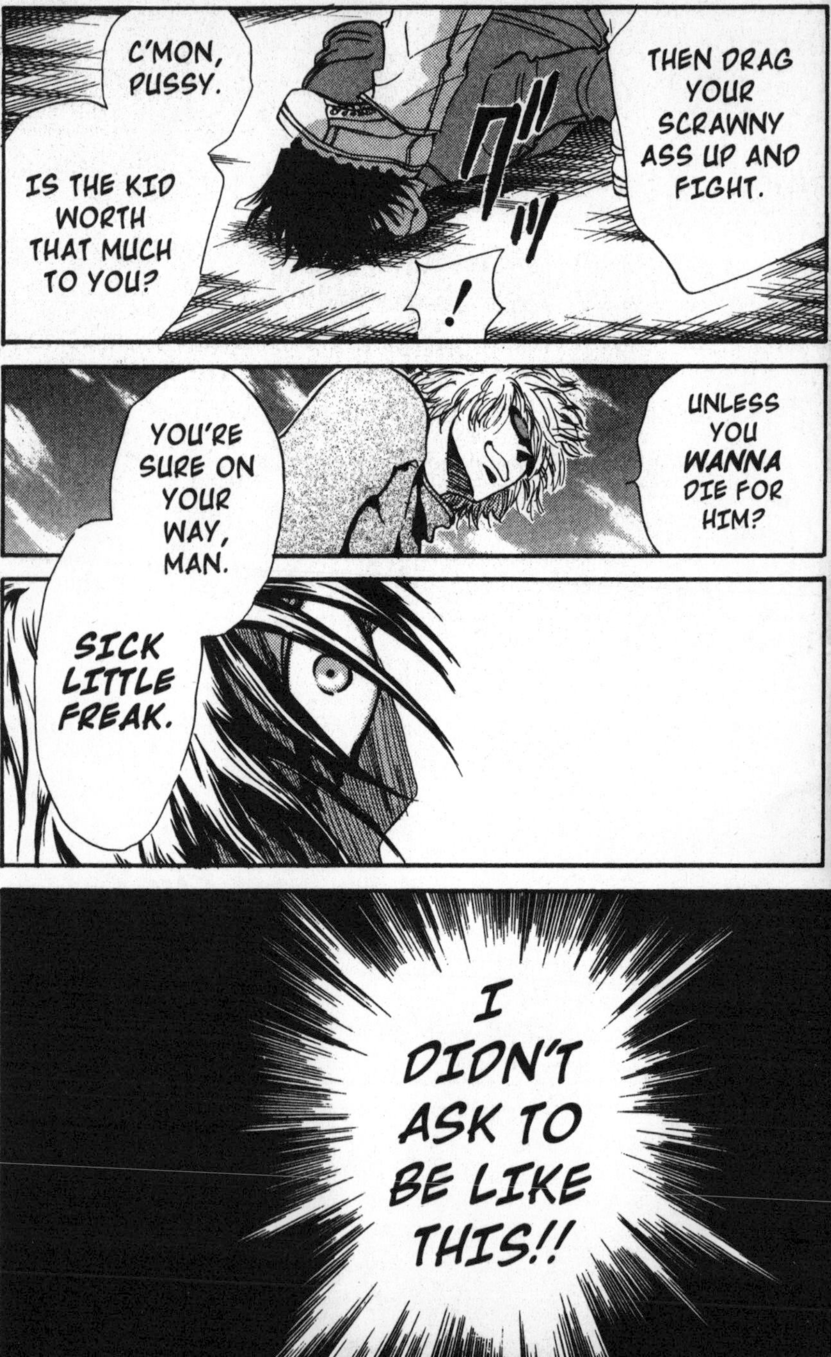
THEN DRAG YOUR SCRAWNY ASS UP AND FIGHT.
C'MON, PUSSY.
IS THE KID WORTH THAT MUCH TO YOU?
!
UNLESS YOU WANNA DIE FOR HIM?
YOU'RE SURE ON YOUR WAY, MAN.
SICK LITTLE FREAK.
I DIDN'T ASK TO BE LIKE THIS!!

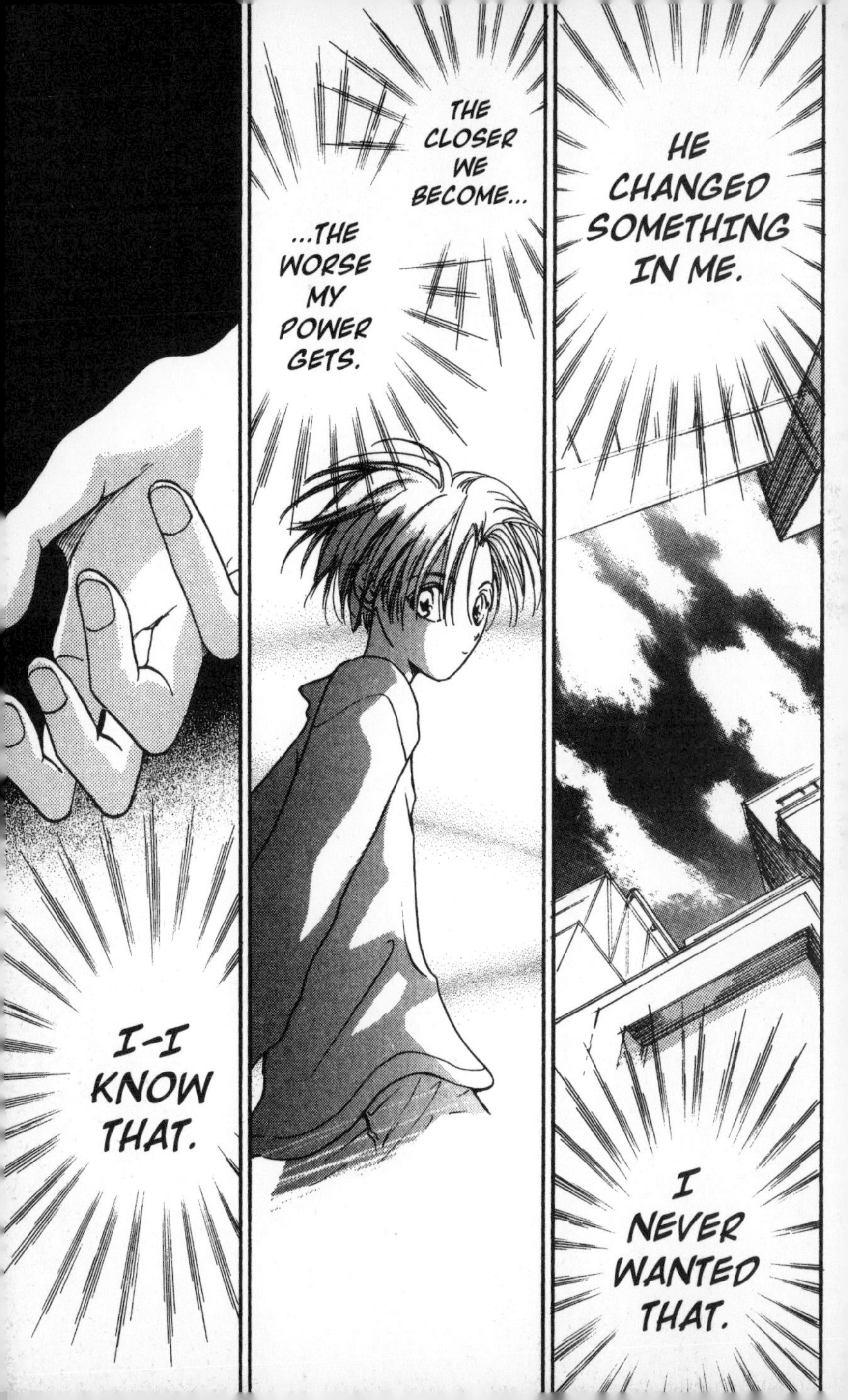
HE CHANGED SOMETHING IN ME.
I NEVER WANTED THAT.
THE CLOSER WE BECOME...
...THE WORSE MY POWER GETS.
I-I KNOW THAT.

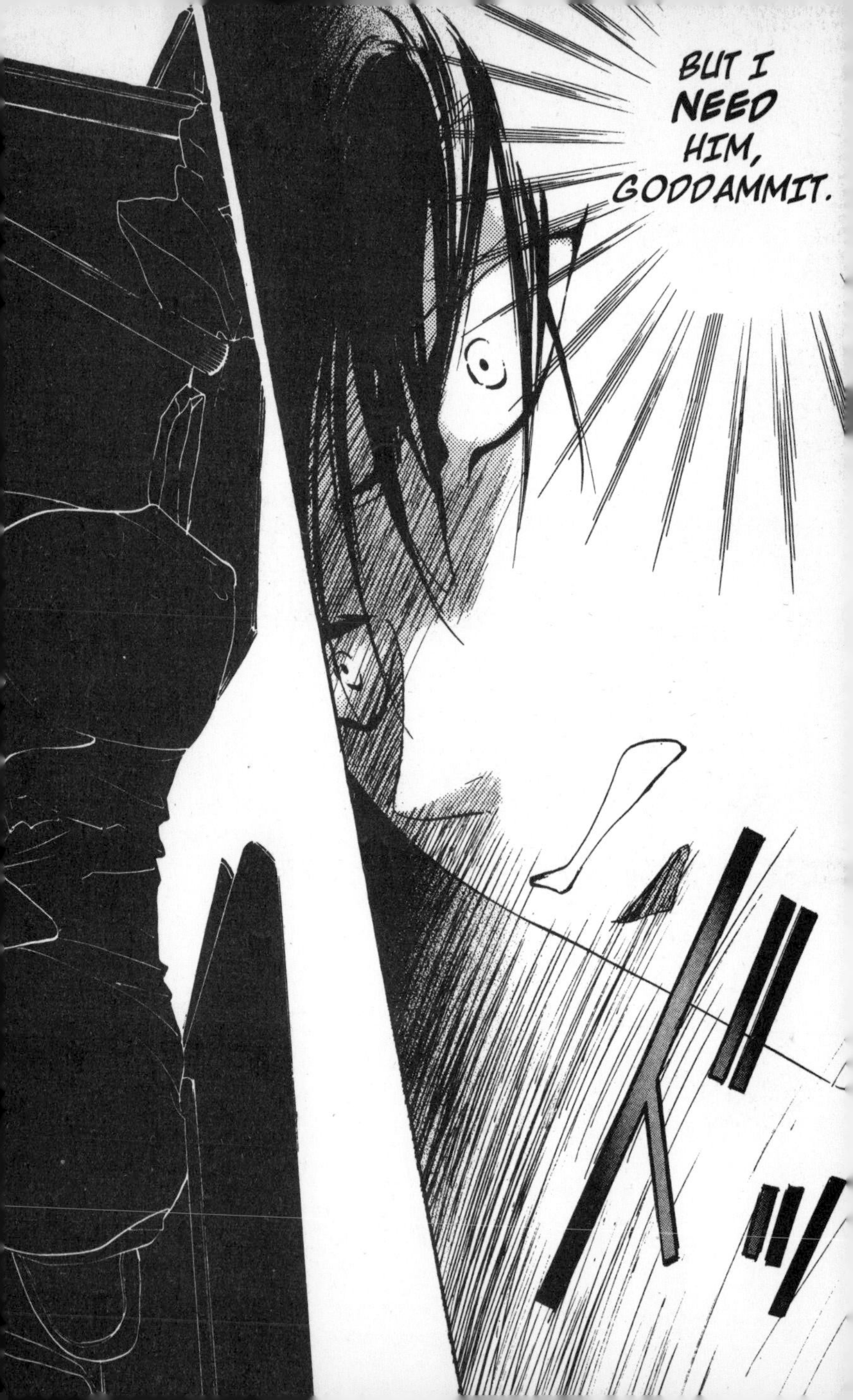
BUT I NEED HIM, GODDAMMIT.

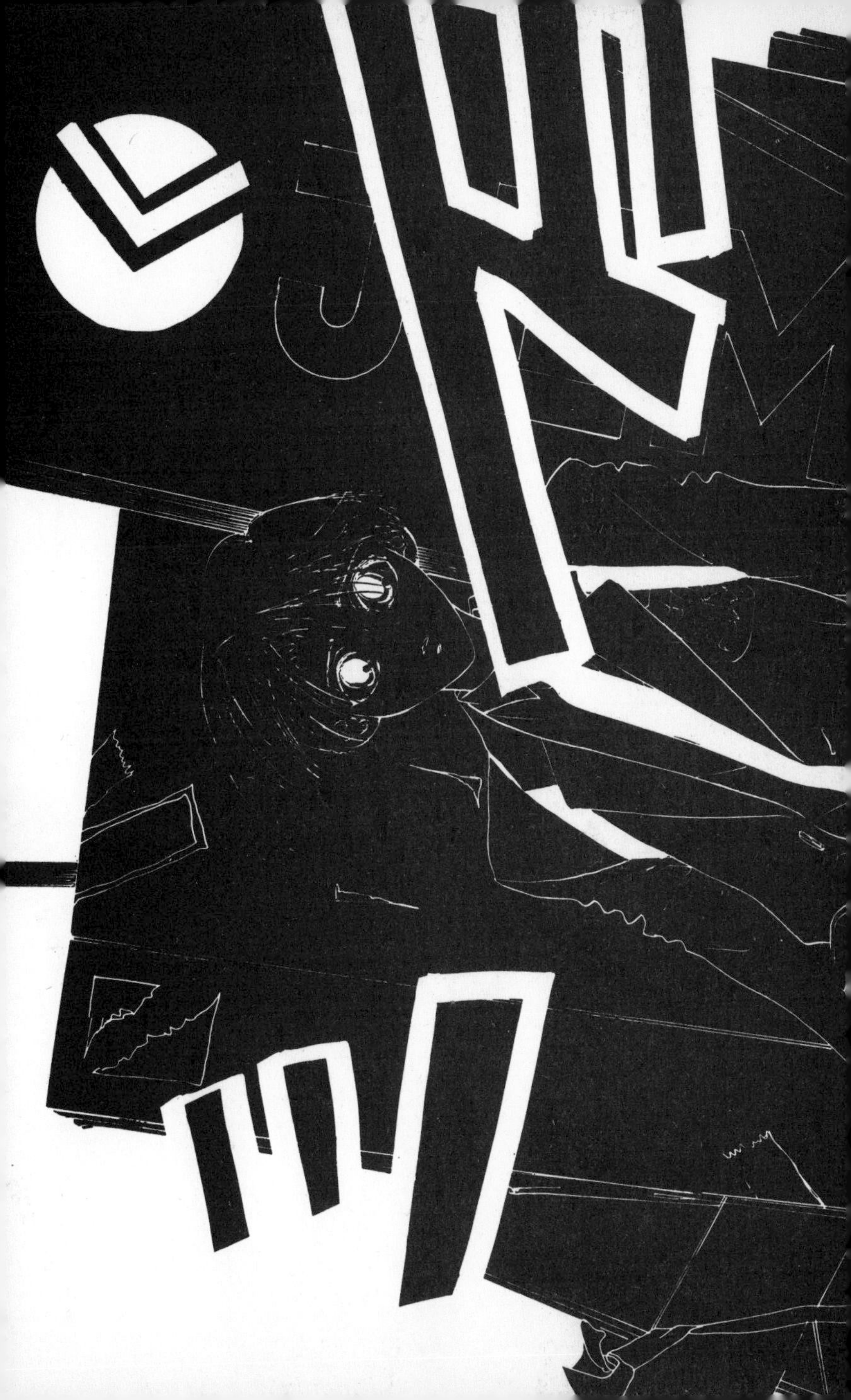

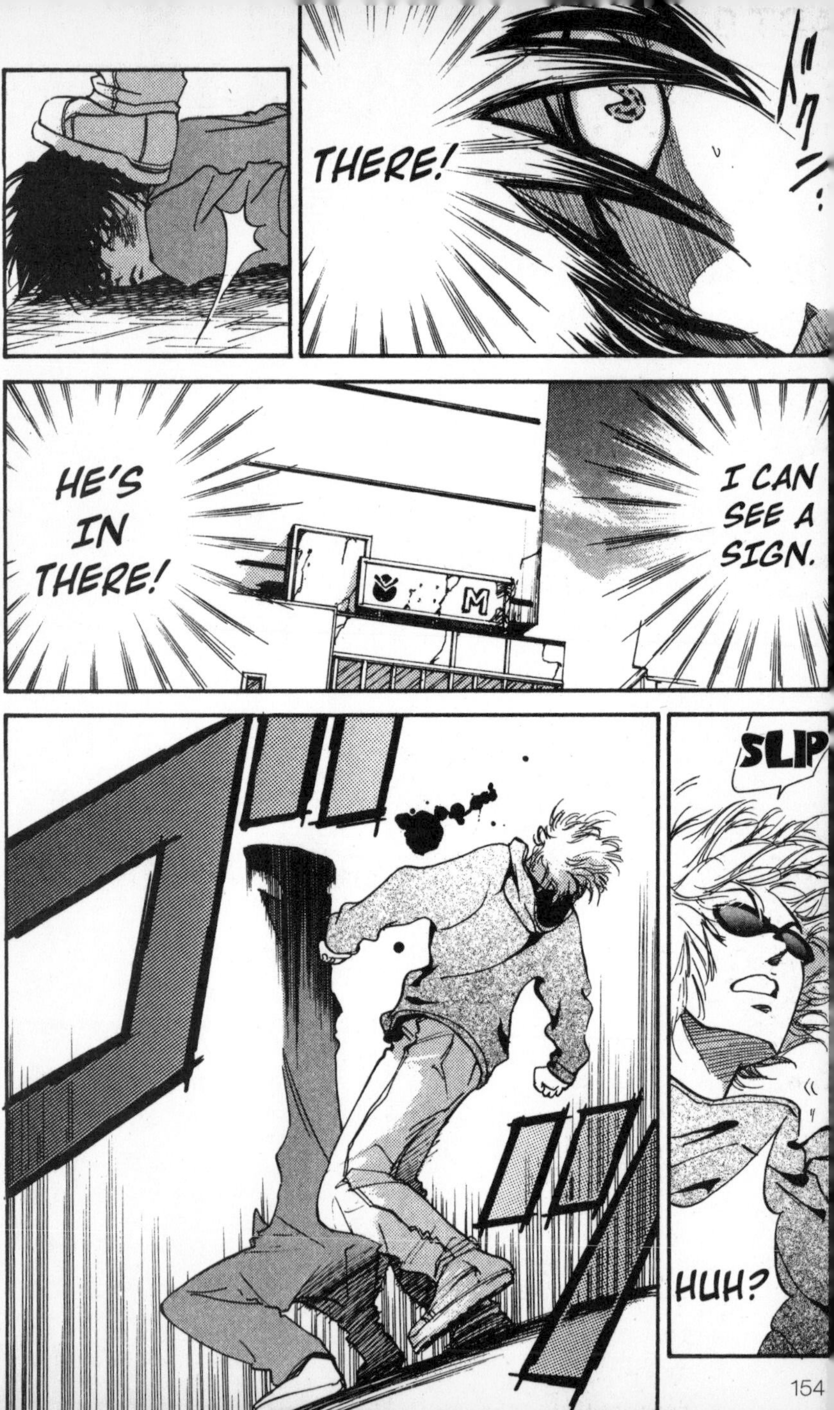
THERE!
I CAN SEE A SIGN.
HE'S IN THERE!
SLIP
HUH?

ACT 9

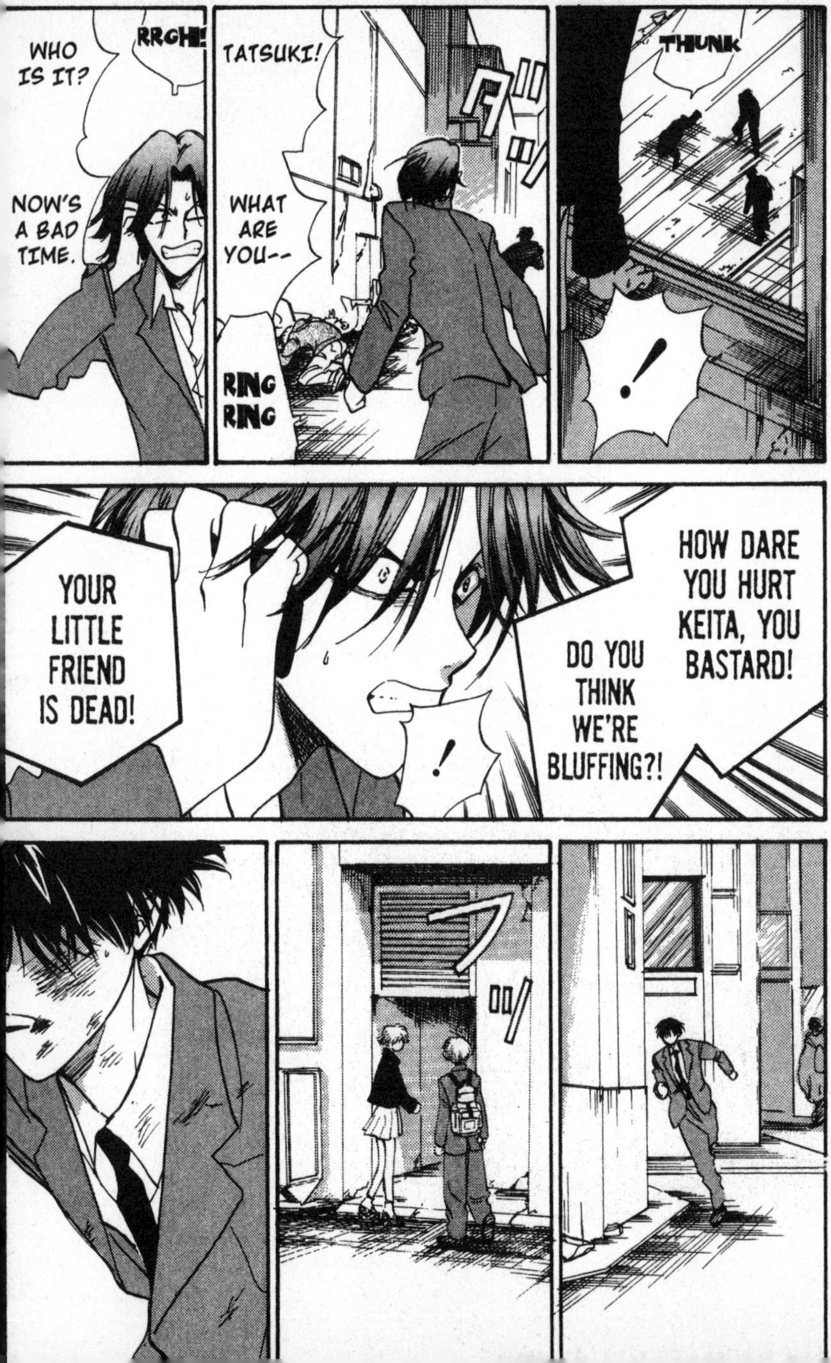
THUNK
!
TATSUKI!
WHAT ARE YOU--
RING RING
RRGH!
WHO IS IT?
NOW'S A BAD TIME.
HOW DARE YOU HURT KEITA, YOU BASTARD!
DO YOU THINK WE'RE BLUFFING?!
!
YOUR LITTLE FRIEND IS DEAD!

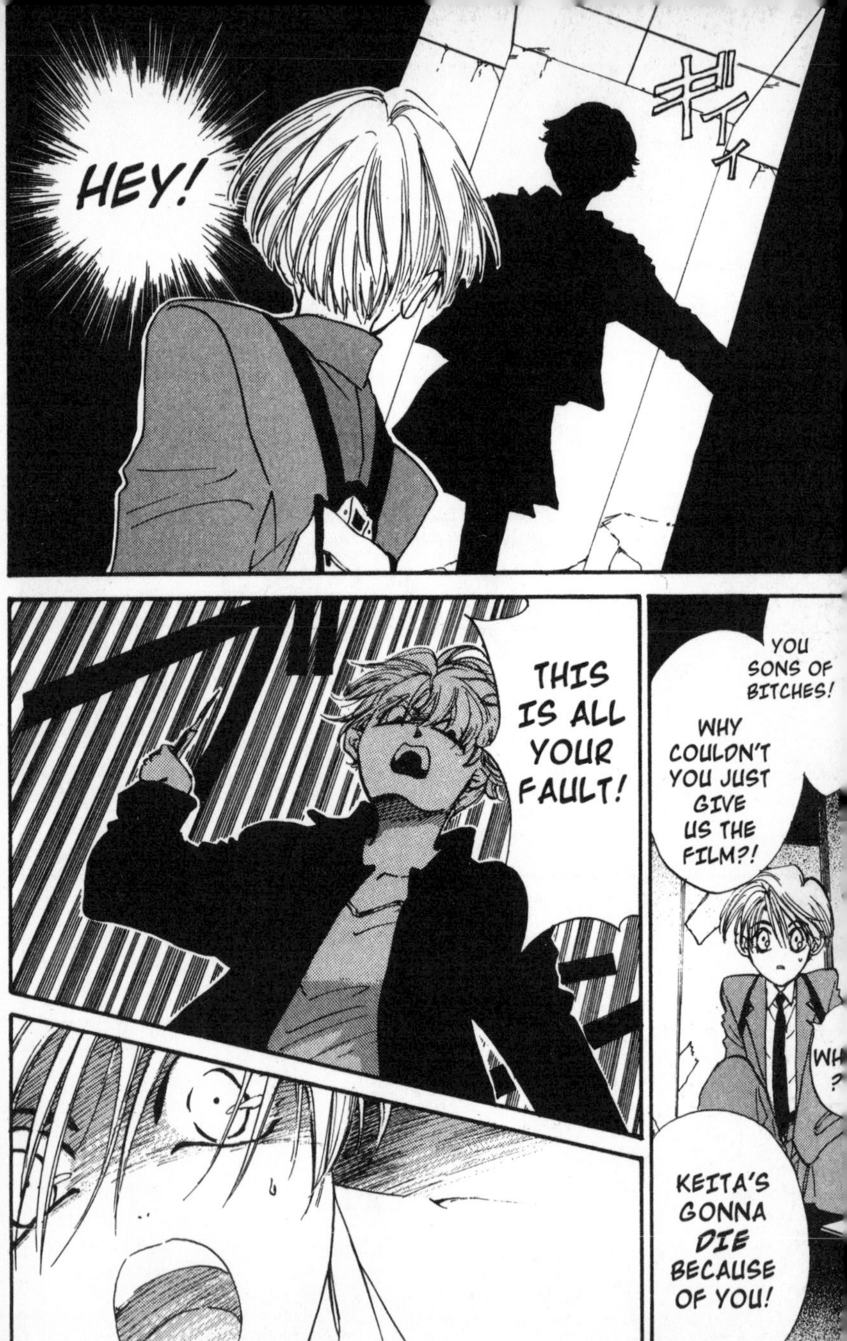
ギイイ
HEY!
YOU SONS OF BITCHES!
WHY COULDN'T YOU JUST GIVE US THE FILM?!
KEITA'S GONNA DIE BECAUSE OF YOU!
THIS IS ALL YOUR FAULT!

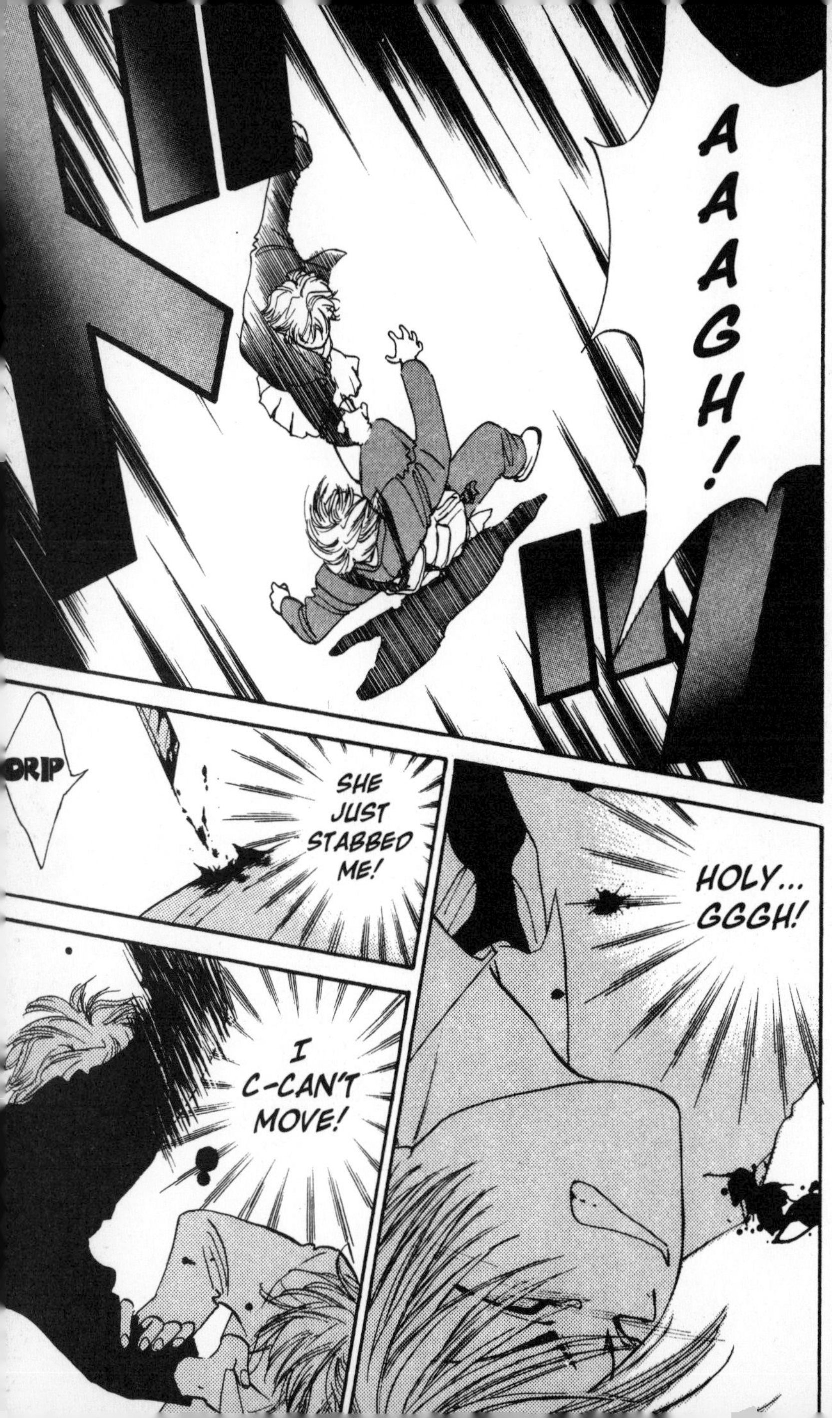
AAAAGH!
HOLY... GGGH!
DRIP
SHE JUST STABBED ME!
I C-CAN'T MOVE!

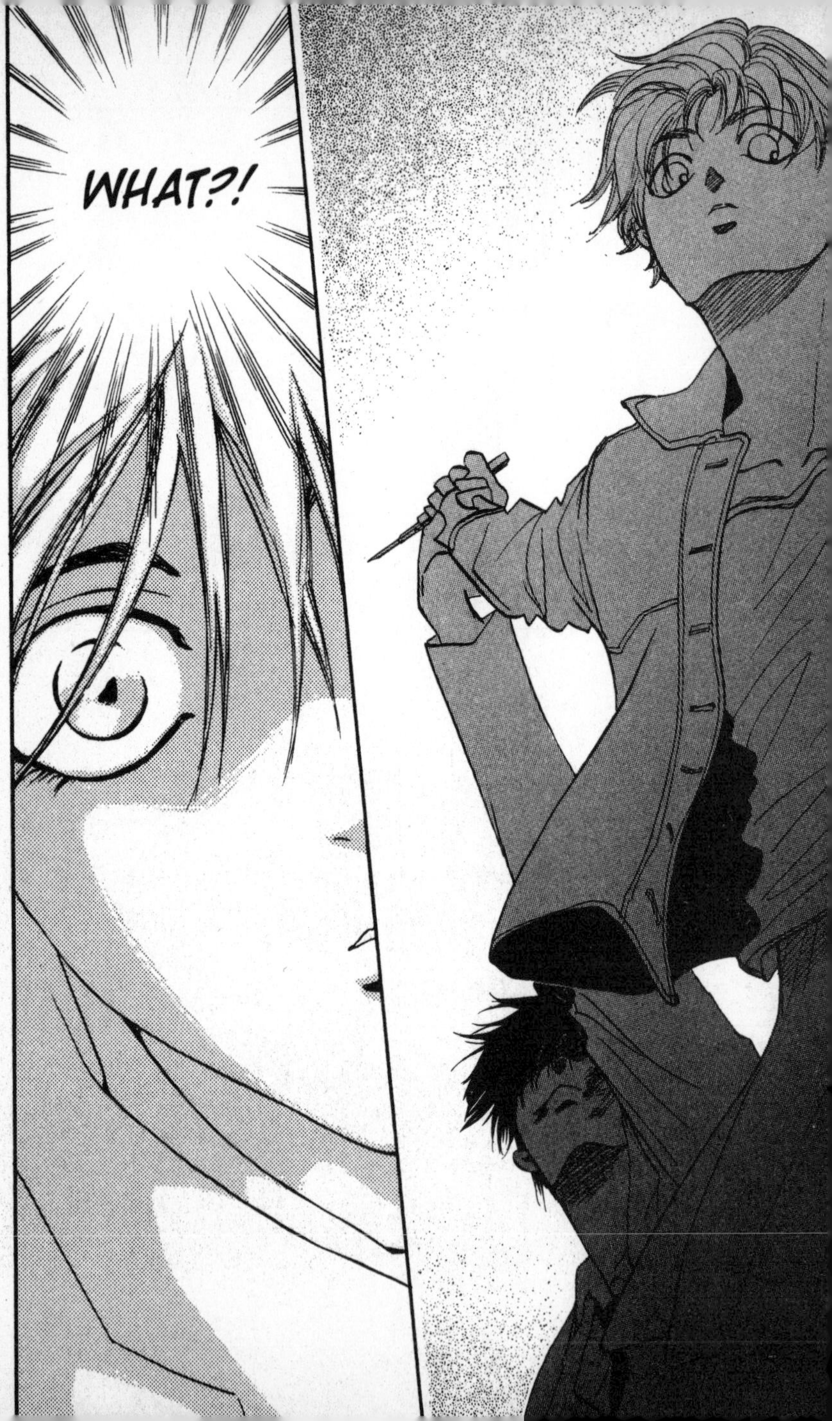
WHAT?!

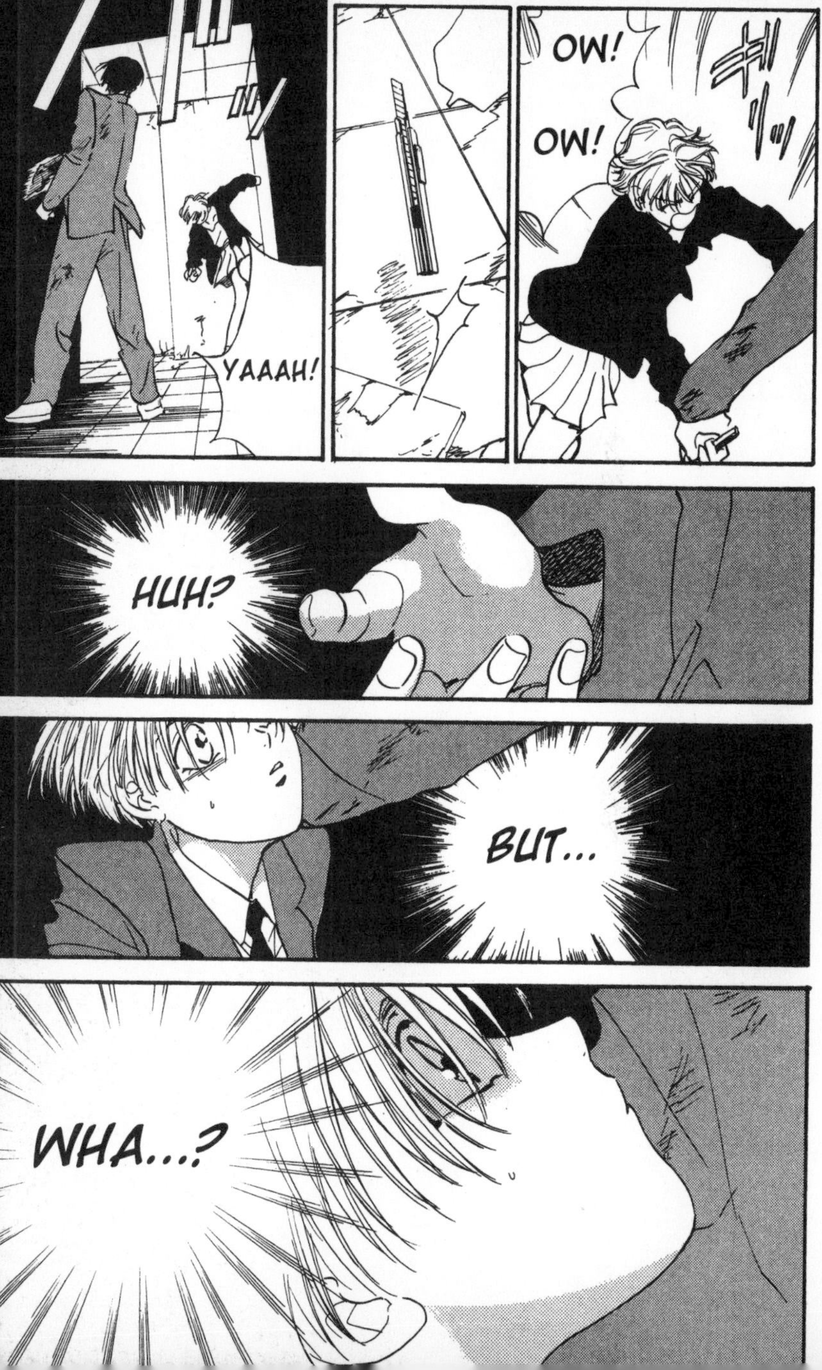
OW!
OW!
ギリッ
YAAAH!
HUH?
BUT...
WHA...?

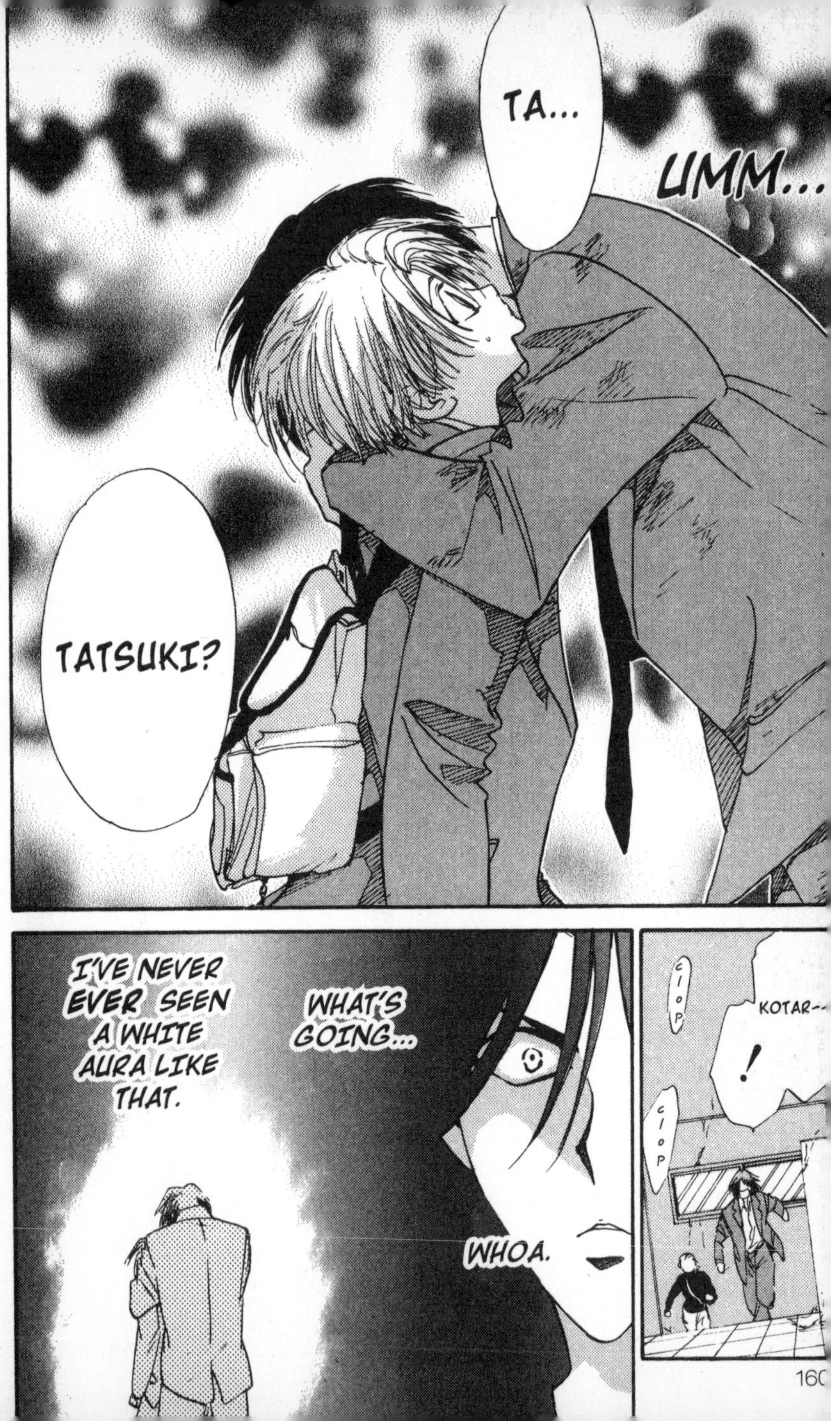
TA...
UMM...
TATSUKI?
clop
KOTAR--
!
clop
!!
WHAT'S GOING...
I'VE NEVER EVER SEEN A WHITE AURA LIKE THAT.
WHOA.

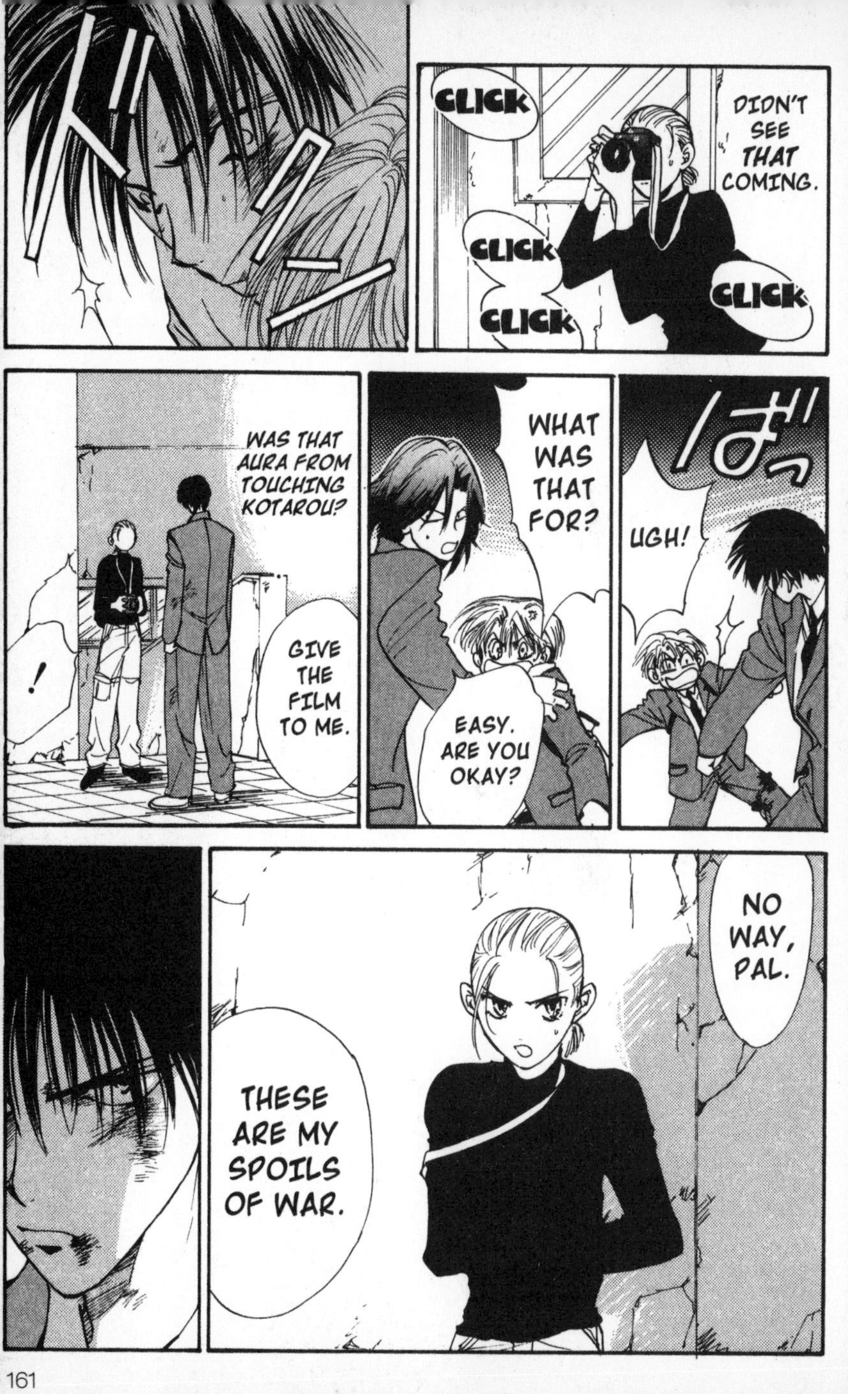

DIDN'T SEE THAT COMING.
CLICK
CLICK
CLICK
CLICK
ばっ
UGH!
WHAT WAS THAT FOR?
EASY. ARE YOU OKAY?
WAS THAT AURA FROM TOUCHING KOTAROU?
GIVE THE FILM TO ME.
!
NO WAY, PAL.
THESE ARE MY SPOILS OF WAR.

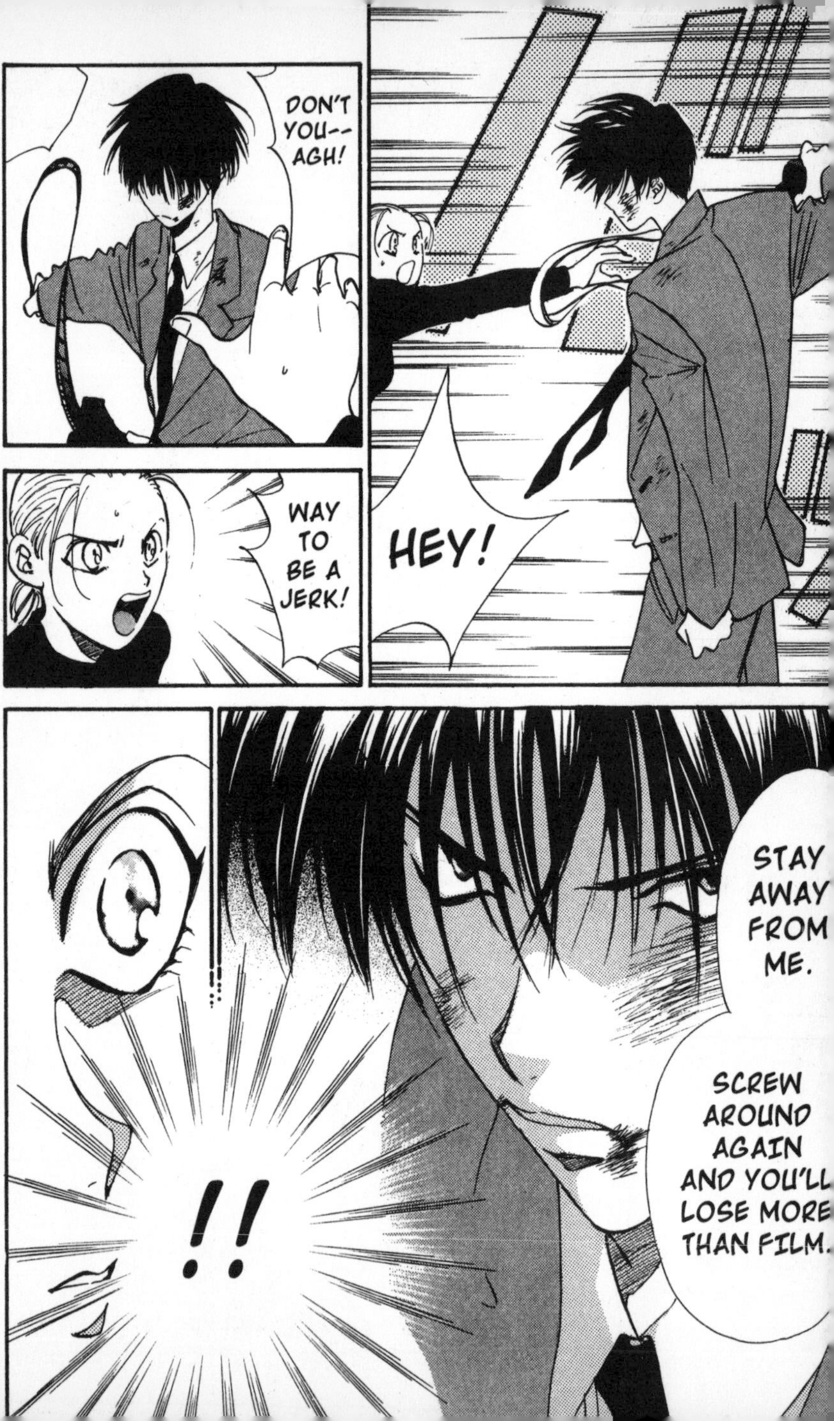
HEY!
DON'T YOU-- AGH!
WAY TO BE A JERK!
STAY AWAY FROM ME.
SCREW AROUND AGAIN AND YOU'LL LOSE MORE THAN FILM.
!!

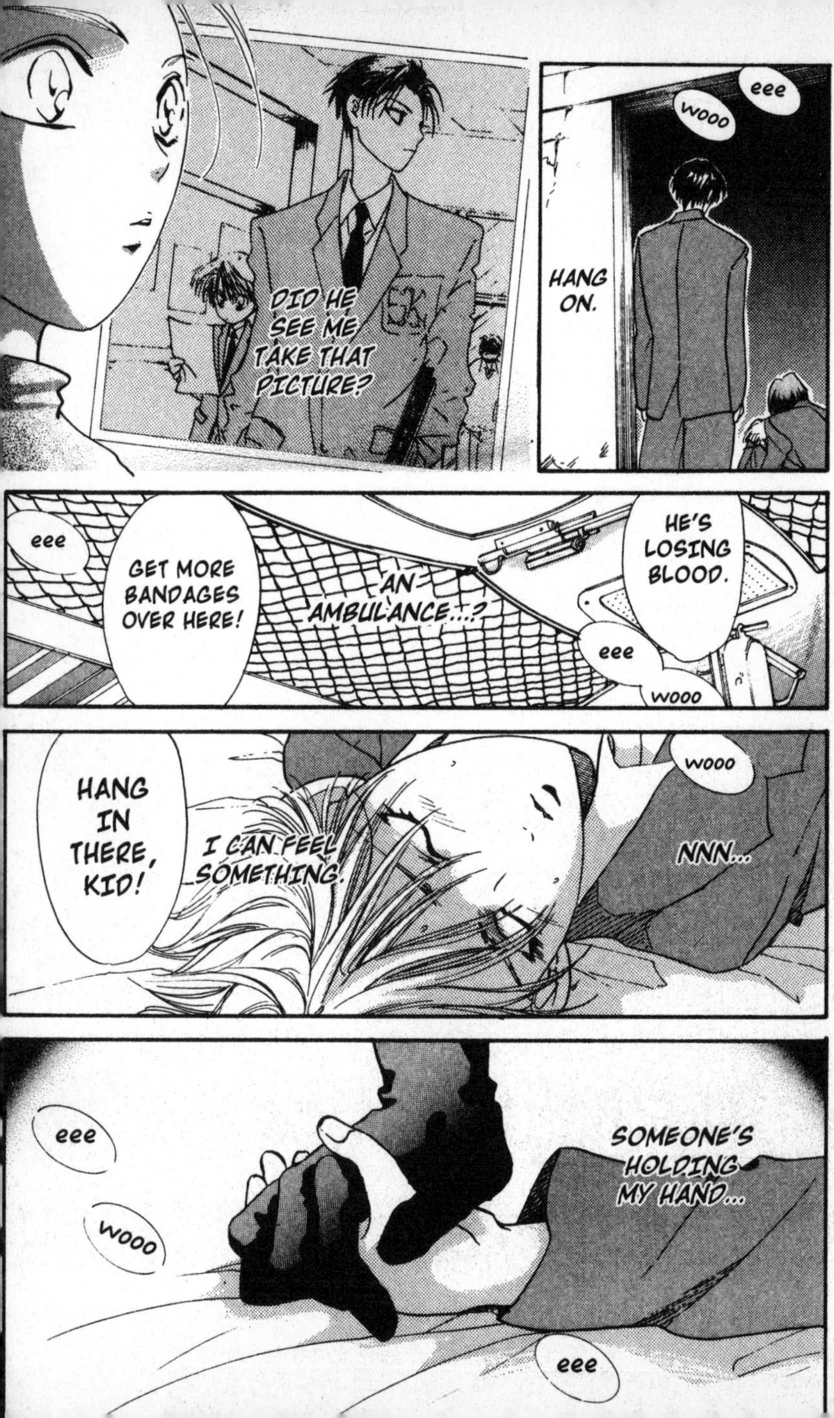
eee
wooo
HANG ON.
DID HE SEE ME TAKE THAT PICTURE?
HE'S LOSING BLOOD.
eee
wooo
AN AMBULANCE...?
GET MORE BANDAGES OVER HERE!
eee
wooo
NNN...
I CAN FEEL SOMETHING.
HANG IN THERE, KID!
SOMEONE'S HOLDING MY HAND...
eee
wooo
eee

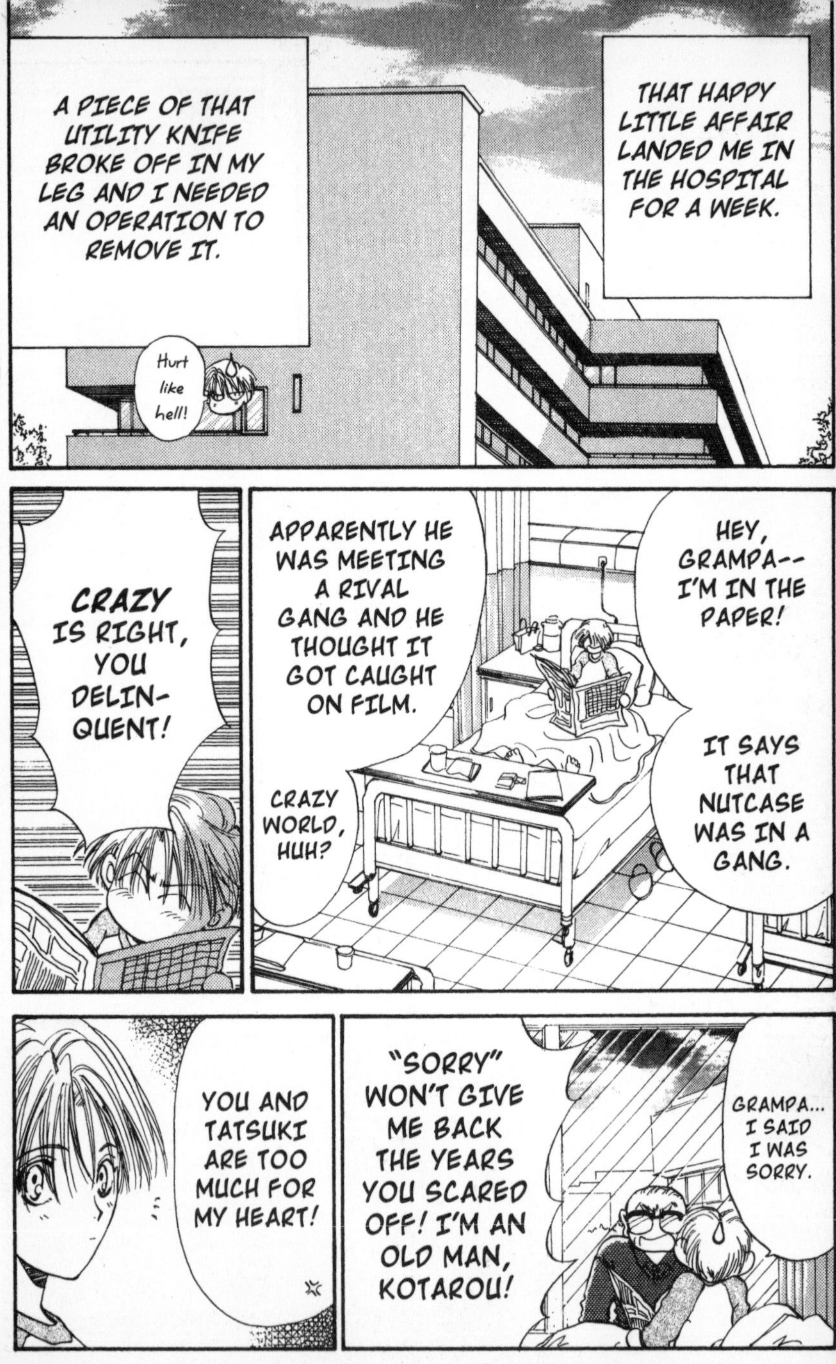
THAT HAPPY LITTLE AFFAIR LANDED ME IN THE HOSPITAL FOR A WEEK.
A PIECE OF THAT UTILITY KNIFE BROKE OFF IN MY LEG AND I NEEDED AN OPERATION TO REMOVE IT.
Hurt like hell!
HEY, GRAMPA-- I'M IN THE PAPER!
IT SAYS THAT NUTCASE WAS IN A GANG.
APPARENTLY HE WAS MEETING A RIVAL GANG AND HE THOUGHT IT GOT CAUGHT ON FILM.
CRAZY WORLD, HUH?
CRAZY IS RIGHT, YOU DELIN-QUENT!
GRAMPA... I SAID I WAS SORRY.
"SORRY" WON'T GIVE ME BACK THE YEARS YOU SCARED OFF! I'M AN OLD MAN, KOTAROU!
YOU AND TATSUKI ARE TOO MUCH FOR MY HEART!

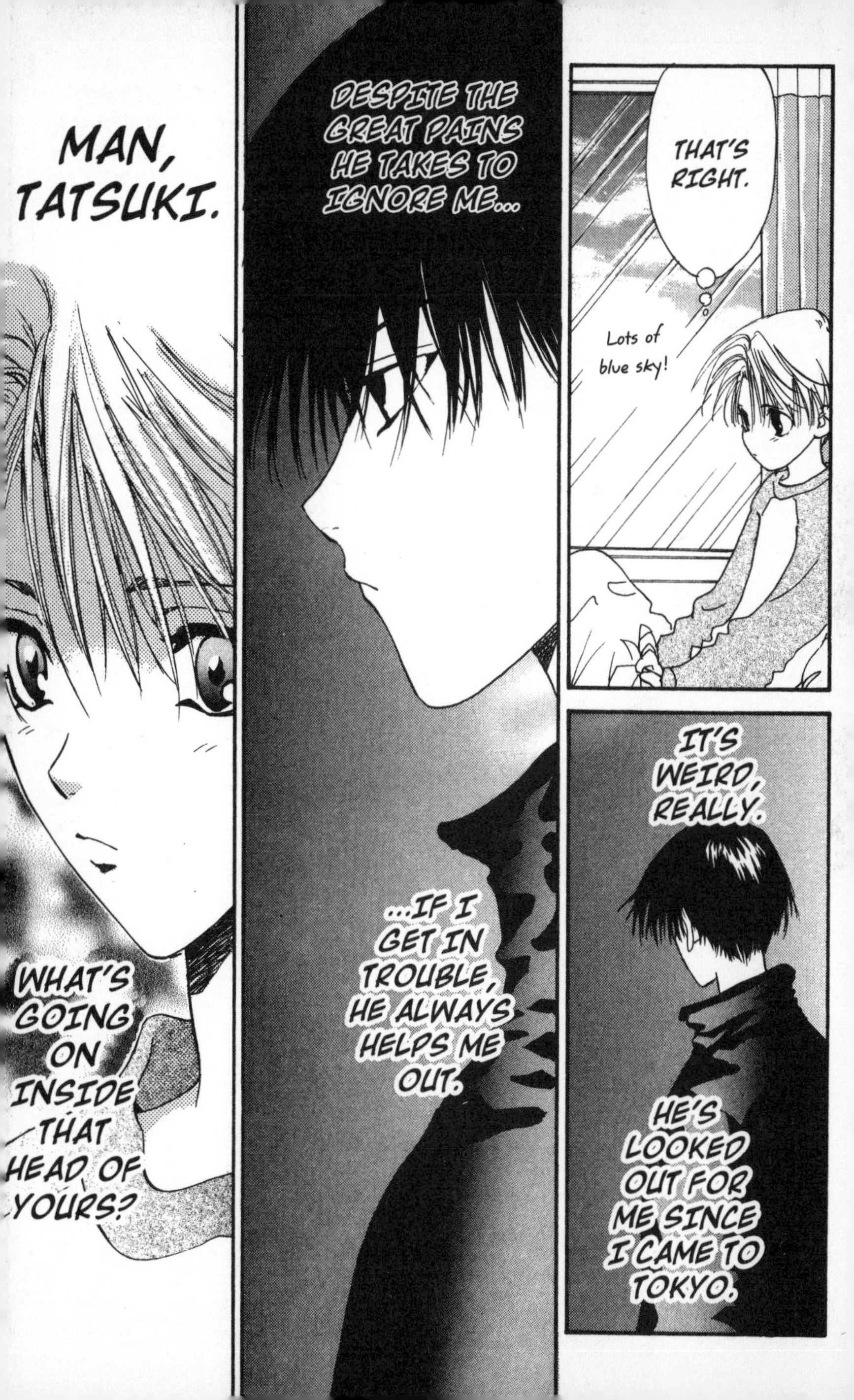
THAT'S RIGHT.
Lots of blue sky!
IT'S WEIRD, REALLY.
HE'S LOOKED OUT FOR ME SINCE I CAME TO TOKYO.
DESPITE THE GREAT PAINS HE TAKES TO IGNORE ME...
...IF I GET IN TROUBLE, HE ALWAYS HELPS ME OUT.
MAN, TATSUKI.
WHAT'S GOING ON INSIDE THAT HEAD OF YOURS?

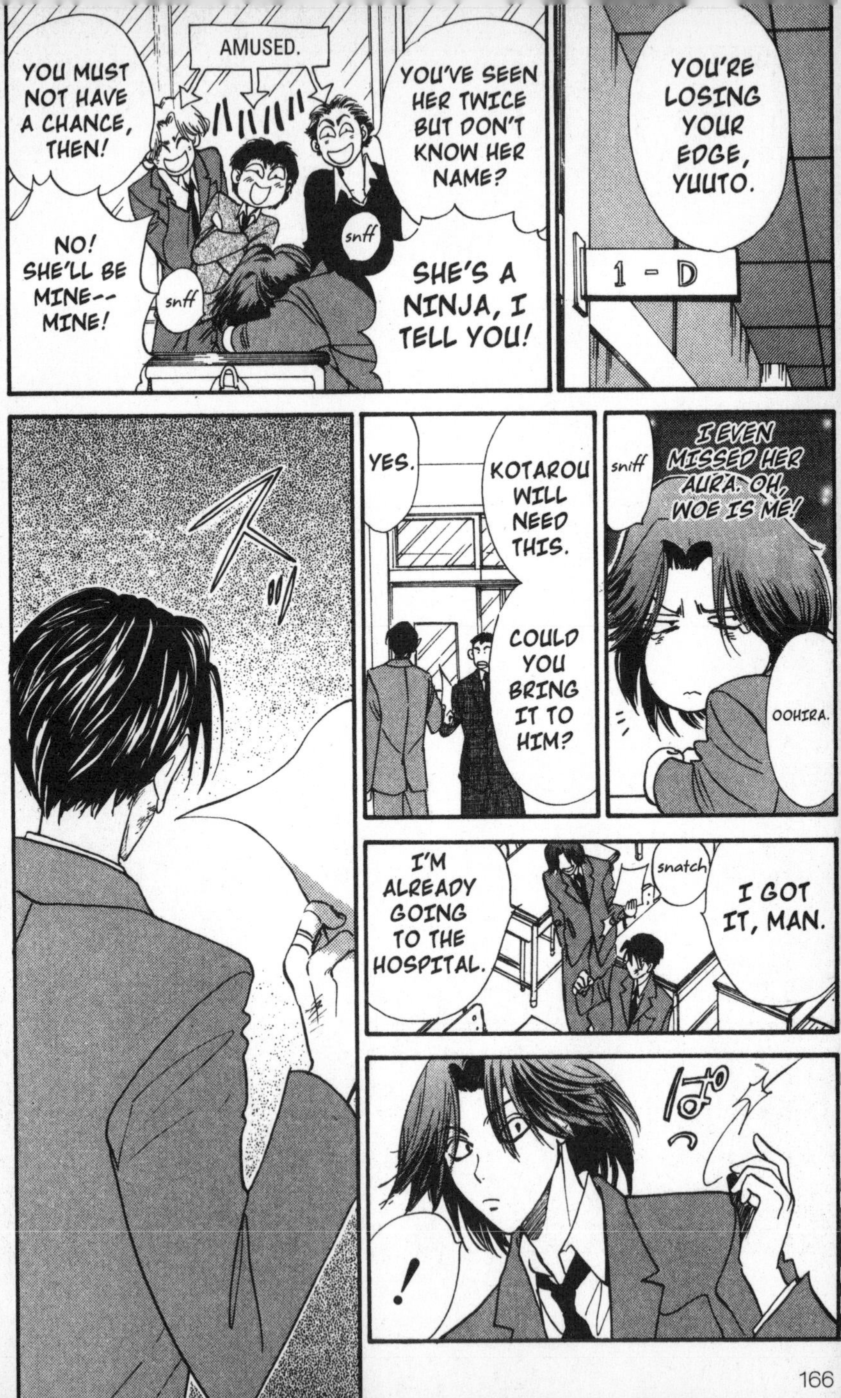
YOU'RE LOSING YOUR EDGE, YUUTO.
1 - D
AMUSED.
YOU'VE SEEN HER TWICE BUT DON'T KNOW HER NAME?
YOU MUST NOT HAVE A CHANCE, THEN!
snff
SHE'S A NINJA, I TELL YOU!
NO! SHE'LL BE MINE--MINE!
snff
I EVEN MISSED HER AURA. OH, WOE IS ME!
sniff
OOHIRA.
KOTAROU WILL NEED THIS.
YES.
COULD YOU BRING IT TO HIM?
I GOT IT, MAN.
snatch
I'M ALREADY GOING TO THE HOSPITAL.
ぱっ
!

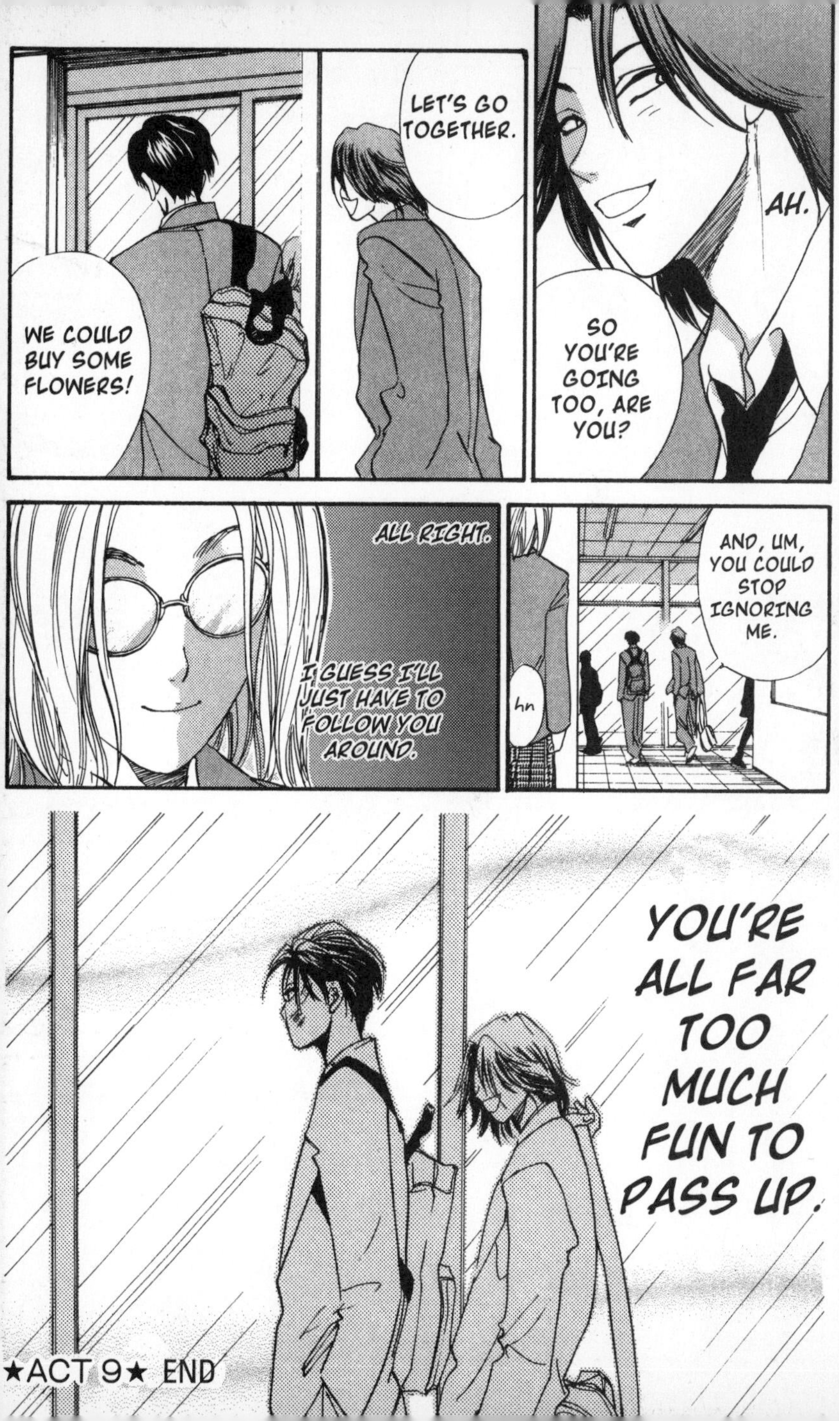
AH.
SO YOU'RE GOING TOO, ARE YOU?
LET'S GO TOGETHER.
WE COULD BUY SOME FLOWERS!
AND, UM, YOU COULD STOP IGNORING ME.
hn
ALL RIGHT.
I GUESS I'LL JUST HAVE TO FOLLOW YOU AROUND.
YOU'RE ALL FAR TOO MUCH FUN TO PASS UP.
★ACT 9★ END

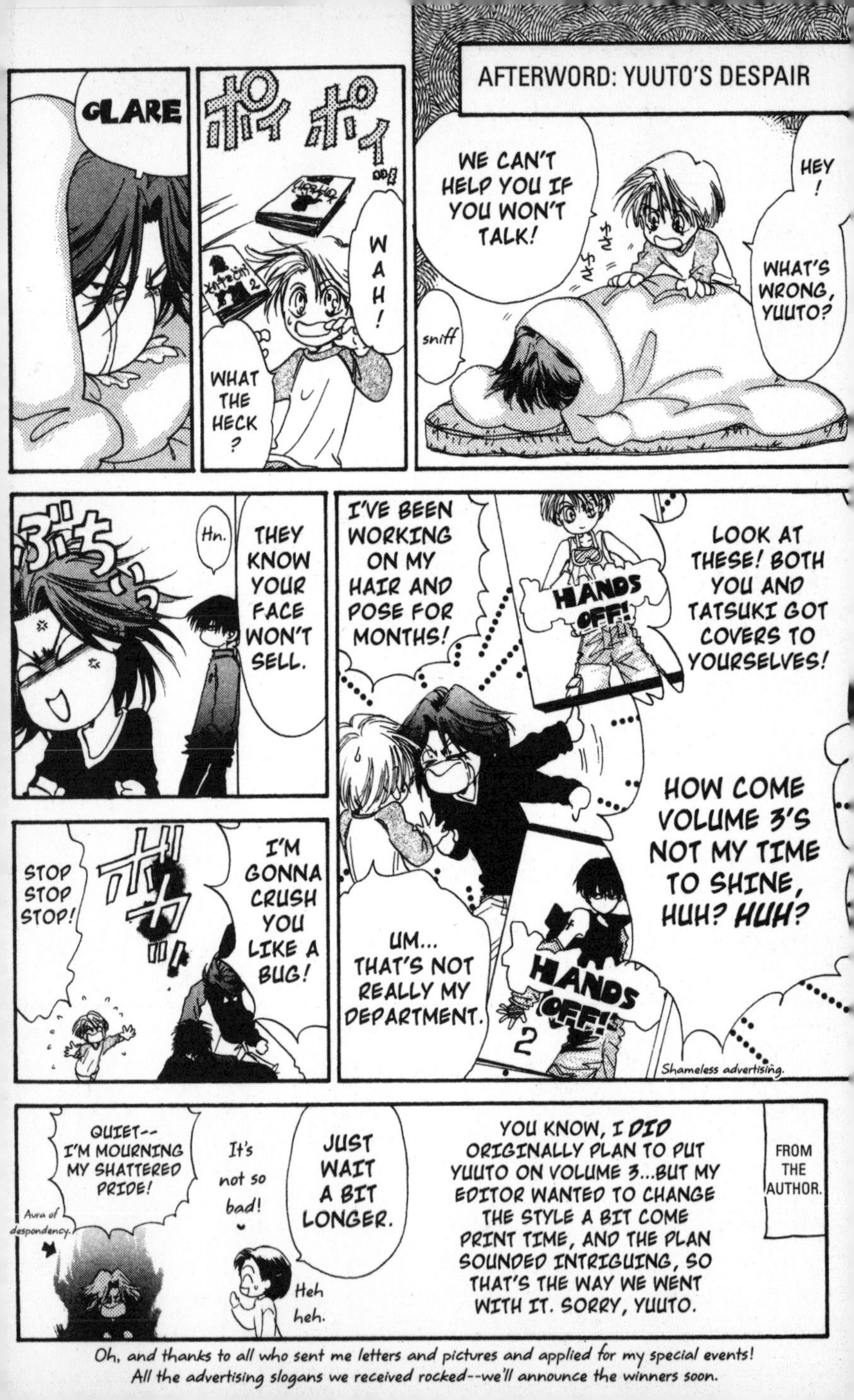

AFTERWORD: YUUTO'S DESPAIR
HEY! WHAT'S WRONG, YUUTO?
WE CAN'T HELP YOU IF YOU WON'T TALK!
sniff
ポイ ポイ
WAH!
WHAT THE HECK?
GLARE
LOOK AT THESE! BOTH YOU AND TATSUKI GOT COVERS TO YOURSELVES!
HANDS OFF!
I'VE BEEN WORKING ON MY HAIR AND POSE FOR MONTHS!
HOW COME VOLUME 3'S NOT MY TIME TO SHINE, HUH? HUH?
HANDS OFF! 2
UM... THAT'S NOT REALLY MY DEPARTMENT.
Shameless advertising.
THEY KNOW YOUR FACE WON'T SELL.
Hn.
I'M GONNA CRUSH YOU LIKE A BUG!
STOP STOP STOP!
FROM THE AUTHOR.
YOU KNOW, I DID ORIGINALLY PLAN TO PUT YUUTO ON VOLUME 3...BUT MY EDITOR WANTED TO CHANGE THE STYLE A BIT COME PRINT TIME, AND THE PLAN SOUNDED INTRIGUING, SO THAT'S THE WAY WE WENT WITH IT. SORRY, YUUTO.
JUST WAIT A BIT LONGER.
It's not so bad!
Heh heh.
QUIET-- I'M MOURNING MY SHATTERED PRIDE!
Aura of despondency.

Oh, and thanks to all who sent me letters and pictures and applied for my special events! All the advertising slogans we received rocked--we'll announce the winners soon.

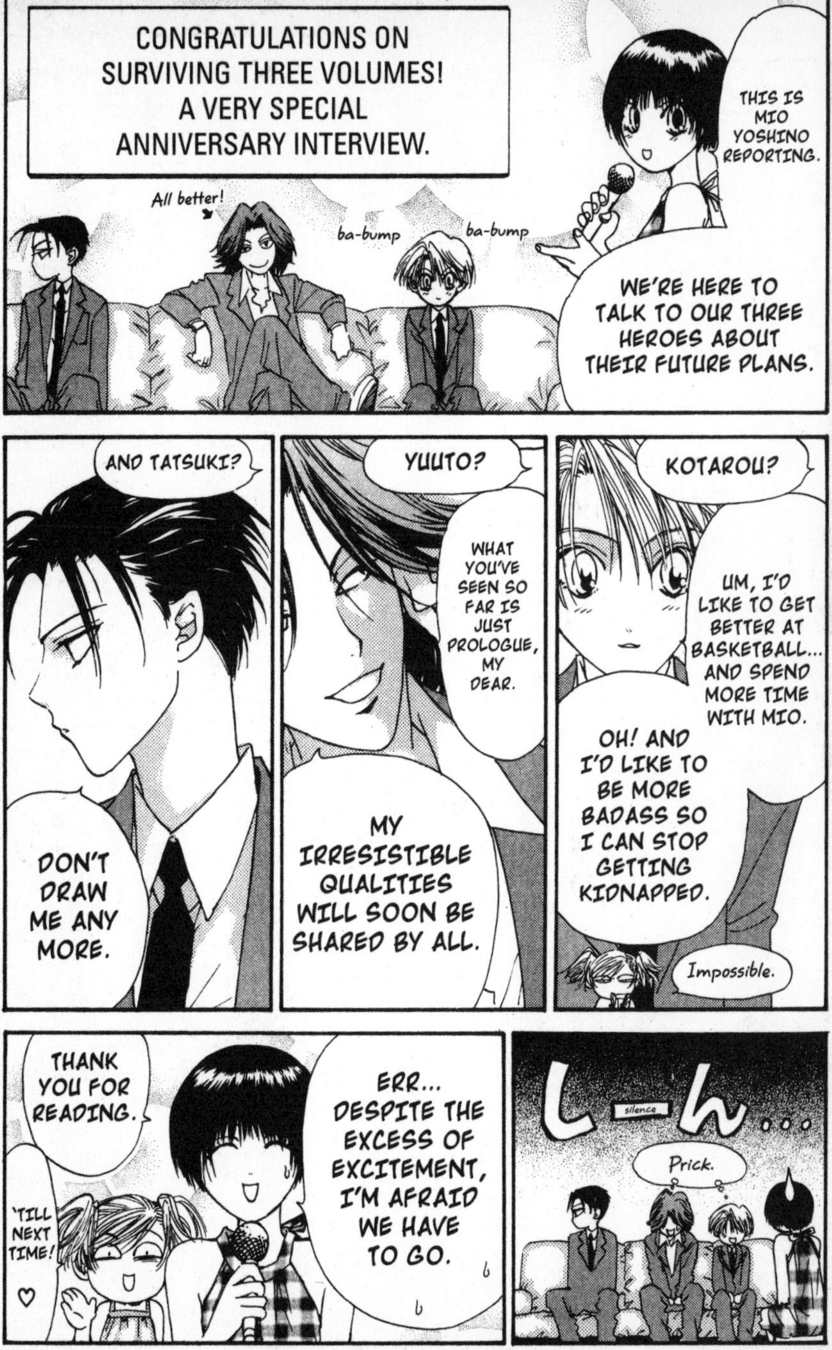
CONGRATULATIONS ON SURVIVING THREE VOLUMES! A VERY SPECIAL ANNIVERSARY INTERVIEW.
THIS IS MIO YOSHINO REPORTING.
All better!
ba-bump
ba-bump
WE'RE HERE TO TALK TO OUR THREE HEROES ABOUT THEIR FUTURE PLANS.
KOTAROU?
UM, I'D LIKE TO GET BETTER AT BASKETBALL... AND SPEND MORE TIME WITH MIO.
OH! AND I'D LIKE TO BE MORE BADASS SO I CAN STOP GETTING KIDNAPPED.
Impossible.
YUUTO?
WHAT YOU'VE SEEN SO FAR IS JUST PROLOGUE, MY DEAR.
MY IRRESISTIBLE QUALITIES WILL SOON BE SHARED BY ALL.
AND TATSUKI?
DON'T DRAW ME ANY MORE.
しーん...
silence
Prick.
ERR... DESPITE THE EXCESS OF EXCITEMENT, I'M AFRAID WE HAVE TO GO.
THANK YOU FOR READING.
'TILL NEXT TIME! ♡

AFTERWORD END

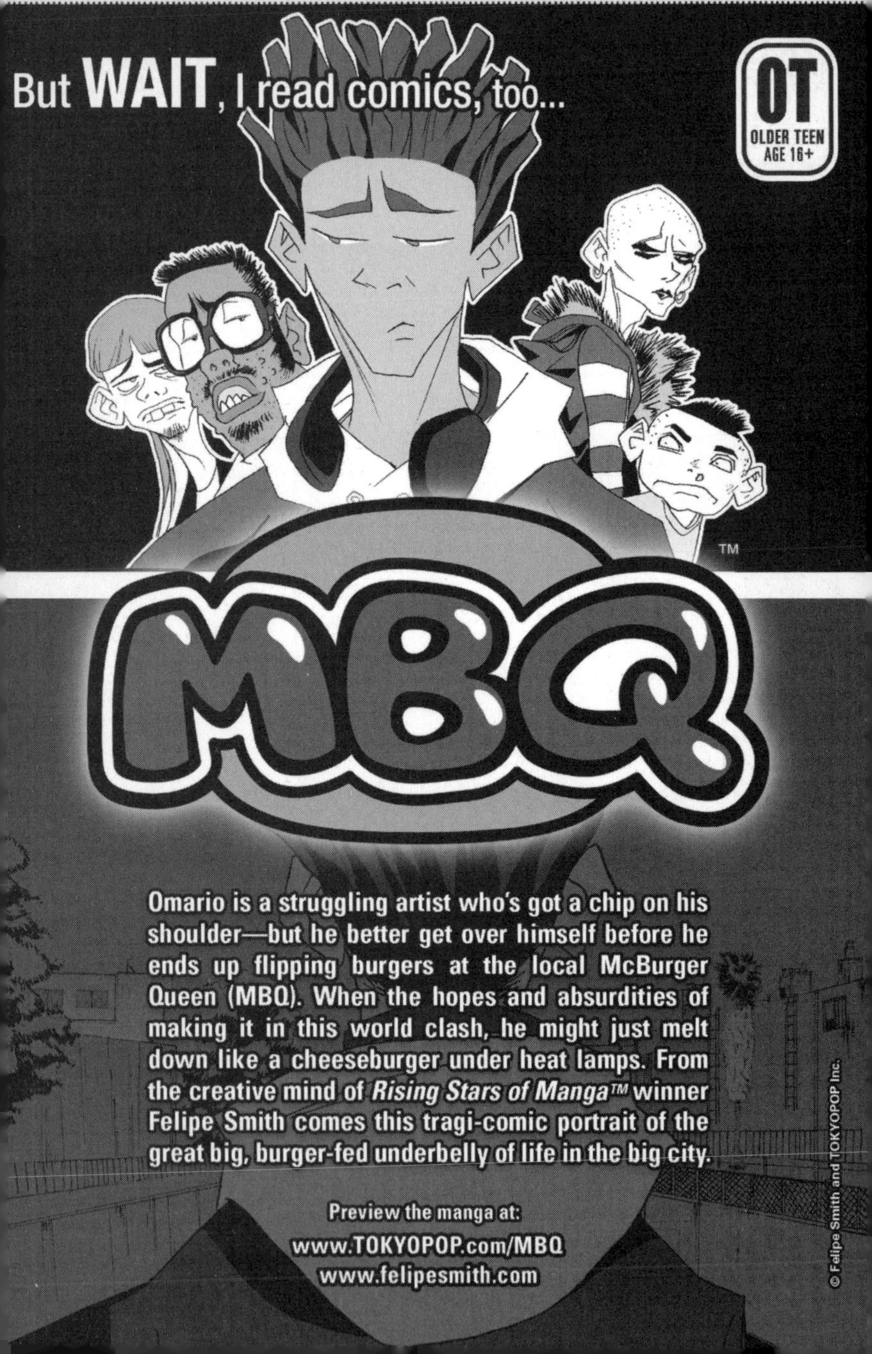
But WAIT, I read comics, too...
OT
OLDER TEEN AGE 16+
MBQ™
Omario is a struggling artist who's got a chip on his shoulder—but he better get over himself before he ends up flipping burgers at the local McBurger Queen (MBQ). When the hopes and absurdities of making it in this world clash, he might just melt down like a cheeseburger under heat lamps. From the creative mind of *Rising Stars of Manga™* winner Felipe Smith comes this tragi-comic portrait of the great big, burger-fed underbelly of life in the big city.
Preview the manga at:
www.TOKYOPOP.com/MBQ
www.felipesmith.com
© Felipe Smith and TOKYOPOP Inc.

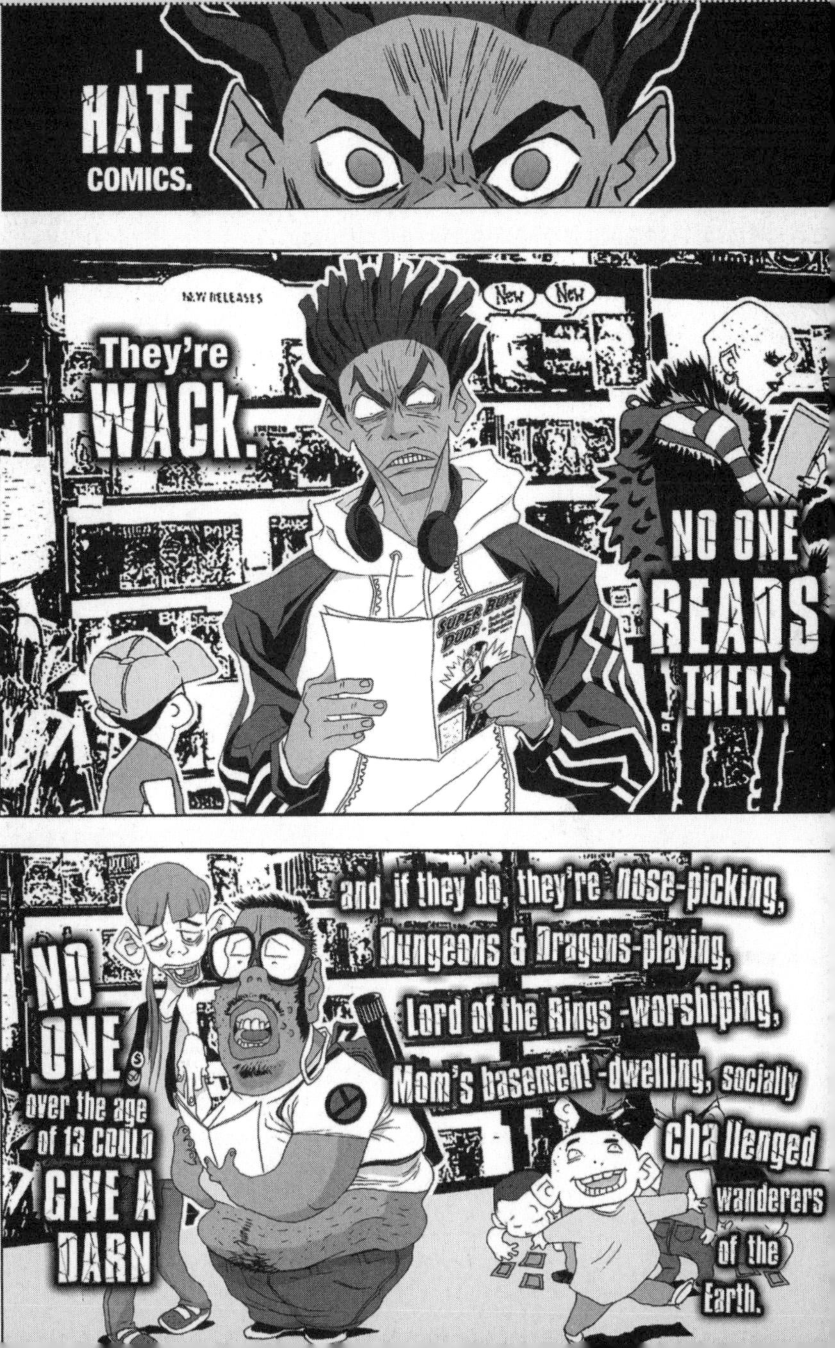
I
HATE
COMICS.
NEW RELEASES
New
New
They're
WACK.
SUPER BUFF DUDE
NO ONE
READS
THEM.
NO
ONE
over the age
of 13 COULD
GIVE A
DARN
and if they do, they're nose-picking,
Dungeons & Dragons-playing,
Lord of the Rings -worshiping,
Mom's basement -dwelling, socially
challenged
wanderers
of the
Earth.

TOKYOPOP SHOP

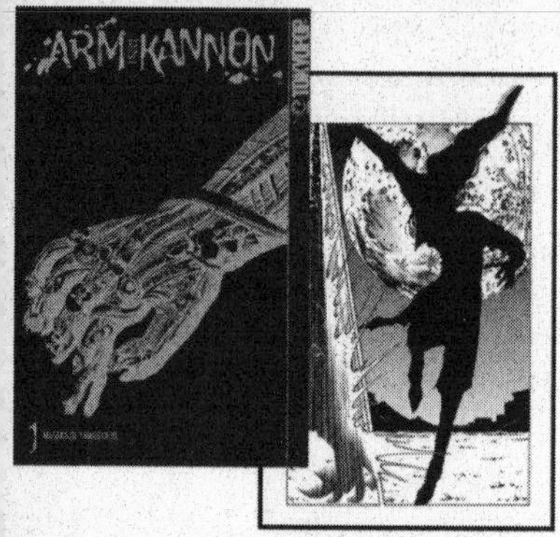
ARM OF KANNON

BY MASAKAZU YAMAGUCHI

ARM OF KANNON

Good and evil race to find the mysterious Arm of Kannon—an ancient Buddhist relic that has the power to bring about the end of humanity. The relic has been locked in a sacred temple for thousands of years. However, it is released and its demonic form soon takes over the will of a young boy, Mao, who must now flee from the evil forces that hunt the arm for control of its awesome power. This sexually charged action/horror story, traversing a vast landscape of demons, swordsmen, magicians, street gangs and government super-soldiers, will make the hairs on the back of your neck stand on edge.

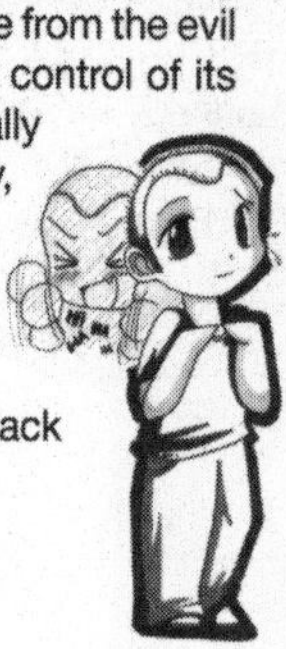

~Rob Valois, Editor

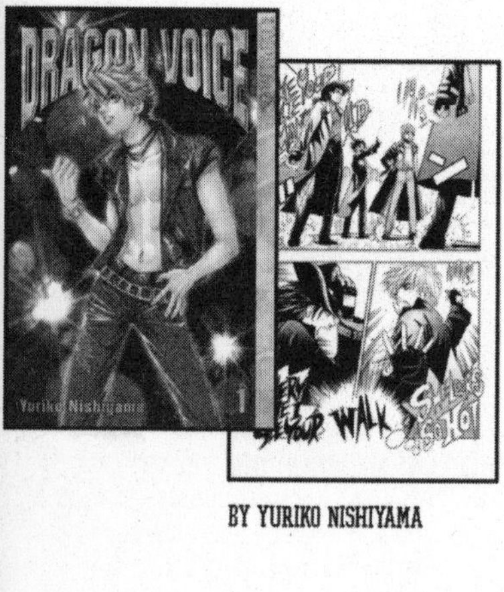
DRAGON VOICE
Yuriko Nishiyama
1
WALK

BY YURIKO NISHIYAMA

DRAGON VOICE

I have to admit that Yuriko Nishiyama's *Dragon Voice* was not at all what I was expecting. As more a fan of action/adventure stories like *Samurai Deeper Kyo*, the singing and dancing hijinks of a Japanese boy-band seemed hardly like my cup of tea. But upon proofreading Volume 3 for fellow editor Lillian Diaz-Przybyl, I found *Dragon Voice* to be one of my favorites! Rin and his fellow Beatmen dazzle their way past all obstacles—rival boy-band Privee, theme-park prima donnas, or TV production pitfalls—and do it with style! This book is one of the most fun reads I've had in a long time!

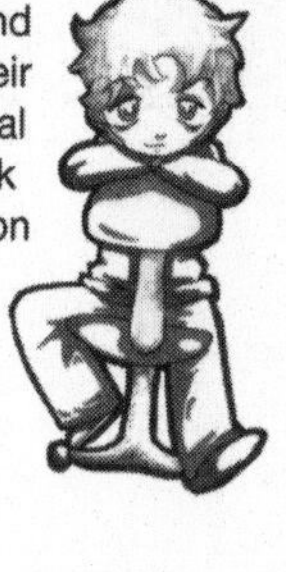

~Aaron Suhr, Sr. Editor

ONE

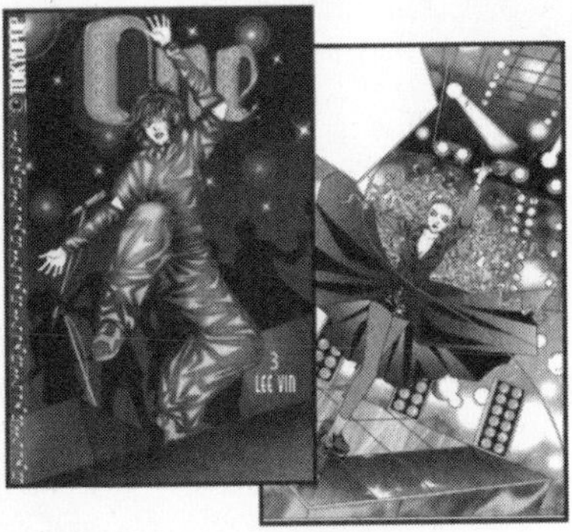
TOKYOPOP
One
3
LEE VIN

BY LEE VIN

Like American Idol? Then you'll love *One*, an energetic manga that gives you a sneak peek into the pop music industry. Lee Vin, who also created *Crazy Love Story*, is an amazingly accomplished artist! The story centers on the boy band One, a powerhouse of good looks, hot moves, and raw talent. It also features Jenny You, a Britney-Avril hybrid who's shooting straight for the top. But fame always comes at a price—and their path to stardom is full of speed bumps and roadblocks. But no matter what happens, they keep on rockin'—and so does this manga!

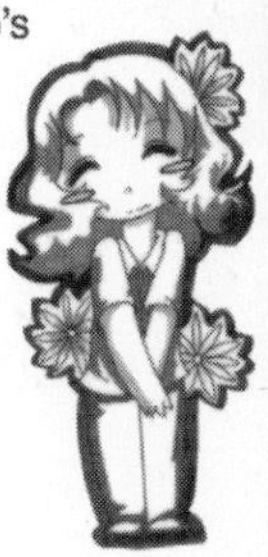

~Julie Taylor, Sr. Editor

THREADS OF TIME

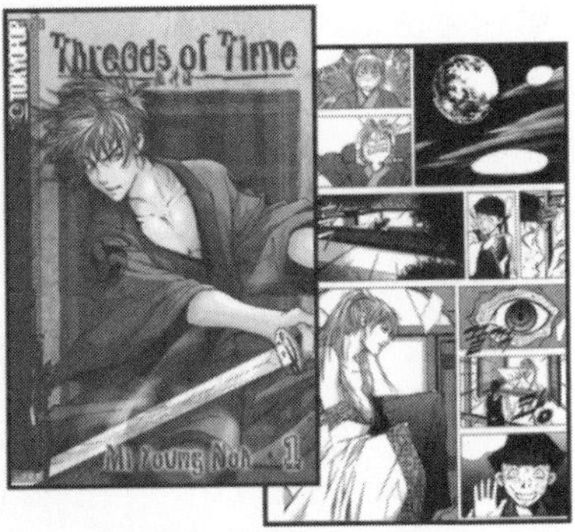
TOKYOPOP
Threads of Time
Mi Young Noh 1

BY MI-YOUNG NOH

The best thing about *Threads of Time* is its richly dramatic depiction of Korea's struggle to push back the Mongol Hordes in the 13th century. The plot focuses on a 20th century boy who ends up back in time. However, this science fiction conceit retreats to the background of this thrilling adventure in war-torn ancient Korea. Imagine a Korean general riding into battle with a battery of twelve men against two hundred Mongol warriors! Imagine back-stabbing politicians murdered in the clear of night. Imagine an entire village raped and slaughtered by Mongol hounds only to be avenged by a boy who just failed his high school science test.

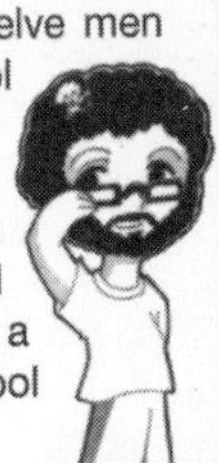

~Luis Reyes, Editor

STOP!

This is the back of the book.
You wouldn't want to spoil a great ending!

This book is printed "manga-style," in the authentic Japanese right-to-left format. Since none of the artwork has been flipped or altered, readers get to experience the story just as the creator intended. You've been asking for it, so TOKYOPOP® delivered: authentic, hot-off-the-press, and far more fun!

DIRECTIONS

If this is your first time reading manga-style, here's a quick guide to help you understand how it works.

It's easy... just start in the top right panel and follow the numbers. Have fun, and look for more 100% authentic manga from TOKYOPOP®!

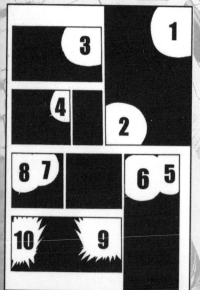